The Bulletin of the
SHAWNEE COUNTY HISTORICAL SOCIETY
*Commemorating the Bicentennial
of the American Revolution
1776 — 1976*

Witness of the Times

A History of Shawnee County

Authors
DOUGLASS W. WALLACE
ROY D. BIRD

Editors
ROBERT W. RICHMOND
JOSEPH W. SNELL

Published jointly by the
Shawnee County Historical Society,
Box 56, Topeka, Kansas 66601,
and the Shawnee County American
Revolution Bicentennial Commission,
July 4, 1976

BULLETIN No. 53
Shawnee County Historical Society

**Kansas Avenue,
North from Sixth Street,
West Side of Avenue.**

535   (Corner) *Bank of Topeka;
George H. Whitcomb, Attorney.*

533   *Crosby Brothers, Dry Goods.*

531   *J. Weiss & Co., Grocers.*

529   *Kitchell & Marburg, Hardware.*

527   *W. L. Bates, Dry Goods;
W. C. Trapp, Merchant Tailor.*

525   *Adams Express; Pacific Express;
J. B. Whitaker, Civil Engineer.*

523   *Swift & Holliday, Druggists.*

521   *Clements & Chaffee, Clothing.*

519   *Guilford Dudley's Bank.*

517   *W.A.L. Thompson, Hardware.*

515   *Investment Banking Co.*

513   *A. H. Sharum, Boots & Shoes.*

511   *John P. Cole, Grocer.*

507   *Greenwald & Co., Clothiers.*

505   *W. B. Kirkpatrick, Boots & Shoes.*

503   *J. W. Farnsworth, Queensware.*

501   *J. K. Jones, Druggist.*

★   ★   ★

435   *Kansas National Bank.*

419   *M. F. Rigby, Confectionery.*

**Kansas Avenue,
South from Sixth Street,
East Side of Avenue.**

600   *Rowley Bros., Druggists & Ticket
Agents for A.T.& S.F. Ry.
Topeka Omnibus Co. Office.*

602   *Abe Steinberg, Gents Clothing.*

604   *W. S. Furman, Boots & Shoes.
Law Office, Schenck & McKeever.*

606   *Conwell & Peasley, Confectionery.*

608   *James B. Hayden, Jeweler.*

610   *S. Ettlinger, Clothing.*

612 - 14   *Crawford's Topeka Opera House.
L. M. Crawford, Bill Poster.*

616   *D. H. Forbes, Hardware & Stoves.*

620   *John D. Knox's Bank.*

622   *August Bros. Clothing.
Drs. Stormont & Alexander.*

624   *H. K. Danenhower, Sewing
Machines.*

626   *Thompson Bros. Hardware
& Stoves.*

632   *Parlor Drug Store.
C. J. Snyder, Photographer.*

634   *Central National Bank.
(later, 700 Kansas)*

COPYRIGHT © 1976 BY THE
SHAWNEE COUNTY HISTORICAL SOCIETY, TOPEKA, KANSAS
ISSN: 0362-1731
ISBN No. 0-916934-03-9

Printed by

H. M. Ives and Sons
Topeka, Kansas
1976

To Our Parents

This Book Would Not Be Possible

Without Them

PREFACE

Thomas Paine once wrote, "It is at all times necessary . . . that we frequently refresh our patriotism by reference to first principles. It is by tracing things to their origins that we learn to understand them, and it is by keeping that line and that origin always in view that we never forget them." And another revolutionary patriot, Benjamin Rush, advised, "the American War is over, but this is far from the case with the American Revolution. On the contrary, nothing but the first act of the great drama is closed."

Indeed, another curtain went up in the 1850s, and this time the scene was set in Shawnee county, Kansas. Then and there on the edge of the great plains a new revolution began, and a land as alien to the settlers as Jamestown or Plymouth had been two and a third centuries before, challenged the new pilgrims to transform the wilderness into a civilization composed of farms and towns and cities.

WITNESS OF THE TIMES captures many of the elements of this revolutionary process. While similar developments occurred in other places, retracing these particular ones in their manifold dimensions refreshes contemporary Shawnee countians. "By tracing things to their origins" our generation acquires a perspective on ourselves. We understand ourselves better by understanding the challenges and accomplishments of our fathers. Providing that perspective has been the goal of the Heritage Committee of the Shawnee County American Revolution Bicentennial Commission. Sponsoring this history in conjunction with the Shawnee County Historical Society has resulted in a work that all can turn to for enrichment.

Larry Wolgast, General Chairperson
Shawnee County American Revolution
Bicentennial Commission

FOREWORD

Undoubtedly many who read this history will notice that some individual, event, or institution has been neglected. For these omissions we do not apologize. From the beginning we recognized that a definitive or scholarly work, though feasible, would be unbelievably lengthy, technical, and dull. A topical approach was thought to be more interesting, as factual, and certainly more entertaining than a chronological treatment. Above all we wanted to avoid, for want of a better term, a chamber of commerce history—one which floods pages with a sea of praise where sins, at best, are ignored.

Thus this work may startle some who expected a quite different book. Certainly, much of this community's glory lies in the past, and a considerable portion or tangible evidence of that past has been ruthlessly or ignobly stripped away. It will remain for the historian of the tercentenary to say kind words about us or not. Nevertheless, from princes to pimps, sinners to saints, ultimately they are the stuff that is history.

Numerous individuals and organizations must be thanked for their contributions. The officers and trustees of the Shawnee County Historical Society, including Presidents Charles J. Scheetz, Pauline D. Beatty, and Kelsey H. Petro, have backed this project from the beginning. Too, it was a major venture of the Shawnee County American Revolution Bicentennial Commission with funding and support through the Kansas ARBC and Ruth Garvey Fink of the Fink Foundation. In particular we must mention Shawnee County ARBC Chairmen Marc Lahr and Larry Wolgast and Heritage '76 Committee Chairman Dr. William O. Wagnon.

We cannot ignore those who helped us in the research and preparation of the book. The manuscript, library, and newspaper staff under Executive Director Nyle H. Miller of the Kansas State Historical Society constantly ran around the Memorial Building digging up odd bits of information—usually without cursing us (which we probably frequently merited). Bradbury Thompson generously designed the cover and end plates while Dan Fitzgerald and Brad Trimble aided in the research of Shawnee county ghost towns; Ruth Snell and Marjorie House saved enormous amounts of time deciphering (not always accurately but with excellent reason) and typing our hand written manuscripts; and Kenneth and John Ives of H. M. Ives & Sons, as always, turned out a handsome product. Larry Wm. Mogge assisted with the index.

Naturally, we do not forget John W. Ripley—who *is* the Shawnee County Historical Society—the director of publications and the acknowledged authority on, among other things, Topeka life and institutions. Nancy Sherbert from the State Historical Society helped immensely in typing and finding materials. Her only payment was learning more than she ever thought she would, or perhaps wanted, about local history and other less decorous items (she also discovered the title for us, from Cicero). Andrea Glenn of Emerson-Franzke Advertising helped greatly in promotion. Finally, we do not leave out the editors, much as we may wish—Robert W. Richmond and Joseph W. Snell of the Kansas and Shawnee county historical bodies. Not only did they receive the honor, such at it was, of reading this work first but also edited out the best, juiciest, or most insulting parts. By now, undoubtedly, neither one—especially the suffering Mr. Snell—can stand our faces.

<table>
<tr><td>June 15, 1976</td><td>Roy D. Bird</td></tr>
<tr><td>Topeka and Manhattan</td><td>Douglass W. Wallace</td></tr>
</table>

CONTENTS

In his later years Sam Reader painted this water color of himself staking a Shawnee county claim. (From the "Autobiography" of Samuel J. Reader)

ON THE BANKS OF THE KANZAS; THE TERRITORIAL PERIOD

"I doubt whether even sunny and far famed Italy can favorably compare with this," wrote Cyrus K. Holliday, a Kansas immigrant of 1854. Many others who pieced together articles about the newly opened territory for eastern newspapers echoed his sentiments. But when people arrived they found Kansas to be no paradise and no Italy. Instead they found a tremendous plain—the "Great American Desert" —which stretched imperceivably to the Rocky mountains. Nothing of its proportion existed in the East or in Europe; for those who stayed, their world would permanently change.

Located on the fringes of the prairies, Shawnee county is a land in transition from the eastern wooded hills to the treeless high plains. Geographically, the Kansas river dominates the 545 square miles that is the county, dividing it in two. Numerous streams feed the Kansas on both sides including the subservient Wakarusa river which finally joins it in Douglas county. A broad flood plain crosses the county on the north side, but the only hill of note, Burnett's Mound (known in the 1850s as Webster's Peak) lies on the south. John C. Fremont climbed to its summit in 1853. His companion of that day, Julia Ann Stinson, remembered: "there was quite a little timber along the Shunganunga [creek], but very little along the river, a great prairie between and high grass."

The very little timber included, in the 19th century, small stands of oak, walnut, hickory, ash, hackberry, cottonwood, and others, all outlining the streams. An early survey reported only 8% forest in the county and the New York *Times,* January 10, 1855, acknowledged the problem of Kansas:

This scarcity of timber is one of the first discouragements of the emigrant-tourist, and the greatest. He is in raptures with the magnificent, rich, rolling prairies, but imagines that the want of material for houses, fences and fuel will long bar its settlement.

The paper had an explanation and a solution: "every Summer a vigorous growth of young trees starts up . . . which is regularly and inevitably killed by the Autumn fires [or] stunted by the same causes." To improve the land, it suggested "a good supply of *Osage Orange Seed* will be a capital investment" for fencing and hedge rows.

Drawing by George Lehman from an earlier sketch supposedly depicting
Fool Chief's Kansa village in present Menoken township about 1830.
(Courtesy Kansas State Historical Society)

Yet, with good soil and evidence of coal underneath, the *Times* concluded that Kansas possessed all the "requisites for a sudden and
brilliant prosperity."

Another requisite, which early settlers propagandized back east,
was the climate. Holliday, who helped organize the Topeka Town
Association, basked in the winter sunshine of 1854. Supposedly he
and his Topeka partners held an informal swimming party Christmas
morning. On the last day of the year he wrote home to his wife in
Pennsylvania that the weather had been like September. "This entire
week we have gone about our work without our overcoats and most of
the time in shirt sleeves. Except to cook our victuals scarcely requiring
fire. Thus it is in Kansas." Reality, however, destroyed such myths;
on a March morning Holliday awoke to find three inches of snow
on his bed. He complained to Mary, "I believe you generally use
snow scrapers *outside* of the house in Penna. Remember that in
Kansas we use them for the *inside*."

Eastern Kansas Indians who never knew of Italy's "sweet clime and
serene sky," were relative newcomers to the area also. The earliest
historic peoples who inhabited Shawnee county were the Kansa,
apparently moving here from the East in the early 17th century. Their
first villages were on the Missouri river, but the Kansa roamed on
hunts as far west as central Kansas. At their semi-permanent villages,
they grew corn, muskmelons, pumpkins, beans, and squash. In the
summer, the men stopped work in the fields to hunt buffalo. On the
surface an idyllic life, it ended with the arrival of the white man.

The French visited the region first when the party of explorer Etienne Veniard de Bourgmont crossed the northern portion of Shawnee county in 1724. French traders-trappers followed him, some temporarily living with or marrying the Kansa. The Louisiana Purchase of 1803 spurred further exploration: one party under Maj. Stephen H. Long's command and including naturalist Thomas Say retraced de Bourgmont's steps in 1819. By then the stage was set for the Kansa to gaze upon the American and the American to gaze upon the Indian. Undoubtedly neither cared for nor understood the other.

After initial contacts, the Kansa bartered away, in a treaty of June 3, 1825, their unrestricted land for $4,000 in goods and horses, an annuity of $3,500 for 20 years, and a fixed reserve astride the Kansas river. Later the government designated 23 sections of land along the north bank of the river, accidentally located in the Delaware reservation, for the Kansa half-breed children. Seven of these half-breed tracts were in Shawnee county.

During the 1820s the Kansa had their primary village near the junction of the Big Blue and Kansas rivers. Several Indian traders lived down the river from it, including Louis Gonville, who married into the tribe, and Frederick Chouteau, who opened his first post in 1829 on Horseshoe Lake, now Lake View, in Douglas county. Opposite Chouteau's was the Kaw Agency where Daniel Morgan Boone, son of famed Daniel Boone, demonstrated farming techniques to the Indians.

Sometime in 1829, for unknown reasons, the Kansa abandoned their Blue river home for sites in western Shawnee county. Internal

Samuel J. Reader's watercolor of his Indianola home in the 1850s. (From the "Diaries" of Samuel J. Reader)

disputes divided them and a sub-chief headed each of the three villages. American Chief and Hard Chief founded their villages south of the river, in Dover township, just west of the mouth of Mission creek. Frederick Chouteau removed his store to the vicinity of American Chief's settlement. Fool Chief established his followers on the north side of the Kansas in Menoken township between the river and Soldier creek. American Chief's village was the smallest with perhaps 100 people. Fool Chief's was the largest with 800. A census taken in 1843 counted a total of 1,588 Kansa, but in future years the population declined.

The more permanent homes of the Kansa were earth lodges arranged in irregular rows, similar to the style of other prairie Indians. The lodges were dome shaped timber frames covered with sod and grass. They were usually 30 to 50 feet in circumferance and generally inhabited by one or two families, the hearth in the center dividing the living quarters. Brothers and their wives and families shared the compartment, one group on the north side and the other on the south. The entry faced the east to catch the first rays of the morning sun.

Such social customs, and the Kansa themselves, offended many whites and few said kind things about them. One who did, Gwin Harris Heap, on the Santa Fe trail in 1853, thought the "Caws" to be "fine-looking men, well proportioned, and athletic." Peter Burnett, traveling to Oregon in 1844, reacted more typically when he met a war party of about 90 Osages and Kansa. They had just killed a Pawnee—a favorite sport—and Burnett saw them as "the most miserable, cowardly, and dirty Indians . . . east of the Rocky Mountains. They annoyed us greatly by their continual begging."

Shortly after the Kansa had signed the 1825 treaty establishing their reservation as a strip 30 miles wide beginning 20 leagues up the Kansas river from its mouth, and with an unspecified western boundary, the Shawnee agreed to a treaty which gave them the remaining portion of Shawnee county south of the river plus much more contiguous land. In 1831 the Delawares secured the north part of the county which was not owned by the Kansa.

As national Indian removal brought more and more tribes to Kansas reshuffling was necessary to make room for them. Consequently the Kansa, in a treaty of 1846, sold the east 30 mile square portion of their land to the federal government for the use of the Pottawatomies originally from Michigan but lately from along the Marais des Cygnes in eastern Kansas. The Kansa were given a one hundred mile square area in present Morris county.

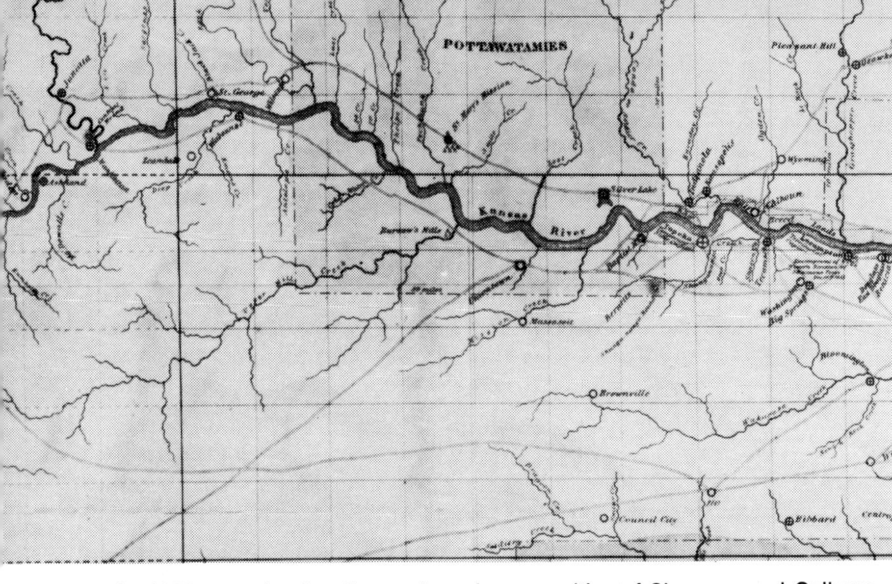

An 1856 map showing the roads and communities of Shawnee and Calhoun counties with Uniontown on the west, Washington the east, Council City (Burlingame) the south, and the high prairies to the north. (Courtesy Kansas State Historical Society)

Advance parties of the Pottawatomies began to arrive in Shawnee county during the fall of 1847 and more came the following year, including the best remembered Pottawatomie sub-chief, Abraham (or Abram) Burnett.

Right behind the Pottawatomies came the missionaries who had done little work among the Kansa but who now fully intended to establish missions and schools. The Baptists, previously in Franklin county, reopened their Pottawatomie mission in Shawnee county, south of the river on the eastern edge of the reservation. Dr. Johnston Lykins and Isaac McCoy were responsible for establishment of the mission and school. McCoy's daughter, Elizabeth, conducted the first classes for 11 Pottawatomie girls, five boys, and one white girl. The first quarters were temporary log shelters, but work quickly commenced on a permanent complex which included a stone school which still survives. In the neighborhood the Rev. Robert Simerwell served as blacksmith to the Pottawatomies and probably, from time to time, hammered out a sermon or two.

The Catholic church also accompanied the Pottawatomies in their move. Father Christian Hoecken put up about 20 primitive log cabins late in November, 1847, on the Wakarusa river near present Auburn. He discovered the next spring that his small settlement occupied Shawnee, not Pottawatomie, ground and so the small flock again moved, this time north of the Kansas to the site of St. Marys. Thus, the Baptists, Catholics, licensed traders, blacksmiths, agricultural experts, and others ventured among the Indians and their farms— for the Pottawatomies lived in log houses and not earth lodges therefore being "semi-civilized"—hoping to bring more benefits of the white man's civilization.

Besides the church, the United States provided a trading post and community within the reservation. In March, 1848, agents R. W. Cummins and A. J. Vaughan selected a site for "the smith & traders," and Vaughan wrote: "I have accordingly stuck my stake and christened it union town"—the first town in what became Shawnee county. The place overlooked the river on a bluff about a mile south and supposedly close to good timber. Unfortunately, the Pottawatomies disapproved of the location, especially those who had to ford the river to reach it. Nonetheless, it served as their official trading center until 1853 when it was moved to a post on Cross creek near Rossville.

Numerous accounts about Uniontown have survived, particularly from overland travelers—a branch of the Oregon-California trail passed over Uniontown's single street. Most writers concurred with Samuel Dundass' view of May, 1849: "the village is constituted of a few Indian huts and log cabins with two or three small stores, reasonable in their prices considering the difficulty and distance of transportation." John F. Snyder, in a letter dated May 22, 1850, counted 50 log houses and reported a high population of 300, "nearly all Indians." He also noted that the "government has stationed . . . a physician, two blacksmiths, a wagon maker, two gunsmiths, and a circular saw mill" there. Two of the inhabitants, later to play roles in Shawnee county history, were Anthony A. Ward, the wagonmaker, and Thomas N. Stinson, a trading post representative who, during his stay, itemized the cost of building his log house, the total being $125.32. Military explorer John C. Fremont was less impressed with the place when he stopped by on October 25, 1853: "Went to Uniontown and nooned. This is a street of log cabins. Nothing to be had here . . . lots of John Barleycorn [whiskey] which the men about were consuming."

Outside of town there were few whites and only clusters of Pottawatomie farms. Snyder declared that the Indians "here have large farms, and seem to be very industrious." Disaster struck them, however, when cholera broke out in the spring of 1849. The Indians suffered severe losses as did the white population. Joseph Chick, whose trading firm had a Uniontown store, lost a sister at the Baptist mission and he and the rest of the family camped out on the Blue river until conditions were safe for a return. The other caucasians apparently followed suit leaving only a doctor in town, but the Indians had no such escape. A legend has evolved that their dead were heaped into a huge common grave near the, now, ancient Uniontown cemetery.

Eventually the government reduced the Pottawatomie reservation to a small reserve in Jackson county. Of the tribe only one member, Abraham Burnett, captured the popular imagination of the white settlers. Born in Indiana in 1812 and educated in the east, he acted as interpreter during the tribe's move to Kansas. In 1843 Burnett married a German girl and later settled on the new reservation just north of a conical-shaped mound which is now named after him. In his last years he usually drove over to Topeka once a week and, legend states, became quite drunk. Topekans would roll him out to his lumber wagon, then, taking a board or two, or three, would roll him up into the bed. Burnett's horses knew the way home and delivered him safely to his abode with no human guidance. "Mr. Burnett," wrote a Topeka newspaper in 1868, "is the largest and heaviest man in the state of Kansas . . . and one of the wealthiest men in the country."

At the time of his death in June, 1870, Burnett weighed over 460 pounds causing the undertaker to make a coffin "twice as large as the largest coffin" he had ever manufactured before.

After the Civil War interest turned away from the "civilized" Indians of the eastern Kansas reservations to the tales of savages in the far west. Well into the next decade, however, Topeka papers reported on the curious events of Indians coming into town. Things had changed indeed when the *Commonwealth*, September 10, 1873, commented: "A couple of squaws were in the city yesterday trundling their papooses in baby carriages. Who can now say that civilization is a failure?"

Undoubtedly on cold winter nights, the white population of Uniontown met in front of a fire and, with John Barleycorn at hand, discussed their future and that of the unorganized Indian territory. Expansion beyond the Missouri was inevitable, only time determining when this would occur. Senator Stephen A. Douglas' committee on territories submitted the Nebraska (later the Kansas-Nebraska) bill to Congress in January, 1854. This measure provided for the creation of two territories, opened them up for colonization and, most significantly, repealed the Missouri Compromise of 1820. For that agreement of balance between slave and non-slave states the bill substituted the concept of popular sovereignty whereby the people of the territories could decide whether to be admitted to the Union as a free or slave state.

President Franklin Pierce signed the Kansas-Nebraska Act on May 30, 1854, and in June appointed Andrew H. Reeder, an Easton, Pennsylvania, lawyer as territorial governor. Reeder took his time coming to Kansas, reaching Fort Leavenworth finally on October 7.

Abraham Burnett (1812-1870), prominent Pottawatomie leader, nearly engulfed the stool on which he sat for this portrait. (Courtesy Kansas State Historical Society)

Some of Topeka's pioneers sitting for their portrait. Standing left to right: James A. Hickey, Enoch Chase, Daniel H. Horne. Seated left to right: Fry W. Giles, George O. Wilmarth, ... Brigdon, and Cyrus K. Holliday. (Courtesy Kansas State Historical Society)

There he assumed his duties and shortly afterwards moved to the Shawnee Methodist Mission, now in Johnson county. Among his first acts was to divide the territory, which stretched to the summit of the Rocky Mountains, into 17 electoral districts. Portions of the third, 12th and 13th became the future Shawnee county. Reeder also created three judicial districts the following year, 1855, with the second district encompassing the area of Shawnee county.

With the territory of Kansas now open and somewhat organized, who were the first settlers and why had they come? Slavery has, of course, long been interpreted as an important, if not primary, reason for settlement. Kansas' neighbor, Missouri, was an old slave-owning state and by being next door many of the earliest pioneers in the young territory naturally were Missourians. This influx of potential or actual slave owners alarmed many persons in the north, especially in the abolitionist stronghold of New England. Therefore, in Massachusetts, Eli Thayer and Amos Lawrence responded to the dangerous Missourians by forming the Massachusetts Emigrant Aid Society, soon afterwards recast as the New England Emigrant Aid Company. It, along with several other similar bodies, provided abolitionist transportation to Kansas where it established communities, schools, mills, hotels, and those items necessary for a strong, anti-slave, Free-State population. At the same time, Yankee to the core, the company was to earn a profit for its investors.

Despite an aura of success that has always surrounded the New England Emigrant Aid Company (partly because its side won the Kansas civil war), it actually sent only a relative handful of immigrants to Kansas. Over a third of the first party, of July 17, 1854, either returned home after a month or two or later permanently left the territory. Loring Farnsworth, a member of the first spring party in 1855 and later first mayor of Topeka, admitted that he "joined the company to save expenses of travel"; it cost him $33. The parties left amid bands and parades and picked up numerous settlers along the way. The company bought blocks of railroad and steamboat tickets which it in turn sold to the travelers. A company representative journeyed with them and another advised the groups where to settle, etc., upon arrival in Kansas. A southern newspaper claimed the New England company "scraped the very off-scourings of their [northern] cities and sent them to this Territory."

There were southern emigrant companies, too, but on the whole they were far less successful, few people wishing to desert the fertile South for the arid Kansas prairies. Late in the summer of 1856 Capt. Henry D. Clayton led over 90 men, women, children, and possibly one or two slaves, from Alabama and Georgia to Tecumseh township. They reached Kansas early in September and were welcomed by Tecumseh officials. Rush Elmore declared "it will afford me pleasure, now and hereafter, to assist any actual, *bona fide* settlers in selecting and locating their claims. Bring out the men with their women and children to Kansas. They will all, who try, do well—We want no more adventurers in Kansas." The Proslave Leavenworth *Herald*, September 13, 1856, happily announced the arrival of this group of "laboring men of industrious habits and high moral character." Clayton computed his costs at $3,740; yet it was all for nought according to the 1860 territorial census, only one of his southern families remained in Kansas.

Not all settlers came because of the slavery issue. One individual explained his motive years later. As a young man of 19, Samuel Reader trekked to Indianola with his aunt and her husband in 1855. He stated:

Rich, cheap farm land was the principal incentive that lured me on from my Illinois home. I had heard and read much concerning the political troubles in the Territory; but the question of a free or a slave state, was a secondary consideration with me at the time. In fact I had given little thought to the subject; viewing the "Peculiar Institution" as a great wrong, but leaving its adjustment to older and wiser heads.

Many men delayed bringing their families or waited to become secured before returning home to marry a loved one. One man who did just that was Merrit W. Atwood, a bachelor who farmed in the Auburn area in 1857. By 1860, at age 20, he was married to a home town girl from Ohio. In June, 1857, he wrote to his sister portraying the backgrounds of his neighbors.

"I have a house of 61 by 20," he stated, "there has been 8 of us keeping bach—in it a good lot of boys." Most were in their 20s and from New York, Ohio, or Vermont. Most of the eight had given up good positions to relocate on the prairie: two had been teachers, one a public school superintendent earning $600 a year, one a bookkeeper for a furnace company with an annual wage of $1,000, one a locomotive engineer, one a conductor for the New York and Erie railroad getting $60 a month, one a farmer, and one 23-year-old with "no occupation in particular."

Besides farmers to be, the new territory attracted large numbers from the professional classes—lawyers, doctors, engineers, teachers, and others recognizing the opportunities in potentially rich Kansas. Land speculators also saw a future and profit by being there among the first. "I bought an interest in Topeka 2 weeks ago for 300 dollars," wrote Hugh M. Moore in 1856. "I refused 1,000 dollars this morning for it. If Kansas is a free state it will make me a fortune."

Cyrus K. Holliday, long noted as a loyal Topeka promoter, commented to his wife Mary in 1855 after an Iowa trip:

> I am much pleased with the appearance of the lands & settlements through Iowa. . . . All the towns have a thrifty and healthy appearance. Hence my trip through this country may be turned to a profitable account; for if things don't go right in Kansas I will have some idea of where else to turn my steps.

The year 1854 and 1855 were important ones for town building in Kansas; the maps became dotted with villages which aspired to become metropolises only to fall back to dust as ghost towns. Six places of some pretense were founded in the future Shawnee county these two years. Three were north of the river: Calhoun, Indianola, and Whitfield City founded respectively by James Kuykendall, H. D. McMeekin, and J. Butler Chapman. Three more were south: Brownville (Auburn), Tecumseh, and Topeka organized respectively by John W. Brown, Thomas N. Stinson, and a group of nine, representative of whom was Cyrus K. Holliday.

Thomas Stinson, the Uniontown trader, had been residing on the Shunganunga near Burnett's Mound in 1852 and 1853 when he staked a claim to the east in the old Shawnee Indian reserve. After farming it for about a year, he moved his family to their new home where the house became something of a landmark and a hotel for incoming settlers called Stinson's Place. Late in August, 1854, Stinson platted a town on the spot, naming it Tecumseh. On December 6, 1854, he, along with Territorial Governor Andrew H. Reeder, Second Judicial District Judge Rush Elmore, and eight other men formed the Tecumseh Town Association to develop the community as a full scale city with business, industry, schools, churches, and the various social amenities.

Under federal law town promoters could pre-empt 320 acres for the village. This the men did, setting aside 240 acres for Tecumseh and 80 for Stinson. They sold town stock at $50 for a full share and $37.50 for a partial. Money generated by sales was to be used for such projects as a brick hotel. Enterprises like a Kansas river bridge company and the Tecumseh Library Association were each given stock to dispose of as they saw fit, namely sell them and plow the profits back into the organization.

Undoubtedly many people inquired about this newly-born community in the fall and winter of 1854. Since Stinson, Rush Elmore and one or two others identified with the town came from the south and owned slaves, those of a similar outlook on slavery discerned a place where they would be comfortably welcomed. Late in November, 1854, several men from ardent Free-State Lawrence visited Tecumseh, examining it as a possible site for a new Free-State settlement. Despite its attractive location, they quickly pushed on spotting numerous huts of pioneers who had settled beyond Tecumseh during the summer. Approximately 25 miles upstream from Lawrence they discovered the site they wanted. It appeared both well watered and well drained, with high country near-by and good timber lands at a not too inconvenient distance. Also, and very important, it seemed a prime location for a steamboat landing, the last one before entering the Pottawatomie reserve.

Thus the men reported their findings and encouraged settlement, partly, of course, to counteract the previously established and Proslave Tecumseh. Early in December agents of the New England Emigrant Aid Company, as well as interested speculators, prepared work up river and built or refurbished an abandoned log cabin near Papan's Ferry on the Kansas river. After this initial labor, nine tired men gathered on the prairie late on the fourth of December, 1854, to form the nucleus of the future capital of Kansas.

Next day, December 5, the nine, C. K. Holliday, F. W. Giles, Daniel H. Horne, George Davis, Enoch Chase, J. B. Chase, M. C. Dickey (New England Emigrant Aid Company representative), C. Robinson (the future state governor and most disinterested of the Topeka founders, a loyal Lawrence resident), and L. G. Cleveland formed the Topeka Town Association. All nine, in varying degrees of intensity, were Free-State men united in establishing a city on the prairies but otherwise complete strangers. At their meeting that morning, Dickey, not knowing the names of all his companions, simply called for "that fellow with the white hat to take the chair" of the association. The man in the white hat was Cyrus K. Holliday and thus he became the symbol of Topeka's founding.

Among the first orders of business, the nine drew up an agreement dividing the townsite into fifty shares with the lots apportioned as the association may direct reserving, however, one-sixth of the lots of the town to be donated to such persons as will improve them as directed by the association, and also one-sixth to be donated to the Emigrant Aid Company . . . as a consideration for the erection of a mill, a school house, receiving house [hotel], etc. . . . The timber and wood on our claims may be used by any member of the association for his own improvement for one year, provided no person shall take more than four thousand feet of timber, board measure, and six cords of wood, except from his own claim.

As the New York *Times* mentioned a month later, the scarcity of timber weighed on everyone's mind.

Contrary to the laws assigning 320 acres for townsites, Topeka founders originally believed four square miles a suitable size; "ample space," wrote Fry W. Giles in his 1886 history, *Thirty Years in Topeka,* "for many quiet people to dwell." Seeing the work ahead of them, they soon reduced their goal to section 31 of township 11, range 16, and a portion of section 30 near the river bank for a total of 684 acres. As protection to the embryo town, several of the men pre-empted claims bordering it.

In order to have clear title to the land, a little over a full section, the Topeka Association contracted with one Isaiah Walker on February 9, 1856, for a Wyandot float. As a part of a treaty settlement, March 17, 1842, for the removal of the Wyandot Indian nation from Ohio, the United States granted 640 acres west of Missouri to each of some 35 blood or adopted members of the tribe, provided the sections not be in any established reserve. Hence the name given to their land, Wyandot float; the property could be located or "floated" nearly anywhere and then sold. Therefore, early white settlers assumed that the purchase of a float, located upon their townsite, would solve any claim or title difficulties.

Complications arose as to Topeka's purchase which prompted a hostilely organized rival group, the Valley Town Company, to block Topeka's move. Topeka Association surveys of late December, 1854, were discovered to be 18°40' out of alignment with later federal surveys. Though the matter was clouded, the association went ahead, raising $1,200 as the agreed price with Isaiah Walker, owner of Wyandot Float No. 20. The Valley Company, backed by Proslave interests including Calhoun's James M. Kuykendall, stepped forward to claim the land under pre-emption rights but gained nothing other than drawing "the members of the Topeka Association more closely to-

Topeka's Constitution Hall, built in 1855, where Federal troops dispersed the extra-legal Free-State government July 4, 1856. (Courtesy Kansas State Historical Society)

gether." Finally, the patent for Float No. 20 was issued on February 14, 1859, and Topekans had little more to worry.

Tecumseh promoters also desired a Wyandot float for their community, and Tecumseh Association members discussed it at a June 5, 1855, meeting. Territorial Gov. Andrew H. Reeder also mentioned it in a letter dated October 6, 1855, adding that "a new assessment of $5 per share [has been made] to pay for a Wyandot float of 640 acres which has been laid on the town" and for the county court house. Either the residents felt comfortable with the *status quo* or were unable to meet demand, as Tecumseh failed to secure a float. Other than the Topeka float, only one other was located in Shawnee county. Number 19, granted to Elliot McCulloch, was placed in Monmouth township.

Other than the pretensions of the Valley Company, the Topeka men faced few obstacles. About the first of the year, a squatter suddenly showed up who proceeded to erect a log cabin at the prairie grassland intersection of Eighth and Topeka streets. Town Association members spoke to him but to no avail. Then, secretly the night of January 8, "when the glare of sunshine was gone and the moon shone dimly o'er the scene," wrote Giles, a wagon team drove up to the claim jumper's cabin and several vigilantes demolished it, prudently hauling the logs away.

Another potential problem quickly dissipated. A. A. Ward had planted the town of Fremont just west of the Topeka site. Giles dismissed it as consisting of just "one man, one woman, one horse, seven chickens, one carriage and a shake shanty," so it offered no opposition. However, Ward had deeded some nearby property to an itinerant preacher named Hummer, an act that he promptly regretted. One night a group of Tecumseh and Topeka men assembled and marched to Hummer's cabin to procure the scrap of paper. While there one of the party, Ike Edwards, picked up a rock and hurled it at Hummer, injuring him. Then the men packed up the squatter's belongings, the woman staying with Hummer, put all in a wagon and sent them on their way "to find relief if they might [on the cold high prairies] or to perish if they must." All in all, it was one of more unpleasant affairs in Topeka's early history.

For some time in the winter of 1854-55, the log cabin finished on December 4 was the only building in the town of Topeka. Its roof was thatched and the unmortared chimney quite low making it easy for cinders to spark the reeds. When one of the men pointed out this danger his companion supposedly commented, "let her rip." Though accounts state it was on the night of December 5, two or three nights later the roof did exactly that. A fire burned all but a few logs by morning. The nine occupants barely escaped from burning and fortunately had a tent in which to spend the nights while rebuilding took place. Unfortunately for the nine the tent proved very confining. In the *Commonwealth,* December 5, 1872, Daniel Horne explained that "when one wanted to turn over, some one had to go out of the tent, and wait until the revolution was complete."

Fire, and sword, would play roles in Kansas the next two or three years, in the age known as Bleeding Kansas, though political life certainly began peacefully enough. The first territorial election, for a Congressional delegate, took place on November 29, 1854, at the Stinsons' home, the third district's polling station. Forty-eight persons voted with the Proslave candidate easily winning, there being as yet few Free-Staters in the district. In fact, the concept of opposing political parties had not yet materialized; in six months it would.

To prepare for the first territorial legislature election, the Reeder administration initiated Kansas' first census, which was conducted during February, 1855. In the third electoral district, which included Tecumseh, Topeka and some area west of the present county boundary but none north of the river, census taker Thorton W. Hayes counted 252 individuals—161 males and 91 females of whom 112 were minors, a high figure for a frontier environment less than a year old. Nearly three-quarters of the citizens were under 30 and five, not enumerated in the census, of course, were slaves, four belonging to Tecumseh township masters. Hayes listed some occupations, including, in order of frequency, farmer, mechanic, merchant, minister, one lawyer and one doctor. Finally, he reported 93 residents eligible to vote.

The 12th district included Indianola and some area outside of present day Shawnee county as did the 13th district to the east. The polling station for the former was the home of R. C. Miller (accounts vary as to whether located on Soldier creek or to the west) and the latter the G. M. Dyer house at Ozawkie. Census for the 12th district showed 104 males, 40 females, 78 voters, one free Negro, and seven slaves. The 13th, which barely touched Shawnee county, had 168 males, 116 females, and 88 (or 96) voters. In all three electoral districts, third, 12th, and 13th, former Missouri residents predominated with 51 individuals from that state in the third. Also, south of the river, were significant populations from Kentucky, Virginia, Maryland, Tennessee, New Hampshire, Illinois, Ohio and Massachusetts as well as England, Ireland, and one family from Switzerland. Only one, a three-month-old baby, Allen M. Horner, had been born in Kansas territory.

Reeder scheduled the election for March 30 and on this occasion Free-State and Proslave factions clashed for the first time. Two days before the balloting Reeder, resting at the Stinson home, found himself surrounded by Missouri border ruffians desiring to lynch him because of imagined wrongs against their political beliefs. He successfully escaped but the incident merely set the stage for the vote a few days later.

Missourians rushed into the territory everywhere, swamping the ballot boxes. The Proslave candidate in the third district, D. S. Croysdale, received 366 votes to C. K. Holliday's four. Thus, the electorate had swelled four times above the population statistics issued the month before. One Free-State observer described the scene at Stinson's house for a Vermont newspaper: "The room was half filled with ruffianly looking men, armed with bowie knives, revolvers, and large hickory bludgeons." When an argument broke out as to voter eligibility, Stinson "rushed into the room and brandished a large hickory club, with both hands over Mr. Burgess' [the only Free-State member of the three electoral judges] head" swearing that he would "smash him through the floor." Needless to add, such stories persuaded Topeka Free-Staters not to enter the polling booth.

Because of these shenanigans Governor Reeder called for a new election to be held on May 22. To this action the southerners objected loudly and abstained from voting. Topeka's Cyrus K. Holliday won 146 votes out of the 149 cast, a more reasonable number. Nevertheless, when the Proslavery-controlled legislature met at Pawnee, they reversed the outcome and awarded the seat to Croysdale. Thus, for the next several years, politics would be confused, complicated, and often violent and dishonest.

During the summer of 1855 the legislature, firmly controlled by the Proslave faction, created Kansas' first counties with that portion of the third and seventh districts south of the Wakarusa river becoming Shawnee county on August 30. These boundaries included the present east and west limits but stretched from the Kansas river south to a line just below present Burlingame in modern Osage county. North of the river the legislature formed Calhoun county with the present east, north, and west boundaries of Jackson county. On September 17 it divided Shawnee county into two townships, Tecumseh comprising everything north of the Wakarusa river and Yocum, everything south. The counties would be altered in 1860 and 1868 but for most of the territorial period Shawnee county possessed the communities of Tecumseh, Topeka, Brownville (Auburn), and Council City (Burlingame) while Calhoun county had Calhoun, Whitfield City (Rochester), and Indianola.

For and in consideration of the sum of four hundred Dollars to us in hand paid by Thomas N. Stinson of Union Town Pottawatomie Nation, we have this day sold unto the said Thos. N. Stinson a certain Negro Man named Moses of the age of Twenty Six years old to be a Slave for Life, we also warrant said Man Moses to be sound and healthy. Given under our hands and seals this 15th day of May 1854—

Alexander Boshman [Seal]
Margret Boshman [Seal]

Witness,

Luke Lea
Indian Agent
Fort Leavenworth Agency.

The first and perhaps only slave sale in what is now Shawnee county. Boshman was Stinson's brother-in-law and lived in present Auburndale. (Courtesy Kansas State Historical Society)

Tecumseh settlers had hoped for, and even believed to have been promised the territorial capital, but a vote of the legislature in August gave the prize to Lecompton. As compensation Tecumseh received the county seat for her loyalty to the southern cause. As the largest town in the neighborhood, many of her civic leaders also became county officials. W. O. Yeager (chairman), Edward Hoogland, and William Yocum made up the first board of county commissioners with John Horner (upon the refusal of George W. Berry) the first sheriff. Thomas Stinson was the first treasurer. As Shawnee county officials they also held certain added responsibilties, such as road maintenance, in Richardson (Wabaunsee) and Weller (Osage) counties for the first several years.

Of the officals, the county tax assessor drew the toughest task, above and beyond traditional reasons. Free-State property owners were reluctant to pay taxes to a Proslave body; hence, between October, 1855, and March, 1857, seven men served, briefly, in that capacity. According to an article by Fry Giles in the *Commonwealth,* July 6, 1876, by early 1857 "affairs . . . had become so confused that no valid business could have been done." With an impasse between the two forces and the situation dissolving into the ludicrous, Giles added that "a large part of the business during 1856 and the first part of 1857, by the tribunal transacting county business, consisted of appointing, qualifying, and receiving resignations of assessors, sheriffs, magistrates, constables and other county officers."

In spite of the mountainous problems confronting a faction-torn county, the board attempted constructive programs. Through a bond issue of $8,500 they erected a two-story brick courthouse, roughly 40 by 50 feet with a portico facing north. Like many of its projects the county never actually finished the Tecumseh courthouse, leaving some walls unplastered and doors unmounted.

In other business county officers oversaw road construction, established ferry rates, licensed wine and spirit dealers, and called for public school meetings. When smallpox broke out in Tecumseh in May, 1857, the board of commissioners appointed a health official to deal with the problem which, in this instance, meant the removal of the victim and family he was staying with "to an isolated spot not to exceed three miles from the courthouse." On some occasions, however, business ceased altogether. The March 16, 1857, minutes simply read: "the clerk was absent and books of the court cannot be found, and on motion the court is adjourned."

Performance and measures of the Lecompton government greatly displeased Kansas Free-Staters so on September 5, 1855, a convention met at Big Springs, then thought to be in Shawnee county, to organize a formal opposition. Out of the meeting evolved the Free-State party (later called the Black Republicans by their enemies) which agreed to hold a constitutional convention in Topeka late in October. Throughout that fall differing groups met in the territory and Shawnee county, sizing up their opportunities or opponents. Also in October, Proslave forces assembled in Tecumseh and other towns organizing "Law and Order" parties. The defiantly pro-South Leavenworth *Herald* declared their aim was to "put down the spirit of recklessness exhibited by fanatics, abolitionists and disunionists, by prompt and energetic measures."

The Topeka convention submitted a constitution to be voted upon, as it turned out, by only a part of the territorial electorate. Pro-South voters stayed away from the December elections, the tally reflected that fact. The constitution was adopted unanimously in the county with 135 ayes in Topeka but only 35 in Tecumseh. Following various preliminaries Charles Robinson journeyed to Topeka in March, 1856, as governor of the extra-legal State of Kansas.

A second event of the previous fall proved crucial to the peace of the territory when Proslave man Franklin M. Coleman murdered Free-Stater Charles M. Dow over a claim.

This incident provoked an affair later called the Wakarusa War in which tensions soared throughout the territory though no more blood was spilled. It induced communities to form militia groups to protect themselves from their adversaries, be they Free-State or Pro-slave. Topeka, Tecumseh, Indianola, and other rural settlements mustered some Free-State men together while a body called the Tecumseh Tigers may have been the southern counterpart.

Thomas Stinson had purchased his one or two slaves as early as 1851 in the first and probably only recorded slave sale within the future Shawnee county. Southerners brought most of their slaves into the territory during the summer of 1855 and established in Calhoun and Shawnee counties two major slave centers, Indianola and Tecum-seh. A very few slaves were brought into the upper reaches of the Wakarusa valley but Tecumseh township was the stronghold.

James K. Waysman, Dr. Duke W. Hunter, Eli Hopkins, and possi-bly Hiram J. Strickler were the leading Tecumseh residents known to own slaves. Judge Rush Elmore, also of Tecumseh, governed the most, having a veritable plantation with 12 or 14. Elmore, from a distinguished Alabama family, brought two or three families of slaves with him when he came to Kansas. He hired out one slave as a barber in Lecompton. Another gave him constant trouble, running away on at least one occasion, before being sold. The Elmore children played with some of the younger slaves. A neighbor, John Freeland, later recalled that the judge's son, Nesbit, often fought with a slave boy named Webster. The latter, being the heavier of the two, usually defeated Nesbit in wrestling matches. This disturbed Mrs. Elmore but her husband said that "if Nesbit puts himself with a negro, he must take negroes fare!"

Was slavery ever profitable in Kansas? The answer must be no. Even many prominent southern politicians, however much they might resent northern dominance in Congress and the country, recognized the institution as a hopeless venture on the Kansas prairies. The vast plantation system of the South required considerable time in building and this it did not receive in Kansas during its short territorial period. Of the three great southern cash crops, corn, cotton and tobacco, the two latter could not be grown in Kansas except under special circumstances and then in limited quantities.

Corn, on the other hand, might have been the key to the successful importation of slaves since it necessitated extensive field work in planting, weeding and harvesting.

One factor—the Kansas weather—doomed, not totally but effectively, the use of slaves. Unlike the South, each Kansas spring brought uncertainty whether the coming summer would be dry or not. The 1850s were not exceptionally good agricultural years, the last ones being disastrous. As yet no one had built up huge farms practical for slave cultivation. With the Free-State-Republican party gaining dominance at the end of the decade, the whole point soon became moot.

Even before the great Kansas drought of 1859-60, slave masters were selling their property. Judge Elmore transported most of his slaves to his brother in Alabama in January, 1859, asking them "to be sold in families; but if they will sell better by separating the larger children only do so. I do not wish the younger ones to be separated from their mother." One boy he praised highly because the lad could "drive a two-horse wagon, any no. of cattle, work and plough." For one woman, Fanny, he asked $1,100 but settled for $400. With his slaves gone by the spring of 1859, slavery disappeared as an issue in Shawnee county.

Yet for the summer of 1856 the problem of slavery and the future dominance of North or South was in balance. All around Shawnee county, especially in neighboring Douglas county, violence broke out with casualties on both sides. Apparently no one was actually murdered on account of political sympathies in the Topeka, Indianola, or

Tecumseh areas, but a number were injured. A Tecumseh transient with the inappropriate name of Pleasant Wood struck with a rock and seriously wounded Deer Creek farmer Erastus Moffet in April, 1856. Moffet, who quickly recovered, belonged to a Tecumseh Free-State militia unit while Wood was a member of what appears to be a loosely organized Proslave miltia group called the Tecumseh Tigers.

Tensions on the Missouri border and inland reached fever pitch during the summer of 1856 with numerous incidents occurring throughout the territory. Lawrence had been sacked in May and Missourians nearly succeeded in closing or reducing trade from the border to the inland Free-State communities. Supplies ran low in Topeka and on one occasion a teamster employed by John Farnsworth was stopped by ruffians "who," wrote Fry Giles, "under threats of death at resistance, took him from his fine team, wagon and merchandise."

Border ruffians, the Proslave legislature and even the federal government heaped, in the eyes of ardent Free-Staters at least, insult upon insult. On July 4, 1856, federal troops under the command of Col. E. V. Sumner dispersed the bogus Topeka Free-State legislature, thus ending its pretenses. Later that summer, in August, the adjutant general of the territorial militia, Tecumseh citizen Hiram J. Strickler, wrote to his friend Thomas Stinson about the battle, or rather, skirmish of Osawatomie on August 29: "All is excitement and confusion," he hastily explained. "Nothing but War Rumour of War are the Order of the day." He then went on: "losses to our side *none* . . . The Southern Division will eat *Breakfast* in Laurence!"

The southerners did not have their morning meal in Lawrence, but they did frighten Free-State settlers. Topekan Franklin L. Crane wrote in his diary on September 1, 1856:

> The affairs of Kansas are in a miserable condition. Yesterday Mr. Updegraff Mr. Tyler Mr. [Erastus?] Moffet and some others of Tecumseh with their families left that place being afraid to stay there longer. . . . The women & children are going to Iowa to remain till the troubles are settled the men will return and help fight the battles of freedom.

To obtain supplies, Topeka settlers sometimes banded together and traveled far to the north, even to southwestern Iowa. Conditions so deteriorated that some Topeka Free-Staters retaliated by raiding several of the nearby Proslave communities, in particular Tecumseh and Indianola early in September. In the process the stringent Free-Staters became little better than their antagonists.

Franklin Crane innocently recorded in his diary for September 4: "Some men went to Tecumseh & returned with goods in five waggons." About this incursion in Tecumseh the pro-South Leavenworth *Herald* exploded, laying all the blame at Jim Lane's feet (actually Topeka's

John Ritchie was one of the conspirators). This "confederated band of savages rode into town" reported the paper, "plundering, threatening to burn the town if the least resistance was effected them." It continued mentioning how all were "well armed and mounted on fine horses" and that they ransacked every store of their goods—*"even down to the brooms!"*

Benjamin Castleman, a leading Tecumseh merchant, soon wrote to the *Herald* about the assault on his place of business. He added that the men carried "Sharpe's rifles, Colt's revolvers, and bowie-knives." For the "advancement of their unholy cause" the Topekans seized a little over $4,000 worth of merchandise. According to the Andreas *History of Kansas,* all Castlemen ever got back from the raid was "a meal sieve and a tin pan, which some conscientious individual returned to him on finding his trademark upon them." One need not feel too badly for him, though, since less than a year later he was advertising his goods "which will be sold *cheap for cash.*" A month and a half after the robbery, Castleman was appointed sheriff.

Indianola also suffered the indignity of a similar visit by Topekans a few days later. Samuel Reader remembered in his autobiography:

> Our neighborhood was badly stirred up. . . . A party of Free-State men . . . took from the most rabid Pro-slavery citizens, their arms and military stores; together with Sundry articles, claimed to be contraband of war. The whiskey was emptied in the street. I had no hand in it; and whether the act was justifiable or not, is not for me to say. It was called a reprisal; but two wrongs do not always make one right! . . . But it was reported that our ruthless enemies [the ruffians] did far worse. Besides plundering, they added, "fire- and sword" and numberless outrages, on Free-State men!

When Free-Staters overheard that border ruffians were preparing to attack Valley Falls, Reader and other Topekans under James Lane rushed out to face them September 13 just over the county line at Hickory Point in Jefferson county. After this minor skirmish, Reader dashed off some lines in his diary that they arrived at Hickory Point about 11:00 o'clock in the morning, "Fired some," and then "retreated to O [zawkie]." He claimed that his side only counted three horses and one man wounded to "Several B.Rs. [border ruffians] killed" (actually only one). With that brief moment behind him, Reader ate some watermelons and in the evening started for home, "sleepy and tired but full of glory."

Glory could never be a description for Kansas in 1856. Following this period of "Bleeding Kansas," the United States established a claims commission to reimburse those whose property had been stolen or destroyed during the conflict. From the report of the Commissioners of Claims (Edward Hoogland of Tecumseh was a member) in

Samuel Reader's view of the Battle of Hickory Point, September 13, 1856.
(From the "Autobiography" of Samuel J. Reader)

1859, the Shawnee county claims totaled over $24,200. To the 22 Pro-slave claimants and the 17 Free-State, this body awarded $22,103.19. Proslave contestants would have received the greatest share, a little over $16,000. Both Proslave and Free-State partisans had property destroyed or stolen by their compatriots—particularly the Free-Staters. One Free-State and two Proslave houses were ruined, 33 Proslave and 13 Free-State horses were stolen, and 60 Proslave cattle and seven Free-State cattle were appropriated. However, the federal government never paid the claims. Until the turn of the century and a bit beyond, people sought relief but this issue, like that of "Bleeding Kansas," passed into history and myth.

A number of Free-State warriors involved in the Tecumseh and/or Indianola raids and other activities were subsequently arrested that fall and imprisoned in Lecompton or Tecumseh. This action stirred great resentment in the northern or Free-State press. Most were acquitted. At one time the jail in the Tecumseh courthouse sup-posedly housed as many as 47 prisoners of whom John Ritchie of Topeka was one. About ten o'clock the night of November 21, 1856, around 30 or 31 of them escaped, "by pegging a hole in the wall and crawling out like rats," recounted the pro-South Lecompton *Union* on December 11. Officers caught one fellow half way out and pulled him back in, his excuse being "I am following the rest."

Shawnee county quieted down following the fall of 1856, but the communities, particularly Topeka, grew very little that year or in the winter of 1857. Beginning in the spring people began traveling to the area from the North and Topeka's fortunes improved. Nearly 450 persons temporarily or permanently were residing there when new blood arrived from the East "well supplied with coin" as Fry Giles put it. Even "men who had invested in Topeka's Proslavery rival, Tecumseh," Giles added, "joined the crowd of greedy buyers at Topeka, and made large investments." Any Proslavery desire spent itself in the next year or two, and Topeka Free-Staters turned their eyes and attention to the courthouse at Tecumseh.

The county seat started losing the population race in 1857 but still appeared economically and politically healthy. Tecumseh's newspaper, the *Kansas Settler,* desperately called out in 1858 "we want 100 masons, bricklayers, and carpenters immediately. Every mechanic, wagon-maker, tinner, shoemaker, chairmaker . . . is requested to 'pitch in' to Tecumseh." Unfortunately, they didn't and Free-Staters captured both the territorial legislature and many of the county government positions. This led to the showdown on the county seat question: was it to be Tecumseh or Topeka?

The Topeka controlled county commission resented meeting in Tecumseh and so occasionally conducted sessions elsewhere. At the same time, inhabitants of Auburn believed their community an excellent choice for county seat. The legislature, now sympathetic to Topeka, designated October 4, 1858, as the date for the election to decide the matter. Topeka won handily, but out of this contest arose an amusing, apocryphal story, often attributed to Chester Thomas, which questions the ethics of that election. Supposedly late on the appointed day a Topekan excitedly rode into town exclaiming that Tecumseh was voting 17-year-old boys there. One Topeka official, however, quickly hushed him up murmuring that "we're votin' 15-year-olds here."

By law the probate judge was required to publish the results, but Tecumseh's Judge Hoogland delayed doing so in hopes of postponing the inevitable. The county clerk, Fry Giles of Topeka, grew impatient and, as he wrote in his *Thirty Years in Topeka,* "became a little revolutionary in turn, and quietly loaded the 'county seat' [the records, etc.] into his buggy and carried it away to Topeka." Hoogland and Tecumseh leaders protested to the legislature but to no avail. In January, 1859, the territory officially acknowledged Topeka as the county seat. Cyrus K. Holliday in a letter dated January 20 referred to the jubilant Topekans firing off their cannon in celebration and the frustration of the people from the village to the east,

Tecumseh. Pleased with their efforts the Topeka county officials promptly repudiated the debts on the Tecumseh courthouse.

Secure now with the county seat tucked under her breast (the first Topeka courthouse would not be completed until after the Civil War), Topeka grew while Tecumseh and Auburn declined.

The year 1859 produced mixed results in territorial life. Settlers heard the news of a great new gold discovery in the western mountains of Kansas as Denver became the new land of fortune. In a letter to his brother dated February 17, 1859, Rush Elmore explained how scarce money was though he expected new settlers and Pike's Peak bound prospectors to improve the supply. But "if all go who are talking about it the country will lose 1/3 of her population (of the males) and we will not be able to produce a sufficient quantity of bread stuff of their support." A month later Elmore concluded "all quiet in the Territory everybody going to Pikes Peak after gold, which I think will in all probability be a wild goose chase to a great many of them."

Shawnee county residents that same year witnessed another phenomenon but one far less amusing than Pike's Peak or bust caravans. Drought struck and lingered well into 1860. Crops failed throughout the eastern section of the territory causing great distress among settlers, especially those still quite new to the land. Rains were spotty and never sufficient. When one of some dimension did occur, Topeka's *Kansas State Record* became quite agitated. "Rain, Rain!" headlined the *Record* February 18, 1860, "We have rain at last." After four months with little more than "two or three light snow flurries" Topeka had one of these "old fashion dreary, drizzley rain storms." Once people "dreaded" that kind but now welcomed it—the rain being more important "than 'color' to the miner."

Such enthusiasm, however, was infrequent and conditions became desperate during the summer. John Brown of Auburn, who had been in the area since the 1840s, claimed that of 40 acres of wheat his yield was nothing and of 100 acres in corn he estimated the yield to be no more than one bushel to the acre. Under the sponsorship of Thaddeus Hyatt, easterners formed a relief agency for Kansas and gathered information about the destitute in the various counties. Three meetings were conducted in Shawnee county in September, 1860, where township residents reported the problems and failures in their neighborhoods.

One farmer, who had planted eight acres, claimed he would not get a single potato nor enough corn "to feed a goose." Another resident in the Tecumseh-Topeka area stated that in eleven months only four inches of rain had fallen. In all the relief agency report estimated that there had been planted and sown in Shawnee county 17,500 acres, "from which has been raised 4351½ bushels of wheat, 5,187 bushels of corn, 11 bushels of potatoes, [and] 10 bushels of beans. . . ." This, naturally, meant scores of farmers faced poverty in the county and needed provisions immediately.

Brown calculated that "there are fifty families in this township [Auburn] that have not two dollars to the family, nor two bushels of corn, and nothing else." The report estimated 100 families had left, most back east no doubt, and the following is an example of their plight:

E. Baily, west of Williamsport, said his teams were idle for want of employment; could not get one dollar per day for hauling; the prospects for crops last spring were good; there is nothing now; he has planted forty acres of corn, and cannot find a mess of roasting ears without worms. He is about starting for the East, with a wife and seven children, and with fifty cents in his pocket; he has already sacrificed his property, except his wagon and oxen, for three dollars and fifty cents.

In the future Shawnee county residents would suffer through more droughts and the opposite problem, floods. Undoubtedly most were ready for the plagues of the territorial years to end. Many eagerly looked forward to glorious years for a State of Kansas.

John and Hettie Thresher in a covered wagon typical of those used in the late 19th century. (Courtesy John W. Ripley)

Topeka about 1858 as drawn by Henry Waugh. The scene is apparently from the Kansas river bank looking south on rut-filled Kansas avenue. One of the flat-topped buildings on the right may represent Constitution Hall. Acquainted with the narrow streets of fire-plagued eastern cities, Topeka founders may have made the avenue extra wide to serve as a possible fire-break. (Courtesy Missouri Historical Society)

Many Shawnee countians, such as Capt. Henry C. Lindsay (later a Topeka police chief), upper right, served in the 18th and 19th Kansas cavalry against the Indians. The man in the top hat may be Wild Bill Hickok who served as scout. The picture was probably taken in Topeka in 1867. (Courtesy Kansas State Historical Society)

SOUNDS OF RIFLE FIRE; MILITARY HISTORY

On July 5, 1859, delegates to the state constitutional convention met at Wyandotte and continued in session until the 30th. The officials had been elected a month before with John Ritchie, H. D. Preston, and John P. Greer chosen to represent Shawnee county.

Under a provision of the constitution written by this convention, the location of the state capital was to be adopted in the following manner:

> The temporary seat of government is hereby located at the city of Topeka, county of Shawnee. The first Legislature under this constitution shall provide, by law for submitting the question of the permanent location of the capital to a popular vote, and a majority of votes cast at some general election shall be necessary for such location.

On January 21, 1861, the U. S. senate voted to admit Kansas as a free state under the Wyandotte constitution. Prior to this seven southern states had renounced their allegiance to the Union and were therefore not represented in congress. Thus Kansas was not subjected to their negative votes on admission. The vote in the senate was 36 to 16. On the 28th day of January the house of representatives passed the Kansas bill by a vote of 117 to 42. The following day President James Buchanan signed the bill, ending the long Proslave and Free-State quarrel on the prairies.

A permanent site for the capital could now be decided. On the last day of the first legislative session, June 3, 1861, an act providing for submission of the issue was passed. An effort had already been made by Lawrence to hold a special, rather than the general election provided by the constitution, but this had failed.

From its inception, Topeka had vied for the honor of being made capital, as had Lawrence and Leavenworth. Fry Giles, in his *Thirty Years in Topeka*, says that Lawrence had particular confidence in the race: "Lawrence, especially, for two or three years before, had felt quite confident of her ability to win the prize. She had repeatedly secured, substantially without opposition, an adjournment of the Territorial Legislature from Lecompton, and had by that means secured considerable prestige as the seat of legislation." In addition, Lawrence had greater political influence, greater population, and was more centrally located than Leavenworth. "In good works for the cause of free Kansas, Lawrence had been pre-eminent, and she enjoyed the measure of gratitude justly due to her," Giles concluded.

Only Topeka's location and the efforts of her citizens could win her the title. To conduct the fight a meeting was called and a "board of managers" elected. Headquarters were set up in the office of Edmund G. Ross' *Kansas Tribune*, and the procurement of funds for the campaign became the chief order of business. It was assumed that $40,000 was the minimum needed to secure the capital for Topeka, but the amount of available funds was so small that the board turned to the country people surrounding the town. The board members resorted to a plan to get subscriptions by sale of town lots and country lands. Urgent appeals continued, but not more than a quarter of the sum was raised.

The election came on November 5, 1861, and the turnout was relatively heavy. The total vote was 14,981. Of that number, Topeka received 7,859; Lawrence, 5,194; and Leavenworth, 815.* Other towns receiving votes were Baldwin, Emporia, the Sac and Fox Indian Agency (present Quenemo), and the previously Proslave towns of Lecompton, Kickapoo, Whiskey Point and Tecumseh. Out of 33 counties in the new state at the time, 22 gave majorities to Topeka and 11 went to Lawrence.

Without the benefit of rapid communications the inhabitants of Topeka did not learn the outcome of the election until the evening of the following day. The selection meant much to the city. Upon acquiring the seat of government, she assumed a new character for all the citizens of the infant state and its prospective immigrants.

"No excitement in regard to value of real estate took place," stated Giles, "but it had at once an assured value in the estimation of holders, that it had not previously possessed." What had been accomplished in the growth of the town so far was the result of its residents' diligent efforts to combine the hopes of individual wealth and position with the overall prosperity of Topeka. It might be supposed that having reached the pinnacle which had been desired since the birth of the town, there would be a relaxation of community efforts and a redirection toward personal benefit. But this was not the case. Rather, becoming the capital was considered a springboard for "further advancing the interests of the town."

The economic advance triggered by the designation of the capital was not slowed later in that year when civil war began. The majority of the inhabitants of Shawnee county were intensely pro-Union, and after the war commenced there was little active disloyalty in the

---

*According to Giles all but 14 of the votes cast for the city of Leavenworth came from Leavenworth county.

county, although there is some evidence of political dissent and southern sympathy. In Tecumseh a resident raised the Stars and Bars over his home, but it was quickly removed when he was visited by local Unionists.

In general, the county was not directly affected by the war during its early days. Two men—W. W. Ross of Topeka and Chester Thomas of Auburn—hastened to join Jim Lane's Frontier Guard in Washington, D. C. in April, 1861, and this unit bivouacked in the East Room of the White House. Many Shawnee countians enlisted in the volunteer regiments raised in 1861 and 1862.

Then in 1863 a disastrous blow struck Topeka's former rival, Lawrence. William C. Quantrill and about 300 guerrillas crossed the Kansas river near Aubrey on August 20. The raiders covered some 50 miles of countryside unpursued and at dawn the next day devastated Lawrence, killing nearly 150 persons.

In early September, Gen. Thomas Ewing, commanding the Department of Missouri (and brother-in-law of William T. Sherman), sent word to Topeka and the surrounding area that Quantrill and about a thousand men were 20 miles south of Independence, Mo., preparing for an encore performance. Topekans were naturally agitated by this news. A public meeting was called to discuss various plans for defense, but all that was done was alert the militia for possible service.

The attack on Lawrence did give Topekans pause, however, so much so that the people met and discussed protection plans for the city. Discussion was as far as the plans went for over a year. The fall of 1864 brought an invasion of Missouri by Confederate Gen. Sterling Price. His original objective was St. Louis, but finding Union defenses stout in the eastern half of Missouri, he turned west. The Confederate army could conceivably have invaded Kansas had it not been defeated during the three-day Battle of Westport.

During the time that Price was on the state border the question of defense once again arose in Topeka, and it was considered necessary to take proper precautions to protect the city "should any stragglers from Price's command come this way."*

A stockade was finally decided upon and a force of woodchoppers gathered elm and cottonwood logs from the south side of the river where the Kansas avenue bridge now crosses. The timber was cut "in lengths of about twelve feet, split in half, and hauled to the intersection of Sixth and Kansas Avenue by Ed Pope, Eberry Papan and perhaps others," said Freeman Sardou, an old resident of the county.

*On July 3, 1869 The *Kansas Daily State Record* carried a story on Price's raid and protective measures adopted by Shawnee county. The defenses had been dismantled only a short time before.

The logs were set in the ground about three feet deep in a circular form with the bark side out. Loopholes were cut in each log—one for firing while standing and one for the kneeling position—and four openings were left, facing each direction, for a small cannon. A single gate was installed on the west side.

The stockade, dubbed "Fort Simple," was high enough to prevent scaling by any but the most able attackers and then "only by a hard effort." All men not at the front were engaged in digging rifle pits in which sharpshooters could lie with relative safety. Reports of guerrillas and rebel stragglers came to the county several times, and at least once the residents of Topeka were so convinced of an impending attack that they buried their treasures and manned the trenches. Among those standing guard at the stockade one night were three women who masqueraded as men. Only the coming of daylight revealed their feminine characteristics.

When it became known that Price was heading toward Kansas, Gen. Samuel R. Curtis, commanding the Department of Kansas, hastily summoned his available troops. Many of his men were with James G. Blunt fighting Indians on the frontier. Curtis urged Gov. Thomas Carney to call out the state militia. Estimates of Price's force ranged in number from 5,000 to 30,000. This threat was enough to convince the governor to follow the advice of Curtis and on October 8 he activated the militia. In order "to give an impetus to Price's departure," wrote Curtis, the governor issued the following proclamation:

Kansas, rally! You will do so as you have always done, when your soil has been invaded. The Call this time will come to you louder and stronger, because you know the foe will seek to glut his vengeance upon you.

Meet him, then, at the threshold and strike boldly; strike as one man against him.

Let all business be suspended. The work to be done now is to protect the State against marauder and murderer. Until that is accomplished we must lead a soldier's life, and do a soldier's duty.

Men of Kansas, rally! One blow, one earnest, united blow, will foil the invader and save you. Who will falter? Who is not ready to meet the peril? Who will not defend his home and the State?

To arms, then! To arms and the tented field, until the rebel foe shall be baffled and beaten back.

A Free-State militia had been organized as early as 1856. It was to "prepare as fully as possible for self defense against the invaders," Proslavery men from Missouri at that time. Elements of the county militia had seen action during the troubled territorial days of Kansas. In revenge for the massacre of Free-State men near the Marais des Cygnes river, in the southeastern part of the state, Lawrence and Topeka area militia had been called out by Jim Lane. The Indianola Free-State

Guards had been formed during the territorial period and took part in the bloodless "Battle of Indianola." By 1864 even some of the former Proslavery men of the town had joined with the Indianola company to make up Company D of the Shawnee county regiment.

Immediately following the sack of Lawrence, the citizens of Topeka feared a like outrage, and immediately organized a militia company to protect themselves. Elizabeth Reader, a resident of Indianola and later of Topeka, said that its members continued to meet and drill until the fall of 1864. The Shawnee county unit was designated the Second Regiment, Kansas State Militia, with Col. George W. Veale commanding. The Second K.S.M. was brigaded with Lawrence and Wyandotte units under Gen. M. S. Grant and was ordered to assemble at Olathe, along with ten other regiments. Each outfit had to provide its own transportation and all rations possible. Individuals were supplied with "two blankets, a tin cup, knife and fork, and a haversack," according to the major general of the state militia, George W. Deitzler. In addition, the Second received new Enfield rifles, in place of the old and nearly worthless carbines that had been issued directly after the Lawrence raid. Samuel J. Reader, a resident of Indianola who reported on the equipping of the regiment, was lieutenant and quartermaster of the Second and the best available source of information on the county regiment.

Two days after the militia was called out General Curtis proclaimed martial law throughout his department and ordered every man between the ages of 18 and 60 years to arms and to the border. On the morning of October 12 the Second moved out for Missouri. They saw combat ten days later.

The regiment had 561 men divided into 11 companies and a battery with a 24-pound gun under Capt. Ross Burns. Captains of the companies were Daniel H. Horne, A. J. Huntoon, J. B. Hannum, Sterling B. Miles, John H. Banks, James Thomson, Harvey McCaslin, William Disney, J. B. Stuart, D. B. Burdick, and J. W. Mossman.

There were also a number of men in the county who had not arrived in Topeka in time to join Col. Veale and the Second. Andrew Stark, major of the regiment, was ordered to remain in Topeka to command the stockade and organize the men still in the capital into a "home battalion." Two companies of infantry, two of cavalry, one of exempts who were in one way or another invalided, one of "coloreds," and another one-gun battery made up this unit. Fry Giles, captain of a Topeka company of infantry in this short-lived militia, said that it was on duty from October 12 to the 26, "when it was last mustered."

Samuel J. Reader's watercolors of the charge "into the Jaws of Death," march into Missouri, and the capture of prisoners at the Battle of the Blue. The men of the Second Kansas Militia came from Topeka, Tecumseh, Indianola, Big Springs, Auburn, and Monmouth. Prisoners of war on their march to southern Missouri subsisted on corn and after fording streams, slept in their wet clothing. Once released and returned home, many died of exposure and pneumonia. (From the "Autobiography" of Samuel J. Reader)

By the middle of the month nearly 12,000 men had answered the governor's call, and martial law was in effect along the border. Gen. Curtis organized his troops into two divisions under Generals Blunt and Deitzler. Portions of Blunt's division engaged Price's Confederates near Lexington, Mo., on October 18, but superior numbers forced them to fall back. Price, whose rear was being pressured by some 20,000 Union cavalry, pushed Blunt's troops back again in a day-long skirmish at Independence.

On October 22, Curtis' entire force confronted the rebels on Big Blue creek, a short distance south of Kansas City, where severe fighting took place at Byram's Ford and Hickman's Mills. The scene of the battle was shifting towards the southeast and Gen. Deitzler made an effort to get his militia into position for the impending attack, but without much success. The Second K.S.M. was deployed at Byram's Ford south of Westport.

Upon reaching the Big Blue, Price found himself in trouble. The Union cavalry to his rear was rapidly drawing nearer and on the border he had run into Curtis. The Confederates attempted to break through the Union lines to the west only to run headlong into the Shawnee county regiment. Sixteen regiments of the state militia took active part in the fighting south and east of Kansas City in the vicinity of Westport, but the Second was in the "thickest of the fighting and was nearly cut to pieces, losing a great many men killed, and a large number wounded, and many taken prisoner. The balance of the militia regiments did flanking movement duty," wrote J. C. Petheridge in his *Kansas State Militia—1864.* The regiment was at one point driving against the enemy when it was outflanked and overrun by a series of cavalry charges led by Jo Shelby. Of particular note was the stand of Capt. Ross Burns and the Topeka Battery. About them Shelby said, the "defense against me was a most gallant one, and was executed with masterly skill and superb courage, and how so small a battery could have held my superior forces so completely in check is a question which has caused me to wonder greatly, my only explanation being the splendid military skill and quick perception by Captain Burns and the bravery of his men." *

The Shawnee county militia lost 24 killed, about 20 wounded, and 88 taken prisoner, among them four officers. The 24-pound howitzer and about 100 horses were also lost. The battery took the brunt of the losses, with all 24 men killed, captured, or wounded. The last man captured was Ross Burns, who was knocked senseless with a rifle butt before being taken prisoner by the Confederates. Colonel Veale

---

*Shelby discounts the rest of the regiment's effectiveness, however, claiming that he swept away all resistance until his cavalry was faced with the Topeka Battery.

reported enemy losses as very heavy, counting some 43 dead rebels on the field shortly after the battle.

The next day the Confederates concentrated their full force along the Big Blue. The ensuing Battle of Westport was the last major engagement in the Trans-Mississippi war. Price's army was broken by the combined efforts of Union ranks before and behind him. By the end of the day the rebels began a precipitous retreat, pursued by volunteers and militia, towards the Arkansas river; on November 8 the greatest battle on Kansas soil was fought at Mine creek. But after the Big Blue, Shawnee countians, with the exception of men in the Kansas volunteer units, were not engaged.

On October 25 General Curtis revoked the declaration of martial law, and the same day ordered the militia back to Kansas. Five days after the battle on the Big Blue, Gov. Carney disbanded the state militia.

Colonel Veale, in his report of the fight of the Second K.S.M., said:

> On the morning of the 24th, we gathered together our dead (our wounded having been already cared for) and took them to Kansas City, where we obtained coffins for them, and on the morning of the 25th, we buried them at Wyandotte, on Kansas soil. From there we marched home to meet our mourning friends, and tell the story of the fallen.

In the four years of the war, Shawnee county contributed a fair share of her men to the armies of the Union. Most notable of the county's military experiences was the departure of the untrained militia from its formation on Sixth street and its movement eastward "in its varied equippage," as Giles said, "and followed by its incongruous huddle of farm wagons and teams, in haste to be a military train. . . ."

When the Second returned from its adventure its members quickly reverted to civilian life. Recovery from the disastrous drought of 1860 had been rapid; so much so that agricultural activities in the county, combined with businesses in Topeka, was sufficient to develop a satisfactory market for the two new banks on Kansas avenue by 1866. That year marked the beginning of a minor boom in the county which was to last through the decade. That year also brought the first train to Topeka.

The war years had opened a market in government military buying and this eventually absorbed most of the county's agricultural output. Farmers began to abandon their log houses for more substantial stone or frame ones.

Despite booming business in the county, money was scarce. Milton Tabor wrote years later that "settlers along what was then the western edge of civilization had to take their produce to the markets in eastern

Kansas. Wabaunsee county was settling up, but the nearest market was Topeka." He told of two farmers who lived near Alma. They loaded two wagons with produce to sell in Topeka. On their arrival, they found they could not dispose of any of their goods, but John Branner (after whom Branner street is named) and Jacob Klein, pioneer cobblers in Topeka, gave them a letter of introduction to a Leavenworth merchant. Five days and 240 miles later they returned home with groceries for the winter.

One of the most dramatic features of the post-war era was the migration of blacks from the South into Kansas, with a substantial number making their home in Topeka. In one decade the total black population in Kansas had risen from a mere 816 in 1860 to nearly 13,000. Whites in the county welcomed the influx of black refugees for labor. The shortage of manpower in the state had become severe because of the war. Sam Reader wrote from Indianola to a relative back east, "it would be a great blessing if more darkies would understand their rights and come to our aid."

Blacks, coming more rapidly after the arrival of the railroads, settled in the less desirable areas of the city and threw up little "contraband" shacks. Despite the labor shortage, some of the new citizens did not feel obligated to work, often equating work with their former slavery. Little settlements such as Tennessee Town and Redmondsville and "the Bottoms" became black ghettoes, but gradually the refugees came to the realization that work was an essential requirement for their survival. They left their shanty towns and sought jobs.

Topeka grew rapidly after the war. It became the center of trade for lumber, supplying areas to the west and south. The Union Pacific, Eastern Division, offered a reduced cost in lumber transportation and made the construction of buildings much less difficult and expensive. The years 1866 and 1868 were big ones for construction in Topeka. It has been estimated that fully 400 buildings were put up in Topeka in 1868 alone.

"But gratifying and encouraging as were the events of 1868," wrote Giles, "those of 1869 greatly surpassed them in importance to the commercial interests of the town." Businesses were established and better stocked than Topeka ever had seen; new homes were estimated at 500; Kansas avenue was graded, curbed, and guttered; and the new Atchison, Topeka and Santa Fe railroad spanned the Kaw with an iron bridge and laid track from the capital to Burlingame.

The railroads, which helped bring prosperity to Shawnee county, had been the final factor in removal of Indians from the area. Railroad interests centered in eastern Kansas cities were the prime factor in opening Indian reservations within the boundaries of the county. Kansas reservations totaled 9,986,442 acres in 1860—approximately a fifth of the total area of the state. One historian states that during the 1860s state and federal officials launched a determined drive to acquire the reservations for white settlement. By the summer of 1863 Indian Commissioner W. P. Dole came to Kansas "and drew up treaties with the Sac and Fox, Osage, Shawnee and New York Indians calling for their transfer to the Indian Territory." Railroad lobbyists wanted Indian land in Shawnee county for right-of-way and sale to new settlers. Only the treaty with the Shawnees directly affected the county, and, even though that tribe refused to ratify its treaty, by 1871 all Shawnees, Pottawatomies, half-breed Kaws, and Delawares had given up their land within the boundaries.*

Local politics were dominated primarily by the Republican party in the 1860s. The outstanding exception to this rule was one of the city's founders and leading citizens, Cyrus K. Holliday. Republicans styled themselves the "Union" party during the war and criticised their Democratic colleagues as "seceders" and "copperheads." Even with the considerable personal influence exercised by Holliday, who served conspicuously as the state's first adjutant general, the Democratic party as a whole emerged from the war a weak minority.

Republican strength in part rested with the Grand Army of the Republic. The first post of the G.A.R. in Kansas was formed in Topeka in December, 1865. It rapidly became a political force in the post-war years. Its members were highly patriotic, placing flags over Kansas schools, helping to make Lincoln's birthday and Memorial Day national holidays, and adopting the motto "One flag, One nation, One language." For a time, when the educational system in Kansas broke down because of political squabbles, schools were run by the G.A.R.

Members of the G.A.R. also helped former soldiers in their relations with the government. Instrumental in obtaining discharge papers and pensions for veterans was Colonel Veale, late commander of the Second K.S.M. Typical of requests made of him was that from O. T. Angell, a private in the Indianola company of Veale's regiment: "Sir will you Please inform me whether the Kansas Malitia have been paid, and if so how I can get my pay &c. I Belonged to the Indianola Co. Capt. Miles. Please give me all the particulars and oblige."

Veale was elected state senator from Shawnee county in 1866 and was soon faced with debts incurred by the Second K.S.M. in its campaign against the rebels. Some of the regiment's equipment and

---

*Although these tribes did not give up their claims in the county until 1871, there were no established Indian reservations within the area after about 1860.

supplies had been paid for in scrip and clamorings for payment of that scrip continued throughout Veale's term in the legislature. Eventually most of the debts were paid by the federal government.

The year the colonel was elected was comparatively quiet in western Kansas because Cheyennes and Sioux went north to carry on their warfare. In 1867, however, the Plains tribes tried to prevent the building of the railroads and prohibit wagon traffic across the prairies. Gen. Winfield Scott Hancock with 1,100 men and some artillery took the field that spring to show the warriors "that the government is ready and able to punish them if they are hostile, although it may not . . . invite war." Hancock tried to find and fight them, but they avoided his large force. George A. Custer and the Seventh cavalry had no better luck.

By summer it became necessary for the state to assist in subduing the hostiles. The 18th Kansas volunteer cavalry battalion of four companies was organized to take the field against them. The 18th was called into service by General W. T. Sherman in June, 1867. Shawnee county provided 70 men for the battalion, including five officers. Nearly half of Company B were citizens of the county, enlisted from Auburn, Eugene and Topeka. The campaign of the 18th began at Fort Harker on July 15 and extended over a wide area of the western counties. At Harker and again at Fort Larned the battalion was stricken by Asiatic cholera. Two companies, B and C, including many Shawnee countians, took the field from Hays on August 12 and fought a severe battle on Prairie Dog creek on August 21. James H. Beach wrote in the *Kansas Historical Collections*, "In all probability these operations prevented a general uprising of the Indians such as occurred the next summer."

In the summer of 1868, from the Texas Panhandle to Nebraska and from central Kansas to the Rockies, murders and outrages became commonplace. Regular troops were inadequate to meet the emergency. Gov. Samuel J. Crawford called a full regiment of cavalry, the 19th Kansas volunteers, into service following a request by Gen. P. H. Sheridan dated October 9, 1868. Governor Crawford, who had seen service in the Civil War, resigned the governorship on November 4 and assumed command of the regiment. The lieutenant-colonel was Horace L. Moore, who had commanded the 18th Kansas the previous summer.

Topeka provided captains for all but one of the companies of the regiment. Company A was made up of 101 Topekans, and its captain was A. J. Pliley, a veteran of the Beecher Island fight earlier in the year. Other Shawnee county men were interspersed throughout the regiment.

The 19th left Topeka on November 5, and on the 28th joined General Sheridan on the North Canadian river in Indian territory. It moved to Fort Hays in March, 1869, having stayed in the field the entire winter, and was mustered out in April. During that time only one man from the county deserted. He was apprehended two days later, and $30 bounty was paid for his return.

Colonel Crawford returned to Topeka from the campaign before the 19th was mustered out. The March 11, 1869, issue of the Topeka *Weekly Leader* stated:

Col. Crawford left here with his regiment, in early winter, and passed the entire time on the plains until about ten days since. His face was bronzed with exposure, but his feelings and good heart looked out through those kind and affectionate eyes. He was gladly glad to get back to friends and family after having been exposed to the snows and grim winter of the plains. And those persons who have never been on our western frontier know nothing of the severity of a north-wester.

The same issue of the *Leader* claimed that the entire winter campaign against the Indians was fruitless. Indeed, nothing had been solved in regards to frontier violence between red men and white. But county men who returned with the 19th felt that though they had not participated in any fights, they had taken part in an instructive campaign against the hostiles.

Shawnee countians also served in the 20th Kansas volunteer infantry during the Philippine war of 1899. (Courtesy Kansas State Historical Society)

"Presented by the People of Shawnee Co. . . . in Grateful Recognition for Patriotic Services in World War." (Courtesy Jerry Clark)

Kansas' 35th Division on parade after World War I, May, 1919. The First Baptist church is in the background. (Courtesy Perce Harvey)

Topeka Army Air Field (Forbes) with B29s and B50s on the flight line during the Korean conflict of 1950s. (Courtesy Kansas State Historical Society)

A Topeka Bus and Baggage Company rig out in the hinterlands near Richland. (Courtesy Mrs. LeRoy Murren)

Alonzo and Annie Thomas of the Santa Fe Watch Co. in Terry Stafford's auto "Old Bill #2." (Courtesy Kansas State Historical Society)

Sam Reader, of Indianola, drew this picture of the Kansas river ferry at Calhoun in 1855. (From Samuel J. Reader's diary)

Kansas Power and Light company's car number 123 heads south on Kansas avenue in North Topeka in 1936. (Courtesy William A. Gibson)

FROM PLACE TO PLACE; TRANSPORTATION

The fertile Oregon country lured thousands of Americans west in the 1840s and 1850s. Settlers crossed overland or on the central rivers to western Missouri and in the spring embarked from St. Joseph, Fort Leavenworth, or Westport over the Oregon-California road. Although never distinctly laid out, wagon roads generally followed the line of least resistance. One branch of the trail, that from Westport, stayed south of the Kansas river until the Shawnee county area where the wagons made the first important and difficult river crossing.

Actually there were two Oregon trails in Shawnee county, the road having divided just east of the town of Big Springs. The older fork turned southwest and then resumed a slight northeasterly course to a river ford just above Uniontown. The second branch curved to the northwest to be closer to the river and cross on the Papan ferry at the future Topeka town site. Since that time nearly all traces of the trail have been plowed under or destroyed.

Crossing the relatively flat Kansas prairies was not a simple matter for wagon trains which often had over 100 ox, or mule-drawn wagons and large herds of cattle. Even small creek banks were hazardous, especially when wet, and each wagon had to be slowly let down and then brought up on the other side. At the ford or the ferry the cattle usually became mired in the soft, sandy river bottom. It took time and patience for everything to be efficiently organized for the Kansas river crossing and then it might require two or three days to get the last wagon of a train off the Papan ferry and on to the north bank.

Sometime in the early 1840s, three French-Canadian brothers named Papan, later joined by a fourth, came to Shawnee county and established in 1843 a ferry service for Oregon travelers. Their initial ferry was crude, being no more than two or three dug-outs tied together by a log platform, capable of carrying only one wagon at a time. A rope strung from a tree on one bank to one on the opposite side served as a guide for the ferryman who propelled the craft with a long pole. Changing river currents and floods such as the disastrous one of 1844 frequently interrupted operation creating more delays and headaches for those Oregon bound.

Apparently their customers did not particularly admire them, one unfavorable account coming from Peter H. Burnett who arrived late in May, 1843. His party included 110 wagons and 263 men "able to bear arms," which for two days crossed on their own platform built atop two canoes. Burnett wrote:

> The committee attempted to hire Pappa's platform (a Frenchman who lived at the crossing), but no reasonable arrangement could be made with him. Before we had finished our platform, some of the company made a private arrangement with Pappa for themselves, and commensed crossing. This produced great dissatisfaction in camp. On the 28th [May] Pappa's platform sank, and several men, women, and children came near being drowned, but all escaped with the loss of some property.

Once on the other side of the Kansas, the wagon parties continued on a single trail to the Catholic Mission of St. Mary's. James A. Pritchard described one incident on that leg of the journey in his diary of 1849:

> Our rout today was along the Kansas bottom principally the bottom being soft made it very heard pulling. We crossed a number of creeks & mud holes, with steep banks. We passed an Indian village about 9 A.M. where their was . . . a temporary bridge across a bad muddy creek by an old Indian [later identified as Peter Bourbonnais] who charged us 25 cts apiece for our wagons.

Capitalism was rampant in the Pottawatomie reserve as a week later a party reached the same toll bridge and was charged 50 cents and still others got by for only a dime.

A second pre-territorial route was the Fort Leavenworth to Fort Riley military road which opened in 1853. It passed through the northern portion of the county, and the towns of Indianola and Whitfield City were founded beside it. The road lacked bridges and was in an unimproved state when this letter was written to the New York *Times* which printed it July 15, 1853:

> It was the roughest and most disagreeable one that ever was traveled by white man or nigger since the days of Moses. It was an incessant crossing of creeks, sloughs, quagmires, swampy bottoms and rocky hollows, the entire route. The man that conceives the idea of opening a road through the section of country we passed over, ought to be trundled over it in a mud wagon, without anything more comfortable to sit upon than a triangular rail, twice every month for five years to give him a quintessence of all the *pleasures* that would be enjoyed by all future travelers passing in that direction.

With the opening of this route, traffic from Leavenworth to Santa Fe, N. M., used the military road to Indianola and then struck south for the Sidney Smith ferry near the Pottawatomie Baptist Mission. Travelers then headed south for the Santa Fe trail in Wabaunsee county.

The Shawnee county commissioners in 1856 tried to correct some of the problems specified by the traveler quoted above. First they divided the county into two road districts and appointed an overseer to each. The overseer hired and directed all work as, for instance, the construction ordered in January, 1856, for the California road from Big Springs to the Pottawatomie reserve line. The county authorized the overseer "to clear said Road of trees, Stones and other obstructions. Construct and repair Bridges: and grade the hills between Said points, So as to render Said road Safe and easy for loaded teams." The commissioners also designated roads for the section and township lines, they to be 40 feet wide, 20 feet on either side of the boundary.

Unfortunately, much of this work was left undone. Residents petitioned and re-petitioned for improvements, but the county usually found itself without the necessary funds. Especially during the years of political fighting between the Free-State and Proslave factions, the tax assessor often came up empty handed for his efforts.

It was in the troubled years of 1856 and 1857 that another important trail was opened in Shawnee county with Topeka the terminus. With the regular routes to Missouri blocked by southern sympathesizers or border ruffians, Jim Lane and other Free-State activists conceived of a road to bring supplies and emigrants down from Iowa and the northeast, to the northern Kansas line and then south through Holton, Indianola, and Topeka. The first party used the trail in August, 1856, and more arrived in Topeka during the spring of 1857 thus swelling the Free-State population.

The Lane Trail was also noted as a minor branch of the so-called underground railroad to bring freed slaves north. Although many inaccuracies have crept into stories about underground railroad activities in the Topeka vicinity, several local freedmen were sent on their way over it. Years later, John Armstrong of Topeka remembered taking the newly freed slaves first to a farm near Rochester (White-field City) for the night and then a stop west of Holton for the following evening. The final destination was Civil Bend, Iowa, a town on the Missouri river.

Town officials were concerned about street and road improvement when they conducted initial surveys of their site. Later, the county required each town to file a town plat showing proposed streets and lots. The Auburn founders laid their community out in the eastern, 18th century, fashion, with city squares and streets on the grid pattern. Topekans made their avenues deliberately wide. Fry W. Giles in his *Thirty Years in Topeka* explained: "It was the mind of the founders to make them so; with land at a dollar and a quarter an acre [for pre-emption], they certainly could afford to, and we have seen few who regretted their action."

The Tecumseh town council assured itself of continual street improvement in 1858 with an ordinance that assessed every able-bodied male over 18 and under 45 to work two days a year on the streets. They could commute that by paying the city marshal one dollar for each day's work, but if they refused both, they were fined five dollars. To keep the roads safe and repaired, another ordinance declared "no person shall ride through any street or lane in the compact part of the city on a Gallop, or at any swifter pace than at the rate of five miles an hour."

Several stage companies operated in Shawnee county during the 1850s. Usually the coaches stopped at one of the prominent hotels in town where they received their passengers. The Kansas Stage Company offered service in 1860 from Leavenworth to Westport and then west through Big Springs, Tecumseh, Topeka, Indianola, St. Mary's Mission, and on to Junction City—all for ten dollars. Henry Tisdale, a Kansas Stage Company employee, later recalled for the Kansas State Historical Society a journey he made from Lecompton to Topeka:

> There were six or eight passengers in the four-horse coach when we got to Big Springs to change horses. The driver and stock tender led out one of the fastest teams on the road, but thin and stiff. . . . We having made good time from Lecompton to Big Springs, the passengers made derogatory remarks regarding the new team. The driver remarked: "They are like cold potatoes, better when warmed up." He then started them on a walk, gradually increased the speed until, about Tecumseh, we were going at about the rate of eight or ten miles an hour, and at every rough place on the road the passengers were tolerably well mixed up inside, making the run in about one and one-half hours. If you want to vex a stage-driver, speak with derision of his team.

Once the railroad boom began in earnest in the 1860s, the importance of stage lines declined in the larger communities. Those towns not on the Union Pacific, Eastern Division, or the Santa Fe, however, still depended upon some kind of stage traffic for freight and mail as well as passenger service. For the remainder of the 19th and into the 20th century, small stage firms ran between Topeka and the rural hamlets of Redpath (Plowboy), Willard, Dover, and Eskridge and Alma in Wabaunsee county. They were tri-weekly or daily runs, and one of the last references to them appears in the 1904 *Kansas Gazetteer and Business Directory* for Dover: "stage daily to Willard, fare 50 cents."

The Papan ferry of 1843 was both the earliest and most famous of a myriad of ferries to be founded over the next 30 years. According to George Root's "Ferries in Kansas," published in the *Kansas Historical Quarterly,* there were at least ten and possibly as many as 15 separate ferry sites within Shawnee county, depending on how one counts them. Even then, Root failed to catalogue all of them. The typical ferry service changed owners periodically and due to floods or business failures, many sections of the county were without a ferry for one or two years.

In 1853 and 1854 several ferries were established in the Uniontown area which relieved the Papans of some of the Oregon-California traffic. Sydney Smith, John Ogee, Lucius Darling, and Joseph Ogee were some of the names associated with the ferries in western Shawnee county. On the east side, Thomas N. Stinson and James K. Waysman began a service in 1854 at Tecumseh. Afterwards it became a link in the road from Fort Leavenworth to the Sac and Fox reservation to the southwest. The territorial legislature charter provided that Stinson operate it "at all times, except at night, and the running of ice so thick and in such quantities as to make the crossing unsafe and dangerous to the boat." It also required that all foot passengers, horseback riders, wagons and teams, the United States mail, and "stock of every kind and description" be carried.

The ferries were still quite active in the county at least until the 1880s. Five owners succeeded Stinson with the Tecumseh ferry, three of them apparently from the same family, including perhaps the only woman operator, Susan Quiet. The Rossville Ferry Company was formed in 1879, serving that area for a few years. The Rossville *Kansas Valley Times,* August 8, 1879, advertised the firm:

> The Ferryman lives in a tent just a stones throw from the landing on the South Side [probably Wabaunsee county]. The rates of crossing are fifteen cents each way for either single or double teams and horseman or two tickets for 25 cents; four tickets for 50 cents; eight for $1. Horns will be placed on each shore to blow for the Ferryman if not in sight.

One of the last recorded ferries was operated in the Rossville vicinity by William Reece of Willard in 1904.

Just as crucial as ferry service was a Kansas river bridge. In 1855 the territorial legislature incorported the Kansas River Bridge Company and granted it "the exclusive right . . . of building and maintaining a [toll] bridge across the Kansas (or Kaw) river, at or within five miles . . . of Tecumseh." As an added financial inducement the Tecumseh Town Association donated 100 lots to the firm. The $70,000 iron bridge to be built in three spans, was begun in the summer of 1857. A rival Topeka paper, the *Kansas Tribune,* March 30, 1857, wished the enterprise well stating the "prosperity of the towns on the south side of the Kansas river depends much upon facilities for crossing that stream." However, the company postponed construction time after time as money quickly disappeared for the venture. In the end it erected only one stone pier.

The "exclusive right" of the Tecumseh company worried Topeka promoters; nevertheless, they too secured, in 1857, a bridge corporation. The Topeka Bridge Company proposed and built a $10,000 pile bridge by using only a small quantity of iron. The piles were made of oak and the planking of cottonwood cut from trees felled nearby. A 100-foot turnspan permitted river traffic to proceed upstream unhindered. Thus, on May 1, 1858, Topeka and not Tecumseh opened the first Kansas river bridge. A few days later Julia Lovejoy passed through on her way home to Manhattan. She wrote: "At Topeka we crossed the Kaw River on a bridge! The go-aheadative spirit of the Yankees has spanned the Kansas River with the first bridge ever built across it." A flood in July completely destroyed the structure.

"As the fragments of the Topeka bridge floated past Tecumseh," related Fry Giles, "satisfaction there at Topeka's disaster was undisguised." Ferry service resumed and Topekans waited until after the Civil War for their second bridge, a pontoon structure which rested on 13 flat boats measuring 15 by 25 feet and spaced 50 feet apart. It served from 1865 to 1870 when the King Wrought Iron Bridge Works of Cleveland, Ohio, replaced it with a $100,000 structure. The concrete arched Melan bridge succeeded that in 1898 and soon after it collapsed in 1965, the latest Kansas avenue bridge was completed.

The remaining Kansas river bridges within the county were all begun around the turn of the century. One little known organization, the Pottawatomie Bridge and Ferry Company, planned in 1866, or shortly afterwards, for a bridge east of Uniontown but nothing was ever completed except an approach. A Willard bridge was finished in 1902, in time for the 1903 flood, the Brickyard bridge in 1901, and the Sardou bridge in 1899. All three were destroyed or severely damaged in the 1903 and 1951 floods and subsequently replaced each time. Thus, the Topeka Avenue bridge, built in 1938, stands as the oldest Kansas river structure in Shawnee county.

A year before the founding of Topeka, Charles K. Barker, captain of the steamboat *Excel,* sailed his boat west from Wyandotte to the confluence of the Smoky Hill and Republican rivers, the site of Fort Riley. The little side-wheeler was the first steamboat to ascend the Kansas river any appreciable distance.

The *Excel,* stocked with supplies for the fort, reached the future site of Topeka on June 16, 1854. Captain Barker had purchased the steamboat in Massachusetts and intended to create a highly profitable business transporting goods on the Kaw. The first trip was successful because the river was running high that summer, but it belied the navigability of the river. Barker reported that green timber was used for fuel, supplemented with drier fence rails pilfered from Indian gardens.

The founders of Topeka were aware of steamboat voyages and these in part, influenced the location of the new community. Only three months after the first cabin was erected, the trustees of the Topeka Association were instructed to provide a landing suitable for river traffic. "Three or four boats came up the river as far as Topeka in 1855," wrote Giles, "and one of them went to Manhattan. Their arrivals were always heralded with satisfaction and sometimes when their whistles were heard a few miles down the river, citizens would walk down and escort them up the muddy bank, dignified by the name 'levee.'" The landing was prepared near the foot of Quincy street. Small amounts of produce were sent on return trips, but the river trade of 1855 was not as heavy as expected.

Santa Fe traders were optimistic over the prospects of sailing on the Kaw. They hoped to shorten the overland haul from Westport to the New Mexico settlements. Some of the steamers traveling the Kansas loaded at St. Louis, sailed up the Missouri, and then attempted to head up the Kaw to Fort Riley, the "head of navigation."

The winter of 1855-56 was unusually cold and deep snow accumulated across the plains. The spring thaw filled the river and brought the first floods which the Shawnee county pioneers witnessed. Missouri businessmen again saw the possibility of profitable shipping as the sandbars and snags disappeared beneath the swirling water. Fry Giles remembered that the river was deep enough for boating in the spring and early summer "and at times there were as many as three boats lying at the foot of Kansas avenue and below, producing quite a business aspect." However, the captains were disappointed with the amount of trade goods available in the year old town. The settlers of Shawnee county were, as one of them said, "almost universally poor." Topeka merchants had no ready sources of merchandise and the county provided only subsistence level produce.

The steamers themselves were not large, drawing between six and 12 inches of water when loaded. Even then they dragged on sandbars except when the river verged on flood stage. They were side-wheelers, usually about 125 feet long and some 25 feet across. When loaded, the boats brought Topekans and others along the river lumber, flour, meats, and other articles of importance.

The *Kansas Settler,* a Tecumseh newspaper, reported in March, 1858, that the *Minnie Belle* had reached Lawrence and that the townspeople informed the captain that Lawrence was the head of navigation. The paper's editor, angered over the events, declared "they [the Lawrence citizens] make proportionate sacrifices to prevent boats from attempting to come up the Kansas any further, although it is well known that the river is generally in better condition between Lawrence and Tecumseh and Topeka, than below Lawrence." The

Settler continued to editorialize: "We trust our neighbors and friends at Topeka, Wabaunsee, Manhattan, St. George, and other places above here will unite with us in making arrangements for a boat or boats which will go past Lawrence in spite of money or bugbear stories."

The *Minnie Belle* was constructed in St. Louis specifically for Kaw river traffic. The *Kansas Tribune* ran an article stating hopes of the steamboat running "nearly the whole of the summer season." She drew eight inches of water and carried light side wheels, so she could run the river "regardless of low water or sandbars." Built in 1857, she plied the Kansas successfully for two seasons, 1858 and 1859.

The *Kansas Settler* reported in February, 1858, that plans for three or four "light draft boats" were being made. They drew more than the *Minnie Belle,* 14 or 16 inches, but "its model will be alike fore and aft, and have two sets of paddle wheels." This latter arrangement was decided so that the boats need not "turn around in narrow or crooked channels." The paper claimed the builders in Pittsburgh, Pa., expected to carry 100 tons of freight. The Tecumseh people, naturally, were pleased to work for this service.

The busiest year of the short-lived river trade was 1859. A Mr. Valentine descended the stream from Fort Riley to Wyandotte in a small boat, and "determined to commence his navigation in the spring," according to a reporter for the *Kansas State Record.* He had two boats under construction at Wyandotte and evidently had had experience in western navigation.

The *Col. Gus Linn,* captained by B. F. Beasley, tried to gain complete control of the river traffic in 1859. The captain operated between Pittsburgh and the headwaters of the Kaw. In April, 1859, the *Col. Gus Linn* was rushing prospectors to the gold fields in western Kansas, now Colorado. During a stop at Topeka a number of the gold seekers washed a few particles of the precious metal from the Kaw. Many citizens of the town grabbed pans and scoured the sand for more. Little came of Topeka's "rush," but the story persisted that any person could discover a few flakes of gold in the sandy bottom.

The *Kansas Valley* was the last boat to ascend the Kaw to Topeka. This was in April, 1861. The following year Giles "issued a policy of marine insurance upon freight from . . . New York to Topeka, *via* New Orleans, the Mississippi, Missouri, and Kansas . . ." but the river trade was dead. On February 25, 1864, the state legislature declared the Kansas river not to be a navigable stream. The commercial advantage of the Kansas was conceivable to many people up and down the river, even though the volume of water often failed to allow traffic in dry years. The legislative closing of the stream received much criticism in Topeka, as well as other towns further west. The legislature, however, was only giving way to progress and facing facts.

By the mid-19th century railroads were the most modern and progressive means of transportation. Even as steamboats plied the river in the spring of 1857, the St. Joseph & Topeka Railroad was being chartered. The board of directors included Cyrus K. Holliday, a Topeka founder. The company was a prominent project of St. Joseph, to continue west from the Hannibal & St. Joseph road then under construction. Though 15,000 shares of stock were authorized only 74 subscriptions were made at St. Joseph and 21 at Topeka. A "railroad circular" envisioned the St. Joseph & Topeka as the distributing line for "southern and western Kansas, Oregon, California, New Mexico and Texas." On April 23, 1860, the first locomotive west of the Missouri river touched track on the company's meager stretch of rail at Elwood, Kansas. This was the Elwood & Marysville R.R.

The legislature chartered the Kansas Valley Railroad in 1855 to build from the Missouri line to the town of Pawnee. Thomas Stinson and two fellow Tecumseh residents backed the proposal, but the road remained merely the dream of zealous town promoters.

The Kansas Central projected a railroad up the Kansas valley and through the county from Wyandotte (now Kansas City, Kansas) to Fort Riley. A route was surveyed to Lawrence on the north bank of the river, and from there to Topeka on the south. Later plans called for the line to come west from Wyandotte on the south side of the Kaw and make its crossing at Topeka. It seemed that Topeka would be the first town in the Kaw valley to enjoy rail service. The *Kansas State Record* explained the prospects of railroads to Topeka in March, 1860:

> The Kansas Central road will not be long behind the St. Joe [and Topeka] in reaching this point, and then we will have concentrated here a railroad interest which will attract capital and trade from every direction, and tend to the aggregation of commercial interests at this point sufficient of themselves to create a city of the first magnitude.

By 1861 many railroad conventions were being held throughout the state, but the Topeka meeting was probably the most important. A petition containing proposals for five lines was forwarded to Washington by the Topeka convention. One of these "would stretch from Atchison to Topeka, and then to Santa Fe." It was obvious that private capital could not finance these lines since many would be built through desolate countryside. In these areas the government would have to bear the burden in some form of subsidization. Atchison was optimistic about the route to Santa Fe, but its plans lasted briefly.

The coming of the Civil War suspended such dreams and directed energy to more immediate problems.

Even though the war handicapped railroad construction, promoters remained busy. One of the most important railroads to be built in Kansas was the Union Pacific, Eastern Division, which had its beginnings as the Leavenworth, Pawnee and Western, incorporated by the territorial legislature in 1855. When the Pacific Railroad Act was written the LP&W was to be one of several eastern terminal branches of the Union Pacific. The Act stipulated that the road was to build "from the Missouri River, at the mouth of the Kansas River . . . so as to connect with the Pacific railroad of Missouri. . . ." The line could, if it wished, build a branch to Leavenworth. On June 6, 1863, the railroad's name was changed to Union Pacific Railway Company, Eastern Division, and it was under this name that it finally commenced construction later that year.

The road was completed to Lawrence in late 1864, with round trips daily, except Sunday. The first passenger train to Topeka arrived on January 1, 1866. Practically the entire population of 1,500 turned out for the welcome, and "there was band music, cheering and booming of cannon to greet the party from Kansas City as the 'Iron Horse' drew the coaches into the little station." The first depot stood in North Topeka just east of Kansas avenue. It was built of native white oak and walnut timber, "much of which was held together with white oak pegs instead of nails." With the arrival of the Union Pacific, products from Topeka could rush to Kansas City in the remarkable time of six or seven hours. By March the track for this road extended to Silver Lake, ten miles west of Topeka. The line became known as the Kansas Pacific railway on March 3, 1869, and on January 24, 1880, it was consolidated with the Union Pacific Railroad Company. The road reached Denver in 1870.

In an 1872 message to the legislature, Gov. Thomas Osborn summarized Kansas railroad construction: "In 1862, not a mile of railroad was in operation in the state. Now we have 2,039 miles in actual operation. . . . Kansas has more miles of railroad than either of 26 states."

Cyrus K. Holliday, who had promoted the St. Joseph and Topeka, envisioned a longer line linking the east with the rich Santa Fe area. He and other Topekans left for Atchison in mid-September of 1860 where they met with Atchison and eastern interests and formally organized the Atchison and Topeka, which later added Santa Fe to the title. In the fall of 1868 Senator Edmund Ross helped the officials turn the first spade of dirt for the railroad on Washington street in

Number 1073, a Santa Fe Prairie class engine, steaming past the Pauline depot. (Courtesy William A. Gibson)

A Union Pacific passenger train pulls up to the Silver Lake depot about 1910. (Courtesy Jessie Van Orsdol)

Waiting at Wakarusa's two story Santa Fe depot sometime in the early 1900s. (Courtesy Joyce Ritchie)

Topeka and construction commenced for a bridge over the Kaw in order to bring the first locomotive over the Union Pacific, Eastern Division, lines to the Santa Fe. The next year, 1869, the railroad opened from Topeka to Burlingame. By 1872 a line was built between Atchison and Topeka while the main thrust continued through the Arkansas river valley. The route north to Atchison covered virtually the same ground as that proposed by the St. Joseph & Topeka.

Both the Santa Fe and the Kansas Pacific sold subscriptions, although Shawnee county bought only Santa Fe stock. Nine hundred fifty thousand dollars in county bonds were voted by Atchison, Jefferson, Shawnee, Osage, and Lyon counties in exchange for railroad stock. Shawnee county subscribed $250,000 of which $150,000 was payable when a line from Topeka to the southern boundary was in operation and the remainder when the northern part of the county received rail service. Topeka also issued bonds to bring the Santa Fe general offices and shops here. There were western rivals for these considerable advantages, but the company proposed a subscription of $100,000 to finally locate their offices and shops in Topeka. A vote in July, 1872, prevailed by a sizeable majority and the bonds were delivered in September, 1874. Santa Fe purchased the King Wrought Iron Bridge company's building near Crane and Adams streets, and a permanent office building was erected in 1883-84 on the corner of Ninth and Jackson streets.

Two Rock Island stock trains collided head-on, October 10, 1898, with four men hurt and 25 horses killed. Within minutes hundreds of spectators arrived at the scene near the foot of Western ave. (Courtesy Kansas State Historical Society)

The last major railroad enterprise of Shawnee county came in 1873. The Lawrence & Topeka Railroad was a result of a series of abortive efforts on the part of Lawrence, beginning in 1867, to build a line from St. Louis to Denver, bypassing Topeka by cutting west up the Wakarusa valley. The Lawrence interests pushed for a pair of lines for this purpose; Topeka would not be a stop on either. Monmouth and Auburn townships wanted to vote for subscription to the stocks of any rail line which might directly benefit them, as would one down the Wakarusa valley. The county commissioners revealed the Lawrence subterfuge to these townships, however, and discouraged any support. Topeka as an important rail junction, already having both north-south connections in the Santa Fe and east-west lines with the Kansas Pacific, would be more valuable to the county as a whole.

The Lawrence & Topeka Railroad Company existed as early as 1868. By 1871 Lawrence had a direct line to St. Louis, making it an important link in western transport; the same year Topeka, Tecumseh township, and the county voted $215,000 to the Lawrence & Topeka. One Lawrence newspaper remarked that Topeka desired a direct connection to St. Louis, *via* Lawrence: "Topeka is trying to follow in the tracks of Lawrence in the matter of improvements. She has got gas, and might get street cars, but will wager a new hat she will not have the Pleasant Hill [St. Louis] extension in a hurry."

The entire situation was so confused that a new firm, the Midland Railroad Company, was chartered in 1873 to incorporate the interests of the previous attempts. In April, 1874, the first rails intersected with the Santa Fe at the corner of Washington avenue and Second street and by mid-July trains connected with Kansas City. Two months later the Midland ran from Pleasant Hill, Mo., to Topeka, and as thus completed was leased to the Santa Fe on June 30, 1875, for a period of 99 years.

Numerous plans for smaller rail ventures continually cropped up during the two decades following statehood. Short lines were proposed in every direction from such towns as Auburn, Silver Lake, Rossville (the Kansas Valley & South-Western Railroad Company, from Rossville to Maple Hill, Newbury, and Alma in 1879), and Tecumseh, and from Monmouth and Soldier townships (the Topeka, Soldier Creek & Nebraska in 1871). Many newly incorporated firms, too numerous to mention, contained the name of Topeka in their titles. Most of these proposed lines were paper projects or, if any surveying or construction were done, were soon taken over as branches of a larger company. The best the country towns received was a local train, usually called the "plug," which made daily runs stopping at each whistle station to let people and freight on and off.

The Santa Fe's first depot and general office building was constructed at Fourth and Holliday streets in 1869. The first Fred Harvey House in Topeka was located on the second floor. (Courtesy Kansas State Historical Society)

The Kansas (later Union) Pacific depot and hotel, 1872-1927, was on the east side of Kansas avenue. The bus waits for passengers bound for south Topeka. (Courtesy Kansas State Historical Society)

The second Topeka Santa Fe depot as it appeared in 1898. Built about 1880, it was enlarged before being partially included in the third depot which was constructed in 1949. (Courtesy Kansas State Historical Society)

The Rock Island depot at First and Kansas avenue was Topeka's most magnificent. Built in 1887 it was torn down in 1943. The Chesterfield hotel is at left. (Courtesy Kansas State Historical Society)

David Zirkle, whose family came to the Wakarusa valley in 1869, wrote that "a railroad was built through our place which provided us with activity for a couple of years." His family watched the proceedings "from the time the first survey was made until the road was completed. . . ." Monmouth township farmers sent their crops to market on locals such as this, while Topeka became a real hub of rail traffic in Kansas.

In time the Rock Island and the Kansas, Nebraska & Dakota (later the Missouri Pacific) railroads arrived in Topeka, along with the possibility in the 1880s of the latter company establishing shops in South Topeka (a separate community until 1887). Enthusiasm over railroad building waned during the late '80s. The Topeka *Democrat* announced, February 10, 1887: "Yesterday afternoon unheralded by trumpets and booming cannon, the great Rock Island reached Topeka." Earlier, celebrations would have broken out, but "those good old days" had passed. The paper concluded that Topeka possessed "new schemes and projects that she has no time to devote to . . . any single event."

The new schemes in part, proved to be the interurban or the street-railway, or trolley. From 1866 to 1956 some 54 street railroad or bus systems were incorporated in Topeka though most were paper organizations and only 18 ever operated. The earliest transit businesses were simple hacks or buses which waited for passengers at the Union Pacific station and then delivered them home or to a hotel on the south side of the Kaw. In 1872, the Southwestern Stage & Omnibus Company offered a bus line, with eight and 20 passenger carriages drawn by two and six horse teams, respectively. These carriages commuted up and down Kansas avenue every hour, on the hour, 8 A.M. to 7 P.M.

Although the company advertised that the buses were "a better arrangement than street cars, because the transit will be more rapid," the public desired a modern street railroad. Even so, the first functioning company in Topeka, the City Railway Company, was not formed until 1881. To this horse-drawn line, the city council granted an exclusive right to lay track and operate on the major thoroughfares of town. Eight years later the city saw the folly in this act, when modern, electric trolley cars were forced to use side streets while the old-fashioned horse cars maintained their right of way along Kansas avenue. The last horse-drawn trolley wound its way from Sixth and Washburn to the State Hospital and subsequently retired in May, 1896.

The first and most important mechanized street system belonged to the Topeka Rapid Transit Railway Company, incorporated in 1887. For power, the firm dressed up a steam locomotive like a miniature

Construction work on the Kansas ave. trolley track, about 1930. (Courtesy The Kansas Power & Light Company)

passenger car. The prospect of these engines running in their midsts distressed some Topeka individuals who believed that horses would be frightened, children killed, and adults maimed. Nevertheless, the transit line quickly proved popular and converted most of the skeptics.

The steam and horse companies clashed for patronage, to the ultimate detriment of both. The Rapid Transit reluctantly settled for running its track on Jackson street. Joab Mulvane, a president of the City Railway Company, later remembered how one year both firms hastily built track to the new Rock Island depot, technically on City Railway right-of-way. "The Rapid Transit people," he wrote, "tore up our track one night and put down some of their own. We promptly proceeding to tear theirs up." The affair reached court "and an injunction stopped the war."

In 1889, after less than two years of operation, the Rapid Transit company electrified its system. Considered a progressive step, the Topeka *Capital-Commonwealth* modestly proclaimed it "Earth's Greatest," when the service reopened after the change over in April that year.

Other firms during the 1880s and 1890s briefly served different sections of Topeka, especially on the east side. In 1892 the Topeka Railway Company purchased a number of these properties, including the Rapid Transit, and emerged as the major transit line for the city until the 1920s when the Kansas Power & Light Company acquired it. For a time, in 1915, gasoline powered jitneys, precursors of modern buses, competed with the trolley company. They, too, followed a prescribed route, with no variance, a fact which occasionally annoyed a passenger or two. Charging five cents, the jitneys grew in popularity, the 50 licensed vehicles in March, 1915, becoming 116 by July. Obviously the Topeka Railway Company became both envious and disturbed over this news and looked for help from the city. The Topeka commission remedied the railway's dilemma and added a good revenue source by raising the license fees from ten dollars to fifty. As rapidly as they had multiplied, the jitneys disappeared from the streets leaving only five for Topeka in April, 1916.

The first gasoline buses entered service in 1925 and for a time in the early '30s an odd sight greeted Topekans, the quiet, speedy, trackless trolley coach. Then on July 18, 1937, the Kansas Power & Light Company ordered the last Topeka trolley off the streets. The internal combustion engine had triumphed over "Earth's Greatest."

Only the North Topeka, Silver Lake & Rossville Rapid Transit Company, of several proposed inter-urban railroads, ever operated. In 1888 Soldier and Silver Lake townships voted $23,000 in bonds for the railroad, but monetary problems continually plagued it and the line only reached Menoken, five miles from North Topeka. For a few years the tiny engine-coach ran up and down the track accomplishing little. Concerning other efforts, after false starts, the Topeka-Southwestern Railway Company graded four miles in 1908 from the Washburn campus and in the direction of Eskridge. Then interest and money dissipated as did the same for the Kansas City, Kaw Valley

A car of the Topeka City Railway Company rounds the northwest corner of Sixth and Kansas avenue in 1884. The tall building housed the Bank of Topeka. (Courtesy John W. Ripley)

& Western Railroad's desire to link Lawrence with Topeka. In the end, the inter-urban never achieved the popularity with Topekans as it did with others and by the turn of the century, the trolleys and railroads found new competition in the automobile.

In August, 1900, a local newspaper reported that Terry Stafford, operator of a bicycle repair shop in Topeka, had completed the city's first auto. It was a very simple machine made by placing a seven-horsepower engine under the seat of an ordinary wagon.

Stafford refined his original car and turned to Topeka businessmen Anton and Clement Smith for the production of autos. The two brothers decided to add automobiles to their diverse line of products when they made an agreement with Stafford in 1901. Two years later the Smith brothers had a factory 45 feet wide and 185 feet long at the corner of Tenth and Jefferson. They managed to sell a few cars that year and in 1904 began production on a significant scale with the "Veracity." In 1905-06 the company produced the "Smith" and in 1907 the "Great Smith" automobile. However, the Smith Company managed only a limited production in less than a decade of business.

Competition, primarily from larger and more efficient rivals in Detroit, along with instability in the auto market sent the Smith Company into receivership on December 2, 1910. The Smiths felt that having their factory in Topeka was a major advantage since they were much nearer their customers. There were also many mechanics in Topeka willing to work for lower wages and less inclined to fall into labor disputes. Still Topeka's automobile factory was at best only a weak challenge to the leading Detroit companies.

A typical service or "filling" station, located at Sixth and Gage, as it appeared about 1929. (Courtesy The Menninger Foundation)

"Art deco" styling for automobiles and showrooms of the 1940s is typified in the agency located at 1000 West Sixth street. (Courtesy Paul Boeger)

In 1909 the Topeka city commission established a downtown speed limit at nine miles per hour and a limit of 18 miles an hour elsewhere in the city. The same meeting created an age limit of 18 for city drivers. One motorist claimed this would discourage owning and driving cars, something he felt Topeka should promote. He said: "The whole business looks like a hold-up to me. . . . The city has no right to make such penalties and create such licenses. The records show that the dangers from autos is not one-half as dangerous as the trolley cars or fast horses." That year Topeka had about 300 cars which increased to 3,000 in six years, justifying the restrictions.

Rural people were no less endangered than city dwellers. George P. Morehouse, state senator from Council Grove, introduced legislation for controlling motorists. He defended the final section of his bill staunchly:

The last provision is the one which our rural communities are most interested in for it is there that the most damage and trouble is caused by careless automobilists. . . . This law protects our farmer friends and their wives and daughters while driving on the highway and hereafter they will not have to run into the wire fence and hang up or into the ditch and give all the road, which has been the custom as sporty automobile drivers were flying by.

The automobile clearly triumphed over the horse and trolley in the following decades. Automotive races (the first in Topeka were held in September, 1902, at the fair), automobile associations, and good roads organizations all appeared very quickly in Shawnee county along with motorized police and the first parking problems. Three important national highway systems crossed the county by 1920 and were given names representative of the area served: Golden Belt Highway, now U. S. 24; Victory Highway (originally the Fort to Fort road), now U. S. 40; and Capitol Highway, now U. S. 75.

Small communities clamored for better and more modern roads too, and in 1916 the Auburn and Dover good roads committees or boosters demanded a modern highway between their towns and Topeka. They wanted one of brick and macadam, 15 feet wide, 24 miles long, to cost $216,000. Ultimately, such projects altered rural life. Lena Baxter Schenck described the changes in Dover, which also applied elsewhere: "With the coming of the automobile and the hard surface road, Topeka became so close to Dover that shopping in Topeka became a habit, and the business at Dover began to suffer as the vacant store buildings there indicate. . . ."

Changes occurred in the city also and businesses responded with a wave of drive-in restaurants, theatres, gasoline stations and super markets in the 1940s. Just as the street railroads created the first Topeka suburbs, so did the automobile, after World War II, the second. By 1960 shopping centers, ringed with parking lots, had become the dominant commercial and retail centers for both city and county residents. And beyond them at ever greater distances flocked the middle and upper classes who, with the aid of the automobile, attempted (and still attempt) to achieve the relaxed, rural atmosphere which that same automobile destroyed.

Just as the car thrilled and touched the public's immagination, so did the airplane and flight. During the teens and twenties aircraft were produced, like automobiles, by dedicated mechanics in small converted shops. Overhead for them was small and work relatively simple for the mechanically minded. Albin K. Longren, a motorcycle builder from Leonardville, Kan., had such a background and with his brother Erenuis and another mechanic built and flew Topeka's first aircraft in September, 1911.

Before Longren's flight, T. C. Mars had demonstrated the airplane's potential in a journey from Topeka to Lawrence, in June, 1910, taking some three and a half hours, 87 minutes of it on the ground at two unexpected stops. Longren's first flight on September 2, 1911, covered only 200 feet, however, he soon got his plane up in the air for rides of five miles and more. With such performances he excited the venturing spirit in the youngest son of Topeka mayor J. B. Billard.

L. Philip Billard was 21 when Longren taught him to fly, and the Topeka papers in 1912 were filled with features about him careening around the capitol dome in his Longren built plane. The *Capital* on December 27, 1912, explained that "Mayor Billard was opposed to his son purchasing the racing biplane, because of the dangers of flying, but Phil wanted something that was faster than an auto, and so purchased it." Soon Billard became an expert and for five dollars (occasionally $15) he gave rides to Topekans brave enough. In his flight records for December 1, 1916, he reported he had carried his brother aloft and that "hair was standing on end when Robert put his feet on the ground." Of his next passenger, T. C. Powell, Billard wrote "Mr. Powell says anybody that is not scared the first ride [they went up 800 feet] is a Damn Liar."

Not all was fun as accidents sometimes struck. Airplanes crashed into the Kaw or, as happened once to Longren, into the side of a cow. Surprisingly, fliers usually survived such mishaps, though a few were killed. One of the earliest air accidents near Topeka resulted in death as the *Capital* wrote on August 9, 1920, the pilot's "body was burned to a crisp before the eyes of many spectators who were on the field." Phil Billard experienced trouble too; once his engine stopped at an altitude of 300 feet. However, greater tragedy came in July, 1918, when as an AEF pilot in France a plane he was testing disintegrated causing his death.

Twice, in the teens and from 1919 to 1926, A. K. Longren tried to establish airplane manufacturing on a sound basis in Topeka, and twice he failed. He built ten craft between 1911 and 1917 but then took a position in Denver. He returned two years later and set the stage for his enterprise in the abandoned woolen mills in Oakland. From the first he had difficulty in manufacturing numbers of planes, but he offered several innovations including a folding wing biplane. Supposedly, in 1922, individuals and the governments of France, Italy, Switzerland, Mexico, China, and the Soviet Union inquired about the "New Longren Aircraft." The Navy also expressed an interest and ordered a plane for testing in 1924. A Tulsa, Okla., man in a letter of May 9, 1924, declared himself "a Longren booster" and "as far as I am concerned they can put all the Jennys, Standards and the like in *Smithsonian Institute.*"

Nevertheless, it was all in vain as neither the interest nor the capital existed in Topeka. There was no way to generate the money necessary to produce any great quantity of aircraft and so the Navy lost interest. The *State Journal* for November 28, 1928, expressed anger toward Topekans for their failure of support. It could have been "one of the biggest airplane producing plants in the entire west," and Longren "went down a martyr to the indifference of a skeptical public." A second venture that year, owned by one Ray Morris shared the same fate for the same reasons. Moribund hopes were revived briefly in 1942 when the Strickland Aircraft Corporation proposed building light transport planes in the old International Harvester building east of town, but they too folded after making only parts.

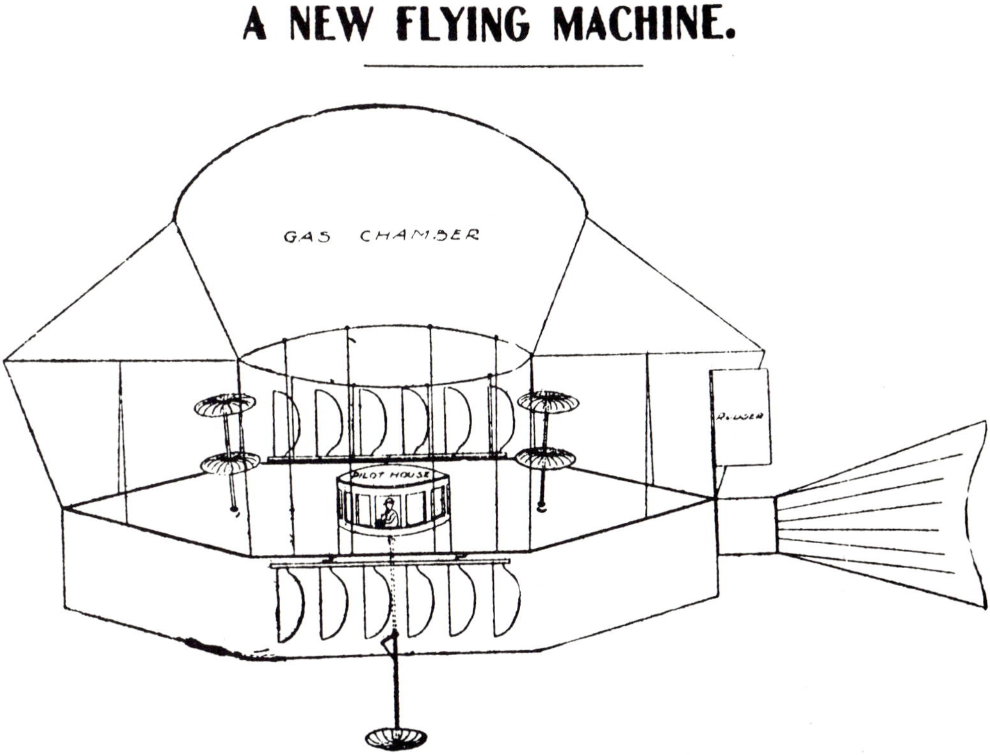

A NEW FLYING MACHINE.

An ambitious if monstrous looking flying machine designed by a Topekan, General Vorhees. (From the Topeka "Mail and Breeze," November 23, 1900)

The "most spectacular trip ever made by an aviator in Topeka," said the "Capital" about A. K. Longren's 20 minute flight over the city on September 11, 1911. Thousands roared "three cheers for Topeka I [the plane's name]" when it soared over the crowded fairgrounds. (Courtesy Kansas State Historical Society)

Digging potatoes in Scott Kelsey's fertile Kaw Valley field, 1916. (Courtesy Kansas State Historical Society)

Hay wagon pulled by Richard Wallace's big grays on the James D. Wallace farm east of Tecumseh, about 1920. (Courtesy James D. Wallace)

The William Kreipe farmstead and orchard east of Tecumseh about 1895. (Courtesy Mr. and Mrs. Gerald Kreipe)

FROM THE LAND; AGRICULTURE

In 1857 Dickey and Young, a mercantile firm located on Kansas avenue between Fifth and Sixth streets, shipped a quantity of corn east by riverboat. "This was the first shipment of corn from Topeka, or from Shawnee county . . ." said Fry Giles. The settlers of that early year were nearly all poor. Merchants such as Dickey and Young found slim pickings; often they could scarcely buy a wagonload of merchandise in one purchase. The entire county operated primarily on a subsistence basis during territorial days.

Agriculture in the county began even prior to the founding of Uniontown or the infant Topeka. Daniel Morgan Boone, grandson of the famous woodsman, operated a government farm for transplanted eastern Indians in the 1820s. Native Americans, however, were little inclined to till Kansas river soil, and squatters were planting crops of corn on Indian reserves before the opening of Kansas territory. Gradually, after 1854, the government allowed settlement of the reserves and previously established squatters could rest content that their rights were recognized. New arrivals added new fields in good bottomland and expanded local agriculture until urban Topeka found itself surrounded by farms and farming communities.

The undulating surface of the county is drained by the Kansas river through its center and the Wakarusa in the south, and between these rivers there are numerous creeks and streams. The *Kansas Daily Commonwealth* reported in 1876 that of the land 31 percent was bottom and 69 percent upland; eight percent was forest and 92 percent prairie. The timber was confined to the water-courses. Springs were "not numerous, but there [were] some excellent ones; good well water [was obtained] at a depth of from 18 to 40 feet." The same article estimated the number of acres in the county as 357,120 "of which . . . 89,418.21 are under cultivation."

An immigrants' guide to northern Shawnee county made the following claim concerning that part of the county north of the Kaw: "No State in the Union can compare with Kansas in point of soil, climate, and in the rapid growth of all kinds of produce. Northern Shawnee is the richest and most desirable part of the State." Some 75 percent of this area was first and second bottom and the remainder gently sloping upland. The depth of the soil averaged 20 feet with no water-holding rock below. This facilitated rapid absorption of water up to almost 80 inches, although normal rainfall averages closer to 20 inches per year. Timber for fuel and fencing purposes abounded along the streams north of the river. Corn was the principal crop raised early in the county's agricultural history and the guide stated that it had "grown fifteen feet high in the Kaw bottom, and from ten to twelve feet on the upland, having three to four large, well developed ears in a stalk, producing from fifty to seventy-five bushels per acre."

To the south settlers discovered the Wakarusa river bottom which "was very rich land, well-watered, and with plenty of timber for firewood and fence material. . . ." The Wakarusa, whose source lies in Waubaunsee county, flows the length of Shawnee at virtually an even distance of one and a half miles from the south line of the county; from there it crosses Douglas to its confluence with the Kaw. In the valley of this stream was found some of the richest land south of the Kansas river. The Zirkle family of Monmouth township located about 18 miles southeast of Topeka in the late 1860s. David Zirkle, son of one of these pioneers, later wrote: "The three families bought a tract of land one-half mile wide and a mile long . . . they paid cash for the land, about $25.00 per acre."

Like the Zirkles, farmers and urbanites alike flocked into the county. Between 1860 and 1875 the population expanded by some 12,000 souls. In the rural areas around Topeka cattle equalled the human population in numbers, and swine surpassed people by over a thousand. By 1875 towns which rivaled Topeka in territorial days had become rural centers. The census of 1870 shows that Shawnee county had a ratio of more than ten persons per square mile. Each year the prairie above and below the Kaw gave way to more fields or became pasture for livestock. No doubt many pioneers felt the same as did Augustus T. Daniels who saw the country for the value it held and bought a farm north of Topeka in 1877, paying $2,500 for it. He wrote of the good land he purchased as well as the "hundreds of prairie chickens flying around." Optimism prevailed among the agricultural community despite many bad years which the farmers faced.

Shortly after Kansas territory became the 34th state the county experienced several hard years. First came the Civil War which took a heavy toll from among the male inhabitants. Sam Reader wrote from Indianola during the war that "a great many farms are not cultivated in this section for want of working men." Such a severe shortage of manpower existed in the entire state by the middle of the war that Gov. Thomas Carney felt it necessary to caution recruiting officers to go slow in their efforts. The war years also reflected the devastating drought of 1860. Crops had failed for lack of rain and relief poured into the area from the East. Some of the less resolute country folk had packed up their belongings in farm wagons and headed back from where they came. The county suffered another drought in 1865 which dropped crop production to slightly below the level of 1860, but by then the war was over.

The drought of the 1860s and the war were only preludes to the next decade. Rapid development of agriculture was curtailed in the early 1870s by three factors: the depression of 1873, grasshoppers, and still another drought. The panic of 1873 had less effect in Kansas than later depressions because expansion was not based upon credit as much as later advances were to be. Homesteaders who came in the 1870s found it unnecessary to borrow much money since machinery was simple and required only small financial outlays for maintenance and replacement.

If the financial depression had little effect on Shawnee county agriculture, the drought that summer most certainly did. Only scattered light showers dampened the dust throughout June, July, and the first two weeks of August. On August 14 the *Commonwealth* printed the following: "Complaints are coming in continually of drouth in various localities in this county. In some portions of the county vegetation is actually parching for want of rain, and unless rain falls soon, corn, potatoes and fruit will suffer severely." Apparently the drought was broken that very night for the paper carried a brief notice of rain on August 15, and two days later reported "the benefits of the late rain to the potatoe crops of the county will in all probability prove to be almost incalculable." However, even at that late date, not all the corn was planted due to the extended dry spell.

The summer of 1874 was the hardest that Shawnee county farmers were destined to face. As though withering weather was not enough, the county was overrun with insects all summer. Charles A. Thresher, a farmer of Monmouth township, noted in his diary on June 12: "Chinch bugs taking the rye—some in the wheat" and on June 18 "millions of Chinch bugs leaving the rye—it is all dead." Those "millions" headed for his corn patch the next day and a week later he noted sarcastically "in the morning next I am going to shovel up & haul off a load of corn & Chinch bugs." Thresher hauled four wagonloads of bugs, corn, and dirt that day and plowed the corn patch up in the afternoon. He noticed that water holes were drying up the same day.

In that year the drought came after the wheat harvest of July and August. The entire state was parched, and the corn crop commenced to fail badly. The dry spell was finally broken on September 5, but another scourge had already descended on the county.

On August 8, 1874, a Saturday afternoon, millions of grasshoppers dropped like a cloud to the earth. The sky took on a peculiar hazy appearance that afternoon; the swarm floated lazily along, with an occasional lone insect drifting to the ground. Suddenly millions of voracious hoppers dropped from the sky and rapidly began devouring everything in sight. Noble Prentis, an Atchison editor, wrote of the invasion: "As a spectacle the approach of the winged destroyers was sufficiently terrifying and the destruction of vegetation was complete."

According to Thresher's diary the grasshoppers moved south-by-southwest across the county. He gave day-to-day accounts of the movements for three weeks in August. Although some writers claim that the pests devoured all vegetation, exempting only castor beans, those in Shawnee county had a relatively sizeable list of plants they avoided—maples, honey locusts, and box elder trees, potatoes or any sort of vines—but most farmer's fields were devastated.* Mr. Thresher's already ravaged corn stalks were stripped completely and he wrote discouragingly of his fine orchard: "Hoppers taken every leaf off of apple trees and eating peaches & plums—not so thick in stalks but worse on trees."

To deal with the state-wide infestations, a special relief agency was created in Topeka. Agents were sent east to collect money and supplies. Gov. Thomas A. Osborn called a special session of the legislature in September after the grasshoppers had gone, and two important relief acts were passed. One provided for the sale of state relief bonds to the amount of $73,000. The legislature decided that relief from the state treasury was not required in most county cases, including Shawnee. Consequently the county issued bonds of its own to provide some assistance for its injured farmers.

The locusts in the plague of 1874 ate their fill, laid their eggs, and moved on south. These eggs hatched in 1875, setting off another migration and causing much alarm. But Shawnee county was not nearly so crippled as it had been the previous year, and the hoppers moved north from where their progenitors had come. Planting was somewhat late in 1875, but the season which followed was one of the more fruitful of the 19th century.

In an attempt to combat the effects of insect infestations, droughts, and economic panics, Shawnee countians formed farmers' clubs and the Shawnee County Agricultural Society. The latter was organized

---

*Most of the potato crop and vined plants in gardens which escaped insects were virtually ruined in the ensuing drought.

in 1860 with H. W. Curtis as president and vice presidents representing each of the communities within the county. It contained regular elected officers as well as directors from all the townships and precincts. For the most part, however, it was merely a conveyance for the annual county fair.

More influential were the local farmers' clubs which began to organize in the late 1860s. Between 1868 and 1873 clubs appeared in Dover, Indian Creek, Silver Lake, Plowboy, Wakarusa, Lynn Creek, Waveland, Monmouth township, and Indianola. The farmers were creating cooperatives for purposes quoted in the Topeka *State Record* in 1871:

> Our object is mutual improvement, the protection of our interests in general and the elevation of our profession to that honorable position that it is worthy of, and we ask and hope that all the farmers in the county will organize and that soon we may have a thorough working county club.

There had long been efforts for farmers to organize for their own benefit. Topeka newspapers were filled with letters on the topic. The numerous clubs were not trade unions but rather cooperative organizations seeing that all received "something like just and fair compensation for their labor," as a letter to the *Commonwealth* pointed out. In addition to struggling against natural hazards the farmers' clubs also opposed "special legislation for the benefit of rich corporations, high freights, and combinations of railroad companies to protect the same. . . ." Subjects of importance to county agriculturalists were also discussed. For instance, the Dover Farmers' and Stockgrowers' Club talked about objectionable southern (Texas) cattle, the profitability of horned cattle, the use of Osage orange hedge for fencing, the best time for breaking prairie, stock diseases and their treatment, uses for dogs on farms, the success of fruit-growing in Kansas, the cultivation of potatoes, and the improvement of various types of stock.

As community farm clubs were approaching their high point in 1872 a new state and nation-wide organization was introduced into the county. On December 4, 1872, nine local granges met and organized the Kansas State Grange; on June 30 of the following year more than 600 delegates met in Lawrence to complete permanent organization.

The principles of the Grange have always been popular. The fraternalism of the Grange appealed to the pioneers as did the outspoken stand of the Grange against unjust taxation, freight rates, interest rates, and government programs—many of the same themes which occupied the local farmers' clubs. The Grange farmers' institutes were forerunners of county agents and the extension service. A State Board of Agriculture publication states that other notable promotion programs were rural free delivery, establishment of experiment stations, county extension agents, the Future Farmer program, parcel post, farm credit, improved farm-to-market roads and women's suffrage. "This long record of development and promotion of sound policies for rural people has no equal in the nation," it concluded.

The Grange in Shawnee county also served as a social organization. When Augustus Daniels moved to his farm north of Topeka, he attended a Grange ball at one of Topeka's opera houses, becoming involved with farm organizations immediately. Grange buildings were constructed in most communities and one of the most popular events of rural society was the annual Grange fair, usually held in late August or September.

From the beginning the Grange carried on a persistent and aggressive campaign against policies and programs adverse to agricultural progress and better rural living. It remained relatively free of political domination. Up to 1976 the Kansas State Grange has had 15 masters. Longest to hold that office was C. C. Cogswell of Topeka, master for 18 years.

Topeka newspapers were active in reporting the statewide farmers' convention in the city in 1873. The meeting was a result of the depression and the rapidly growing farmers' movement across Kansas. The Kansas State Agricultural Society, which called the convention, had done more, according to one article, than any similar organization in any state. The notice continues with a mention of a Topekan, Alfred Gray, secretary of the society, and "the pains-taking supervision which [he] . . . takes of every line that is publised by the Society." The farm movement had by then been growing for over five years, and all the organizations combined had done much to help county, as well as state, farmers to benefit from their produce as much as possible. That year one paper estimated some 10,000 persons attended Topeka's convention in an attempt to alleviate agricultural problems in the state, but little if any long-lasting effect was accomplished.

Ten years previously, on January 16, 1863, Andrew Stark (major of the Second regiment, K.S.M.) was secretary pro tem of the first "Farmers' Meeting," the progenitor of the Kansas State Board of Agriculture. Topekan F. G. Adams helped to draft the Board's constitution. He was also Secretary of the Board in 1863 when the first issue of the *Kansas Farmer* appeared. It was organized "in the open air, in front of the old Topeka House, . . ." in the words of the Board's 44th annual report in 1961. From its inception the State Board of Agriculture utilized the talents of Shawnee county men in its offices. At the time the farmers' convention was called in 1872, H. J. Strickler was president of the Board. Publisher J. K. Hudson served as secretary during 1880-1881. Elmer McNabb of Richland became president in 1950 and remained on the Board for many years afterward.

The last major agricultural organization to appear on the county scene was the Farmer's Union. This group, originally Texan, arrived in Kansas in 1906. The state had a large enough membership in the Farmer's Union to entitle it to one delegate to the organizing convention in 1905. James Butler of Topeka was elected to the Board of National Farmers' Union in 1906, even before the state group was chartered. Edwin H. Hewins of Topeka was the second president of the Kansas Farmers' Union. Martin Byrne of Shawnee county was president of the state organization in 1961. State headquarters were for a time at Topeka, but were moved to Salina in 1909. After 40 years in Salina, the offices were moved briefly to St. Marys, then returned to Topeka where they are presently (1976) located. H. N. Gains, a former State Superintendent of Schools and thereafter editor of the *Farmers' Advocate,* published in Topeka, was an early member. He promoted the Farmers' Union through his newspaper. The most obvious institutions of the Farmers' Union today are the co-ops, located in nearly every county community.

The early pioneers arriving in Shawnee county would struggle for nearly a decade before any attempt was made to organize. In that decade and for several years thereafter the settlers' original crop was sod corn. This hardy, broad-leaf maize produced few ears, but the thick root system, sowed with a minimum of soil preparation, broke up the sod for tilling and for the next year's crop. The State Board of Agriculture first gathered crop statistics in 1872. As claimed in its

The Shawnee county fairgrounds in 1871. Some of the buildings housed the Exodusters at the end of that decade. Notice the single wing of the state-house at upper right. (Courtesy Kansas State Historical Society)

annual report "corn was the main crop with 41½ million bushels produced. Over production of corn was causing trouble in those days and the crop was of very little value. In fact, corn was sometimes used for fuel."

County agricultural statistics reported in the *Kansas Daily Commonwealth* of July 29, 1870, showed the total number of acres planted in corn was 11,543 with an aggregate production of 439,502 bushels—an average of 33½ bushels per acre. Wheat acreage was 2,860 amounting to a production of 37,286 bushels. A newspaper reporter wrote of his personal crop observances, comparing corn and wheat:

> In passing through the county I observe that crops, while not so promising as they were at this date last year, yet betoken a good yield of winter wheat. Corn also will be a good yield. The grazing was never better, and the late rains insure the hay crop. As to the condition of the spring wheat I can only say as some one else said, that it's short, but thin.

Wheat has been grown in Kansas since the territory was thrown open for settlement and in a limited way at the missions in pre-territorial days. As late as 1878 farmers debated whether wheat could be successfully raised in the state. According to the *Cyclopedia of Kansas,* this prediction was made that year: "It will be safe to say that the day will not be far distant when Kansas will stand at the head as the greatest and best wheat growing state in the Union."

Shawnee county is not in the Kansas "wheat belt." This cereal grain, however, is one of the most important crops in the locality. The first soft spring wheat planted came from Ohio, Pennsylvania, Maryland, and other eastern states. When the hardier Turkey Red wheat seed became available in the late 1870s, sowing of spring wheat declined drastically and almost disappeared by 1885. Mennonites from the Crimea brought small quantities of hard Turkey Red wheat for planting in their new homeland, passing through Topeka on their way to central Kansas. They did not choose the county for their farms, but by 1890 the wheat they brought with them was well on its way as a superior variety for planting in all of Kansas.

The growing of wheat became something of a farming cultural rite by the turn of the century, lasting until progress produced modern self-propelled combines and large farm trucks. Threshing occurred at the end of June and early July. It usually took three days to a week for harvest, depending on the size of each field and the individual farmer's crop. This included all the involved processes of cutting, binding, heading, and threshing. Augustus Daniels paid $20 for the rent of a thresher to work his crop. About his father, David Zirkle wrote that he "never took anything he could not see his way through." That early pioneer was progressively inclined, however, for he "bought one of the first self-binding machines that came out." Harvesting by 1910 was done almost exclusively by the header. The headers were unloaded into two stacks of unthreshed wheat heads, between which was stationed the threshing machine. Threshers fed the grain heads and some short straw into the threshing machine. With so little straw attached to the heads no straw stacks developed. A few producers did not bother to stack wheat heads but had the heads fed in directly from the header barges.

"Gangs" of threshers banded together around a single farmer who owned a threshing machine, or they purchased a machine jointly. Threshing bees during harvest moved from farm to farm cutting and threshing grain. By the 1940s, combines had taken the place of threshing gangs, allowing the individual farmer to harvest his own grain with only the help of his own family.

The financial depression of 1893 curtailed agricultural pursuits once more, but by 1896 eastern Kansas had recovered. Sorghums were introduced by the Department of Agriculture and by experiment stations. Kaffirs were first introduced in the county around 1875. Milo was probably imported around 1885. In 1873 only a little over 4,000 acres of sorghum were growing in the entire state, but by 1893 the acreage of kaffir was greater than that of all other crops except corn, wheat, and alfalfa. In Shawnee county sorghums rival wheat in crop production.

The sorghums captured wide attention in the 1880s during a sugar boom in the county. Both the federal and state governments and farmers gave much attention to the saccharine types of sorghums for the production of sugar and syrup. In August of 1888 the Topeka Sugar Company began operation. Mary Davis Sander wrote, in an article for the Shawnee County Historical Society *Bulletin* entitled "Sweets and Sours":

Farmers on both sides of the Kansas River had been encouraged to grow cane. Eri Hansford, Sr., who owned land across the river, operated a pontoon bridge, so that cane could be taken across to the plant. . . . This pontoon bridge was constructed by the stockholders of the Topeka Sugar Mill in 1888. High water and drift destroyed it in April, 1889, according to records of the company, now in private hands. After that, he had three cable ferry boats (each about 60 X 30 ft.) for transporting cane and passengers. He loosened the south cable about 1902; these boats were lost in the 1903 flood.

A year after its opening the Topeka Sugar Mill was destroyed by fire; however, it was again operating by October 2, 1890. Sugar beets were tried in the county then but were found to be unprofitable. By November of 1891 the mill was in the hands of a receiver and the property of the company had been sold. Two other mills were chartered in the county during the 1880s. The Topeka Sugar Refining Company, of Topeka township, filed in 1882. It was located one mile east of Topeka. C. K. Holliday was one of its directors. The National Sugar Manufacturing Company which filed for its charter in 1888, was directed by Boston merchants but never functioned.

By 1910, about half a million acres across Kansas were planted to non-saccharine sorghums. Farmers in the county learned much about types of sorghums which could resist drought, produce larger yields than corn, and be harvested with relative ease. Sorghums were a certain crop and could be depended upon when corn or wheat crops failed. Should wheat land fail to produce a crop, it might be plowed up and produce a good stand of short-termed sorghum for stock-feed before winter came on.

During the twenties farmers gave preponderant attention to diversification of crops, better farm management, rotation, and legumes in soil building. There was more attention paid to circumventing damages from insect pests, in evading tricks played by the weather, and in warding off diseases which decimated herds. Diversification of crops had begun sometime earlier during the last decade of the 19th century. Fields of legumes and soybeans appeared to supplement corn, wheat, and sorghums.

At the same time that county farmers were varying their plantings with these new crops, another important and valuable feed source, grass, came into use. The *Kansas Valley Times* of November 21, 1879, evaluated different kinds of grasses. Bluegrass and timothy were ranked failures, rye was "vastly superior," orchard "still preferable," alfalfa was "fast becoming favorite."

Alfalfa production, relatively heavy in the county, has grown with civilization. This hay came to Kansas from southwestern Asia, where it grows wild in Iran. Seed was shipped to Marion county from San Francisco in 1868. From there alfalfa spread west and east. Noble Prentis wrote in his *History of Kansas*:

> One of the discoveries of agricultural Kansas for the year 1891 was that of alfalfa. In the spring of that year the Secretary of the State Board of Agriculture received such reports of its value, that he arranged a place for it in his statistical rolls, and the assessors were requested to give the acreage of alfalfa separate from other tame grasses. Since, it has occupied an enlarging space in the agriculture . . . [of] Kansas.

By 1893, there were only three counties which did not produce alfalfa. Because of the more acidic and less well-drained soils in eastern Kansas this forage crop was slower to increase in Shawnee county. Use of lime and development of better varieties increased alfalfa production in the county over the next 30 years.

The drought of the 1930s depleted hay stocks all over the midwest. Cattlemen and farmers who had used alfalfa and prairie hay were forced to feed their livestock wheat straw in the emergency. To make the straw more palatable and nourishing, cottonseed cake was added, carrying many cattle through the winters. Around 1937 molasses was being used as an ingredient of mixed feeds to increase palatability. This molasses was a residue from the manufacture of cane and beet sugar. The popularity of alfalfa grew more after the depression, with many farms producing mostly that crop. Plants in Rossville and Grantville process some of the local alfalfa, but the majority of the crop is today turned back into the farm as livestock feed.

The drought of the '30s helped another county crop along its way to oblivion. During the '20s, '30s, and '40s, there was a slow but steady decline in both Irish and sweet potato production. Irish potatoes for the market were grown mostly in the Kansas river valley. Kaw valley potatoes enjoyed a modest amount of fame for a few years, but the agricultural slump following the first World War, the depression, and the drought of the 1930s pushed profitable potato crops out of local markets. The 1951 flood wiped out most of that year's potatoes and virtually wiped out the industry, although the next year brought a sizeable crop.

The *Commonwealth* of August 30, 1872, reported that the Topeka nursery firm of Rosse and Grant was then preparing a catalog of fruits, flowers, and some ornamental trees. The catalog had 18 woodcut plates, 15 colored lithographs and about 80 pages. The *Kansas Valley Times* ran articles in the 1870s encouraging the planting of trees and shrubs around houses to add value and refinement to families' homes. These are two examples of the campaign within Shawnee county to timber the prairie. Augustus Daniels cut timber from his farm north of the river and sold it to Shawnee county in 1877. "Receive of County Treasurer $152.25," he wrote in his diary, "for lumber for Soldier Creek Bridge." This provided him with cash to work his farm when he first arrived in Kansas. Other than woods along watercourses, all of the county was open grassland so farmers were urged to forest the open spaces with trees of all kinds.

By 1867, notices were appearing in local papers concerning orchards. One orchard was owned by Elliott Carriger, on the Wakarusa. He proposed saving "at least one hundred bushels of winter apples" and 500 bushels "set on his trees [but many] dropped off as they will from young trees." Tecumseh's Mrs. Julia Stinson displayed some of the apples raised on her farm that same year. The largest weighed 17 ounces and the smaller ones a full pound. The next fall H. W. Martin, also of Tecumseh, presented the publishers of the Topeka *Weekly Leader* with a bushel of the freestone variety of peaches grown in his own orchard.

Indian Creek Grange Hall. Grangers hauled the stone and helped lay it, completing the building in 1909. (Courtesy Kansas State Historical Society)

To facilitate the planting of orchards, four brothers from Gettysburg, Pa., named Taylor, bought the lands surrounding the abandoned Calhoun county courthouse with the intention of producing and peddling apple seedlings. Lewis R. Taylor purchased the property on which the courthouse stood in 1869, but before he got into the seedling business the grasshopper years of the 1870s sent him back to Pennsylvania. He kept the land, however, and returned in 1879.

The seed of the hardy champagne apple of northern France was imported in the 1880s, and the superiority of the Kansas valley stock quickly found favor among apple growers. A hundred thousand young seedlings could be produced on a single acre of soil here, and for years they had a ready market. When the business was at its height several large scale growers and numerous smaller ones became engaged in it. J. H. Skinner of Topeka, whose groves are still in operation, and F. W. Watson at St. Marys farmed considerable acreages. They were independents who grew for their own accounts. Other nurserymen grew on contract in Rossville, Grantville, Soldier township, and Silver Lake. Local farmers could buy direct from these nurseries, but some believed that better trees could be had from back East.

In 1921, E. R. Taylor, son of one of the Taylors who originated the industry, wrote for the 23rd report of the State Board of Agriculture:

The growing of these seedlings has reached its perfection in the Kaw valley. The success has been so phenonomenal here that the growing in other sections has practically ceased, and fully 90 per-cent of this important stock, both in the United States and Canada, is grown here in the Kaw valley.

The disappearance of the seedling industry dates back to the depression of the 1930s. Competition from Washington and Oregon growers, state regulations and insect pests contributed to the eventual decline of the Shawnee county seedling business.

Attempts at growing other crops were made within the county. Dick Mann wrote about some of those experiments in the *Kansas Farmer* in 1961: "When the Kansas State Agricultural Society was organized in 1857, and farmers began meeting to compare notes, glowing reports were made on the production of grapes, tobacco, and cotton." A Mrs. Parsons of Tecumseh mentioned "a basket of grapes, very fine, and bottled for future use." Although fruit, cotton and tobacco were tried in much of eastern Kansas, no successes with these crops were reported.

As the 19th century brought hardships and progress to farmers, stockmen were developing their own businesses. The *Kansas Daily Commonwealth* of October 20, 1870, printed this notice: "A large drove containing about 200 head of fat, native cattle, passed through the city yesterday in a northerly direction." The cattle trade commenced in earnest after the Civil War. One of its originators was Col. George W. Veale. By 1866 he was deeply involved in the cattle industry, trading to the army at Fort Riley and shipping cattle east as soon as the railroads arrived at Topeka. Another was Andrew Wilson of Kingsville, who in 1872 had "from 2,600 to 2,800 head of domestic and Texas cattle on his farm. . . ." During September of that year he purchased "300 head of three-year-old steers, for which he paid $65 a head." The *Commonwealth,* which printed the notice, also wrote that "Andy has great faith in cattle." A. C. Sherman of Rossville was at that time shipping six car loads of cattle each week to Chicago, and Wilson was shipping to Pittsburgh and Louisville. A. M. Coville of Mission township had 700 head of Texas cattle for shipment.

In the early days of the local cattle industry much of the county was still open prairie. Augustus Daniels "drove the whole herd to our herding ground on Half Day Creek 9 miles from Topeka." Community pastures were the order of the day. David Zirkle wrote:

When I was a boy, a large body of open prairie extended to with in a mile of our home and other homes along the Wakarusa bottom. All of the settlers used this open prairie for grazing of their livestock. . . .

Farmers such as the Zirkles did not deal in cattle to any large extent. Cows were never sold. No one sold cattle before they were mature. In the fall of the year buyers would come through the country buying three-year-olds. The price was usually around five cents per pound.

A dedicated stockman would pay but a minimal cost for the production of good beef in the mid-19th century. Cattle grazed about eight months of the year on the rich and free prairie grasses and the other four months on hay put up from these grasses at a trifling expense, interspersed with a little corn from the crops raised around the ranch. Nearly all the income of the stock-raiser, if he owned his cows rather than having to buy feeder cattle, was profit with very little trouble. In addition, railroads were bringing the market right to the cattleman's door. Cattle buyers came to the county paying the stock-men for their animals right at home, often even paying shipping costs.

Andrew Wilson was easily the most famous of Shawnee county's stockmen. He raised thoroughbred shorthorns which the *Common-wealth* termed "the finest herd of cattle in the Union." He owned a bull of that breed named Minister, which took more prizes than any other bull exhibited in the area. Mr. Wilson also owned 15 other bulls, many of which he bred on his own farm. One article about the "Cattle King" gave a vivid opinion of Wilson's herd:

> We have no hesitancy in saying that this is the best collection of thoroughbred animals in the western country, and in fact, we know of no better collection any-where. While every state in the west will be represented by stock men, anxious to purchase and carry these animals off, it would be a great damage to the state of Kansas to allow one of them to be taken out of its limits.

Cattle of good breeding and ordinary steers arrived in the county from different parts of the country: Texas, Colorado, Kentucky, Ohio, Illinois, Missouri, and elsewhere. Until the advent of barbed wire in the mid-1870s, many different types of fencing were used to encircle the animals. Due to the relative lack of timber in most locales rail fences were unfeasible. An abundance of native limestone in the area led many farmers and stockmen to build corrals of stone, but stone fences around their entire land-holdings meant much time-consuming and difficult work. Some rural men did build stone walls, but another popular form of local fencing was connected with the forestation of the prairie.

An 1872 newspaper article made this statement: "The value of the Osage orange as a hedge plant for Kansas, and in fact for all the middle and southern states . . . is now . . . well established." David Zirkle wrote in *Yesteryears and Yesterdays* of fencing materials used at the time of his parents' arrival in Monmouth township.

> Fencing material was quite an item at that time as barbed wire was not manu-factured for a good many years after my folks came to Kansas. Lots of fences were of stone. Wooden rails were also used extensively, and some hedge fences were planted about this time.

The coming of barbed wire solved the problems of enclosing pasture land and eventually brought an end to grazing cattle in open meadows. Stock raisers found it cheaper and easier to string wire of many different types to surround wayward steers. By the end of the century, barbed wire was the exclusive fencing material, and is still rivaled only by electric fencing, even easier to string but in the long run a drain on power and income.

Land encircled by these fences was at first natural prairie grass pasture. In 1916, however, Sudan grass, a member of the sorghum family, came into the state. This new comer proved itself able to resist dry weather and furnish pasture in August and September when other pastures were short. Feeding cattle on this grass fattened them more than did ordinary grasses and good results were obtained by those who kept the seed pure and planted it a considerable distance from other sorghums. Another pasture introduced was known as Johnson grass. It was an excellent hay. Its drawback was that it was not an annual like Sudan grass, but a perennial. As a result it proved very difficult to eradicate, and has come to be regarded as a pest.

Cattle raising in the county is no longer the big business that it was during the days of Veale, Coville, and Wilson. Mostly, it is relegated to farmers branching into stock-raising. Cattle are still an important part of county agriculture, however, as can be witnessed at any livestock auction around the county. Agricultural statistics presently include over 30,000 cattle and 4,500 dairy cattle in Shawnee county.

An 1870 estimate placed the whole number of hogs in the county at 2,232. Swine production has grown greatly over the century since. After 1960 the State Board of Agriculture reported 12,300 hogs in Shawnee county valued at $209,100. The *Commonwealth* issued the following article in 1872: "The pool of polluted gore in front of the K. P. depot was occasioned by the train running into a large sized porker at noon yesterday, and making a short division of his body by two." Luther Woodford surely had one of the largest swine ever reported in Kansas: "Luther Woodford of Tecumseh . . . killed a Chester white hog a few days ago that weighed, after being dressed, 706 pounds. The rendered lard from this hog just filled a forty gallon cask. Beat this if you can." Andrew Wilson was also involved in the hog business. "Mr. Wilson's Berkshires," wrote the *Commonwealth* of August 13, 1873, "are very fine animals and ought to command lively competition among purchasers." Today (1976) hog prices are generally stable and nearly 15,000 hogs and pigs are being raised each year in the county.

Spraying potatoes in the fertile Kaw bottoms near Silver Lake, 1924. (From Silver Lake centennial book, 1970)

The raising of sheep has never been of extreme importance to local agriculture, although many are raised within the vicinity. In 1960, 3,500 sheep were in the county. Today the number is about the same, with a value of approximately $55,000.

The first Kansas Poultry Association was organized at Topeka in 1887. Since that time a number of different poultry organizations have come and gone. Today the poultry industry, with its allied branches, is represented by the Kansas Poultry Association presently located in Manhattan. The poultry industry has changed from one of small mongrel flocks that were left to rustle for themselves and roost wherever they could find a place, to one that is scientific and highly specialized. Fifty years ago the average hen laid about 100 eggs per year; the recent average for all birds is over 200 eggs per bird per year. A quarter-century ago there were almost 200 breeds and varieties of chickens, but there was no real difference of performance. Modern geneticists have concentrated on developing specific cross-breeds for either egg production or meat. Twenty-five years ago it took some 15 to 18 weeks for a broiler to grow to about two pounds; today broilers weigh three to four pounds in half the time, eating half the amount of feed.

The Topeka *State Journal* made this comment: "It has been said that Shawnee county has more poultry breeders, fanciers, and judges to 'the square inch' than any similar territory in the United States. Topeka is known all over the country as a poultry center." At the time this was written, in May, 1914, the poultry industry of Shawnee county was being revolutionized. The scrub hen was disappearing from the farms for farmers were finding that pure bred fowls were more profitable. The poultry industry was growing, particularly in its commercial aspects. By the same token, there were a large number of poultry fanciers in Topeka and the surrounding territory and local birds were awarded prizes at leading poultry shows across the country. The majority of those interested in strictly show birds kept poultry simply as a side issue, depending on other sources for their livelihoods. Many of these birds, however, brought high prices, some as much as one hundred dollars apiece. At one time there were over a hundred fanciers raising particular breeds of chickens around Topeka.

Topeka boasted in the 1920s of possessing one of the greatest poultry concerns in the world, the Seymour Packing Company. That one firm handled almost 600 carloads of poultry and eggs annually. The Beatrice Creamery, the Topeka Packing Company, and the Continental Creamery also were deeply involved in poultry shipping. The poultry industry in Topeka did not depend entirely upon Shawnee county for its supply since it processed the enormous sum of one billion eggs per year. At the industry's highest point poultry of all kinds in the county numbered 185,000 and was valued at $140,000. By 1960 the number had dropped to 92,000 birds, with a value of $65,320. The poultry industry, of which Topeka was a one-time center, has slowly been deteriorating, although in Kansas generally it has expanded into modern high-production business.

About the same time the poultry industry was being revolutionized the entire face of agriculture was undergoing a change. Fred L. Parrish wrote that the coming of the 20th century saw the natural fertility of the soil decline, and work animals and equipment had been strenously used. Farmers had previously known and used comparatively little knowledge of the principles of agriculture. "For them it seemed that the only prospect was to keep doggedly at the time-honored ways of farming or to get out of the business entirely," he wrote. The late 19th century saw the extensive introduction of windmills into Kansas. Rain sometimes fell in sudden showers, which meant most of the moisture ran off unless there was a deep porous subsoil. Too much cultivation could be disastrous because the wind blew the soil away. The lister, which threw soil into ridges, was used in the fall, thereby allowing the soil to stay in a rough condition to catch the moisture. Listing and plowing were done at right angles to the prevailing winds. Should the fall have been dry, stubble was often left on the land to hold the soil. When rainfall was light, the ground was often summer-fallowed during alternate years, but this could be done as seldom as every three or four years.

The first 30 years gave increased attention to soil management. Commercial fertilizers were still largely unknown. Soil was rebuilt and restored by fallowing and the rotation of crops, using legumes to restore nitrogen and phosphorous. In some hardpan areas of the eastern part of the state there were some experiments in the use of explosives to get moisture down to the roots of the plants.

In 1933 the legislature passed a law for the purpose of controlling and eradicating bindweed and other noxious weeds. Controls for small areas were the use of sodium chlorate and heavy pasturing with hogs. Intensive fallow and a smother crop were used for larger land areas. In 1937 the state Noxious Weed Law was passed, and a noxious weed division of the state government was established. A relentless battle against bindweed was inaugurated. If landowners refused cooperation in stamping out the pest, the county could treat the weed and collect costs as taxes. The cheapest weed-control method was cultivation. By 1942, all but three Kansas counties were active against bindweed and other troublesome plants. In Shawnee county, county,

The sugar works on the Rock Island line west of Topeka about 1888. Later they were destroyed by fire. (From "The Capital City, Topeka, Picturesque and Descriptive," 1888-9)

city, highway, and railway officials cooperated in the movement and brought it under control by this year.

After the turn of the century, hitching posts at the market square in rural communities fell into disuse. Across the state the horse population dropped below one million for the first time in 1921. By 1924 local farmers were being "bothered" by tractor and truck salesmen. There were those who contended that the only fool-proof motor for field-work was a mule. Many believed a horse could do every conceivable type of work more cheaply than a tractor.

When the first gasoline traction engine was used in Shawnee county is not known, but there were evidently several by 1910. The truck took the place of the horse and wagon after World War I. Shortly thereafter, power lines began supplying farms with electricity around the county. The growing use of farm power machinery obligated the farmer to learn how to keep it in good working order. By 1925, all the rural villages had gained some sort of electrical service. The problem of bringing electricity to the service of individual farmsteads was tied to the cost of distribution in small quantities. Kerosene lamps were still used in many farmhouses. Following the Second World War, the use of power controls on farm machinery was a significant new development. It allowed the farmer to operate machinery attached to the tractor by means of a finger-tip controlled hydraulic cylinder.

Most farm loans had been of the mortgage type, and those depended considerably upon the local banker. Land was regarded as a sound basis for credit. The federal government under the Wilson administration took steps to improve rural credit by means of a flow of credit from the newly-created Federal Reserve system. This system of credit was made available through Federal Land Banks, farm mortgage companies, and life insurance companies.

After World War I the federal government returned to a *laissez faire* policy, with a subsequent decade of declining farm prices. The national government tended to favor big industries until the world-wide depression carried not only American industry but also agriculture to an all-time low. Farmers and stockmen had been initiated to depression conditions prior to 1929 and therefore, despite the financial collapse, continued to improve livestock breeds and develop new varieties of crops through the '20s, '30s, and '40s.

The two world wars initiated much world control over Americans. Producers of food had an abundance of statistics about production but very little about the consumption of their products. In order to become enlightened in the business of food production, statistics were needed not only from county and state but even world markets. In spite of what farmers believed, agriculture had become a global industry and remains so today. It had to be conducted as an industry.

A laboratory was established in Topeka in the early 1950s to provide complete analytic facilities for many kinds of testing. Included in the many services performed by the laboratory was the testing of seeds.

The *Kansas Valley Times* of March 7, 1879, quoted prices for farm goods to settlers at Rossville:

A good farm wagon, $75; a new set of double harness, from $26 to $32; a harrow, $10; a good team of heavy farm horses from $150 to $165; cows, $25 to $38; plows for breaking, $25. Household furniture, dry goods, groceries, etc., at about eastern prices. The choicest cuts of beef, 10¢ per pound; flour $2.50 to $3.00 per 100 pounds.— Boots and shoes fully as cheap as they can be bought in any eastern cities.

The costs of farming and of living are no longer so inexpensive. County agriculture in 1976 is a big business. Its importance to the county has grown with the county through drought, insect depredations, and financial depressions. Corn, wheat, sorghums, alfalfa, cattle, hogs, and chickens all contributed to farm expansion in 120 years since pioneers sowed their first crops of seed corn.

Harvesting wheat near Silver Lake, 1940. (From Silver Lake centennial book, 1970)

Dressed for work, these Santa Fe shop workers posed for their portrait shortly after the turn of the century. (Courtesy James D. Wallace)

THE WORK OF A PEOPLE; INDUSTRY

"The Santa Fe Railroad is the boss of all Topeka things," wrote Joseph G. Waters in 1883. He saw the firm as the focal point of Topeka enterprise. Shawnee county industrial history, however, stretched back well before the territorial days. Oregon bound travelers noticed in the Pottawatomie reserve several small circular saw mills which were operated either by or for the Indians. At least one was located north of the river though Uniontown and the Baptist Mission were the centers for small craft industries like blacksmithing, gunsmithing, and wagon making.

Settlers required the sawmills for the lumber, shingles, and lath to go into their homes, churches, and businesses. The territorial towns frequently boasted of a mill before they did a public school, and Topeka was no exception. In the spring of 1855 Topeka acquired its first steam sawmill from the New England Emigrant Aid Company. Unfortunately it proved too small for the task, and, besides, the best timber lay inaccessible in the Kaw half-breed tracts north of the Kansas river. Eventually the community, as did Auburn, Indianola, and Tecumseh, obtained a suitable mill which doubled as a grist mill on behalf of the neighboring farmers.

Until after the Civil War Topeka business was predominantly commercial. An 1868-69 directory listed six blacksmiths (who were also carriage makers), two gunsmiths, and two steam mills but also 16 groceries, 12 dry goods emporiums (some of the firms being groceries as well), and numerous small scale merchants like milliners and tailors. Perhaps the most unusual concern was H. B. Middaugh's washing machine company. Guaranteed to perform the work in one-fourth the usual time, the *Kansas State Record,* July 7, 1860, declared that "this machine was no sham." It would make household tasks "comparatively light and trifling" and the paper asked for the town's patronage.

Heavy industry came to Topeka in the 1870s, a decade of economic instability. The *Commonwealth* later bemoaned that in 1870 "lots were unsaleable, rents were exorbitant, streets and offices were bare of customers." To correct this depression the city tried to lure industry by selling municipal bonds. In the process it increased the city's indebtedness and ruptured relations between north and south Topeka, both rivals bidding for industrialization.

Zenas King of Cleveland, Ohio, approached Topeka businessmen during the fall of 1870 proposing to move his iron bridge manufactory to Kansas. To this he attached a proviso—Topeka had to raise $10,000. The city proposed to do so with an $11,000 bond election, a plan warmly endorsed by the *Commonwealth*. Others, however, were not so sure; some believed that the money was already subscribed, thus making an election unnecessary. One man complained to the paper, December 25, 1870, that "the bonds are to be given to Zenas King . . . as a present to him." He feared the city's high debt would go still higher and "if we are anxious to give away eleven thousand dollars at this time, let us give it to our own mechanics to enable them to run the foundaries and machine shops which are now idle for want of a little capital."

The *Commonwealth* replied to the criticism: "We can't do better than involve ourselves a few thousand more [dollars] . . . to secure commercial prosperity to this city." The bond issue passed by a comfortable majority late in December. In the first ward (North Topeka) it sailed by, 209 for and only 45 against. In the second ward (East Topeka), however, the vote stood 50 in favor and 16 against, and in the third (the residential West) the proposition lost, 90 for and 102 against. Already, some people on the south side began thinking the North Topekans were interested only in their own prosperity and not that of the city as a whole.

Despite the victory, King accepted $50,000 worth of bonds offered by Iola, Kan. Yet, a year and a half later, the company again knocked at Topeka's door. Though spurned once before, local businessmen petitioned for a new bond election, this time one of $100,000. The *Commonwealth*, August 10, 1872, featured a long discussion of its merits and explained that the 1870 proposal had contained "a provision Mr. King would not accept." This second offering divided both the townspeople and city council. Fry Giles later commented that "great mistrust was entertained by citizens as to the ability of the company to carry out in good faith its proposition, even if the aid asked for was granted."

Public meetings were held before the election; that at the African Baptist church received the greatest coverage in the *Commonwealth* of August 9th. Most speakers concurred with William Brooks that the shops "will benefit the laboring man" and "if we [the colored men] want employment, we must work for the interest of the city and work to build it up." A. M. Carter dissented:

We voted once to establish this bridge manufactory here, but Iola voted more and they went there. Now they propose to leave Iola and come back here, provided we will give them more bonds. It isn't treating Iola right. If they show bad faith with Iola, why will they not with us? We hear a great deal about their employing colored men. I am a mechanic, am a harness maker, but can't work at my trade in the shops, because I am a colored man. Don't flatter yourself that you will get work.

Regardless of any doubts, the bonds passed by 200 votes. Significantly, the three wards south of the river (a new ward had been created since the first election) rejected them, the second and fourth very narrowly and the third by 171 to 79. North Topeka, however, swamped the balloting, 338 in favor to one against—no question as to where they believed the shops were to be located. The *Commonwealth,* elated over the outcome, declared Topeka would "unquestionably have the largest manufactory establishment west of St. Louis." For now "the company is entitled to the good will and co-operation of every friend of the city." The paper concluded, "let us have peace."

Throughout the fall of 1872 the newspaper reported on the shops' progress, employing all kinds of statistics and descriptive adjectives; in their words, the shops "look like a modern Babylon." The King Wrought Iron Bridge Manufactory and Iron Works opened with a flourish and almost immediately rumors spread about the firm's insolvency. Despite soothing words from the *Commonwealth,* mismanagement, the general economic collapse of 1873, and the high price of iron shipped to Kansas sealed the company's doom. Too, the U. S. Supreme Court ruled against the validity of the original Iola bonds, thus placing Topeka's in jeopardy. Bridges had been built in Wamego, Wyandotte, Kansas City, and elsewhere, but creditors quickly stepped in and removed the company's machinery. The bridge shops, which were to have made Topeka the "Indianapolis of Kansas," withered after less than a year's existence.

Shortly before the bridge shop election, in July, 1872, the city held an even more important vote—whether to issue $100,000 in bonds for the permanent Santa Fe shops and general offices. This puzzled many who thought the A.T.&S.F. shops were already in Topeka and that no money need be provided. However, Emporia had offered $200,000 and other towns along the rail line were equally interested in procuring them. The *Commonwealth,* July 9, 1872, explained that the present structures were merely repair shops employing only 55 men. If the bonds passed at least 200 men would be employed at "an average of $3 per day."

The bonds won approval in every ward though only 83 voted in North Topeka (80 in favor). Little was accomplished until the Santa Fe bought the empty bridge shop complex in 1878 and erected more buildings on the site. In 1883-84 the company built their general offices on Jackson street.

A third industrial project of the 1870s, the Topeka Iron and Steel Company, or rolling mills, benefitted from $150,000 in bonds and was to manufacture railroad rails. The first major problem was its location. On April 3, 1873, the *Commonwealth* announced the works were to be on the south side. "Tenement houses will soon be looming up in that vicinity," prophesied the paper but the next day it was not so certain. Still later the city learned that the rolling mills were to be located in North Topeka.

This period was one of intense rivalry between the two sections of town. North Topeka possessed several advantages including the Kansas Pacific railroad with its connections to the east. In 1871, a secessionist movement raised its head in the first ward. After several angry meetings the North Topeka *Times,* December 14, 1871, stated "the South Topeka folks are afraid the secession movement will prove disastrous to their interests, and they are at work to discourage it." The deannexation cause sputtered out in the state legislature in February, 1873. It left bitterness between the two sides each of which cajoled industry to locate in its area.

The *Commonwealth,* April 9, 1873, expressed disappointment that the south side lost the rolling mills. Three years before, the editors, supposedly, had not cared where the bridge shops were to be located: "North Topeka is part and parcel of Topeka." This time, however, it blamed the loss to South Topeka's "indifference and illiberality." The "Kansas Pacific took a lively interest in the project" while the Santa Fe gave it "the cold shoulder."

Against an unfavorable supreme court ruling on bonds and the 1873 panic, the plant opened in April, 1874. Almost immediately a major potential customer, the Northern Pacific, failed. Off and on for a few years the mills produced rails. The *Daily Blade,* August 7, 1875, sarcastically wrote that the factory "shuts down on the merest shadow of an excuse." The Kansas Pacific purchased the complex in 1880 only to have a fire in April the following year destroy it.

The failure of two highly touted industries, along with that of the First National Bank of Topeka* in 1873, soured many Topekans. In 1878 Charles Curtis, better known then as a north Topeka jockey, forcefully asserted: "The infernal [rolling] mill has been a worse drawback on our gallant little city than all others, and has caused it many undeserved curses." The *Blade* asked not for "great overgrown Bridge shops" but "smaller and more practical manufactories." Finally, reflecting upon the disaster of pet projects, the *Commonwealth,* October 1, 1873, calmly reflected: "After all, virtue is purer than a bank account, and contentment far better than riches."

---

*Not the same institution which does business under that name in 1976.

Unlike the 1870s, the 1880s proved to be one of the most prosperous and exciting eras in Topeka history. Much of the business activity centered upon a real estate and building boom but industry played a significant role. In value of product the ever expanding Santa Fe railroad topped the list, followed by an important publishing-printing trade and flour milling. The *Commonwealth,* June 13, 1886, outlined the community's economic health with a few statistics on selected industries. Topeka had ten cigar manufactories; nine flour, feed, and oil mills; seven each of metal roof plants and tailors; three each iron-foundries and machine shops, publishing-printing shops, stone works, and harness and saddle works; two each sash-door-blind factories, vinegar works, and electric light plants; and one railroad car shop, packing house, candy manufactory, gas works, preserved fruit works, file factory, soda-bottling plant, and tent and awning factory.

Total value of industrial products, excluding the Santa Fe, approached $2,500,000, and the plants employed 1,580 men, 36 women, and 18 children. The printing trade hired the most women, 31. The cigar manufactories, by nature small hand crafts, had 56 men and two women but the most children, 13. Other industries hiring women included the candy factory and the fruit works.

While some wages fluctuated, most were fairly stable during this period. Common laborers, according to the reports of the State Board of Agriculture, averaged around $1.25 or $1.50 per day. Stone masons and bricklayers received $2.50 as did blacksmiths, harness makers, and bookbinders. Wagon makers and tinners got $2.25, tailors and printers only $2.00. Milliners and dressmakers, on the other hand, obtained only $1.25 per day and seamstresses $1.00.

This is a sampling of the industrial base. Some businesses, like the asphalt paving works, achieved near instantaneous prosperity in a city bent on civic improvements. Others turned out carriages, crackers, boilers, plows, shirts, shoes, starch, fire escapes, soap, and trunks and valises. L. V. R. Smith and his two sons Anton and Clement (the brothers later known for their Smith automobile) manufactured artificial limbs, braces, crutches, etc. When business slackened, they switched to filing knives and saws or making bows and arrows. Unlike many of the above mentioned enterprises, the Smith company survived to eventually become Petro's Surgical Appliances.

An important source for the business concerns of the day is a booklet entitled *The Leading Industries of Topeka, 1882.* In it is mentioned the Kaw Valley Manufacturing Company, makers of "Climax Washing Powder" with this enthusiastic comment: "[The washing powder] contains no poisonous ingredients; is good for the bath and shampooing; does away with rubbing and boiling; will not injure clothes; and is guaranteed to be the best washing compound ever made."

Another publication, *The Commerce of Topeka, 1880,* reported that Kraemer Brothers cigars, founded in 1873, made 30,000 cigars a month with a trade in Kansas and Colorado reaching $25,000 to $30,000. Kraemer's was only one of ten or 12 small firms; Charles S. Eagle, which supplied the bulk of Topeka's cigars during the 19th century was the best known. With a handful of workers, who turned out 250 or 300 smokes a day, the companies sold different shapes and sizes for five or ten cents apiece. Arthur Conklin in the Topeka *Capital,* October 10, 1947, rolled off their colorful and magical names: Rose Tint, Eagle Smoker, Silver Statue, Big Tromp, Little Tromp, Seal of Kansas, Little Joe, Modoc, Buck Skin, Head Clerk, Little America, Gold Bug, 310, Jolly Fellow, and many, many more. The machine age and growing expenses killed the art in Topeka with most factories closing before World War I.

Economic reversal plagued the country late in the 1880s, though Topeka apparently was not affected until two or three years later when the city's population stopped cold. Building was still fairly strong by 1890, but soon after land sales and development collapsed, bankrupting a number of persons. The *Capital's* response to these problems is indicated by an 1894 plea: "If all Topeka merchants would confine their trade to the Topeka [paper box] factory twenty girls would find steady employment, as it is eight or nine are employed." Conditions were growing better by the end of the decade as civic improvements—the high school, courthouse, Kansas avenue (Melan) bridge, etc.—helped the economy. As Topeka prepared to enter the new

This 1880 lithograph shows at the lower left the old King bridge shops, bottom center the rolling mills, and extreme upper right a distillery in the Redmondville district. (Courtesy Kansas State Historical Society)

century, the city's Commercial Club in its *Glimpses of Topeka* (1899) examined the community's financial health and wants. One of the latter was a wholesale harness and horse-collar manufactory.

These growing Topeka industries required more and more energy resources. Initially using their own or animal power early settlers quickly harnessed wood and coal for fuel. Shawnee county streams were too slow running or too shallow to be used though one grist mill north of Rossville obtained water power from Cross creek. Fortunately businesses and private consumers could tap nearby coal fields in extreme southern Shawnee county and in Osage county. While coal long remained an important fuel, by January and February of 1870 the Excelsior Coke and Gas Company had introduced gas lighting to Topekans. A *Kansas State Record* reporter affirmed that it was "far superior to coal oil."

The company manufactured its gas in a works at First and Monroe. The first use came in the lighting of Kansas avenue, but very soon problems developed because of the quality of the generating coal which produced unpleasant sulphurous odors. The company switched from Osage county coal to that from southeastern Kansas but at the same time, faulty pipes reduced gas pressure. The *Commonwealth,* September 23, 1870, caustically remarked: "Last night it was so bad that we understand the party whose duty it is to extinguish the lamps on the street, had to procure a lantern to assist him in finding them."

Nevertheless, once the problems were corrected, everyone in town wanted gas lighting. The system expanded in 1882 with new and better gas works, but it was not until 1905 that the Kansas Natural Gas Company piped natural gas to town. After several corporate changes, the distributor became, in 1935, the Gas Service Company which continues to today (1976) with the Kansas Power and Light Company serving Rossville and Silver Lake.

On November 25, 1881, in the press room of the *Commonwealth,* 16 carbon arc lamps were set up in a row and switched on to the awe and excitement of Brush Electric Company Stockholders. In the next day's paper a writer stated: "Each individual carbon seemed to vie with its neighbor in an effort to cover itself over with glory." Soon, Kansas avenue merchants, including Manspeaker's grocery, Crosby's dry goods, and the Dutton House hotel, installed one or two lamps to astound and delight their customers.

By 1889, Topeka had five-power plants serving different sections of town—Brush Electric Light and Power, Edison Electric Illuminating, North Topeka Light and Power, the Rapid Transit, and the city of Topeka stations. Though lighting was the primary and almost only purpose, competition in the late 1800s was fierce and led to franchise wars and desires for municipalization. Early in the '90s several parties, including outside interests, were involved in damming the Kaw for hydro-electric power. One dam was proposed up river from town and a second down stream at Oakland. Some work, apparently, was done at both places before the idea was abandoned during the economic uncertainities of mid-decade.

Electrical demand grew enormously during the first quarter of the 20th century, outstripping the Topeka Edison Company's ability to supply it from the downtown Van Buren street station. Thus, in 1923 the company, a successor to Brush Electric, Rapid Transit, and the others mentioned above, planned a new, $4,000,000 power plant near Lecompton. To finance the project the Edison company merged, March, 1924, into a totally new corporation, The Kansas Power and Light Company. This firm selected a plant site at slumbering Tecumseh and commenced operations at the generating station in October, 1925. Over the years, as KP&L acquired other electrical systems in northeastern and central Kansas, it added generating units to the Tecumseh plant making it (in 1976) the second largest on the system.

One of the worst industrial accidents in Kansas history took place at the Tecumseh power plant on December 9, 1948. Natural gas, collecting under the plant, exploded causing a secondary explosion which ripped out windows, doors off their hinges and heaved huge concrete slabs. Nine men, some of them employed by a building contractor, lost their lives.

Out in the county, people acquired gas or electric service much later than their city cousins. In 1901 one Rossville newspaper editor asked for gas street lighting since "the Northern lights we are using at the present time are two remote to be of much service." Even when the town hung up gas lamps that year or in 1902, they were so dim the same writer demanded "some Jap lanterns" as replacements. Several enterprising individuals organized small operations to generate electricity, like the Rossville Electric Light and Ice Company, before they were replaced by KP&L. Some of the more progressive farmers in the 1910s and 1920s owned a small farm generator though others, even living in the shadow of the Tecumseh power plant, lacked service. To aid the latter and as a part of Franklin Roosevelt's New Deal, the Kaw Valley Electric Cooperative was formed in 1937. It built a distribution system throughout western Shawnee county to Auburn and Dover as well as parts of Douglas, Jackson, Osage, and Wabaunsee counties.

A Monmouth township farmer wrote to the *Commonwealth,* March 25, 1873, about a need for new manufacturing interests. Farmers

The Topeka Woolen Mill in Oakland, later the home of the Longren aircraft factory. (From the Topeka "Mail and Breeze," February 4, 1898)

Several cigar makers operated in Topeka and sold their product in boxes such as these. (Courtesy Kansas State Historical Society)

would plant flax, he explained, if suitable oil mills, rope and starch factories, and coarse linen textile plants be established. "Let us have manufactories," the writer concluded, "to manufacture the things we can *produce*, rather than manufactories of imported things [e.g., iron for bridge shops]. Until then, our county will not be in a very sound condition."

Agriculture, therefore, became an important cornerstone in Topeka industry. Early saw mills ground wheat as a sideline, and the Shawnee Mills of the late 1860s was the first major flour operation in town. The *Commonwealth*, May 13, 1873, naturally enough, warmly embraced this home enterprise: "The proprietors . . . are scrupulously careful in material used and workmen employed." It produced the "celebrated" XXXX brand of "family flour" which was "prized by all housekeepers." The industrial pamphlet of 1880 mentioned that the firm shipped products, annually totalling over $200,000, as far east as Chicago, north to Iowa, south to the Gulf and west to Colorado.

The history of the major firms and elevators in Topeka may be found in Euphemia Page's (a daughter of mill owner Thomas Page) history of milling in the March, 1948, *Bulletin* of the Shawnee County Historical Society. Besides the Shawnee, they included the Inter-Ocean, Topeka Mill and Elevator, Crosby Roller, Mid-Continent,

Kaw, and Forbes. Most were located on or near the river bank adjacent to the Union Pacific or Santa Fe tracks. A few smaller operations, like Emil Utz's corn meal mill at 17th and Fillmore, were found elsewhere. The *Capital* in its year-end review, January 1, 1890, boasted: "The number and capacity, of our mills, together with their annual output, placed Topeka at the head of the list of western cities, and it is only surpassed by Minneapolis in the northwest." Yet, by the time of Miss Page's writing there were only two. Only one operation remains replaced, in part, by the huge grain elevators strung along the U. P. line west of town.

Besides milling, packing achieved some prominence with Seymour's (founded 1892) in poultry, Hill's (founded 1907) in horse meat pet food, and General Foods (1971) in dog food. Wolff Packing Company with its "Honey" brand hams and "Old Fashion" lard was, perhaps, the best known. Founded as a butcher shop in the early 1870s by Charles Wolff, in 1898 the slaughter house averaged 12 cattle and 150 hogs a day with 25 or 30 men doing all the work—butchering, smoking and curing, sausage making, and even packaging and shipping. By the 1920s the weekly cattle kill numbered from 300 to 500 while 7,000 hogs were slaughtered.

The *Daily Capital* featured Wolff's in an article, July 30, 1922. An old time employee recalled the early operations and some of the problems when, for instance, a bull got loose in the killing room and "treed" all the workers. For its readers the *Capital* followed step by step the 1922 modern assembly line process or "endless chain" of butchering. "A hog would certainly enjoy it," the old timer asserted, "if he could but see with what thoroughness and dispatch he is handled. It would do him good to see the many expensive machines and labor saving devices which were purchased for his sole benefit." At the end of day, when the last pig was killed, the good news was shouted and "everybody takes it up, until the whole plant is ringing with the cry 'all dead, all dead!' "

The Morrell packing company succeeded Wolff's and in 1940 added new buildings to the complex on lower Kansas avenue. While the firm contributed greatly to the area's prosperity the 1951 flood swept mud and debris into the plant and forced the company to halt its Topeka operations. Several attempts to revive the packing trade collapsed and the Wolff-Morrell buildings eventually became warehouses.

Disaster of some kind often struck Topeka enterprise when least expected. The 1880s was a time, according to Mary Davis Sanders, of "Sugar Fever." Boston capitalists subscribed one half of the stock and Topekans the other half in the Topeka Sugar Company's plant west of town. Fire destroyed the investors' hope early in August, 1889, leading the *Capital* to wail: "It is unfortunate that the fire fiend does not confine himself to remote fields such as Pacific coast cities and the forests in the Rockies."

In 1884 Will Ripley opened his Kansas Preserving Works which produced jams, mincemeat, catsup, sauces, pickles, and other similar items. Butters Manufacturing Company took over the business and in 1893 Otto Kuehne purchased Butters. Kuehne's Topeka Vinegar and Preserving Works became the city's best known such enterprise and sold a large line. Mary Sanders in her "Sweets and Sours" described them:

There were three grades of products: Silver Leaf, Home Made, and Green Leaf. In the early 1900s, the first grade Silver Leaf products included: pickles, olives, vinegar, sauerkraut, cider, catsup, mustard, extracts, syrups, preserves, apple butter, mincemeat, salad dressing, and other table condiments. Gypsy Queen Baking Powder was also their product.

Kuehne exhibited his produce everywhere and by 1904 had plants at Kansas City, Mo.; Denver and Fort Worth. Both the 1903 flood and a 1909 fire damaged the north Topeka premises so that after 1917 the company ceased its activities.

One of the few cotton mills in the west, the Topeka Cotton Manufactory, was incorporated in 1887. West of Topeka it constructed an impressive two story stone structure, 76 by 164 feet. Short-lived, if it functioned at all, one goal, according to the *Capital,* January 1, 1889, was making "flour sacks to supply the grist mills of this city and state." Five years later Topekans laid the cornerstone for another textile factory, the two story brick plant of the Topeka Woolen Mill in Oakland. One speaker at the ceremony forthrightly declared: "This industry is the opening wedge to a new Topeka. An old fashioned Topeka, we have been dormant for a few years, but now we are making another start forward." Unfortunately, the machinery was not installed until three years afterwards with the plant starting up in December, 1897. It operated for about ten 'years turning out blankets, skirts, flannels, jeans, and yarns during the summer and fall and the "celebrated Sunflower pants" in the winter.

Whether the farmer appreciated or not the "new manufacturing interests" which sprang up, certainly industry stayed close to the markets and transportation systems of Topeka with little out in the country. Most sections of the county, other than the sparsely settled extreme north, had their small grist mills and blacksmiths serving local farmers. Many families built private mills for sorghum molasses or apple cider and butter; others made their own cheese to sell or barter. Auburn, Dover, and Richland were particularly important for cheese manufacturing around the turn of the century with the Dover Cheese Factory and Vassar Creek Cheese Company on the west side and the Richland Creamery Company on the east.

Rossville and Silver Lake, as the two largest communities in the county outside of Topeka, naturally possessed considerable business activity which was aided by being on the main line of the Kansas Pacific. In 1872 Rossville residents chartered the Rossville Manufacturing Company "to manufacture all kinds of Furniture, Agricultural Implements, Wagons" as well as to conduct a "General Mercantile business." Two years later Silver Lake people incorporated the Silver Lake Distilling and Mill Company to make both flour and whiskey. Despite grand plans local industrial efforts declined over the years with much of the activity gone by the turn of the century. H. F. Kellner established in Silver Lake in 1909 a river jetty manufactory, the Kellner Patent Steel Jetty Company, which attained some success during the 1920s selling $800,000 worth of products in 22 states.

Though Topeka attracted industry, on a small scale, a few major plants were founded on the outskirts of town as can be seen by the recent large industrial acquisitions, Goodyear and DuPont. For wartime production, the U. S. government sought in the summer of 1944 a site in Kansas for a synthetic rubber plant, eventually choosing Topeka over Kansas City and other towns. On the eve of V-E day, in March, 1945, the plant commenced production on large sized combat and tractor tires. After the war the Goodyear Tire and Rubber Company assumed control of the plant located, at that time, well north of the city in Soldier township. In 1952 the company greatly enlarged the Topeka plant and expansion has continued since then making Goodyear the largest industrial employer with 3,950 and a plant worth in eight figures. Such statistics, naturally, have turned city commissions envious as they tried various devises to annex the property. In retaliation, company officials hinted at curtailments of further expansions.

E. I. DuPont de Nemours searched for a site to build a cellophane plant in 1957 and chose Tecumseh over 34 other communities. Its complex cost over $25,000,000 and employs 500 workers. The greatest drawback to the industry is a by-product, hydrogen sulfide, with an odor of rotten eggs, which drifts over the countryside. Fortunately for Shawnee countians, the prevailing southerly winds usually carry the smell over Grantville in Jefferson county. Drawbacks or no, both Goodyear and DuPont contribute abundant tax dollars to Soldier and Tecumseh townships respectively, making them far and away the wealthiest in the county.

One of the first major flour mills, Shawnee Mills was located on the northwest corner of Third and Kansas. A boiler explosion on September 3, 1883, killed one man. (Courtesy Topeka Public Library)

Brickyard near Gage boulevard and the Brickyard bridge in 1904. (Courtesy Mrs. C. W. Koch)

Topeka's short-lived cotton factory, located at Tenth and Randolph streets, about 1888. (From "The Capital City, Topeka, Picturesque and Descriptive," 1888-9)

The Wolff Packing Company, later Morrell's, in the 1920s, from the Kaw. (Courtesy Kansas State Historical Society)

Thomas Page's Mid-Continent Mills in North Topeka was built in 1892. (From the Topeka "Mail and Breeze," May 22, 1896)

North Topeka's industrial district in the early 1920s. (Courtesy Kansas State Historical Society)

Joseph G. Waters, Topeka lawyer and writer, recounted in an 1883 description of the town: "If there is a marriage or a funeral, it is a Santa Fe employe; and if you meet a good-looking man on the street, it is hit or miss . . . that he does not belong to that institution." Both the railroad and the city of Topeka grew up together, with all the problems of such maturation. Both had the same father, Cyrus K. Holliday who soon disappeared from active direction of his creation as corporate officers were replaced by eastern capitalists. However, no other community became so identified with the line. Charles M. Chase of Vermont in his *The Editor's Run in New Mexico and Colorado* (1883) expressed it succinctly: "If Topeka is not a friend to the A.T. & S.F. railroad it is because she does not know on which side of her manna the oleomargarine—butter is scarce and strong—is spread."

Important Santa Fe construction began in 1869 with its combination depot and general office on Washington street. The following year the *Commonwealth* announced plans for a two-story, brick machine shop to measure 65 by 100 feet. However, in the 1870s the railroad delayed significant shop improvements in Topeka in favor of its track program in western Kansas. Original buildings included a six stall round house and a 20 by 24 foot storehouse. Candles or torches served as lighting but heating and ventilation were practically nonexistent. All car repair was made on a side track under the open sky.

After it acquired the abandoned King Bridge shops in 1878, particularly in 1881, the Santa Fe started an extensive expansion with several new brick and stone shops. Slowly this bustle moved west into an area that shop superintendent M. J. Drury remembered for the *Santa Fe Magazine* in 1917 as "covered with homes and boarding houses, gardens and shade trees." According to a feature by Tom MacRae in the July, 1911, *Santa Fe Magazine,* the city passed an ordinance in 1881 vacating four acres so that the railroad could erect $200,000 worth of buildings.

Accounts vary as to the number of shop employees during this formative period. A *Daily Capital* reporter counted, October 17, 1885, some 537 men in the cab department, tin shop, machine shop, boiler shop, brass foundry, new machine shop (or new car erecting shop), store house, carpenter shop, paintshop, round house, and locomotive erecting shops. They came from all backgrounds, the 30 men in the cabinet shop being German except for four Swedes. Wages ran as low as 90 cents per day for boys and up to $1.50 for unskilled laborers. Skilled craftsmen averaged $2.25 to $2.75 with blacksmiths as high as $3.00 per day. The hours were long, usually nine or ten

The Santa Fe shops late in the 1800s showing the King bridge shops tower and a portion of the roundhouse at the extreme left, the coal chute left center, and the paint shop on the right. Most of the stone structures which survive date from the 1880s. At this time the Topeka shops were one of the largest railroad facilities in the West. (Courtesy Kansas State Historical Society)

The Railroad YMCA provided wholesome food and entertainment for tired railroad workers. (Courtesy James E. Simons)

hours a day, and the heat and noise almost unbearable. The reporter stated that in the boiler shop "the din . . . is almost deafening. The hearing of the workmen is seriously impaired by long continued work at this trade." The company oversaw their labor before time clocks by a system known as "block time" which was described in Andreas' *History of Kansas*:

> The Block "Time" system . . . is as follows: Each man, as he enters upon his labor, in passing through the office is handed by the block clerk, a small block containing his number. . . . On going out of the office, at the close of the days labor, this block is returned through a hopper at the front of the counter. A register of the time the employee receives the block and when it is returned is kept by the clerk and thus a complete computation of time and wages is made and recorded for each man; ten hours being considered "block time"; all over time is paid for, and all lost time deducted.

For a time, beginning in 1881, the Santa Fe built its own road engines at Topeka, the 4-4-0 American class engine "Cyrus K. Holliday" being the first. The second, the "William B. Strong," cost the company $8,587 but saved it five thousand dollars compared to a locomotive builder's price. Soon, however, economy dictated that the Santa Fe purchase their more complicated engines from other locomotive works. They kept, of course, the repair and maintenance shops at Topeka for the eastern division with occasional experiments like the building of the monstrous and unsuccessful Mallet class of engines. The Santa Fe also built baggage and passenger coaches, the latter requiring considerable artistic skill. The first Topeka passenger car was built in 1882 at a cost of $5,665.

Around the turn of the century the Topeka shop district attained its greatest size and was at the height of its activity and importance. In 1901 the Santa Fe erected a mammoth machine and boiler shop which measured 152 by 850 feet. It still dominates the property with its distinctive saw-tooth profile designed to let in natural, north light. Six years later the shops covered new ground east of Branner street with its low, 900 foot long freight car repair building, later destroyed by the 1966 tornado and then rebuilt. By 1911 the Topeka shops covered nearly 120 acres.

Zenas Potter in *The Topeka Improvement Survey* (1914) counted (as of October, 1913) 2,540 shop employees, 40% of the total Topeka industrial work force. Of these 233 were apprentices; 305 unskilled laborers; 75 foremen; 88 clerks, time-keepers, fire marshals, and instructors; and 1,839 skilled craftsmen. One innovation, which Potter discussed at length, was the apprentice school. Begun in 1907 on a large scale, each department had a school for on the job training for boys aged 16 to 22. The Santa Fe preferred youngsters right out of the elementary schools because they presented fewer problems than better educated boys. The apprentices had classroom study in arithmetic, mechanics, free-hand drawing, etc., for two hours, two days a week. They received wages and the company estimated the average cost per student per day—including wages, equipment, instructor's salary, etc.— at $2.39. Since the Santa Fe considered an apprentice about two-thirds as efficient as a journeyman who got $3.80, with the rate of $2.53 the line actually made a 14 cent profit on the apprentices!

Despite criticism which Potter leveled at certain Santa Fe working practices, the railroad provided several fringe benefits designed to promote worker loyalty. One of the first activities was a railroad Y.M.C.A. association to which the company donated an old passenger coach in 1882. The "Y" offered various recreational and educational programs to off-work employees such as billiards, cards, plays, a library, and classes in different vocational subjects. After a fire destroyed the facility in 1902, the company built a substantial brick building the following year for which President Theodore Roosevelt laid the cornerstone on May 1, 1903. Membership rose to over 1,500 in 1916, one of the largest on the Santa Fe system but declined after the first World War.

The railroad also contributed to its employees' physical well being by forming regional hospital associations in the 1880s and '90s. Each worker paid a monthly fee of 25¢ to $1.00 to the association. Its first hospital was in Las Vegas, N. M., and the Topeka unit was established in 1895. By 1916 it was the largest of seven Santa Fe hospitals with patients coming from a wide region. The old Victorian, baronial pile was demolished in 1953 and replaced with a modern hospital. The line relinquished its authority in the 1960s and the hospital was renamed Memorial.

Such institutions, naturally, captured the workers' loyalty, but they never solved fundamental questions like wage improvement, shorter hours or better working conditions. Here entered the employee's allies, and occasionally his enemies, the union and the strike.

Early 19th century unions, reminiscent of medieval guilds, acted as a protective society for their members. Topeka butchers, for example, organized in March, 1873, to guard "against imposition and loss from unreliable patrons." Anyone who bought meat but did not pay had his or her name entered in a little black book. A marginal note reported "the extent of his unreliability" and fellow members were notified.

Among the first Topeka unions were typographers (1869), cigar-makers (1881), Brotherhood of Railroad Trainmen (1884), carpenters (1886), and machinists (1889). Even before most of these craft associations there existed the Topeka Workingmen's League, the meetings of which were regularly reported by the *Commonwealth* in the 1870s. During the 1880s the Knights of Labor enjoyed a brief popularity in eastern Kansas, especially among railroad men and miners. In March, 1889, several Topeka craft organizations met and formed the Trades and Labor Assembly of Toepka. It advocated the traditional goals of fair wages, shorter hours, woman and child labor laws, factory inspection, and union recognition. Also, it provided a library for members and helped organize retail clerks in 1890.

The Topeka Industrial Council succeeded the above and by 1914 had 25 affiliated unions, including the bakers, barbers, electrical workers, flour packers, garment workers, horse shoers, musicians, painters, plumbers, pressmen, printing press feeders and assistants, tailors, theatrical stage employees, typographers, etc. Twelve, including bricklayers and masons, railway car men (two locals), locomotive engineers, firemen and engine men, laundry workers and plasterers, were not affiliated.

While the Council frequently published pamphlets disclosing those acceptable firms which recognized organized labor, their greatest weapon, of course, was the strike. Because the Santa Fe shops played an overwhelming role in Topeka's economy, a strike there received great attention. The first important stoppage came in 1877 when the shops were "peacefully picketed." The next significant strike began in New Mexico in January, 1893, and by April had spread to Topeka. It started as a wage dispute but then evolved into the question of union recognition. Topeka shopmen peacefully went out on April eighth but reached a compromise in two weeks. A few men wanted to go out during the 1894 Pullman crisis, but apparently the general manager simply closed the shops for a few days allowing emotions to cool.

The Gillette and Nicholson Lumber Company at First and Kansas, about 1912. The old gas works is in the background at left. (Courtesy George L. Whitlock)

The 1904 machinists' strike, however, was not resolved so easily. On March 23rd the International Association of Machinists submitted a list of 20 rules they wanted enforced by the Santa Fe. The company management promptly expressed disapproval over some of the proposals. Any action on their part would mean union recognition as at that time the Santa Fe maintained an open shop. Thus, while employees could join a union, they were not required to do so. A strike was called for on May second, and in retaliation—and protection of property—the railroad temporarily closed the shops.

The *State Journal,* May 5, declared that many machinists opposed the strike but "now that it has been called, they will probably stand by the union." Although a majority of the machinists walked out, many stayed on the job when the shops reopened. Too, the Santa Fe countered the strikers by enlisting strike breakers to take over vacant jobs. The union bitterly resented and criticized this action but to no avail. By mid-May management curtly stated that those not soon back on the job were to be considered as discharged. President E. P. Ripley added that the shops were to be completely open—and no union. Some strikers quietly returned to work, but it was several years before the union representatives admitted defeat.

An anti-union stance, however, lasted little more than a decade. With the first World War came railroad nationalization and the government's acceptance of the unions and brotherhoods. The *Capital* headlined on February 12, 1918: "Organization of Union in Shops well Underway." The United States paid well, too, but when peace came railroads lowered wages. Several roads faced strikes from the brotherhoods during the summer of 1922 and once again Topeka shopmen walked out.

Actually the most serious difficulties arose in the Shopton, Iowa, facility and in the deserts of Arizona and New Mexico. Despite conflicting reports from various sources, apparently Topeka employees slowly resumed work in a week or two. As an inducement to stay on the job, the Santa Fe management stated before the walkout that strikers would lose pensions, death benefits, and seniority. From the other side rumors spread that pensioners were rehired along with women. The strike tore deeply at many of the men. L. L. Waters in his Santa Fe history quoted one young Topekan faced with the dilemma: "In each man's heart there throbbed an unfailing sense of loyalty to his fellow workers engaged in his craft and inversely, in most cases, there was, also, a sense of loyalty toward the management of the railway shops."

As the Santa Fe hired new men to replace the shop strikers, an agreement was eventually made to rehire some old workers as new employees. Still, the crisis of 1922 ripped through not only the railroad but also the city of Topeka and many families. This especially included those from the German-Russian community who lived literally in the shadow of the giant boiler shop. Most of them attended the still new (1917) Sacred Heart parish just east of the shop district; 100 families, nearly half of the parish, moved away after 1922 to Chicago or Horton. The strike divided homes, father against son or brother against brother, and for several years the Santa Fe refused to hire members of some families.

In place of the German-Russians and Germans came unskilled or semi-skilled Mexican workers from the Southwest and Mexico. Probably fewer than 25 Mexicans lived in Topeka as permanent residents before 1900, but the Mexican-American population inched its way up the Santa Fe tracks, working at menial jobs and living, at best, in shacks or railroad cars. They did the same near the Topeka yards with one or more families to a dilapidated frame boxcar. Employed at first and for long afterwards in the lowest paying jobs, the Mexican-Americans slowly filtered into the old German-Russian neighborhoods vacated after the 1922 strike and re-established a strong Catholic community.

The depression and World War II era made up the final chapter in steam motive power for American railroads. After steam came diesel, which the Santa Fe pioneered, but not in Topeka. With this change the Topeka locomotive shops switched to the manufacture of freight cars. For those acquainted with the activity of the '20s and '30s, the shop district appears starkly deserted. Despite the Santa Fe's continued role in community affairs and its strong impact on the economy, Topeka seems to be in some backwater off the mainstream of the road's activities. No more can one say "the Santa Fe Railroad is the boss of all Topeka things."

The Tecumseh power plant, about 1950. (Courtesy The Kansas Power and Light Co.)

The second Topeka courthouse, 1896-1965, was on the northwest corner of Fifth and Van Buren streets. (From the Topeka "Mail & Breeze," May 22, 1896)

The Tecumseh courthouse, 1856-1859. The tower was probably never added. (From an 1859 lithograph of Tecumseh)

(From "Kansas Democrat," April 6, 1891)

THE BALL AND CHAIN GANG.

Do the colored people want any more work on the streets like this?

THE ELECTORATE'S NIGHTMARE; POLITICS

From the very first, Topeka was one of several towns vying to be the center of Shawnee county's political affairs. The same year that she became the county seat, the Lecompton legislature granted the city a charter for municipal government. It was incorporated on February 14, 1857. The territorial legislature was Proslave at that time, and since Topeka was a Free-State town to ask "any favor of that body, or to recognise any of its acts as of legal efficacy," as Giles wrote, "was regarded by Free-State men as closely akin to treason to the Free-State cause." There was a desire in the legislature to mollify Free-State elements in the territory whenever possible. It bestowed such favors on various Free-State centers as it might while yielding none of its status as the legal government of Kansas. Topekans were surprised, and to some extent indignant, when they learned that the Proslave legislature bestowed the municipal charter. Giles wrote that "the disinclination on the part of the citizens to organize under the 'bogus' Territorial authority was so great, that they might not have done so at all but for some further legislation upon the subject by the Free-State Legislature of 1858."

Organization of the city's government began early the next year when there appeared the following proclamation:

To all whom it may concern:

By virtue of an act entitled "An act to incorporate the city of Topeka," and all acts in aid thereof, know ye, that we, Franklin L. Crane, Thomas G. Thornton, Loring G. Cleveland and Samuel T. Walkley, do hereby proclaim and make known, that we have this day constituted and appointed Loring Farnsworth, J. C. Miller and A. F. Whiting judges of election for the purpose of organizing the municipal government of said city of Topeka.

Given under our hands, this 11th day of January, 1858.

The same day this announcement was issued the judges called for an election of a mayor and nine councilmen for Topeka to be held on January 28. Loring Farnsworth was elected mayor and L. Housel, H. W. Farnsworth, G. S. Gordon, J. G. Bunker, James A. Hickey, W. W. Ross, Guilford Dudley, and J. Fin. Hill were elected councilmen. This first city council fixed the second Tuesday of March as the date for annual elections. The first public work by the council was grading Kansas avenue from the river to First street, costing $150. The same year the first city tax was levied to pay for continued grading of

Kansas avenue from Third to Fourth streets (what paving might have been done from First to Third streets is not mentioned), but only a portion of this was ever paid.

The population of Topeka at that time was 512. As the number of inhabitants in the city grew during the next decade, so did the amount of public works. The city council levied taxes, issued municipal scrip, built sidewalks, erected school buildings, and even adopted an ordinance in 1861 prohibiting swine from running at large in the city, evidently a welcome law in Topeka.

During the years of 1863-1867 Topeka experienced an uninterrupted increase in population. In 1867 she became a city of the second class, with a population of 2,810.

Walt Markley, in his *Builders of Topeka,* told the continuing tale of Topeka's municipal government:

Topeka continued under the mayor and council form of government until 1909. In 1907 the legislature authorized the commission form and at a special election November 2, 1909, this form was adopted. The first municipal election under the commission form was held April 5, 1910. William Green, who had been elected mayor in 1907 and re-elected in 1909, resigned in order to clear the records. His move cost him his office, as J. B. Billard was elected the first mayor under the new commission form.

An article in the Topeka *Daily Capital* praised the decision of Topeka to adopt the new form of government:

Kansas, always progressive, was the first to authorize adoption of the commission form of government from Galveston, Tex., and Topeka was the first city in the state to adopt it. Now a score of the leading cities are being governed by this form, the old council and ward system of city politics having passed on.

The Club of Topeka was organized to draw up the commission charter which was approved in May, 1907. In March, 1909, the state

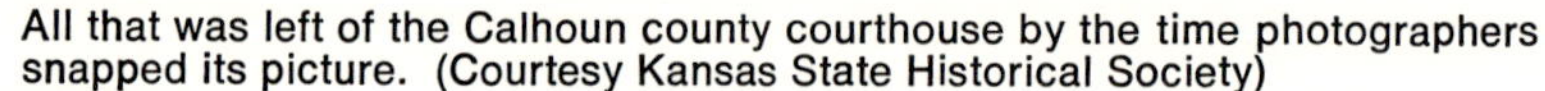

All that was left of the Calhoun county courthouse by the time photographers snapped its picture. (Courtesy Kansas State Historical Society)

The 35-room Dutton House hotel which was built in 1879. The "Commonwealth," January 1, 1880, noted that it had "all modern improvements, including the telephone." During the 1890s Kansas Populists used it as their Topeka headquarters. (From the Topeka "State Journal," October 30, 1935)

legislature amended the charter act to provide for non-partisan primaries and elections, city civil service, the initiative and referendum of ordinances, and the recall of commissions. Under the commission form the city was ruled by five commissioners, one of whom was the mayor, elected every two years.

Following the 1909 changes, in 1929, 1952, 1962, 1964, and 1969 the city electorate defeated proposals to alter again the city structure to a city manager-council or city manager-commission form of government. Partly due to impatience and personality clashes in city hall, the most recent interest in changing the government occurred in 1975-76 with a group of Topekans succeeding in obtaining state legislation for a possible vote in 1976 for a strong mayor-city council structure. Four councilmen would be elected from districts and three councilmen would be chosen at large. Supporters of the proposed change, who would endow the mayor with veto power, have from time to time charged opponents with representing "special interests" ignoring the fact that they, too, are a "special interest."

Topeka had no regular city hall for its first 25 years. City offices were kept wherever the council was able to obtain room, and rental fees eventually totaled nearly $1,500 per year. In December, 1878, during the administration of Mayor M. H. Case, a site for a municipal building was purchased at the southwest corner of Kansas avenue and Seventh street for $7,300. A city hall costing about $38,000 was erected and occupied early in 1879. The council rented out parts of the structure not then needed, collecting a total of $2,360 each year, "enough to pay the interest on the whole investment," according to Markley.

The city maintained its jail in the basement of this building for several years. In 1872 the present site at the northwest corner of Fifth and Jackson streets was purchased and a building constructed for around $9,000. It originally accommodated the offices of city engineer and city attorney as well as the headquarters for the police and municipal court. In the 1930s the city prison was remodeled, adding a new courtroom and a women's ward in the second story. The next municipal building was described by Markley: "[A] City Hall was built in 1900, along with the City Auditorium, the two buildings costing $19,200. The contract price for the City Hall and Auditorium was $76,611. It was remodeled in 1918 and again in 1927."

Until 1877 Shawnee county commissioners were elected for two-year terms. After that year they were elected annually for three-year terms. The register of deeds, a self-supporting office consisting of that officer and five deputies who preserve real estate records, business records, and many important private documents, is also elected for two-year terms. The office of county surveyor was appointive by the commissioners in 1855, but it was made elective by an assembly in 1858. Since 1916 the clerk of the district court has usually been held by women, one of the few such instances until recently. The county assessor has bounced back and forth between being an appointive and an elective office. Since 1910 it has remained an elective post with two-year terms, but the pendulum threatens to swing back to an office of less importance. The county also maintains offices for attorney, auditor, clerk, coroner, Topeka court clerk, district judges, Topeka judges, and Topeka court marshal. Zula Bennington Greene described the most competitive county post:

Other county offices attract modest competition, but there is always a race for sheriff. In the primary election in Shawnee County in 1932 there were 18 candidates for sheriff. The tougher the year, the larger the numbr of candidates. A graph made of the number of candidates each election year might furnish reliable information of the economic state of the county. Until a change in the state constitution made in 1964, a sheriff was limited to two consecutive terms. Now he may hold the office for as long as he can be elected.

County politics have been predominantly Republican and conservative in the party tradition of Kansas. Republican candidates for most offices have largely upheld the status quo and supported large-scale business organizations and ventures, and they have remained the overwhelming favorites in local, state, and national elections. Two major breaks have occurred in this traditional party affiliation, the rise of the Populists in the 1890s and the national sweep of the Democrats in the 1930s. Most early community leaders in the county were Republican, the outstanding exception being C. K. Holliday.

More than any other city in Kansas, Republicans truly felt Topeka to be "their" capital. Though it occasionally lost city elections, the party dominated the political life of the community until after World War II. Republican oriented professional classes easily out-voted the working class of Topeka's major industry, the Santa Fe. With growth in industry, government, and the social service industries in the 1950s,

Democrats started winning more and more county and state legislative elections.

In the 1890s blacks in Topeka became involved to a major extent in municipal politics. In 1891 the black vote in the mayoral election made the difference between A. B. Quinton and incumbent R. L. Cofran. A contemporary newspaper article told much of the story: "The Quinton strikers boast that they have registered every colored male and female vote in the city and ask defiantly: 'What are you going to do about it?' Well, just wait, Br'er Quinton and see. The good people of Topeka will see you later." Despite the majority of black votes for Quinton, Mayor Cofran was returned, but with a plurality of less than 200 votes. About the same time blacks appeared on the Shawnee county sheriff's posse and in the county's court-rooms, in the persons of Elisha Scott and Lutie Lytle, one of the nation's earliest Negro women lawyers.

At a convention assembled in Topeka in 1890 delegates representing the Farmers Alliance, the Industrial Union, the Patrons of Husbandry, the Knights of Labor, the Farmers' Mutual Benefit Association, and the Single Tax Clerks organized the "People's Party," as it was known in Kansas, or the Populist Party. W. F. Rightmire, G. C. Clemens, and Dr. Stephen McLallin of Topeka provided important leadership for the new party. In the state election of 1890 four tickets were in the field: Republican, headed by incumbent Governor Humphrey; Democratic, led by ex-Governor Charles Robinson; Populists, with John F. Willitts nominated for governor; and Prohibitionists, headed by the Rev. A. M. Richardson. Democrats and dissatisfied Republicans united with the Populists to elect John N. Ives as attorney general, but the rest of the Republican ticket filled all other state offices. However, the legislature was heavily stacked with 90 Populists, as opposed to 27 Republicans and seven Democrats.

The tower of the Federal building and post office on the northeast corner of Fifth and Kansas dominated Topeka's main street from 1884 to 1934. (Courtesy Mrs. Ralph James)

The first Shawnee county courthouse located in Topeka was built on the southwest corner of Fourth and Kansas avenue. It served from 1867 until 1896. (Courtesy Kansas State Historical Society)

Topeka's city building on the southwest corner of Seventh and Kansas in 1879. The fire department headquarters are seen at the extreme right. (Courtesy Kansas State Historical Society)

The Hotel Throop, once Topeka's most magnificent, was located on the northwest corner of Fourth and Kansas in 1887. For many years it served as headquarters for Kansas Democrats. It burned in 1950. (Courtesy Kansas State Historical Society)

The Copeland hotel on the southeast corner of Ninth and Kansas burned down in 1909. Known as "Copeland county," it was Republican party headquarters. (Courtesy John W. Ripley)

The legislature began its regular session on January 13 and adjourned on March 13. With the Populists in control in the lower house and both houses on joint ballot, "the proceedings of the session were watched by the public with great interest," Noble Prentis related.

In 1892 the entire Populist ticket for state offices was elected and the party took five of eight congressional seats.

The Kansas senate assembled on January 10, 1893, but the Republicans and Populists each organized their own house of representatives. Both speakers occupied the same desk, and during the first night of the session even slept under the same blanket behind the desk, each with a gavel in his hand. Governor Lewelling recognized the Populists as the legal body, and the senate did the same, with Republican senators formally protesting.

When the Republican house charged L. C. Gunn with neglecting to obey a mandate it had issued and ordered him arrested, an uproar ensued. Scuffles occurred, and the Populists barricaded the door of the hall of representatives. Governor Lewelling authorized a call for the militia if it became necessary. On the morning of January 15 the Republicans brushed aside the guards, smashed in the door with a sledge hammer, and took possession. "Governor Lewelling called out several companies of State militia," wrote Prentis, "guns were brought out of the State arsenal; a Gatling gun and artillerists were ordered from Wichita." Sheriff Wilkinson, of Shawnee county, announced himself the regular peace-keeper in the county and marched a force of his deputies to the State House to join the large force of Republican sergeants-at-arms. The Republicans were soon besieged; provisions

Topeka's combined fire department headquarters, city hall and auditorium was built in 1900 on Quincy between Seventh and Eighth streets. (Courtesy Kansas State Historical Society)

were taken into the capital building by means of baskets passed through the lines.

Two days later negotiations resulted in an agreement that the Republicans would continue to meet in the hall while the Populists adjourned to another room in the capitol. During the "legislative war" the Kansas City *Star* made an interesting proposition:

> The strained situation at Topeka suggests a new use for Kansas avenue; too wide for a street and hardly wide enough for a cornfield, it would make a fairly roomy battlefield for the close and desperate fighting in which the Republicans and Populists will doubtless indulge if they ever get at it. The contending "Houses" surging back and forth across the avenue while the blood quietly trickles down the gutters into the Kaw would be a sight to stir the blood of age and a new feature in representative government for a free and intelligent people.

Despite the *Star's* suggestion bloodshed was avoided through the prudence of militia head Col. J. W. F. Hughes who had received an executive order to remove all Republicans from the House not recognized by the Populist speaker and clear the corridors of all persons except troops. Hughes assumed that the governor had no jurisdiction over the legislature and therefore could not clear the lower house of Republicans. On top of his decision that the governor's order was illegal, Hughes was a Republican and not inclined to evict his compatriots.

J. K. Hudson, editor of the Topeka *Daily Capital,* bitterly accused the Populist governor of being a socialist and communist and of attempting to destroy the American lifestyle. Lewelling's administration, however, marked the high tide of the Populist movement. The "legislative war" ended when the Kansas supreme court ruled that the Republicans represented the legal legislative house. So much time was consumed in settling the dispute that few laws were enacted during the session. In 1894 the coalition between Democrats and Populists split and the Republicans regained control of state government, holding it, with one exception, until the 1930s.

Until fire destroyed it in January, 1909, political observers called the Copeland Hotel at Ninth and Kansas the state's 106th county—Copeland county. Here, before legislative sessions commenced, Kansas' Republicans gathered. In its rooms and corridors legislators legislated and lobbyists lobbied. Underlings reported to their political masters relaying the opinions of unseen power brokers who inhabited other rooms in Topeka. In short, political careers from that of the lowest chairman to governor and senator were fashioned and unfashioned there, and for the convenience of Republican patrons a turn-of-the-century Topeka newspaper noted that the Copeland "makes running arrangements with a joint drug store."

One would assume that after the "legislative war" of 1893, Topeka would have had enough of political combat. But in 1909 a new city "commission war" broke out which hotly contested the administration of Mayor J. B. Billard and the mayoral race became an old-fashioned mud-slinging campaign. Most of the mud was slung at Billard and his suggested police force was slandered as being made up of jointists, drunks, and harborers of prostitutes. A vote for him was considered a vote for open saloons by his opponents. Even the clergy entered the battle when a minister, the Rev. Robert Gordon, was arrested and fined three dollars for driving on the wrong side of the street. Billard tried to stand on his record as a citizen and bitterly complained that his opponents had left all pretext of debating the issues and were conducting an emotional campaign. Despite former Mayor William Green's hope of winning 75% of the votes, Billard was elected.

But the most spectacular comment dropped like a bomb during Billard's re-election campaign of 1911. Reported the Kansas City *Star*:

> The issue is almost wholly religious or rather non-religious, for Mr. Billard, as his enemies proclaim, is not a believer in a Divine Being. In other words, the opposition says of him that he is an atheist and for that reason he should not be chosen to rule over a Christian town.

Billard claimed that it was not up to him "to discuss that unless there is an open accusation. Then I shall have something to say. But not until then." The *Star* supported this view and wrote that the mayor had led an "exceptionally clean and upright life" and had been "unusually successful in business, having built up a comfortable fortune without making enemies with those with whom he dealt."

The inimitable Colonel Hughes reappeared in the 1911 election as a primary mayoral candidate. His campaign was confused when both temperance and wet interests introduced petitions supporting him and claiming his support. The *Capital,* however, informed voters that Hughes stood only for "clean streets and clean alleys, clean men and clean morals," as opposed to the moral turpitude of Billard.

Mayor J. B. Billard in his office in the city building about 1911. (Courtesy Kansas State Historical Society)

But Tom McNeal wrested the Republican nomination from Hughes on a prohibition platform. He declared that a vote for Billard was a vote for open saloons. He stated that Billard's Democratic party had formerly stood for wine, but had since cleaned up its reputation. Topekans evidently assumed that atheism and alcohol were not necessarily detrimental to the mayor's office, for they returned Billard to his post.

The change of Topeka's city government from council to committee form represented the reform movement embodied in Progressive politics. Although the Populists failed to implement many of their programs, the slack was soon taken up by an element within the Republican party known as the Progressive wing. After the failure of the Populists, many liberals re-entered Republican ranks. The liberals espoused a program aimed at achieving political reform, economic justice, and social betterment. They worked for the people. Republican policies were directed toward the upper classes and big business; the Progressives intended to benefit the lower and middle classes.

Several Topekans were intimately associated with Kansas progressivism in the first two decades after the turn of the century. In the 1902 election the railroad interests which dominated state politics, were opposed by David Mulvane of Topeka, a Republican National Committeeman. James Troutman, once mayor of Potwin, was a leading reformer; Charles Curtis, whose family owned the property on which Eugene was founded, represented the conservative element of the Republican party.

A factional fight erupted in the 1903 legislature between politicians who favored railroad interests and anti-machine men. Wrote William Zornow in *Kansas: A History of the Jayhawk State:*

The *Topeka Daily Capital* said the session was distinguished only by the amount of private legislation enacted, but such new laws as those providing for the popular election of the railroad commissions and a proposed amendment for the direct election of the state printer were significant. A special session was called in July, 1903, to deal with problems created by a flood which had inundated the state.

Both the *State Journal* and the *Capital* remarked about the corruption of the 1903 legislature and stimulated a movement for reform. Secret meetings were held in town during the summer to form an anti-machine combine which was sometimes known as the "Roosevelt Republican Club."

In early 1906 the Kansas Civic League was formed to combat railroad conniving, but it met defeat at the Republican convention. On July 18, 1906, reformers convened in Topeka, and James Troutman was a member of a committee which recommended the creation of a permanent organization known as the Kansas Republican League. "The objective of the organization," wrote William Zornow, "was a 'Square Deal' in Kansas. The widely distributed *Square Deal Handbook* attained its four-point program favoring equitable taxation, two-cent railroad fare, direct primaries, and the abolition of [railroad] passes."

The *Capital* pointed out that opinion varied as to the strength of the Square Dealers. Some 60 Republicans in the state house of representatives were members of this group; and the small gubernatorial vote for the conservative editor of the Marion *Record,* Edward W. Hoch, disappointed him. He lost Shawnee county, home of Troutman, who was one of the big men of the reform movement, as well as several other important counties. Some claimed Hoch's enforcement of prohibition during his previous administration cost him support.

By 1907 a new alignment of political forces arose in the state. The railroads became a paramount problem. The Republican convention was dominated by the 1902 anti-machine men such as David Mulvane, but in 1906 these were the spokesmen for the railroad business. Mulvane claimed to control 800 of the 1,024 delegates at the state convention. Conservative Topekan Charles Curtis was nominated to fill an unexpired term in the U. S. Senate.

Local progressives at first favored the incoming national administration of William Howard Taft, but by the end of term they exhibited a bent toward Teddy Roosevelt's progressive reforms and a growing conviction that Taft had betrayed the policies of his predecessor. When the *Capital* conducted a poll in 1911, T. R. ran far ahead as a popular choice. After the state central committee met in Topeka in March, 1912, Emporia editor William Allen White replaced Mulvane as national committeeman.

In 1918 Arthur Capper, prominent Topeka editor and state politician, was elected to the U. S. senate. Zornow writes of the condition of politics after the vote:

> An era in Kansas politics came to an end. . . . Many great and lasting reforms had been effected in the political, economic, and social life of its people by the Boss-busters, Anti-machine Republicans, Insurgents, Progressives, or whatever name one wishes to call them. But a new era was at hand.

On the street level, progressivism introduced a pair of the nation's first policewomen to Topeka in 1913. Elizabeth Barr and Eva Corning received appointments under civil service rules and became the first "missionary policewomen in the county." The Kansas City *Star* had this to say about the female officers a week after their swearing-in:

> Both the new policewomen took the examination outlined by Dr. Charles M.

Eva Corning (1871-1963), one of Topeka's first policewomen. (Courtesy
Kansas State Historical Society)

The Republican Presidential Campaign of 1928.
(Courtesy Bernard Bower)

Sheldon, who has undertaken the task of converting the Topeka police force into a missionary force, devoted to the prevention of crime rather than its cure.

Miss Barr and Miss Corning are the first representatives of a type which Dr. Sheldon has pictured as the policewoman-as-she-ought-to-be. Both are women of wide experience and public spirit and have devoted much of their time to social work.

The work of the girls included such diverse duties as settling neighborhood rows, serving as truant officers, rescuing men from wily women, investigating a "Home for Working Girls" and the financial bequest of a dying man to the "other woman," regulating boys in pool halls, and probing into the lives of girls without work.

In 1928 Charles Curtis was elected vice-president. He was part Kansa Indian, the only person with Indian blood to rise so high in national government. He, with President Herbert Hoover, had the misfortune to be in office at the time of the Wall Street crash and received the blame for it. They were defeated for re-election by Franklin D. Roosevelt in 1932.

It was during these hard times that two transplanted Topekans, Arthur Capper and Alf M. Landon, became well known. In the 1920s Capper was a strong friend of the Kansas farmer in the U. S. senate. He was a leader of the band of congressmen which struggled to help farmers and he remained the foremost fighter for agriculturalists into the 1930s. The senator endorsed most of the New Deal programs that Roosevelt offered despite the fact that the majority of Republican house members were not entirely sold on the New Deal.

Meanwhile Alf Landon was the Republican winner of the 1932 gubernatorial race. His opponent had been Omar Ketchum, the capable and personable mayor of Topeka. The national Democratic organization did not back Ketchum strongly but it was highly unlikely that he could have defeated Landon under any circumstances.

Just eight years after one of her native sons had been placed in the vice-presidential seat, Topeka proferred the adopted Landon to the nation as Republican candidate for president. Throughout his second term Landon had been discussed as a possible presidential candidate but no one could have defeated Franklin Roosevelt in 1936, his image was too solid for any Republican to combat.

In a way Landon was a sacrificial lamb, a moderate offered up by religiously conservative party supporters. Though many Kansans were enthusiastic about his candidacy and thousands jammed the statehouse grounds on July 23, 1936, the night his nomination was made official, he was not able to carry even his home state. Of the nation's 48 states, only Maine and Vermont fell to the Republicans that election.

Former Kansas governor and recent Topekan Harry Woodring served as secretary of war in Franklin Roosevelt's cabinet while Georgia

Neese Clark of Richland served as treasurer of the United States under President Harry S. Truman. Mrs. Clark, a former actress turned banker, had long been active in Kansas democratic circles. Now (1976) Mrs. Andy Gray, she and her husband moved their bank to Topeka when Richland was destroyed by a federal reservoir.

Gov. Alfred M. Landon (right) and daughter Nancy visiting Sen. Arthur Capper at the latter's annual birthday party, July 14, 1935. Capper held a grand picnic for Topeka children who could ride free over the trolley system to Garfield Park and then partake of amusements and refreshments there. (Courtesy Capper Publications)

Suffragettes appealing for the vote near the Santa Fe depot, 1916. (Courtesy Kansas State Historical Society)

Crosby Brothers' office staff in 1913 was made up mostly of women. (Courtesy Eileen Charbo)

THE PARADING MISTRESS; WOMAN'S SUFFRAGE

> I have been for years an advocate of "Negro suffrage," and since the question of "Female Suffrage" has been before the people of Kansas, I have given it also my heartiest support. In fact, were I obliged to confess the truth—I should choose the latter, as the most important.

So wrote Samuel Reader in the spring of 1867. The suffrage movement gained its impetus in the West and not the East possibly because women took upon new and difficult hardships in founding a home during times compounded by the Civil War. They kept the family together while the men were gone but also, during times of peace, stimulated cultural and moral interest on the prairie. Thus, the suffrage movement began in earnest in Kansas immediately with the conclusion of the Civil War.

Woman suffrage, naturally, divided communities with not even all women supporting the cause. Its first important push occurred in 1867 when the legislature placed the issue on the ballot as a constitutional amendment. For the November election, woman supporters actively began recruiting votes, a number of them from both in and out of Kansas, hectically canvassing the state making speeches day after day. Topeka newspapers took up the cause with extensive reports, letters, and editorial replies. The *Kansas State Record* backed the measure, with a section of the paper specifically "Devoted to the Social, Financial and Political Interests of Woman," while the *Weekly Leader* did not. On the eve of election, the latter described a suffrage meeting at Tecumseh:

> Mrs. [Clarina] Nichols [prominent Kansas suffragette] spoke at Tecumseh last Monday night on woman suffrage. She made an exhaustive arguement of two hours duration and succeeded admirably in exhausting the patience of the audience. After she had concluded Dr. Jas. Fletcher . . . was called out, and in a brief, but witty and conclusive speech, completely demolished all the arguments put forth by Mrs. N.

Female suffrage, however, was tangled up in the 1867 election with Negro suffrage, another explosive issue. Therefore, explained the *Leader,* certain individuals in the legislature "helped engineer" woman's rights "for the distinct and well understood purpose of defeating negro suffrage." Some Republicans did come forth on behalf of Negro rights though not woman's, but both issues were doomed for defeat. In Shawnee county, according to the *Record,* November 13, 1867, the two questions lost by large margins, especially the female suffrage.

Defeat in 1867 did not deter Topeka women and while the fervent activity of that summer dissipated, the cause continued. Very shortly following the election in November, city women met organizing the Woman Suffrage Association of Topeka. This body generally consisted of upper class women whose husbands, like John Ritchie and Judge Alfred L. Winans, were prominent Topeka leaders. Far from revolutionary, the by-laws of early 1868 used the masculine gender in the following case: "any officer, guilty of a misdemeanor in the duties of *his* [italics added] office. . . ." The husbands, or men, played a large role during the association's life, usually occupying one of the minor offices. Of the 193 members, many were men who joined individually or with their wives, with Franklin Crane, John Ritchie, and J. B. Billard among the best known. Only one person seems to have been expelled from the body—Hale Ritchie, John Ritchie's son.

Many of the meetings, recorded in the surviving society minutes, appear free from harangue, at one point declaring "Woman Suffrage is not Universal Suffrage." On several occasions the assembled ladies and gentlemen discussed holding picnics and peach festivals, a big problem September 4, 1868, being "to ascertain if the price of the peaches for Festival could not be reduced, on account of the poor quality of the same." They conducted serious business such as writing the *State Record* column or sponsoring prominent speakers. Susan B. Anthony spoke at Union Hall, January, 1871. Mrs. Carrie Winans, in particular, attempted to get women to vote in the first ward for superintendent of public instruction (this they could do since legislation of 1861) only to have their vote refused. Some interest in the Topeka association faded during the early 1870s and the minutes cease in November, 1875, when the body probably reorganized as an affiliate to a national suffrage organization.

Suffrage work continued, of course, with women facing several problems, particularly that of pay. Naturally, the Topeka group wanted equal pay for equal jobs; anything else "fosters a spirit of arrogance in man and of servility in woman." The *Commonwealth*, August 2, 1870, took up this idea applauding the appointment of Miss Lizzie Town as principal of the new Lincoln school. "It must be admitted," wrote the paper, "a *good* female teacher is better than a *poor* male teacher . . . , a *first rate* female teacher is better than a *second rate* male teacher in every respect." It added, apologetically, that "ladies ought to receive the same pay as gentlemen for the same work, but they do not and for the present the situation must be accepted."

Mrs. H. H. (Ella) Miller, the first woman mayor of Rossville. She died in 1894. (Courtesy Clyde H. Miller)

Kansas' legislature came to the rescue in a small way in 1887 by passing a bill allowing women to vote in municipal elections, a right only granted in Washington territory. One of its first tests proved to be in Topeka with its city election on April 5, 1887. The *Capital,* April 6th, declared the law "a success;" with a total registration of 5,494, some 1,406 were females. About 1,200 women voted, a quarter of that number black, and the newspaper estimated that three-fourths of them went with the Republican mayoral candidate, D. C. Metsker. Opponents of suffrage had "predicted . . . that the vote of the degraded and ignorant class of woman would overbalance 'that' of the respectable ladies." But this never materialized; in fact, according to the *Capital,* women "almost held the balance of power."

Generally, most of the women cast their ballots after dinner, often escorted by husbands, family, or "sweethearts." Regardless of the paper's support, the scene astounded the *Capital* reporter as the "ladies went to the polls with as much freedom as if they were going shopping" and "formed up in single file, in the same manner as the men, walked up to the window and deposited their ballots."* One man stopped

---

*Women could only vote for city officers; thus, justice of the peace and constable were not on the ballot for ladies.

and challenged all women at his polling station; his explanation being that as his naturalized wife could not vote (or so he thought), "he did not want other women to." With the exhilarating experience over, the *Capital* interviewed one 70 year old matron: "I have belonged to equal suffrage clubs ever since I was a young woman. . . . Today I see my hopes realized. I am now ready to die."

With that success behind them, women continued to exercise their newly won prerogative. In the 1891 city election women made up approximately a third of the electorate and in the first and fifth wards there were half as many females registered as males. However, the import of the new law fell upon the town west of the capital, Rossville. When its municipal election was held, April 1, 1889, complacency was so widespread that with votes of 44 or 45 each, an all woman ticket captured the offices of mayor, city council, and police judge (one of the council women elect was disqualified while the police judge elect declined, saying the office was a man's job).* The Rossville *Times,*

*The first woman mayor in the United States was Susanna Medora Salter of Argonia, Kansas. Rossville's woman mayor was Mrs. H. H. Miller.

William A. Johnston (second from right), later chief justice of the Kansas Supreme Court, and his family in their residence at 700 Topeka boulevard, May, 1900. His wife, Lucy Stone Johnston (right) was long a leader in the fight for women's rights. (Courtesy Kansas State Historical Society)

April 5th, proudly proclaimed that "this new departure will again bring our city into prominence in the eastern states, where for a long time 'Rossville' has been a household word in the annals of temperance. It will now be spoken of as one of the 'van' cities of the great Sunflower state."

Rossville's all woman council apparently justified the *Times'* confidence by passing, a month or two after taking office, an ordinance which outlawed gambling devices and gambling dens in the city. With that accomplishment behind them, the women declined re-election the following year. Their male replacements, who received 102 to 107 votes apiece, inherited, stated the *Times,* April 11, 1890, "a healthy exchequer and the aroma of a good, honest administration, and to posterity a knowledge of the fact that from April, 1889, to April, 1890, the city of Rossville was wisely governed by women." In summation, the newspaper recommended women as judges of elections since with theirs "there was no unseemly jostling, no profane language, no clouds of tobacco smoke, and no nauseating expectoration."

QUINTON AFTER THE WOMAN VOTE.

Mayoral campaign of 1891. Quinton was a Republican, cartoon in Democratic paper. (From "Kansas Democrat," April 6, 1891)

The Hall of Fame saloon, location unknown but supposedly in Topeka, was typical of many Shawnee county joints. (This and other pictures on this page courtesy W. R. Lafferty)

Fritz Durein stashing the booze.

The lavishly decorated upstairs drinking room.

The rear of the saloon, where the "respectable" people would enter.

DRINK; THE TEMPERANCE MOVEMENT

No social crusade was more thoroughly identified with Kansas than the temperance movement. Politically and spiritually, Topeka stood as prohibition's very corruptible capital. Temperance evolved from a number of 18th and 19th century impulses into a liberal reform, all in the spirit of Victorian self-improvement. Initially at least, it strove for moderation and not abstinence; however, drunkeness so repulsed some that they formed bodies like the Independent Order of Good Templars, founded in New York in 1851. They hoped to correct certain human frailties: eliminate the grog shop and you eliminate poverty; eliminate the saloons and you eliminate divorces; outlaw drink and you keep families together and the father will bring home a full pay check to mother and child. All these ideas swept many of the first Topekans into the movement.

On March 12, 1855, the Topeka Association adopted the following resolution: "No member of this association shall be permitted to buy, sell, or give away where profit accrues, any intoxicating liquors of whatever kind, nor permit them to be bought, sold, or given away where profit accrues upon his premises. . . ." Should no profit accrue, the code gave no instruction, but an enterprising businessman could sell "such liquors for medical, mechanical or sacramental purposes."

Two months later the town enforced the law against a certain Mr. Jones. Joseph Miller referred to it his diary for May 15, 1855, saying the man had

in defiance of the will of the people, and contrary to the conditions of the association (as they make it a condition in the distribution of lots, that liquor shall not be sold), been selling intoxicating drinks, and that too not only to the Whites but to the Indians, thus arrouseing in their savage breast a demon, which on the least pretext, might endanger our infant settlement.

Back in the days of Uniontown trade, Joseph Chick recalled for an interviewer that some merchants illegally sold whiskey to the Pottawatomies. Chick's Uniontown store supposedly never indulged in the business, but Abram Burnett was undoubtedly somebody's very good customer.

Whether Topeka founders liked it or not, nothing could halt the importation of whisky. Giles asserted that the first dram shop opened in the spring of 1857, but someone sold the stuff, openly, well before then. This flaunting of the town code so incensed the sober element that they retaliated on July 11, 1857, by smashing the kegs, casks, and bottles of the establishment. They followed suit in two or three other places, only to meet serious opposition at their last stop. This confrontation developed into a fight between a pro- and an anti-temperance man. Their bloody battle ended, wrote Giles, when "one of them, quite regardless of the rules of the ring, brought his antagonist to bay in a manner that it would be indelicate to relate."

Similar legends about mass liquor spillings, led by women, have been nurtured for Indianola and Tecumseh, both well-known for their saloons. Samuel Reader, who dubbed Indianola "Whiskeytown," frowned upon drink and those associated with it. He mentioned in an 1861 letter to his brother:

> It is a significant fact that the 4 groggeries which Indianola can boast of every-one is kept by a "Secesher" [secessionist]. Intemperance is the special vice of this neighborhood and it was fortunate for me that I belonged to the Temperance Society before I came to this wild and lawless region as it has kept me perfectly free from this baneful habit so far.

A couple of years later, before the North was assured of a military victory, Reader implied that his "whiskey friends" were traitors. They were "all noisy for peace by any and all means."

Tecumseh truly earned its reputation for drunkeness and saloons though later stories exaggerate the number of dram shops in town, the figure running from nine to 13 or 14. Tecumseh probably had no more than two or three fullfledged saloons in hotels or in connection with local merchants. One place, the Wigwam saloon or the "wickedest place there ever was, this side of hell," achieved considerable notoriety in Shawnee county.

A Methodist minister called it "a rowdy's resort and gambling hell;" one incident reflected the truth of his words. Late in January, 1858, a man named Andrew Kerr rode into town seeking refreshment, eventually falling into the company of two other men, Edward Adams

A late 19th century photo supposedly of the first store in Topeka built by J. W. Jones in 1855. Here the first whisky in town was sold. (Courtesy Kansas State Historical Society)

and Charles O'Hara. After a card game and considerable drinking at the Wigwam, the three started quarreling which led to Adams shooting and seriously wounding Kerr. The action so aroused the townspeople that they quickly convened a trial, with a jury, according to the *Kansas Settler,* February 3, 1858, composed of "24 of the most respectable and reliable citizens of the county—some from Topeka, some from Tecumseh, and others from the neighborhood." The paper added that "a large party of citizens forcibly took the prisoners from the Sheriff's custody and conveyed them before the jury." Apparently the court safe-guarded the defendants' rights, but the guilty verdict was inevitable. Fortunately for Adams and O'Hara no hanging occurred. Unfortunately for Tecumseh's drinkers, the town regulated the sale of alcohol to one individual who, in one account, had to keep shop outside the city limits.

Regardless of Giles' sentiments ("Topeka has always been most decidedly a temperance town"), saloons quickly sprang up—like the Wallapus in 1871, a place "for either 'square' or 'fancy' drinks." Generally, Topeka city administrations simply licensed the saloons, though the poorly enforced regulation often disturbed the saloon or billiard hall owners. The restrictions also disturbed Topeka's heavy drinking Indian, German, and Swedish populations, groups which were frequent targets of the city's newspapers. Interestingly, even the temperance-prone journals advertised or gave notice to these saloons. At the same time they usually inserted a paragraph or two with a pointed moral. For instance, the *Commonwealth* stated, February 5, 1870: "We saw a woman drunk on the street yesterday. It is bad enough for a man to be drunk, but a drunken woman—ugh!" Or July 18, 1871: "R. T. Tedford was so overcome with whiskey, yesterday, that he chose the front of a gentleman's residence for an indecent exposure of his person. He was fined $10 and costs."

Temperance received a great push when John P. St. John won the governor's chair in 1878. He worked for a prohibitory amendment, and the 1879 legislature voted to put it on the ballot. The Kansas electorate concurred and then enforcement problems began.

Before and even after prohibition several breweries and distilleries operated in Topeka or in the Silver Lake area. The *Kansas Valley Times,* February 28, 1879, featured a long story on a new distillery west of North Topeka. Its complex apparently contained a three-story main building, 86 by 40 feet; a cistern room; a bonded warehouse and an engine room with an attached corn shed. This plant of the Topeka Distillery Company would consume 300 bushels of grain—corn, rye, or barley—every 18 hours, producing three and a half or four gallons of liquor to the bushel.

Radge's city directory for 1883 (three years after adoption of the prohibition amendment) still listed three breweries. Herboldsheimer maintained the largest and oldest of these at Crane and Madison. He opened for business in 1864 and for years his brewery was a local landmark in the bottoms. The building had a series of three stone cellars, and according to a July 29, 1908, *Herald* feature, a tunnel led from the deepest "dungeon" to a nearby "women's drinking parlor." Radge's 1885-86 directory finally noted that the breweries were "not in operation, owing to the prohibitory law."

Prohibition has been called, perhaps too ardently, a total failure leading either to gangster empires or smug hypocrisy. In Kansas the latter prevailed since one big loophole, up to 1909, allowed liquor to be sold as medicine over the counter in drug stores. Still the purchaser had to sign a form indicating the disease whiskey could cure. To say the least, people of the 1880s had innumerable complaints which were relieved by whisky.

With Kansas officially dry, a few complacently rationalized that demon rum had been dried up. Others who overheard them simply headed for the nearest bar. Many of the latter included state legislators, but a few naively upheld Mary Jackson's belief that "today [1890] . . . not a saloon is to be found. They are all gone. A drunken man is now a rare object." Evidently she neglected to look in the right spots, namely lower Kansas avenue. One area resident divulged to the *Mail*, September 28, 1894, that for the two or so blocks south of the river bridge there was nothing "but drinking, carousing and gambling from one end of Smokey Row [his name for the district] to the other."

Immediately after the institution of prohibition, individuals and groups sought resubmission of the issue to Kansas' electorate, hoping they would reconsider the consequences. In response to this, temperance leaders held anti-resubmission meetings; some attended one on December 10, 1889, at Topeka's Grand Opera House. To Miss Jackson, it gave "proof enough that prohibition will still live in Kansas." Unfortunately, time and again these people had to resort to extensive temperance revivals to maintain enthusiasm against the demon rum. Charles M. Sheldon, along with State Historical Society Secretary F. G. Adams, spurred renewal with a crusade and meeting in the early summer of 1894. The Sunday before, Sheldon preached a sermon at his Central Congregational church describing his visit to a half dozen dives and joints in the seedier part of town. It generated interest and arrests, before the status quo was resumed.

Concerning this Topeka temperance convention during the summer, the Republican *Daily Capital*, July 27, 1894, took aim

The Senate saloon on Kansas avenue between Third and Fourth. This photo was taken in 1882, two years after the adoption of prohibition. (Courtesy Kansas State Historical Society)

at a convenient target. "For years," stated the paper, "Topeka was free from joints and dives" until the Populist administration of Gov. Lorenzo D. Lewelling came along "with its policy of pandering to the whiskey sentiment for votes." Actually, the state's Democrats caught the brunt of blame with the Republicans masquerading as the party of sobriety. With little to lose in overwhelmingly GOP Kansas, Democrats usually took a moderate stance in the liquor question, asking for resubmission to please some, like the Germans. Eventually the image became fixed—the Democrats were wet and the Republicans, *on the surface,* dry.

Local Republicans, therefore, reflecting the *Capital* opinion, conferred on themselves any success in enforcement. Charles Curtis asserted in his unpublished autobiography, covering his days as attorney for Shawnee county (1885-87): "On the night of February 15, 1885, the last saloon closed its doors and there were no more saloons in Topeka during the four years I was County Attorney." Yet the *State Journal,* March 30, 1891, reported the police closing a joint which had been in operation since 1883—hidden away in the bowels of a Fifth and Kansas avenue building, a joint which cleared $500 a month.

The joints fell into three general categories—drug stores, clubs and "dives." The *Herald,* November 10, 1903, estimated that of Topeka's 44 retail drug stores "fully one-half are directly engaged in the liquor traffic and rely, in a great measure, in obtaining their profits from this source." The Atchison *Globe* in 1907 was more blunt; some stores completely dispensed with other services as they "refused to take prescriptions." Several jointists employed cappers, or decoys, who

Wein- und Bier- SALOON
von
Georg Kimmerle,
North Topeka, Kas.

Die besten Weine, die feinsten Liqueure, sowie ein ausgezeichnetes Glas Bier und gute Cigarren werden unter der zuvorkommendsten Bedienung verabreicht.

(From "Kansas Staats-Anzeiger," February 14, 1880)

State of Kansas, County of ______, ss. Date ______ No. 2

I, the undersigned, do solemnly swear, that my real name is ______ and that I reside at ______, ______ County, State of ______ that ______ of ______ is necessary and actually needed ______, to be used as a medicine for the disease of ______; It is not intended for a beverage, nor to sell, nor to give away; and that I am over twenty-one years of age. I therefore make application to ______ Druggist, for said liquor.

______ Applicant

Subscribed in my presence and sworn to before me, this ______ day of ______ 189__

______ Pharmacist

After Kansas adopted a prohibition amendment in the 1880s only drugstores could sell whisky and that for "medicinal" purposes. J. Higgins swore he needed a half pint to cure his ague in this affidavit. (Courtesy Kansas State Historical Society)

A liquor spilling conducted by Topeka ministers in 1914. That same year police made 681 arrests for drunkeness. Some were taken in for just having the smell of whisky on the breath. "Sh-h," cautioned one writer. "Don't laugh out loud, or you'll be [considered in] Topeka drunk and disorderly." (Courtesy Kansas State Historical Society)

directed strangers to the proper establishment for refreshment. In most instances, of course, the pharmacist never asked questions.

The *Herald,* in its crusade, told on August 13, 1904, the sad tale of one James R. Pigg, the sickest man in Topeka. During June and July Pigg bought from Frank Keith's Postoffice drug store "228 bottles of beer for his stomach, 93 for his indigestion, 52 for his kidneys, and 16 for his dyspepsia." To this astounding prescription, the newspaper added how "it is a wonder that he pulled through." Pigg, who in 1905 was listed as proprietor of the Owl Cafe, probably resold most of his beer medicine to equally ill customers.

Clubs or dives differed from the drug store in that the customer consumed his drink on the premises. Most were low quality joints rather than exclusive establishments like the Topeka Club, the haunt of the city's professional elite. For the clubs, in theory, an individual paid nominal dues though owners rarely enforced the "by-laws." When Sheldon took his 1894 jaunt among the saloons, he discovered one where membership cost $1.00 with a 50 cents monthly charge. In another membership simply consisted of a 50-cent charge for six beers, good for 24 hours. Some proprietors claimed "social" or "companionship" clubs where dues went to a fund for disabled members. When the police raided a saloon on West Sixth street, above a blacksmith, the owner insisted his place was a literary society. As proof, he offered several *Police Gazettes.*

While found all over town, the majority of the clubs or dives were located one or two blocks either side of Kansas avenue below Eighth street. To discourage prying eyes, many were on the second and third floors. If on the ground floor some "respectable" business like a pool hall, cigar store, or restaurant fronted them. The lower classes entered from the street while in many cases the "well dressed" people sneaked in from the back late at night so as not to mix "with the disreputable loafers."

After climbing a narrow flight of stairs, the visitor found himself in a small lobby or room which was the heart of the club. Few managers decorated their places to any extent so the drinking room was fairly bare, a few tables and chairs and a partition at one end masking the refrigerator or ice box. If in a large place, a hall might subdivide the club, with craps and poker rooms off it. Topeka's white and black populations segregated themselves, with Nick Chiles' hotel at 116 East Seventh being "the leading negro joint of the city." Nick Longergan, on the other hand, opened his 115 East Sixth street pool hall to everyone. A *Herald* reporter visited it in November, 1903:

> At the rear of the pool room is a partition with cheap gaudy paper. This partition separates the bar room from the pool room proper indicating to the look

out who is on duty at the door that one wishes to enter, the door is opened and a
big barn-like room is disclosed. Here on the left is a long cheap counter which is
used for a bar, while at the end is a large ice box—the only respectable looking
piece of furniture in the entire place. No attempt at cleanliness is made. The bar
is foul smelling and dingy; the walls bare and covered with dirt and cobwebs; the
ceiling dilapidated and broken in many places. Ranged along the bar is a mixture
of whites and blacks, poorly dressed—some almost in rags. The language used is
coarse and vile, oaths predominating. Fierce arguments and fights are of frequent
occurrence, but little attempt being made to preserve order. . . . That there is
money in this joint business is evidenced here by large receipts, particularly on
Saturday when they frequently exceed $100.

Police raids, even when frequent, rarely stopped the liquor trade.
Either advance warning gave the proprietor time to hide his stock, or,
as at Longergan's, the joints "resumed business again when the police
are hardly out of sight." While breaking up the joint, the police sometimes uncovered liquor in the strangest places. Early in July, 1888,
they pounced upon the Capital Resort, a new dance hall on the
southern terminus of the Rapid Transit in Quinton Heights. In one
of the outhouses, above a false ceiling, they found 14 pint flasks of
whisky.

Chief Frank Stahl's raid on the night of October 1, 1904, was
probably typical of police experiences. He and two men first visited
the Amity Club at 118 East Seventh. Given a key by a disgruntled
ex-member, Stahl quietly unlocked the door and discovered a brisk
trade—men and women drinking and playing cards. Here they captured a 16-gallon keg of beer and some wine and arrested the bar-
tender. Next Stahl struck a couple of drug stores and four joints,
apprehending among others Andy Rupree "the champion negro
jointist of Topeka" at 116 Kansas. At the Chesterfield Hotel the
police encountered some opposition where, according to the *Herald,*
October 3, 1904, "the joint was protected with an oak door and five
minutes were consumed in chopping through this. Whenever the
police stopped to rest, they could hear the men inside breaking bottles."
Once inside all they uncovered was a keg of hop tea (beer).

Stahl's last raid of the evening occurred at the German-American
Skat Club, 502 Kansas avenue. In the process of seizing the whisky
and beer, Stahl accidently ran into District Court Judge Z. T. Hazen
sitting at one of the tables. Probably embarrassed at such a meeting,
Hazen quipped to Stahl, "I see you are using the Carrie Nation
method!" To which the officer retorted, "I am not sir, I raided this
place according to law." "But your methods are very similar," returned
the judge. Thereupon an angered Stahl answered, "you are a liar."
At that moment the two prepared for a fight only to be stopped by the
intervention of others. No harm of any kind came to Hazen but a

few days later a Wamego man summed the affair up in a letter to a Topeka minister:

> The district judge it seems to me ought to make some arrangement with the police officers so that they may be notified when he is frequenting those places, this would enable the Chief to with hold his raids until the judge had had his toddy, and would save the Chief the annoyance of running on to the Judge. The little altercation the other day . . . did not occur through any design on the part of either, they both seem to have made a raid on the Skat Club having the same object in view, both trying to confiscate the intoxicating liquors therein stored.

As to the quality of the whisky or beer sold at these places, little can be said in its favor. The fancier, higher class clubs offered good whisky; those on the bottom did not. The *Herald* once commented on how Topeka booze was known from coast to coast. "Outside of Kansas it is used only as material for jokes. In Topeka it is used for sickness." Supposedly during the 1903 flood a bottle of Topeka joint whisky floated down the river into a bankside orchard. There it broke and, so reported the Holton *Recorder,* "the stuff spilled, and now all the trees in that locality are said to be dying."

Interest in busting the joints died down except for periodic raids to keep everyone on their toes. Just as it did other facets of life, the automobile changed the nature of the saloon. By the 1930s and 1940s more and more of them were found out in the country for both atmosphere and protection. These road houses, as Nick Longergan's pool hall, were barn-like rooms with panelled walls and tables or booths ringing the central dance floor.

Generally, those who wanted to drink knew where they could find it. The short-lived *Topeka Magazine* for October, 1946, printed a small expose about Topeka's liquor traffic claiming "Topekans drink— and drink heavily." They also paid heavily with a fifth of whiskey priced between $6.50 and $15. The magazine published photographs of some of the nightspots, along with some of the patrons, and the editor blamed the problem on the Republicans. "The raids make big headlines in Republican papers," he stated, "but amount to merely election propaganda and the dry hand is actually well greased."

Kansas' electorate repealed prohibition in 1948 thus ending that element of hypocrisy. Various statutes provided for private clubs permitting consumption of alcohol, which were quickly formed. The two tallest commercial structures in downtown Topeka as well as several of the major hotels have private clubs—the Topeka Town Club atop the First National Bank building looks down upon the site where the poor Mr. Jones, over a century before, stood accused of selling spirits.

This view, taken from Topeka's city building in the late 1870s, looks west and shows the newly completed Grace Episcopal church at Seventh and Jackson. (Courtesy Kansas State Historical Society)

In their Sunday best at the Auburn Methodist church about 1900. (Courtesy Mrs. E. L. Forsyth)

The awesome gothic splendor of the Grace Cathedral design of the late 1880s along with the Guild Hall to the right. This ambitious church project dramatically depicts both the ecstasy and the collapse of Topeka's boom of 1887-8. Only the Guild Hall was built. (From "The Saturday Evening Lance," December 22, 1888)

A PEOPLE'S FAITH; RELIGION

Religion trailed immediately behind the frontiersman so that by the time the United States government opened Kansas in 1854, the missionaries had long been at work. By statehood, most of the major Protestant sects had formed or met in Topeka and Shawnee county. Of the principal denominations Methodism emerged as perhaps the largest or most important in the community.

Sometime very late in 1854 or early in 1855, two Methodist clergymen, the Revs. William H. Goode and James S. Griffing rode into what became Shawnee county from the south. They first stopped at 110 Mile creek, now an abandoned site in Osage county, where the two stayed the night in the home of a "good 'border ruffian.' " There, according to Goode in his *Outposts of Zion,* they found their cabin with "a comfortable fire, a large stock of arms, and an imposing array of well-filled bottles with a *carte blanche* liberty in the use of their contents." After a "good Kentucky supper" the two preachers talked at length with residents of this tiny hamlet. One of their conversations brought them a report of a man in the area who was eaten by wolves as he staggered home drunk.

The following day the ministers left for the Wakarusa, passing the grave of the devoured settler, and by afternoon reached Brownville (Auburn). There, wrote Goode, "we found friends, had an appointment circulated, and I endeavored to preach the Word to a few 'sheep in the wilderness.' " Next day they entered the Pottawatomie reserve, "passing the residence of the lordly old polygamist Chief," and headed for Topeka. While in that new settlement, Goode spoke to "willing hearers" who "enlivened the exercises by excellent singing from a well-trained choir."

Goode, and supposedly Griffing, too, spent the night in Topeka's lone house where he was "honored with a *superior* position" in the log cabin—an upper bunk. In the morning the two gentlemen, before getting on their way, breakfasted on corn meal mush, or hasty pudding, and then journeyed straight east. Goode then concluded his narrative of Shawnee county communities:

Passing through Tecumseh, and visiting Christian families on the way, we stopped at the cabin of a German Methodist [possibly Francis Grassmuck]. . . . Meeting was agreed upon for the evening, and brother Griffing set out at a rapid gait upon his pony to notify the settlers. Taunts had been thrown out in this neighborhood, our pretensions to influence had been ridiculed by those in a different interest, but the evening brought a goodly number of quiet and willing hearers. I addressed them from Mark XVI, 15, and organized a society of nine members; others having attempted an organization of a different character and failed.

From the above account, therefore, may be dated the origin of the Methodist church certainly in Tecumseh and possibly in Auburn. The Topeka organization came later. The spring of 1855 brought considerable church activity what with the first Methodist Episcopal Conference quarterly meeting held in Kansas March 31 in Osborn Naylor's Tecumseh home. In April the first Kansas Sunday school class was formed at Auburn. These Methodists, however, faced severe competition from some of their own, the Methodist Episcopal Church, South.

At an 1845 church convention several ministers from the south broke away from the parent body over a dispute concerning a Bishop's owning, however reluctantly, a slave. With the influx of Proslavery influence, if not slave owners themselves, in Tecumseh and the Wakarusa valley areas, the church, South, possessed considerable support. The attempt at organizing, which Goode mentioned, undoubtedly referred to the Rev. Learner B. Stateler who supposedly conducted a Tecumseh service, under a tent, on October 10, 1854.

Tecumseh Methodists, of both north and south persuasions, constructed and/or completed their churches in 1857. Appropriately, they stood back to back, one church facing east and the other west. For a very short time, the "South" congregation predominated, and in 1859 the Rev. Cyrus R. Rice readied his 30 by 40 foot brick church for the fifth session (the fourth on Kansas soil) of the Kansas Mission Conference, M. E. Church, South, which was to be held on September 29. For the occasion, Tecumseh Methodists hauled pine lumber from Leavenworth for the ceiling, wainscoting, and pulpit platform. With the outbreak of war and the eventual northern victory, the South church quickly lost strength. A few members clung to it well into the 1870s and '80s. Most Tecumseh Methodists rejoined the older branch, selling the South's building to the local school board.

Though the Methodists organized first, March 21, 1855, Congregational minister S. Y. Lum preached Topeka's first sermon late in December, 1854. Giles remembered that it took place in A. A. Ward's cabin northwest of the townsite. Lum described the service in a letter from Lawrence, dated December 23:

> I preached at this new point [Topeka] last Sabbath to about 25 as attentive listeners as I ever addressed, and was happy in being the first to declare the truth as it was in Jesus, upon a spot where thousands will yet congregate in the worship of God. . . . Our sanctuary was a small log house of Indian construction, formerly

used for a dance house, but now as a store room. It is entirely without windows
or means of light except the crevices left when building.

Because of the predominating New England background of so
many early Topeka residents, the church naturally gained a strong
position within the community, a position soon challenged by the
Methodists. Yet the New Englanders suffered a number of potentially
disheartening setbacks. The Rev. Lewis Bodwell, who arrived with
great hopes and enthusiasm in the summer of 1856, dejectedly remarked
in October:

> I cannot say that the prospect is very flattering. Our forces [of 13 members]
> are diminished by very [various] causes. Of our three trustees, one is just (& slowly)
> recovering from a severe illness; another has gone East to spend the winter; and
> the third [John Ritchie] is a prisoner and now on trial at Lecompton, with the
> Free State men.

Initially church members, of what ever denomination, met in
individual cabins, but by 1857 or '58 they were sharing facilities at
Constitution Hall, the Free-State legislative building. Bodwell mentioned that in 1858 five "different orders, with more or less frequency
and regularity" used it, they being the Congregationalists, Methodists,
Baptists, Moravians, and Unitarians.

Hard luck plagued the Congregationalists in their construction of
a church. Like most of the other primitive church edifices in the
wilderness, the Congregationalists planned a simple one-story, one-
room stone chapel with a short bell tower. Work commenced in the
fall of 1857, the men sparing what time they could from their personal
labors, but a wind storm or small tornado in 1859 smashed all the
work leaving behind a $1,000 pile of rubble. Work resumed but again
in June, 1860, a storm struck damaging the walls. Finally, with
parishoners perched on make-shift seating, the first sermon was given
on January 1, 1861.

Most of the major Protestant churches organized before statehood.
The Methodist Society, formed in March, 1855, and the Episcopalians
organized in 1857, the Rev. Charles M. Callaway sharing his duties
between Topeka's Grace church and Tecumseh's St. John's. The
Baptists arrived in March, 1857, and the Presbyterians in December, 1859. In March, 1862 the Catholics founded the Church of
the Assumption and five years later, April, 1867, the English (First)
Lutheran church was organized. After these major foundations, and
with an expanding population, came the smaller bodies like the United
Presbyterian (1870), Christian (1870), Unitarian (1883), and others
including the synagogue Temple Beth Sholom, orthodox Jewish (1920).

Once successfully established, the larger churches colonized different sections of the community or the county. During the 1850s

Topeka's Congregationalists founded separate bodies in Rochester, Mairestown (southern Tecumseh township), and Topeka where a Freedman's church was established. The Rochester and Mairestown churches soon died. The Baptists, however, fared much better with their North Topeka Baptist Church (now Pilgrim Baptist) formed in 1869. Located on Laurent and Harrison streets, the church itself was begun in 1871 and completed in 1879, at a cost of $11,000. It is, in 1976, the oldest church structure in Shawnee county. Presbyterian activity heightened during the pastorate of the Rev. F. S. McCabe of the First Church. Bethel Church, a stone chapel, was organized in Tecumseh township in 1871; Pleasant Ridge Church, also stone, was founded nine miles northwest of Topeka in 1876; Wakarusa Church, frame, was established twelve miles south in 1877; North Topeka, stone, on Quincy street in 1878; Third Presbyterian, a stone edifice built in 1882, at Third and Hancock streets in 1880; and Mission Center six miles west of town in 1880.

An 1880 Topeka newspaper listed 26 churches, but less than a decade later a city directory gave the names of 50 organizations of both major and minor denominations, colored and white. The incoming German, Swedish, and Negro populations of the 1870s and 1880s required religious teaching so many of the newer church bodies of that era reflected these communities. Though sermons in German had been presented before, German Methodists organized in 1870 with the German Lutherans, Evangelicals, and Catholics soon following. The Catholics, under the leadership of Father Henry erected Topeka's most impressive ecclesiastical edifice, St. Joseph's German Catholic Church in 1899.

Topeka Swedes chose services among the Evangelical Lutheran, (the earliest in 1869) Baptist, and Bethel churches. The latter organized in 1872, completing their handsome brick structure at 522 Polk in 1885. Since area Swedes spoke their native tongue until well into the 20th century, services were conducted in Swedish. Indeed, the Bethel church was the only Swedish congregation that did conduct its Sunday school and services partly in English. A writer in the *Journal*, August 7, 1915, praised Bethel church's work in Swedish: "The religious ideals that the Swedish people hold are best preserved in their mother tongue. And the young people growing up, although they are educated in American schools and universities, are realizing that they can best serve their community and country by adhering to the churches that their fathers have founded." To him, adoption of English proved "but one good way of crippling an active church." Time, however, was even then running out.

Negro churches date to the Civil War period, primarily as Freedman's churches under the supervision of a stronger, white organization. The Congregationalists had, in 1864, only three male and four female Freedmen members but 30 in a Sunday school. By the early 1880s there were approximately a dozen Negro churches in town, St. John's African Methodist Episcopal of 1868 being the oldest. Methodist and Baptist bodies predominated. At one time there were colored Second, Third, and Fourth Baptist churches, but Negro Presbyterians and Episcopalians also formed their own congregations. The Episcopal members of St. Simon the Cyrenian (founded 1885) at one time were considered, like their white Episcopalian counterparts, aristocracy in their community. Unlike the Swedes or Germans, the black denominations maintained their identity, merging if necessary though St. Simon's, in a different move, joined the nominally white parent church, Grace Cathedral.

Country churches also grew up, but did not thrive, during the economically disastrous, grasshopper-plagued 1870s. Most well established communities had at least one church served by either a resident or a circuit preacher. The Methodists and Baptists dominated the scene but local Presbyterians and country Episcopalians also felt a spiritual need. If they could not support several churches, then the congregations built together as did the Auburn Baptists and Presbyterians with their Union Church of 1877, a structure which still stands. In May, 1869, Mission Creek Baptists dedicated a neat little stone church while in 1878 their brethren in Silver Lake completed the handsomest stone church in the county, complete with tower and spire.

Rural Episcopalians were exceptionally rare in Kansas. Yet in the early 1870s Monmouth township Episcopalians persuaded the church to build a mission church, dependent on Topeka, away from any population center. The first services were conducted in a local family's parlor. A 25 by 50 foot gothic house of worship, costing approximately $1,500 was begun on October 21, 1870, with Bishop Vail from Topeka laying the cornerstone amid hymns, prayers, and addresses. Two days later the *Commonwealth* stated: "Seldom has a more delightful picture been seen than was presented by that company of glad, earnest country people as they stood in the wide prairie, gathered around the bishop, in the light of one of our autumn sunsets."

Life for a country parson lacked the grace or pleasantries often experienced by a well established city clergyman. Frequently he was assigned a long circuit which required that he spend much of his Sunday on a horse. During the 1870s the Tecumseh preacher had a two week schedule. On the first Sunday he met an 11 A.M. appointment at Wakarusa station (six members), at 3 P.M. was at Lynn Creek (24 members), and at 7 P.M. at Tecumseh Creek (ten members). The following Sunday he preached at Lecompton (11 A.M., 18 members), Pleasant Hill (3 P.M., four members), and Mt. Pleasant (7 P.M., 25 members). Then, occasionally at someone's home, he spoke to people on Deer Creek or at Pauline.

Considering all that work, he earned very little and according to the Rev. J. W. Clock in the *Kansas Methodist,* August 29, 1883, had "to hunt some dilapidated shelter somewhere on the charge, clean out the bed bugs left by some former inhabitant, and then pay the rent" which "took the cream of the small salary" while "the preacher lived on skim milk." Before he completed the Tecumseh parsonage in the early 1880s, Clock and his family of four made do with one room where they all cooked, ate, washed, and slept. Some were in even more desperate straights than Clock. A previous incumbent, stated the Topeka *Blade* in 1875, had "not received $50 during the last year." He appeared before a church conference "in his last clothes—somewhat seedy looking" offering his resignation. The church leaders promptly subscribed money to keep him in office but could do little about the drought, chinch bugs, and grasshoppers which created the poverty of area farmers and in turn the minister's.

Not everything was shrouded in gloom in 19th century religious affairs nor was all activity depressing. Witness, for example, this lively discourse from an exciteable teenage girl, Ovella Dunn, in 1870 Topeka:

> I was at the Methodist Sociable last evening, had the gayest of gay times, it met at one of the members of our church on Harrison St. between 4 and 5th st. they live in a very large Red Brick, double Parlors, four large rooms up stairs, We young folks occupied one room up stairs, and we did occupy it too.   there were no less than sixty young men there, and no more than five young girls, so you may imagine our fun 12 for each one of us.

Most Topeka and Shawnee county churches sponsored, partly as money raising enterprises, dinners, oyster suppers, festivals, plays, dances or balls, concerts and parties. In the 1860s and 1870s strawberry festivals and ice cream socials were particularly important events late in the spring. Churches, like the Presbyterian in June, 1869, hired one of the halls or rooms in downtown Topeka and decked it out in bunting or ribbons. Here they sold dishes of strawberries, cakes and ice cream while one of the local brass bands performed. In one evening the Presbyterian festival netted $250 which went toward the purchase of window blinds.

Women contributed greatly to these fund raising drives, often constituting a Ladies Working Society or some similarly titled body.

A baptism in the Silver Lake, 1913. (From Silver Lake centennial book, 1970)

The Silver Lake Baptist church, completed in 1878. (Courtesy Jessie Van Orsdol)

Emmanuel Episcopal church gave an unique English pastoral vision to Monmouth township. (Courtesy Kansas State Historical Society)

They sponsored the socials and performed most or all of the work. Minutes for the Tecumseh Methodist auxiliary have survived indicating that their irregularly held meetings usually commenced with a noon lunch. The sessions continued well into the afternoon as the women worked on their quilts which were then sold at a festival. The August 25, 1898, assemblage was probably typical, the secretary writing that "needles flew as well as tongues; everyone seemed to be in good spirits and a jolly good time was the result."

People attended church services or entertainments not merely for religious instruction but also for general intellectual edification or even courtship. Martha Van Orsdol, writing in her diaries for the 1880s, alluded to her church visits with an ecumenical air. On one Sunday she attended the Swedish church with the preaching and singing in that language; it was "quite novel to me." At a Congregational evening meeting Miss Van Orsdol saw a magic lantern show about India while on another Sunday she went first to the Christian church in the morning, then to Catholic vespers in the afternoon, and finally to the Methodist assembly in the evening. However, her greatest thrill came when boy friend John Shaw started walking her home after Thursday night Christian church meetings. When one Sunday he showed up at service, Martha declared "I felt he was there for my sake"—love blossomed in the sanctuary.

Social business, though a pleasant diversion, was not the church's main purpose. Following the Civil War tent revivals or camp meetings restored fallen religious enthusiasm. At some time many, if not most, of the country churches carried out such revivals temporarily unifying local churches and increasing their membership. Both the Tecumseh and Auburn Methodists especially implemented such programs. Unfortunately the aura of this good work rarely lingered.

For three weeks in March, 1872, the Rev. Edward Hammond conducted revival meetings at Topeka's Union Hall, this activity stirring both strong support as well as dissent. He held services in the morning and evening with his hymn sessions being most popular. Besides simply preaching to the flock, Hammond normally visited the city jails and less desirable districts in town. People trailed behind him, often with a total lack of interest in the world of saloons and houses of ill repute. He faced few problems in Topeka though on one occasion a fist fight broke out in front of his eyes.

He encountered, of course, opposition from the less "evangelistic" faiths and those opposed to the closing of Topeka schools during his stay. One individual wrote to the *Commonwealth*, February 28, before Hammond's arrival: "I protest against the interruption of our com-

A tent revival near the fairgrounds in the 1930s. (From a watercolor by Charles L. Marshall)

mon schools for the furtherance, supposed or real, of any other interest whatever." Eventually the school board gave in to the desire of the revivalists and operated only half days for two weeks. Nevertheless, another writer hinted that Hammond's greatest concern in the Kansas revivals centered upon his funds and the lack thereof.

Revivals or no, Topeka churches served the community's religious needs though most lacked suitable facilities until the 1880s. The *Commonwealth* in April, 1873, complained that while the city had many fine buildings, "we haven't one respectable church building in Topeka." Most were still using churches constructed in the territorial era, relatively small, one room affairs with possibly a stubby tower or spire at the front or the side.

Church construction, coming with rising prosperity, widened during the 1880s as all the major denominations required a suitable edifice to show their position, and in turn wealth, in the community. The Congregationalists, Presbyterians, Lutherans, and Methodists all completed impressive structures, the latter, as described by Mary Jackson, perhaps the most stunning with its two towers:

Lots were purchased on Sixth and Harrison, and in 1881 and 1882, a church edifice was completed, at a cost of $35,000. The building is 116 by seventy feet, exclusive of steps and areas. . . . The auditorium is sixty-eight by fifty-seven feet, with a gallery around three sides. It is forty-nine feet from floor to ceiling. . . . The style of the exterior is English Gothic, built of stone. The building is heated throughout with steam. There are two towers; the tallest one at the corner of Sixth and Harrison streets, 124 feet high, contains the bell and clock.

Topeka parishioners of Grace Church, after using Constitution Hall, the third floor of Ritchie's block and the first hall of the Episcopal Female Seminary, moved into their new home at Seventh and Jackson in 1865. They enlarged it ten years later by adding a high spire, and on June 5, 1879, a church convention elevated Grace Church to a Cathedral for the diocese of Kansas.*

Such an honor deserved a more imposing church. The *Capital*, August 19, 1887, announced a $100,000 cathedral to be erected beginning that October. Unlike anything else in Topeka, it was to measure 150 by 140 feet with a central tower and dome 34 feet square. A second newspaper implied there would be at least four other towers. The ensuing economic decline wiped out the glorious dream of an enormous monument. Using the Guild Hall as cathedral, the diocese in 1909 resumed a building project which painfully inched its way to partial completion in 1917 when the cathedral was consecrated by Bishop Wise. The towers were not finished until 1955.

Possibly the handsomest Gothic church in Kansas, the cathedral contained numerous artifacts of value as well as of great beauty. Its stained glass was probably the most notable in the city with the carving of the high altar, pulpit, and lectern of the highest order. Bishop Millspaugh brought back as adornment stone from the Holy Isle of Lindisfarne, the ancient seat of Christianity in Northumbria, and glass from the Collegiate Church of St. Peter at Westminster (Westminster Abbey) for the East Transept Rose Window (the glass with the date 1722 affixed, signifies the year the Dean at Westminster had been exiled for his Jacobite sympathies). Its greatest treasure,

---

*At that time the diocese of Kansas included all of the state. In 1901 it was divided in two, Salina being the other Cathedral town.

Left to right: the First Presbyterian, First Congregational, and First Methodist churches, all built in the 1880s and along Harrison street making it Topeka's "Street of Churches." Only the First Presbyterian remains. (From "The Saturday Evening Lance," June 9, 1888)

however, was an engraved baptismal spoon which, by tradition, dates back to 16th century Norway.*

Beautiful as the churches of the 1880s were, by the mid-20th century they had shrunk because of shifting population, decaying neighborhoods and inadequate parking. The impressive First Methodist church burned in 1921 and was rebuilt in a similar Gothic mood on the same site. First Congregationalists moved from a downtown site on Harrison street to the suburbs in 1948. The First Baptists moved several times, most lately to a structure overlooking the Shunganunga valley.

Generally, these modern churches deserted the traditional designs for those reflective of a newer spirit in Christianity. Here and there for sentimental reasons some maintained a spire or bell tower harking back to New England days. Only a very few of the 1880s churches survived, the largest being the First Presbyterian which is without its spire. The cornerstone was laid May 5, 1884, and the church dedicated April 12, 1885.

Religion also had another indirect function in the community, the establishment of Topeka's first true hospital in 1884. Mrs. Ellen Bowman Vail, wife of the Rt. Rev. Thomas Hubbard Vail, first Episcopal Bishop of Kansas, not only lost her ten-year old son early in 1878, but nearly died herself from a prolonged illness. When she recovered, Mrs. Vail completely lost her sight. Partly because of these trials, her attentions turned toward providing proper medical care for Topeka. Though to be Episcopal sponsored, Mrs. Vail purchased property west of the Bethany school grounds. Bishop Vail pledged to raise $10,000 with the hope Topekans would do likewise. He envisioned a 42 by 100 foot, four story structure which would be named Christ's Hospital.

Unfortunately, the scheme generated only modest funds; so, Bishop Vail reduced his goal to a two-story frame hospital. The Topeka *Capital,* September 2, 1884, described the structure which had just opened. It had, the paper said, "six private rooms and four wards housing six patients each." There was a resident physician, and the terms were $7.00 per week for bed patients and $6.00 for convalescents. Improvements were made over the years with the founding, for example, of the Christ's Hospital Training School whose first nurse graduated in 1894. All of this, naturally, taxed the church's financial position. As early as 1892 the trustees required that "all patients in private rooms must pay in advance or make satisfactory arrangements with the Superintendent to pay their bills weekly, or after two weeks . . . be removed to the wards receiving like care with ward patients."

---

*On Thanksgiving eve, 1975, possibly through the work of arson, fire destroyed the Cathedral, the great carved works, and windows

Despite economic woes, which would soon force closure of Bethany College, a new 100-bed Christ's Hospital building opened in April, 1927. Yet with the depression of the following decade, the church could not provide the necessary hospital services by itself. The same was true of the private Jane C. Stormont Hospital in Potwin. Both had nursing schools and both offered duplicate services. The obvious answer was to merge. This came about in April, 1949. Because the name Christ's seemed inappropriate to a community hospital—the city of Topeka having taken over the Christ's property in 1950—Bishop Fenner suggested the name Vail as an appropriate substitute. Since then numerous additions, particularly beginning in the late 1960s, have constantly enlarged and improved Stormont-Vail facilities.

Radge's 1909 city directory listed some 21 hospitals, asylums, and homes in Topeka several being private hospitals like Bethesda General and Maternity, Keith, Long, and City Detention which have long since dissolved. One which did survive was the Jane C. Stormont Hospital which was founded in 1894. Its promoters had two goals in mind, one to provide a place particularly for women patients and secondly a hospital where the poor could be treated. Mrs. Stormont, widow of Dr. D. W. Stormont and a Topeka philanthropist, offered $10,000 for construction. In 1925 the hospital added a four story addition containing 24 private rooms, two operating rooms, X-ray room, and laboratory. In 1976 the addition is the only remaining building from the old hospital and has been used as a nurses' home since the merger with Christ's.

Other Topeka hospitals over the years include the Santa Fe which formerly admitted only employees of the railroad though is now open to all. The Sisters of Charity, Leavenworth, constructed St. Francis Hospital in 1909. Since the 1960s, it, too, has undergone extensive alterations and improvements. State and federal hospitals comprise the remaining important institutions in the city, they being Topeka State Hospital, Veterans Administration Hospital (formerly Winter General Hospital) and the Kansas Neurological Institute.

Christ's Hospital. The first building (right) was built for $25,000 including site. (Courtesy Kansas State Historical Society)

Stormont hospital with horse-drawn ambulance in front. (Courtesy Kansas State Historical Society)

Reminiscent of a chateau along the Loire, the Santa Fe hospital at Sixth and Jefferson was built in 1898 at a cost of $125,000. (Courtesy Kansas State Historical Society)

Policemen of 1874. (Courtesy Topeka Police Department)

Horse drawn paddy wagon and the city prison in 1914. The jail was built in 1882 at a cost of $9,000. (Courtesy Kansas State Historical Society)

MAN'S FOLLY AND PLEASURE; CRIME AND VIOLENCE

From a Topeka newspaper, March 23, 1869: "The 'house with green blinds' paid the usual fine. This time it amounted to $47.50." Patently, the "green blinds" hid an ancient profession which proved as strong, as dynamic, and as profitable in a maturing metropolis as it did in the wildest cattle or mining town.

Topeka's first prostitute undoubtedly arrived well before statehood and, once the city secured the capitol, the institution thrived. Victorian morality supposedly precluded discussion of sex or sexual deviation; such was far from the truth. Western newspapers like the *Commonwealth* unabashedly acquainted the public with prostitution, rape, incest, and murder—all to point a moral.

Houses of ill repute in the 1870s were located in every section of town though they predominated on the river bottoms, north or south, and on either side of Kansas avenue. Several were in the suburbs or old sections like South Topeka.

Police raids kept the prostitutes constantly on the move. A certain Mrs. Banks, according to the *Commonwealth*, July, 1872, switched from a house on Crane street to one in the Huntoon Addition. Next she flew to an 800 Jefferson street address. " 'Hooped' out of that," Mrs. Banks ended up in the First Ward where police again apprehended her.

The really important houses, or so it seemed, concentrated on Madison, Monroe, and Quincy streets. A writer in the *Commonwealth*, July 8, 1871, commented on the popularity of the location: "I understand that there is now a great rivalry between the keepers of the two bagnios, as to who shall have the largest den and employ the most prostitutes."

Soiled Dove, demi-rep, demi-monde, and nymph du pave were the names people gave them; the ranche, house of easy virtue, *maison de joie* their homes. Most of the women lived in very ordinary quarters, often in a room above some store. Usually the girls worked for an older, experienced madame like the big three of the 1870s: Margaret (Maggie) Preston, Joe King and "Long Alice." Maggie, at one time, employed at least three girls including a Miss Haas, the "Italian Beauty," while Alice had four. On one occasion, at least, a prostitute made a house call. State Attorney General A. L. Williams recorded in his diary in 1871 that he climbed the stairs to the law office above his and found there a prominent attorney in a compromising position with the "Italian Beauty."

Either local talent or transients going to or from the western boom towns, Topeka prostitutes might have started out like this couple the *Commonwealth* complained of in 1872: "Two women reside in the first ward who are in the habit of exposing their naked forms, at the windows of their room, while trains are passing. Such unmitigated and inescusable indecencies should be stopped." The paper, May 29, 1875, outlined the sad career of a young Topeka girl, Jennie Shidler, who degenerated into the life of a prostitute. With her father dead and her mother keeping a large family at home, Jennie helped her as best she could washing as a servant in Topeka's better homes. Though modest and pretty, she was, unfortunately, weak minded and thus fell easy prey to villains. Against her mother's protests she started bringing men home, "thieves and rascals, who found harbor at her quarters." The *Commonwealth* warned that if nothing was done for the family her sisters now peddling fruit would follow Jennie's footsteps as would a brother recently arrested for vagrancy.

Staggering down Monroe street drunks frequently accosted respectable citizens by inquiring "where does Maggie Preston live?" Once there, guests always chanced being caught by the police. City officials hauled in both resident and visitor, the costs, equally for both, ranged from five dollars to $15 with a possible night in jail. Often, if the girls lacked necessary funds, the judge released them on the promise they would quickly leave town. Naturally, the embarrassed men hid their identity as best they could. If the newspapers unmasked them then their stories and names made the headlines, such as they were.

On August 22, 1872, the *Commonwealth* reported on the persistently unlucky Mr. Patterson, a Santa Fe time-keeper. First rounded up at Joe King's, he paid his $12, saving enough to visit Daisy Deane the next evening, only to be spied again. Promising never to go back, the following evening found him, the second time, at Daisy's. As he left, bound for police court, Patterson begged Daisy for a loan. "She said she was not a broker," the paper recorded. About then he learned he had lost his job.

A prostitute's life was not an easy one. Her Dolly Vardan, a brightly colored dress, weighed her down, and being overly dressed it "was such that the broad avenues and walks of the first ward did not afford sufficient area for their perambulations." If that were not all one girl lost her $600 wardrobe at a fire in Maggie Preston's in

1871. Even worse befell them.   If Joe King's pimp caught her riding away with another man for instance, a beating was sure to follow. And if despondent enough some committed suicide. When a Topeka physician revived an east side prostiute in 1872 the paper quietly rebuked him.

Naturally, police raids put a crimp in business. The *Commonwealth*, February 4, 1873, happily recounted the following battle against an invasion of Lawrence soiled doves:

The police then proceeded to the Lawrence ranche, located on Van Buren street, between Tenth and Eleventh, commonly termed the "Peach Orchard." What connection there is between a peach orchard and a lewd woman from Lawrence is a difficult problem to solve, and is respectfully referred to the Topeka Scientific Institute. . . . However, the police approached the house, . . . and one of the party knocked politely at the door.

"Who's there?" shouted a female form divine.

"Police," responded one of the officers.

Whereupon the orchard fairy commenced discharging the contents of a wicked little revolver, and with a rapidity which clearly demonstrated that she meant business. The officers surrounded the house, followed from window to window by the nymph, who fired in all five shots, without hitting anybody. The back door was finally forced open, and Miss Lawrence flew out and lodged in a snow-bank, where she was caged by a policeman, brought back to the house and relieved of her revolver. She gave security for her appearance today stating that she thought there ought to be enough Lawrence men in town to defend her.

Prostitution often touched very close to home when important community leaders were unveiled by such a raid. Citizens objecting in 1882 to a house at 114 Quincy street accused a deputy city marshal of being the owner, implying that he knew about the business conducted there and that he should know more about the law. An even worse predicament befell the South Topeka city marshal, E. B. Lull, in 1886. Mayor John Ritchie first asked for a resignation and then fired Lull explaining his reasons in the city minutes for February third. First, the marshal knew but did not act on the fact that "certain persons . . . were violating the law by living and cohabiting together, pretending to be man and wife."

Secondly, Ritchie charged him "with being found and seen at dead of night in a house of ill fame with his boots off and lying in or on the bed with one of the inmates, a lewd woman. . . ." Yet, within nine months, Lull was appointed to a vacancy on the town council. In 1891, while serving as a Topeka council member, he was discovered in a secret Topeka liquor joint!

City ordinances in the 19th or early 20th century did not discriminate between males and females in the house; indeed, the papers frequently complained that the women too often got off easily. Also, the general reputation of certain houses in town was enough evidence for a conviction. A Topeka police report covering the 46 months from April 1, 1889, to February 1, 1893, documented some 560 arrests for prostitution with 512 convictions. Few were for keeping a house of ill repute, most were of "parties guilty of prostitution in a private way, and at no established places."

Everyone, of course, knew where those places were. Samuel Radges obliged those who didn't by marking the girls in his 1882 Topeka city directory with an asterisk. He offered no explanation but in all probability none was needed. Local newspapers, however, quickly revealed the designation and began referring to the girls with the symbol.

Prostitution repulsed respectable women who felt nothing could be done about the *. An idea emerged by accident, when a conversation at a September, 1899, Equal Suffrage Association meeting shifted to a possible practical solution, the creation of a legal red light district in Topeka. A member, who did not give her name to the *Capital*, explained on September 23, how, under the present system with the lewd women residing upstairs of downtown buildings, men easily slipped into the rooms unnoticed. However, they "would be ashamed to go into a district known to contain nothing but women of low character." Her suggestion was that prostitutes "should be driven to the suburbs, confined to one strip of territory and examined by a competent physician every two weeks." While never forced to congregate the prostitutes did finally make it to the suburbs on their own.

Theoretically sin swirls in the big city but not in the pure country. While little is known of rural activities, certainly prostitution was there. Tecumseh was a natural place with its Wigwam of the 1850s and Indianola women wrestled with a nymph there in 1862. A tantalizing feature in the *Commonwealth,* January 18, 1872, mentioned a "brace of 'soiled doves' " from Rossville in town probably to do some shopping. Should any community entertain special visitors, as did Silver Lake in 1876 when "Don Castello's Great American Circus" played there, Topeka courtesans were sure to enjoy the revelry and the customers.

In North Topeka, resident housewives took affirmative action when a neighboring wife, whose husband was at home with their children, seduced the husband of a friend. The "lady" bragged to a servant girl who in turn told the story to four of the neighborhood ladies who, the *Kansas Daily Commonwealth,* April 13, 1872, reported: "seized her and bound her hands and feet with . . . rope. Being then at the mercy of her captors, they first tarred her ears, eyes, mouth and nose, after which her lower limbs and abdominal parts were well plastered with the extract of pine. Not satisfied with these applications, they applied ground red-pepper to the most salient points and left her to her fate."

A son of the sinning woman found the miserable creature and freed her. Two of her tormentors were arrested. The *Commonwealth* continued: "We are assured, however, that the provocation given by Mrs. . . . will mitigate the punishment of those who tarred her." One of the arrested ladies was, "owing to her peculiar condition," fined ten dollars and costs while her mother, "quite an old woman," was fined one dollar.

Dealing with hardened members of the opposite sex often led to brawls, tumults and exciting fist fights among disappointed suitors. About one of these encounters the *Commonwealth* on November 10, 1869, headlined: "Passion, Jealousy and Blood" involving "a naughty painter and insulted chamber-maid." It seems a Tefft House boarder dropped by the maid's room, an action which eventually brought out her boy friend who promptly defeated the painter on the field of honor. "His offense was expiated in blood, which flowed profusely from his mangled face." Not all fights, of course, involved local ladies of the evening. Sometimes they just happened like the time a row occurred between a Mr. Davis and a Mr. Humphries who threw or beat each other over the head with everything in Smith's Sixth street saloon. The two ended up in the streets before they concluded "one of the gamest little fights that ever occurred in the west or any other place." As a proud trophy, the saloon exhibited "a handful of Humphries' whiskers."

For the month of November, 1870, the *Commonwealth* claimed the city prison swelled with 12 arrests for selling liquor without a license, 23 for drunkeness and disorderly conduct, one for assault and battery, one for carrying concealed weapons, three for being found in a house of ill fame, five for being inmates of the same, and three for keeping houses.

Periodically it also warned Topekans to be on the lookout for robbers, thieves, and gamblers. Coming in on the scheduled trains, often in squads, they headed for the nearest saloon to bilk the locals out of their earnings. Dressed in light gray woolen clothes, this disreputable lot supposedly was easily recognizable.

Topeka's *Commonwealth,* naturally, provided helpful hints in dealing with the unruly element. The January 17, 1873, edition advised: "The best policeman a citizen can have about his premises to prevent burglary is a good revolver, and enough nerve to shoot straight." Emphasizing its advantages, an early copy reported an incident concerning a Mrs. Morgan. While walking along Tenth street a "villainous desperado" accosted her. She "struggled manfully" but the "incarnate fiend made indecent overtures to her." Quickly breaking away Mrs. Morgan pulled out a revolver (from where the paper did not say) which so frightened the robber that he "ran away like a deer."

Gambling and pool halls were another significant source of vice frequently censured by the press. Occasionally it reported events at them like the time late in January, 1868, when two "propellers of the ivories," according to the *Leader,* proposed a week long match, ten hours a day, "for a peck of peanuts a side." Generally, though, the *Commonwealth* frowned upon such frivolous loafing. It noted in 1872, for instance, a raid on a gambling establishment in North Topeka. It was located in the basement of the bank of the north side's most prominent citizen, Maj. Daniel M. Adams. The police then publicly burned the faro bank and poker tables at Fifth and Kansas. A brief paragraph in the *Commonwealth,* January 1, 1871, summed it all up: "Billiard halls manufacture lazy idlers, saloons, drunkards; but that young man who attends Pond's business college a few months does a thing which is an honor to himself and to his friends, and may become a blessing and not a curse to the world."

Next to murder perhaps the most serious crime in society would be rape and/or incest, both of which Topeka newspapers fully recorded. Again the stories were printed not as pornographic pieces but rather to point out, graphically, a moral and in the process greatly shame the participants. The *Capital,* August 21, 1888, called the crimes "so black that the darkest crime in the decalogue blanches beside it, a crime so dastardly that it was not even forecast in the commandments of Sinai."

As to murder, nothing else received greater headlines. Some papers played them up, some down but usually one related everything in sparkling detail. Certainly the most sensational murder in early Topeka, with several implications, revolved around a middle aged Negro named Mary Jane Scales who had been born a slave in Virginia and at one time was owned by Jefferson Davis, later president of the Confederacy. Ignorant and superstitious she had "married" during bondage. She escaped in the first stages of the Civil War and married again, to a James Ford, but they soon separated as she moved to Kansas, finding employment first in Lawrence and later in Tecumseh. While in the latter place in 1863 she was married for a third time. Her new bridegroom was her employer, a widowed minister named Burnett Scales.

Mr. and Mrs. Scales next left for a home just west of North Topeka. The marriage, however, never prospered, partly because she had not "been taught the importance of a pure life." Her ex-brother-in-law soon came to live with the couple arousing some gossip in the community. Evidently the brother-in-law, Lewis Ford, impressed Topekans. The *Commonwealth,* August 17, 1871, stated "his general bearing is that of a gentleman, though without culture." Distraught with her husband and feeling for Ford led the two to murder Scales in mid-November, 1870.

Convicted of the crime Ford and Mrs. Scales were sentenced to be executed at Topeka on August 17, 1871. A day or two before the execution workmen completed the scaffold, an enclosed structure 24 by 28 feet, 14 feet high, and connected by a passageway to the back of the courthouse. The *Commonwealth* commented: "Yesterday being the last day for visitors to see the condemned, a constant stream of men, women and children poured into the jail the whole day. Jailor Disbrow acted as usher at the outer gate. . . ."

The sheriff responded to the growing and eager crowds by pushing up the time of execution, but, fortunately for the couple, if not expectant Topekans, Gov. James Harvey commuted the sentences to life imprisonment. By a matter of a few hours, Mary Jane Scales missed entering history books as the first and only woman legally hanged in the state of Kansas.

Infinitely more sensational was the June 4, 1889, murder of Alphonso T. Rodgers, a prominent merchant. The Rodgers family lived in a large and handsome brick home at Third and Fillmore streets where a little after four in the morning a noise disturbed Mr. and Mrs. Rodgers. Thinking it to be their daughter who was ill, Mr. Rodgers rushed out into the hall only to come face to face with a burglar named Nathaniel (Nat) Oliphant. The two men struggled and Oliphant fired a .38 Smith & Wesson revolver, mortally wounding Rodgers. The two continued fighting some time after the shot, the intruder being struck twice with the butt of the gun. Oliphant immediately fled the scene and Rodgers died two hours later.

Police quickly mounted a search for the assailant, first checking the railyards and hobo jungles as well as other parts of town. Two officers boarded the seven a. m. Santa Fe "plug" to Tecumseh, where they stopped and began walking the rails back to the city. Not far from the rural station, one of the men spied someone in the thicket near the river. The police caught and marched the highly bruised man to Topeka where they identified him as Oliphant, the chief suspect.

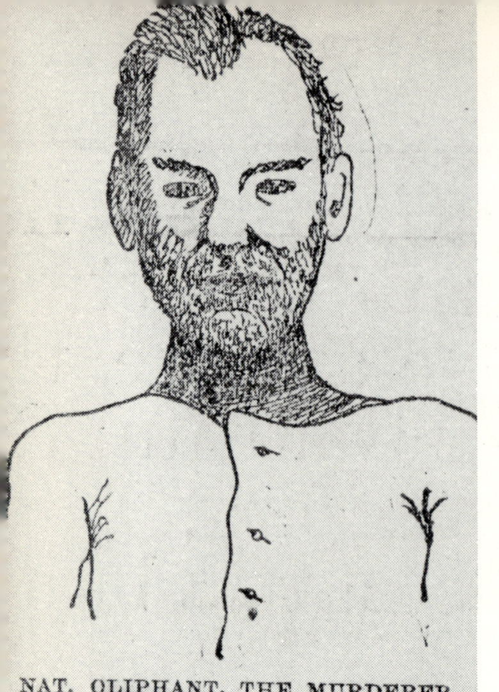

NAT. OLIPHANT, THE MURDERER.

This artist's conception of the Nat Oliphant lynching appeared in the Topeka "State Journal," June 5, 1889.

It was then about ten, half an hour after Rodgers' death. The police became concerned over Oliphant's safety and so moved him to the nearby Shawnee county jail. Only three years old, one newspaper called the new calaboose "an impregnable mass of stone and steel." A special 10:30 edition of the *Capital* carried the news to all sections of town and a crowd began to gather in front of first the city jail and then the county jail.

There the mob stayed, growing all the time. Some reports put the number at 15,000 by early evening but probably there were no more than 10,000. People crowded everywhere up Fifth and Van Buren to Kansas avenue and beyond.

Attempts to break up or quiet the mob failed with officials finally becoming a bit desperate. With the crowd's spirit on the verge of eruption police officers quietly and prudently retreated inside the jail. Nothing could stop the inevitable, the immediate execution of murderer Nat Oliphant. About that evening, June 4, Martha Van Orsdol wrote in her diary: "Mr. and Mrs. Stauffer went and I kept their children. Mr. Shaw staid with me till 10:30 when he went down in time to see the hanging. I could hear the pounding and hear the shouts of the mob, which was enough for me." Such an outpouring of anger had been simmering for some time. Kansas had not conducted a legal hanging since 1870.* Topekans would have an illegal execution in 1889.

---

*There had been at least 36 illegal hangings since then, Oliphant's being number 37. Capital punishment had not been abolished but Kansas governors never enforced the statute or sentences.

Instead of charging the bolted front doors, several enterprising souls began digging at the basement foundation walls. Quickly prying out a hole large enough for a man to crawl through, over 100 men squirmed their way into the jail where they proceeded from cell to cell hunting for their prey. Other prisoners pointed the way. With chisels and sledge hammers they cut their way through two steel doors, meeting no opposition. They removed Oliphant and dragged him with a rope around his neck to the northeast corner of Sixth and Kansas less than an hour after their first entry into the jail. After a Baptist preacher remonstrated against the crowd, the rope was thrown up over an electric light pole on Sixth street. By 11:15 Oliphant was dead.

Around 11:30 the vigilante group cut the body down. The light pole "was whittled into small pieces by souvenir hunters before the body reached the morgue."

The local press quickly seized upon the incident and suggested reasons why such a thing could happen. Both the *Capital* and the *Democrat* blamed the unenforced capital punishment law for arrousing people. The Kansas City *Times,* on the other hand, believed it was "the fruit of Kansas' prohibition craze" which kept the police spending all their time rounding up whisky tipplers instead of more serious criminals. Regardless of the problem's roots, the *State Journal* complimented those involved in the act: "No drunken men were

Crowd waiting to view Nat Oliphant's body at the mortuary, June 5, 1889. (Courtesy Kansas State Historical Society)

The day after the lynching a souvenir hunter climbs the pole on which Nat Oliphant was hanged. (Courtesy Kansas State Historical Society)

seen; no loud or unseemly language was indulged in. It was hardly
to be called a mob. It was simply 'we the people' performing what
they deemed a public duty for the public good."

Officials took Oliphant's body to a near-by mortuary. Martha Van
Orsdol described the scene there the next day:

Went in P. M. Wednesday, June 5 with Hannah Peterson to Stoker's Undertaker's office to see Nat. E. Oliphant, burglar & murderer, who was hanged last
night by the mob. It was a dreadful sight: thousands of people in line, passing
thro' to get a look at him and not one with a thought of pity; all seeming to think
he got what he deserved. Poor man, tho' he did a dreadful thing, *he had a soul* to
save and seems like he ought to have been spared and given a chance to become
a better man. There are other punishments.

It was rumored that soon after his secret burial in Topeka Cemetery, a few persons, objecting to the remains being interred near those
of loved ones, quietly removed the body, leaving behind only the
shroud and coffin.

In 1898 a young University of Kansas student from Topeka, named
John S. Collins, found himself in need of money to court a girl at
school. So desperate was he that he tried to hire someone to kill his
own father so that he might reap the insurance proceeds. Failing in
that he committed the crime himself, blasting his father with a shotgun.

When Collins' trial began late in November it made the headlines
every day and the courtroom was packed with spectators. When the
trial ended Collins was convicted and sentenced to hang. The governor
failed to sign the execution papers and nine years later Collins received
a gubernatorial pardon.

On December 24, 1894, the Topeka *State Journal* narrated the story
of another sensational murder, that of Mrs. A. D. Matson and in doing
so it detailed a feature of human nature which emerges after most
disasters, whether large or small:

All day yesterday a crowd was gathering at the house at 1435 Monroe street,
where Mrs. A. D. Matson was murdered. People of all classes and conditions flocked
to the place, stood in the yard and discussed the tragedy, peered into the windows
and when the doors were finally opened by the colored man who is in charge of
the house the people swarmed in and examined every object with interest.

Then each had his own story to tell of how and where the unfortunate woman
met her death. They gathered around the awful stains on the floor of the south
west room with a somewhat awestruck appearance and then went away satisfied.

The street in front of the house was so filled with carriages that it was almost
impossible to drive through but few of the occupants went into the house. They
contented themselves with looking at the exterior of the rough stone building.

On September 21, 1933, the *State Journal* revealed the planned
kidnapping of Peggy Anne Landon, 16-year-old daughter of Gov. Alf
M. Landon. The story disclosed that 11 persons, six of whom were
behind bars at the state penitentiary and five on the outside (one a

woman), plotted to capture the girl and hold her in a Montgomery county farmhouse for the release of the six prisoners. Connected with an Oklahoma gang, the group originally intended to take the governor himself, apparently watching his every move and hoping to grab him between his office and home. However, a secret service agent overheard them at a "Kansas City underworld joint" and tipped off state officials.

Learning that Landon knew something of their plans, the gang changed their plot to kidnapping the daughter instead. This, too, the police knew of so for three weeks they unobtrusively trailed her. Nothing materialized, fortunately, and the governor's office released the story to the press. When she first heard of the plot Miss Landon declared "Oh, boy! Won't that be a lot of fun." Discovering that armed guards followed her everywhere—to school, to parties, and to the theater—her initial enthusiasm changed to "I'm getting tired of being the hearse in a funeral."

During the 1930s a number of second-rate midwestern hoodlums exploded into national headlines and captured the nation's imagination. Some of these involved Topeka.

One such incident occurred in the Topeka post office at Fifth and Kansas avenue on April 16, 1937, when G-men and robbers held an old fashioned shootout. One FBI man, Wayne W. Baker, was killed while one of the robbers and two bystanders were wounded. Scars from that episode still (in 1976) are visible in the elevator doors of the federal building.

It all happened because Robert Suhay and Glen Applegate had robbed a bank in New York state of $18,000 and were picking up mail in Topeka. The G-men had been tipped off and agent Baker apprehended them. Unfortunately, though, the FBI man was not careful enough. Suhay pulled out a gun and began firing at Baker who returned the shots. Bullets seemed to be flying everywhere, searing the walls and elevator doors, as the pair made their escape. At Sabetha the bandits kidnapped a doctor to treat Suhay's wounds but late that same day the two were caught in Nebraska. Convicted in June, 1937, they were executed at Lansing on August 12, 1938.

Just as exciting, to some, was the home-grown, minor-league Bonnie and Clyde from Topeka, Benny and Estelle Dickson. Their stock in trade, like that of so many others, consisted simply of holding up small town or rural state banks, kidnapping the bank teller and making a successful escape.

Dickson's background, on the surface, belied such a violent career. His father, James Dickson, taught chemistry at Topeka High School and his in-laws firmly believed "no one could have asked for a finer son-in-law. He didn't drink and he didn't smoke. He didn't even use a profane word."

Dickson's crime career began in 1929 while he was still a high school student. He stuck up a taxi cab, was sent to the Hutchinson reformatory, and later spent time in the Missouri state penitentiary. In 1938 he married 16-year-old Estelle and that summer and fall he started his greatest crime spree by striking several South Dakota banks. On October 31 the couple robbed a Brookings, S. D., bank of $17,592, and compelled the vice-president and assistant manager to ride a few blocks with them as hostages.

Benny and Estelle apparently made several visits to her parents who knew him in Topeka as Johnny O'Malley, a Chicago insurance man. However, on Thanksgiving, 1938, county and state police lay waiting for him outside the Gee Cabin Camp on U. S. Highway 75 just south of town. Next day, the 25th, the *Capital* reported that when Dickson appeared outside the motel police shouted for him to halt. Instead of obeying Benny dashed to his waiting car and in a hail of bullets escaped without his wife (who fled on foot) but with his pockets stuffed with money. He received only a scalp wound and in North Topeka seized a car from an Iowa couple. Police later found blood stains on the steering wheel.

Several days later Mrs. Dickson rejoined her husband and the couple disappeared from view. The FBI now classified them as "public enemy number one." One policeman declared "they'll never get Benny alive; he'll shoot it out to the end."

(Courtesy Topeka Police Department)

15833

IDENTIFICATION ORDER NO. 1283

FEDERAL BUREAU OF INVESTIGATION
UNITED STATES DEPARTMENT OF JUSTICE
WASHINGTON, D. C.

WANTED

BENJAMIN JAMES DICKSON, with aliases: R. CRAIG, BENNIE DICKSON, BENNY DICKSON, BENNIE DIXON, JAMES DUNCAN, WILLIAM HARRISON, JOHN O'MALLEY, JOE TRENT.

FBI No. 385908

KIDNAPING

BANK ROBBERY

NATIONAL MOTOR VEHICLE THEFT ACT

DESCRIPTION   Photograph taken July, 1931   CRIMINAL RECORD

Benny Dickson

Dickson's end came four months later at a sleazy St. Louis hamburger stand. Federal agents had been trailing him for sometime and on April 6, 1939, from a signal by his companion, "a lady in brown," ordered him to "stick 'em up." As a natural reaction Dickson reached for a revolver but the FBI agents gunned him down before he could do anything serious.

His bride of a year was later arrested and sentenced to ten years in the penitentiary, thus exterminating the careers—one permanently—of Topeka's most notorious husband and wife.

But perhaps Topeka's best known public enemy was Albin or Alvin "Creepy" Karpis another of the cheap but somewhat romantic hoodlums of the 1930s. Born on the east side, Karpis graduated from Branner street grade school in 1923. At the age of 18 he burglarized a Holton tire shop and sold the merchandise to a Topeka junk dealer. As his aptness at crime grew Karpis joined the infamous Barker gang. At last he had made the big time.

Back in Topeka, in February, 1934, he and several other men terrorized the Ron Hasselbrock family one night, hoping to gain access to the National Bank of Topeka through Hasselbrock, a teller. The caper proved futile, however, and Karpis left town. On several occasions police quietly waited for him at Topeka joints but always to no avail. Finally FBI Director J. Edgar Hoover personally supervised Karpis' capture on May 1, 1936.

Of Karpis' image in his Branner school class photograph, a *State Journal* reporter wrote: "He looks much as the rest of the class, with one exception. His mouth lacks the firmness of most of the other children's mouths. There is a lack of purpose, an apparent weakness." The writer claimed this feature still existed in 1934.

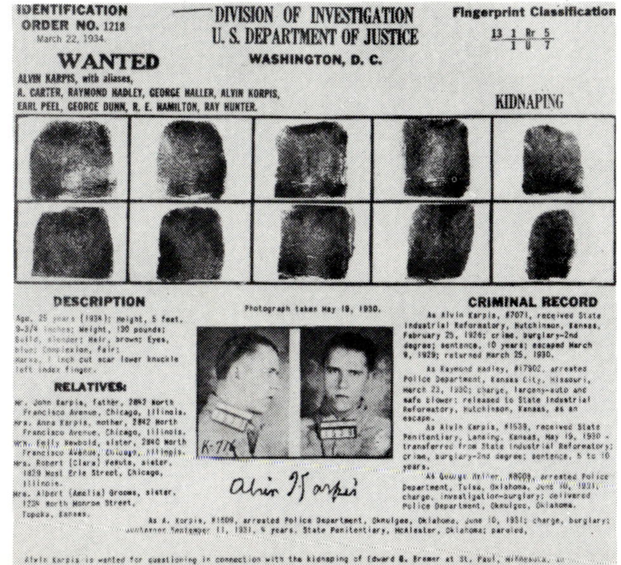

(Courtesy Topeka Police Department)

A snow fort at Oak Grove grade school in the early 1900s. (Courtesy Mrs. Mildred Kreipe McAnaw)

The Dover grade school about 1900. (Courtesy Zercher Photo)

The interior of Oak Grove grade school east of Tecumseh about 1910. This one room schoolhouse was built in 1871. (Courtesy Mr. and Mrs. Gerald Kreipe)

THE INTELLECTUAL REALM;
COUNTRY SCHOOLS

Elizabeth Eddy, a well-known county educator, once wrote: "We will not forget the little Red School house of other days when Kansas was struggling for her place in the union." Few, if any, of local rural school buildings were red, and, indeed, schools in early county history were seldom even frame. A *Kansas Daily Commonwealth* reporter, a native of New York state, made a note of one of the schools in Monmouth township in 1869: "Here they have a log school house, which forcibly reminded us of a (to us) well known, similar institution, nestled far away amid the hills and maple groves of the old Empire State."

The majority of educational buildings in the regions surrounding Topeka proper were stone. By the 1870s native limestone structures, which could be built with little expense from easily available material, took the place of log school houses in existing districts or became the original building in newly created districts. Pleasant Hill school in Auburn township near the town of Auburn seems to have been typical of rural schools in the county. "This District," reported the *Commonwealth,* "has built one of the best school houses in Kansas. It is of stone, 22 x 34, with patent seats, and all the appointments of a first class modern school house." Tice school in Williamsport township "has been lately completed and is a model of neatness, and convenience. It has white ceilings and a *black* blackboard, (in some of our school houses it is *viceversa*), a Webster's dictionary, outline maps, globes, mathematical blocks, etc."

In the spring of 1872 the cost of constructing a new rural school in the county is what was later exemplified by the following article about Berryton school:

> Nine bids for building a new schoolhouse in the 39th school district were opened yesterday by the board of education. They ranged from $1,814 to $2,250. No award was made from a lack of funds. It was decided to either reduce the bids or the size of the house, and here the matter rested.

County school statistics of November 5, 1871, reported 66 school districts in Shawnee county, an increase of 10 over the year before. Of those, 34 were frame, 18 stone, five brick, and one remaining log structure. Eight frame and four stone schools were built during that year.

A description of a school in Topeka township gives another view of the inside of the one-room school. In a letter to the *Commonwealth,* a local school patron wrote: "We have a No. 1 school house a brick structure of 28 x 40 feet and the best house in the county (the city excepted, of course), furnished with Sherwood's patent folding seats, desks, etc., two stoves, and everything handy and convenient." David Zirkle wrote of his own school near Richland:

> The big coal-burning stove took up a lot of room. This stove was alternately too hot or too cold. At recess and noon we played hard doing lots of running. When the bell rang calling us in, we took our seats and the fire in the stove got low, of course, we cooled off quickly. The result was that most us had colds most of the time, and as handkerchiefs were a luxury, coat sleeves and shirt sleeves served as a substitute.

The *Congregational Record* of July, 1865, praised one of the local rural school houses when it reported on Waveland's neat stone building: "The man who settled at ...., [*sic*] Kansas, and 'had been swearing a whole week, because there was no place where his children could go to meeting or school,' should, for his own and his children's good, move to Waveland."

Education has always been an important factor in the history of Shawnee county. In the mid-19th century a discussion sprang up in newspapers of the eastern part of Kansas concerning the first schoolmaster in Kansas after its organization as a territory. At that time a Topekan, J. B. McAfee, claimed to have opened the Leavenworth Collegiate Institute on May 14, 1855. The first country school in the state began in February, 1855, three miles north of Lawrence. A decade later the number of school districts in Shawnee county, including Topeka, stood at 33, although Pleasant Hill school near Auburn had not yet begun operation. The total number of students was 1,980. According to the *Kansas State Record* this amounted to all of the children between the ages of five and 21 residing in the county. Auburn, Tecumseh, and Indianola, in that order, were the largest rural districts in the county.

County sentiment towards education was depicted quite well by a letter describing a visit to one school just east of Topeka: "Its patrons are wide-awake, active men, who believe that district schools may and should become the most successful educational institutions of the State." Settled areas of the county improved existing schools, and new settlers saw the need for educating their children. When a region became populated, one of the first requirements for the pioneers was a school. Silver Lake offers an example of the educational urge reached by the summer of 1870:

> In the township of Silver Lake alone, where, less than five years ago, a single furrow had not been turned, seven schools, costing in the aggregate about $13,000.

Berryton Rural High School in the late 1910s. (Courtesy Kansas State Historical Society)

have been erected within the year. At the *village* of Silver Lake the school now numbers seventy pupils, and is one of the most successful and best conducted in the county.

The rapid expansion and growth of Shawnee county necessitated a commensurate growth in the number of schools. By 1870 there were 4,500 children of school age residing in the county. Of these, 3,000 were enrolled in public schools and the remainder probably represented the older ones who had set out on their own and felt no need for further education. Over $70,000 of bonds were issued for schools in that year, for the maintenance of the 52 existing buildings and construction of 10 new houses. A year later there were 150 more pupils in 66 school districts.

Still with all this active interest in public education, many parents needed their children at home to help with farm work or household duties. A letter from a Monmouth township teacher to the *Commonwealth* demonstrates the concern which rural educators expressed regarding this neglect:

We feel a deep interest in those placed under our care, and labor earnestly to promote their best interest and happiness. Teachers can accomplish very little in comparison with what could be done provided they procure the cooperation and assistance of the parents. Could parents realize how much their children lose by such absence or tardiness and the trouble it gives both the school and teacher, we think there would not be as many who "have to stay at home and nurse the baby while Ma washes," or "to chop wood," or "go on errands," or to be absent from school a week to have a boot or shoe patched.

On the opposite side of the argument, another letter from the same area demonstrates a manner of instruction advocated by some:

> Every elector should read his county paper or papers and every school officer, every teacher, every parent, and every young man or woman who expect to act a *successful* part in the great drama of life.
>
> In fact I shall rejoice when the worthy county paper shall supplant the *Fifth* and *Sixth* Readers in our public schools. Then our young men and women will know less of "Greece and Rome," perhaps, but vastly more of "what we do and say at home."

A typical day at a country school was described by a correspondent from Menoken school who visited there in 1873. The school opened with reading of the Scriptures, beginning with the teacher who was followed individually by all the students who could read. A bell then sounded, and the classes recited in order: first a primary class in the alphabet, printing and reading letters as they wrote them; following that was a class in the primary reader; then scholars using slates and the second reader. Finally, the upper level pupils copied definitions of uncommon words from dictionaries. During arithmetic session, the youngest children learned addition by counting kernels of corn while the older class members did multiplication problems. "While standing in the class, one read and those who had the same results were seated." Those yet standing read in like manner until all were seated. The teacher then read the correct results and those who agreed rose, continuing until all had the correct results. Those in the spelling class spelled off their lesson as they had previously written it on their slates, then again as the teacher pronounced it, followed by the class in concert. Thus, reading, writing, and arithmetic were learned as each term in the rural school passed.

In each individual school there were good and bad teachers, as well as good and bad students. Things did not always go so smoothly as they may seem. For instance, Topeka papers often printed items of local interest such as this one from the *Commonwealth* of May 21, 1873: "The following is the 'Role of Honor' in Linn Creek school (No. 39) for the month of April: Ettie Thresher, John A. Thresher, George Thresher, George Berry, Agnes Hogue, and Alice McQuiston." By the same token, there existed mischievous students such as Robert M. Forbes, who attended Indianola school:

> As a small boy Mr. Forbes had one teacher who was in the habit of getting drunk, week ends. To revenge themselves for a thrashing they did not deserve, he and another boy poured ink on the teacher's new butternut suit, as he was lying drunk in his room in the [Clinton] hotel. The suit had to be dyed black.

This humorous tale of the school master at Union school, near Indianola, in 1871 shows what some parents dreaded in teachers and deserves to be quoted at length:

> The teacher in district No. 47 also had a "new way" which we cannot so highly recommend, (in the school room), being, it would appear, especially anxious to

gain the affections of his pupils, which means in his particular case, the large girls only. Accordingly he passed most of his time at said girls' desks "doing sums," so he claimed. And in class, he would lean upon their shoulders to the disgust of those sensible girls, to their credit be it said, who on several occasions promptly requested him to "lean upon his dinner, if he had any." He would, also, while away an otherwise weary hour in dictating killing verses to them, etc., etc. Well, he was informed that his "system" didn't suit. He was, therefore, promptly relieved and sent to his wife in Kentucky, where it is hoped he will stay. A teacher for his school is wanted; "No Kentuckian need apply."

Kansas took stock of its educational resources in 1874. Rural school districts had grown in number since 1861 from 214 to 4,181; the school population from 4,900 to nearly 200,000. This was a rapid yearly increase, including the Civil War era, with "no year being marked by a falling off or a cessation of growth, showing that the people of Kansas were not to be diverted by any vicissitude from the upbuilding of the common and public school," Noble Prentis wrote. Shawnee county was caught up in this education boom. District schools dominated rural learning in the county until consolidation a century after Kansas became a state.

Though only a few blacks resided outside Topeka, it is interesting to note that racial difficulties took place there when black children attempted to attend classes. Research material on this topic is minimal, but we do have an excellent account left by Sam Reader in his diary. At Indianola, in the fall of 1864, an attempt by some "Negro children" to attend the same school as whites resulted in the parents of the latter withdrawing their children from the school and in the white students "throwing stones at the colored."

The school was the source of nearly all social activity of the community. Spelling bees were popular, as were local lyceums. The lyceums consisted of questions placed before the audience followed by a debate and a resolution being derived from the discussion. The rural school building itself was the meeting place for many different organizations. Political party gatherings such as the one mentioned above met in the schoolhouse in farming localities. Many church services and revivals were held in the school house. Victor school was the meeting place for the Western Bohemian Fraternal Association (Z.C.B.J.) prior to 1909. The list of uses for the structures throughout county history is long and varied.

Surely the big event for the scholars in the country was the end-of-school picnics. "The first school in District 32 has just closed, the examination having taken place last Friday," the *Commonwealth* reported. That Friday was the last day at Waveland "so people in that district had a dinner at Reynold's Grove with a table filled with cakes, pies, chicken, etc." Most often the teacher requested the parents in the district to arrange something nice for the school on the last day. As a result a dinner accompanied by speech-making ensued and a pleasant party assembled in an equally pleasant grove "with a most delicious repast, which did credit to the heart as well as to the culinary abilities of the ladies of the district." This was followed by literary exercises by the pupils and speeches by prominent citizens. It was at this time that the teacher was awarded the position for another year, if she or he was to receive the appointment.

Other than holidays such as Christmas and Easter, a festive day in the rural school, across the state including Shawnee county, was Kansas Day. Elaborate programs were prepared, essays were read on various periods in Kansas history, Kansas songs were sung, and Kansas poems were recited. "On these festive occasions," wrote Noble Prentis, "the walls are decorated with the national colors, the motto of the State in evergreen letters, and everywhere the sunflower."

By the 1890s county schools had nearly grown to their largest number. The *Shawnee County District School* of October, 1893, reported 102 districts having mostly one-room schools with a single teacher. Eleven schools were large enough to merit a pair of instructors; three had three instructors; two employed four teachers; and District 36, Highland Park, had five. School was taught from six to nine months per year. Salaries for teachers ranged mostly from $30 to $60 per month. This was no increase from twenty years before when the average salary per month was $50 for male mentors and $45 for females.

At this time a report by Commissioner Harris of the Bureau of Education showed that Kansas had the greatest proportion of her school-age population enrolled in the schools of any state in the U. S.— 87.66 per cent. The large proportion of attendance in schools shows the interest felt by the people of Kansas in education, and the report claims that this was not the result of the compulsory laws. Kansas received most of its settlers from states in the east where a system of free public schools was an established fact, and the system was successfully maintained in their new home.

Unfortunately, Harris did not realize that the rural schools were really in a sorry condition. Many of them were staffed with incompetent teachers using antiquated methods of instruction. As witnessed above, salaries remained too low to attract superior teachers. Boys and girls lost interest in school and dropped out while they were still quite young. As farmers began to wake up and do something about their agriculture they discovered they were far behind in educational facilities for their children. It didn't take farmers long to understand that the most important crop they could produce was young people. Fred L. Parrish once wrote "if youth could receive a scientific education, perhaps they would be more content to seek a future on the farm, and follow agriculture as a way of life." By 1912 there were 103 school districts in the county and the average salary for teachers rose to $55 per month (with the highest being a phenomenal $111.11).

From the turn of the century until the 1930s, consolidated schools began to increase in number across Kansas. Gradually the district school became "standard" or "superior" by raising certification requirements of the teacher, modernizing the school building and grounds, and upgrading school facilities such as maps, charts, globes, and libraries. The Russell Sage Foundation graded Kansas rural schools as 24th in the nation. It was only with difficulty that rural communities were shaking off the "education-for-the-pioneer" complex Parrish said they had, and it was equally difficult to achieve the willingness to spend enough money for the modern rural school. Education came to be regarded as necessary to qualify the youth for citizenship, rather than to help him make money.

Conditions inside the schools had changed only a little during the century until consolidation in the county became a fact. Girls' dresses all had long sleeves. No nice girl would consider wearing a dress which had sleeves coming above the elbow. With the slow change of style to short-sleeved dresses came the habit of girls carrying handkerchiefs. Most of the students in the small rooms had colds, and the windows were tightly closed, so there was not much chance for a well person to stay healthy.

There was often no well or other means of securing water on the school house grounds. The water consumed by drinking and washing had to be carried in a bucket from the nearest home. The older boys were permitted by the teacher to go for a bucket of water. This was considered quite a favor since it gave them an opportunity to be away from school during the time it took to make the trip.

.The school was often divided into three groups, within which were the regular eight grades. These groups would constitute primary, intermediate, and advanced levels of learning. The first level learned the basics of reading and writing, simple arithmetic, and the spelling of fundamental words. The intermediate group moved on to the more improved areas of these studies, and the third group advanced into history, geography, and refined arithmetic.

After World War II the interest in consolidation of country schools increased and the number of schools declined. They were closed one by one throughout the late 1940s and early 1950s. From 103 schools in 1912 the number in Shawnee county dwindled to 32 in 1951 when Clifford Watson became county superintendent; four years later only 18 remained. Watson, quoted in the Topeka *Daily Capital,* said: "I'm afraid it's only a matter of time until they all will be gone. . . . But I think it's for the best. In the average case, while attending a larger elementary school, a child gets a better education."

In most cases, closing the small schools was not a matter of choice for the property owners of the district. They had to vote to annex to a neighboring district because their school no longer had enough pupils to be eligible for state aid. Even when the property owners preferred to keep their school, they could not do so by raising their taxes because the maximum levy they could impose on their land was set by law. Without enough pupils and enough tax money, nothing could be done but disorganize because state aid usually made up almost 40 percent of the rural school's income.

By 1957 only Sunbeam, Williams, County Line, North Fairview, Union, Howard, Golden Rule, Elevation, Milliken, North Highland, Priddy, and Capitol View schools remained in operation. H. A. W. Kesler, the new county superintendent, estimated that the one-room schools would disappear before 1960. About 35 or 40 had existed after the war, Kesler told the Topeka *State Journal,* "but indications appear to prove the schools will be little more than a memory in Shawnee county before long."

Children enjoying the giant stride, pole swing, at Milliken school, about 1924. (Courtesy Harriet St. John Johnson)

Playing shinny, or shinty, on a country road beside Oak Grove school, about 1920. (Courtesy Mrs. Mildred Kreipe McAnaw)

This was, indeed, the case for less than a decade later, students in rural Shawnee county attended schools in the Seaman, Washburn Rural, Shawnee Heights, and Silver Lake unified districts which consolidated one or more townships into one large school district. Such school unification prompted considerable controversy when first proposed in 1963 and 1964. Twice in 1964 rural voters turned down unification plans which would have created one school body north of the river, one south of the river, and one for the city of Topeka. Residents in wealthy Tecumseh township were especially adamant; an anonymous individual circulated a letter declaring that the law "was so conceived by selfish leadership to grab tax money from unsuspecting farmers through the ruse of better schools." Nevertheless, school unification went through for Tecumseh and elsewhere regardless of local sympathies.

No matter the politics of the 1960s, rural school districts still adhere to the ideas of the "little Red School house" as expressed by Elizabeth Eddy: "While the practical side of an education is of vast importance we want the children to go forth from the school, as nearly as possible a perfect man or a perfect woman, standing always for what is high, noble and true. No less than this should be the high aim of our cooperative efforts."

SHAWNEE COUNTY SCHOOL DISTRICTS
1912 - 1913

No.	Name	No.	Name	No.	Name
1	Auburn	35	Highland Park	68	Forest Bluff
2	Six Mile	36	Oakland	69	Golden Rod
3	Wakarusa	37	County Line	70	Vidette
4	Pleasant Valley	38	Benham	71	Haskell Creek
5	Mowers	39	Berryton	72	Pauline
6	Reed	40	Tice	73	Kingsville
7	Tecumseh	41	Decker	74	Twin Rose
8	Rice	42	Shorey	75	Rock
9	Twinville	43	Rochester	76	Lux
11	Sunnyside	44	Fairview	78	Shenk
12	Deer Creek	45	Independence	79	Lipp
13	Sunbeam	46	Silver Lake	80	Capital View
14	Ivondale	47	Union	81	Bolz
	Pierce	48	Half Day	82	Fairview
15	Dover	49	Ayer's	84	Glenwood
16	Williams	50	Seal	85	Willard
17	Waveland	51	Pleasant View	86	Science Hill
18	S. Pleasant Hill	52	Cedar Bluff	87	Kaw Valley
19	Pleasant Ridge	53	West Sixth	88	Seabrook
20	Indian Creek	54	Golden Rule	89	Walnut Hill
21	Wallace	55	Elevation	90	Liberty
22	College Hill	56	Lone Rock	92	Dawson
24	N. Pleasant Hill	57	Pleasant Valley	93	West Indianola
25	Berry Creek	58	West Union	94	Clover Hill
26	Oak Grove	59	Lyman	95	S. Highland
27	Disney	60	Richland	96	Harrison
28	Matney	61	Belvoir	98	Mud Valley
29	Mission Center	62	Lyon	99	Kelsey
30	Menoken	63	Milliken	100	One Hundred
31	Lone Tree	64	N. Highland	101	Victor
32	Blacksmith	65	James	103	One Hundred Three
33	Wanamaker	66	Priddy		
34	Rossville	67	Valencia		

The Topeka High School girl's basketball team of 1903. (Courtesy Kansas State Historical Society)

THE INTELLECTUAL REALM;
CITY SCHOOLS AND COLLEGES

Despite their concern, Topeka founders could do little to further public education in the mid-1850s. The first schools, like those in Auburn, Tecumseh, and elsewhere in Kansas territory, were privately organized in a home or church or store. Miss Sarah Harlan held Topeka's first class or "day school" in a shake shanty during the fall of 1855. It soon closed, but the *Kansas Freeman,* November 21, complimented Miss Harlan on her "courage during the continuance of her School, as the house was rather open, and the weather very often inclement."

Following Miss Harlan's footsteps in the late 1850s were a number of Topeka women who conducted informal or irregular schools. The New England Emigrant Aid Company fulfilled an earlier promise in 1857 by erecting Topeka's first true schoolhouse, a 35 by 20 foot, two-story brick structure. A few students attended that school free, owing to their family's poverty, but it required tuition and voluntary contributions for survival. Several private academies came into existence at the end of the decade with one preparatory school offering, in 1860, the traditional curriculum of spelling, reading, grammar, mathematics, and history, along with geology, astronomy, book-keeping, political economy, Latin, and Greek. Costs ranged from $3.00 per term for primary subjects up to $10.00 for extras like piano—all in cash, in advance.

Progress suffered, of course, with the drought of 1860 and the Civil War. Peter MacVicar, county school superintendent and later a president of Washburn College, complained in 1862 that while Topeka possessed "two excellent select [tuition] schools and a female seminary [Bethany College]," it desperately needed a "Free Graded School" like those in Leavenworth, Lawrence, and Manhattan. The same year county commissioners formed Topeka as school district number 23 though it was not until three years later that the city appropriated money for a schoolhouse which was built on a Harrison street site donated for school purposes back in 1856. The *Congregational Record,* July, 1865, applauded the city's action and declared that it was about time:

After the lapse of a few years of indifference and neglect, during which the children and the cause of education have been hindered and injured, Topeka, the capital of Kansas, is building a public school-house, somewhat in keeping with her position and her wants. We trust that new facilities and improvements . . . will efface some of the effects and disgrace of years of culpable neglect, and that Topeka will speedily remove herself from any nearness to the reported condition of a sister city: "Fifty grog-shops, and not a school-house."

The first session of Topeka's new board of education met in May, 1867, and at an early business meeting contracted for a stone privy, eight by 16 feet, for the Harrison street school at a cost of $167.50. Lacking funds to construct suitable schools, the board resorted to the leasing of rooms in buildings throughout the town. By 1870 the city owned four schoolhouses and rented four others for a grand total of 15 classrooms. Even then it was not enough; classes averaged 44 pupils per teacher.

Classrooms were often dark, unventilated, and poorly heated though one school superintendent complained that in some of his schools sunlight "roasted" children's heads and blinded them to the point of making them "dull scholars." Perhaps, in part, that explained why, in 1870, of the city's 1,850 children, only 1,416 were enrolled with an average attendance a scant 709. To correct these problems, the board completed the $40,000 Lincoln school at Fifth and Madison streets late in 1870. It stood as Topeka's most impressive public edifice, three stories tall with bell tower, seven classrooms, and a large hall or auditorium on the top floor. The *Commonwealth,* December 4, 1870, fully described with drawings and words Topeka's pride. It also calmed parents' worry over one crucial matter:

> The objection is often made by parents that there is too much familiarity between boys and girls in our public schools. No one can object to Lincoln school on that account. The girls and boys have separate play grounds, enter the building by separate doors, and while the boys have ample wardrobes in the corridors for hats and coats, the girls have large dressing rooms connected with each school room where their paraphernalia can be adjusted, in the utmost privacy, before entering or leaving school.

Newspapers thoroughly reported school progress and affairs, especially the periodic school examinations. These tests were publicly held, and reporters unabashedly seized the opportunity to express candid opinions on teaching methods and the teachers themselves. A *Commonwealth* writer in 1869 stated that one instructor was "a failure, she talks too much for one who does not talk too well," and another was "not adapted to make children love her, being rather unpleasant." Such outbursts, naturally, displeased or stung the board and fellow teachers. To that attitude, the *Commonwealth* asserted "that a teacher who fears to have his or her school pictured in the columns of a newspaper is not a teacher to be employed in the schools of this city."

School growth accelerated in the 1880s with an increasing popula-

Clay street school, like most others, separated the boys from the girls on its playground in 1879. (Courtesy Kansas State Historical Society)

Lincoln, Topeka's first large grade school, was built in 1871 at Fifth and Madison streets. (Courtesy Kansas State Historical Society)

Miss Louise Becker instructs her State Street school fifth grade class in penmanship, 1944. (Courtesy Ruth M. Snell)

tion. By 1887 there were 17 schools, six of them exclusively black (Lane, Madison, Washington, Adams, Buchanan and Douglas) with an enrollment of 9,996 and 86 teachers. The system was divided into the primary department with grades one through four, grammar department of grades five through seven, and a high school of four years. Each elementary grade was subdivided, in turn, into an "A" class and a "B" class with the "As" usually the more advanced.

The school year began late in September and ran for 36 weeks. The morning session was held from 9:00 A.M. to 12 o'clock. Class resumed after lunch at 1:30 and closed at 4:30. This included two 15-minute recesses during the day. All children above the age of seven were entitled to attend free, but the high school students paid a $10.00 tuition. A school manual outlined programs for each grade as well as rules of conduct for teacher and pupil. The manual permitted corporal punishment under certain circumstances, and required children "to be properly prepared" with those "not properly clad, or uncleanly in person" sent home. Too, teachers were to "keep out of their schools all sectarian or partisan questions."

Kindergartens and the high school were later establishments of the school system. Late in 1892 the Rev. Charles M. Sheldon and others discussed educational needs for Topeka's poor, especially those living in Tennesseetown, an area north of Sheldon's Central Congregational church. This led to the formation of the Topeka Kindergarten Association which opened its Union Hall on April 3, 1893. It enrolled 200 children for the kindergarten and also provided a free reading room and library for Tennesseetown residents.

Sheldon claimed, in the *Daily Capital*, January 28, 1893, that there were 2,700 boys in Topeka who neither attended church nor Sunday school and were "living in more or less barbarism" with "the prospect of criminal and irreligious careers." By organizing half a dozen or so kindergartens, it would lessen "the number of vagabond children, of 'gangs' of 'tough' boys who have formed their ideas of life from the trashy fiction so easily bought."

Within a year the idea had spread throughout town though the Tennesseetown experiment remained the only free kindergarten. Bethany College and Parkdale residents both operated kindergartens. By 1894 the latter was nearly self-supporting. Its backers proposed "to send a free hack to gather in the little ones from the surrounding districts." Free kindergartens became a part of the public schools in 1908 with the inclusion of Sheldon's and one at Parkdale.

Although a *State Record* reporter in December, 1868, visited a "high school" class in one of the public schools, Miss Lizzie Towne of

Sheldon's Tennesseetown kindergarteners celebrate Washington's birthday in 1899. (Courtesy Mrs. Leland Schenck)

the Harrison street school organized Topeka's first, authenticated high school during the spring of 1870. It had but five students who were taught algebra, geography, botany, and French. The board, however, postponed permanent implementation of the high school until the fall of 1871. Thereafter it shuttled the school from building to building (including Lincoln and the original Washburn College buildings), running out of space in one and fighting damp and cold in another. Finally, in 1887, the system acquired rooms above street level in the Hudson Building, a commercial block in downtown Topeka.

During the same period enrollment grew from Miss Towne's five to over 130 in 1885 and the faculty tripled from one to three. While the Hudson Block initially appeared adequate—the *State Record*, September 10, 1887, declared "the new rooms . . . are the most suitable rooms ever furnished to the high school pupils of this city, being commodious, well lighted, and centrally located"—within five years people were labeling it a fire trap. While one paper retorted that there was "no point in anyone indulging in . . . exaggerations to make votes for a new high school," the city passed a bond issue in 1893 for a high school to be built at Eighth and Harrison.

The new Topeka High that opened in 1894 had everything desired in a modern, functional school: 17 classrooms, library, assembly hall, chemistry and physics laboratories, and two lavatories. However, school population continued to spiral, forcing the board of education to build in 1905 a second structure, for manual or vocational training, across Eighth street for $100,000. Other additions were periodically made, including an administration building in 1927. With the passing years the old north building slowly deteriorated. A fire marshal in 1925 stated it was "one of the biggest fire traps in the city." The auditorium, added in 1915, became so crowded during pep assemblies that an instructor warned in 1928 that "if the stamping keeps up, we may find ourselves in the basement."

For its new school, the board chose a site on the Bethany College grounds, and November 6, 1928, the electorate voted overwhelmingly for a $1,100,000 bond issue to pay the bill. Architect Thomas Williamson copied Thomas Wolsey's and Henry VIII's Hampton Court Palace in design and added a 155 foot bell tower. The school's first class entered in the fall of 1931. The 1894 structure became the home of the Shawnee County Welfare Department and a few transients. On May 18, 1935, a fire swept through the old high school, completely destroying it.

Over the years numerous changes have occurred in the curriculum, administrative practices, and social activities of public schools. For example, Greek and astronomy, long a part of a classical education, are no longer taught. Athletics, too, evolved over the decades. In one of the earliest recorded football matches, in 1893, a Topeka High team defeated a Washburn College squad six to four. The team lost its next game to arch-rival Lawrence, 74 to nothing. Around the turn of the century both football and basketball teams played colleges such as Washburn, Campbell (Holton), Lane (Lecompton), and Haskell. A girls' basketball club, active at this time, defeated a KU girls' team in 1901, 18 to 14.

From 1867 to 1873 the Assumption Roman Catholic church oversaw a preparatory school and seminary. Not until 1911 did the Catholic High School open its doors with 17 students in its first class. Up until then, and even afterwards, many Catholic families sent their children to schools in St. Marys or Leavenworth. The present high school, built

Topeka High School was built on the northwest corner of Eighth and Harrison in 1893. It survived as a school until 1931. (Courtesy Kansas State Historical Society)

as Capitol Catholic in 1939, was augmented by a second high school on the west side in the 1960s, named for Father Francis M. Hayden, its founder.

Highland Park High School grew out of county school district number 35, southeast of Topeka. High school courses were added in 1909 and conducted at several places until the school board completed a building in 1935 which in 1976 is Highland Park Junior High. Students came from the nearby countryside including Tecumseh township. One of its graduates, Ronald Evans, was the only Topekan to have traveled to the vicinity of the moon. The present high school dates from 1951, and the Highland Park system was taken into Topeka's in 1959. As the city expanded southwestward during the 1950s, the Topeka board added a third high school in 1961 at 21st and Fairlawn streets.

Of the major divisions, the junior high came last when, in 1914, the seventh, eighth, and ninth grades were departmentalized at Quincy school. A building boom began in the 1920s with Boswell, Curtis, Roosevelt, Holliday, and Crane junior highs constructed. Though three more were built in the 1960s, the junior high system became the victim of a declining birth rate, increased costs and the whims of local educational planners. Along with several grade schools, two were closed in 1975.

Fry Giles in his Topeka history mentioned that a Miss Maybe taught colored children in a small wooden place rented to the city in 1865. The next year, when white pupils moved into the school, the colored children were pushed up to the attic.

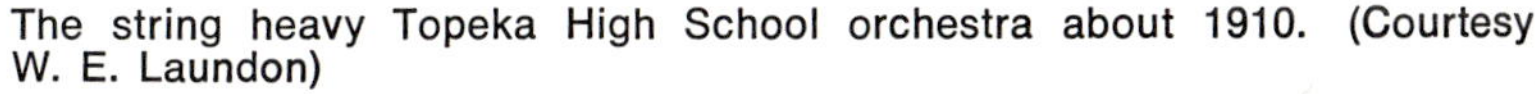

The string heavy Topeka High School orchestra about 1910. (Courtesy W. E. Laundon)

In 1916 the matter of language came into play when the board ordered a special room at the Branner school to be provided for the children, aged six to 14, of incoming Mexican workers. Here classes taught in Spanish introduced the bewildered youngsters to a new way of life. Eventually set up in a separate Branner annex, it was closed in 1942 at the suggestion of Mexican parents.

During the 1870s Negro education remained in flux. Early in January, 1871, six children sought admission to Lincoln school. The board directed the superintendent "to keep the colored schools full in the two churches on the bottom, and to grade into the other schools any colored children living remote from those churches." The problem persisted and the *Commonwealth,* September 12, 1873, reported a rumor "that all the colored children west of Kansas avenue are compelled to attend the school on Clay street, or stay at home." The newspaper then expressed an opinion:

Schools of Topeka are supposed to be free schools; they are not free schools if a class distinction is made and they are not public schools if scholars living within a stone's throw of the Harrison street school building are compelled to have their ideas taught in the Clay street temple of learning.

Other journalists did not concur, the *Daily Blade,* September 20, 1873, felt the Negro community preferred the *status quo* and hinted that agents had "been through the state to stir the negroes up." An observer in the Rossville *Kansas Valley Times,* October 17, 1879, supported segregation in Topeka. It was "a good move; each has their rights, and they should be respected, as they now are, and in most of the wards have been, by separate school houses."

State law allowed the option of segregation for the larger cities, and Topeka followed it in grade and junior high schools. However, Topeka High was never so divided, partly for economic reasons and partly because in the early days few Negroes attended it, there being no requirement or advantage in doing so. According to the *Capital,* September 6, 1942, a Mrs. Harriet Freeman Tarbet was the first black alumna. She graduated in 1882. Likewise, Washburn College was open to all. The *Congregational Record,* October, 1865, claimed: "Although the institution, four years ago, would not have been closed against persons of color, yet the public mind was not so fully prepared for the easy and wide swing of college doors to all classes as it is now." In the high school, whites and blacks rarely met, each possessed separate social and athletic organizations such as the Panthers, the Negro basketball team. The board integrated these school activities in 1949.

The U. S. Supreme Court's 1896 *Plessy vs. Fergusson* decision sanctioned separate but equal school treatment for black children.

Topeka continued as before, but by the late 1930s there were rumblings of discontent. At a June, 1939, board meeting a Negro group requested certain changes in the colored grade schools which went up only to the eighth grade. Their children were "handicapped a great deal when they enter the high school" by having no gym, home economics, or other special classes. In 1941 a youth, Oaland Graham, petitioned to enter a white junior high.

That summer the school board listened to two groups from the Negro community, one desiring changes and the other preferring things the way they were, wishing the "Board to let them alone." A spokesman for the latter, according to board minutes, believed that "colored teachers [all in the colored schools] know the psychology of the colored children better than a white teacher could" and the "time is not ripe yet to make a change" to schools where the majority was white. The board pondered whether to keep things the way they were, create a departmentalized black junior high, or open all junior highs. They chose the third alternative and in the process dismissed several Negro teachers.

The seeds of the Supreme Court decision that ultimately turned American education upside down sprouted in February, 1951, as a suit filed on behalf of several Negroes against the board of education. Local Negro organizations and individuals participated, but outsiders conducted much of the work. On June 25 and 26, 1951, a three man tribunal heard the case in Federal district court. One mother explained how her family lived near Randolph and Gage elementary schools (both white) yet her daughter traveled 24 blocks to Buchanan school (colored) on crowded buses, not to mention the long bus waits on cold winter mornings.

The court ruled the Topeka schools were not unconstitutional. The judges, according to the *State Journal,* August 8, 1951, acknowledged that segregation had "a detrimental effect upon the colored children" but said that facilities and programs at the four Negro schools were equal to the white. The school board, also, provided free bus service, an option not given white children.

Of course, the issue went to a higher court as did similar cases in Delaware, the District of Columbia, Virginia, and South Carolina. The Kansas case achieved prominence partly because it was from a non-southern state but more significantly, and unlike Clarendon county, South Carolina, because the Topeka schools were separate *and,* as nearly possible, equal. After some reluctance, late in 1952, both the school board and the State of Kansas became active defendants, largely on the question of state sovereignty.

Originally the plaintiffs in the Topeka case numbered 13, the best remembered being one Oliver Brown. Actually Brown entered the affair after most of the others; however, as the plaintiffs' names were alphabetized in the documents, Brown came first. Hence, Brown *et al,* . . . *versus* the Board of Education of Topeka.

Many educators felt that in a short time, if let alone, the Topeka schools would have integrated peacefully with only a few ripples in the white and Negro communities. Yet, ten years after the decision, the school board wrestled with the problem of whether or not to assign black teachers to white schools. Racial separateness, of course, continued, especially in the high schools, and disturbances occurred in the late 1960s in the form of fights and arson. In 1973 Topeka schools were accused again of segregation, this time *de facto* segregation. Committees quickly sprang up hoping to find some solution rather than busing but usually coming to no other conclusion. The school board, for instance, hired an outside educationalist, told him in effect to discover any answer but busing, but found his solution for all practical purposes was just that.

Topeka's school leadership, concerned about possible loss of federal money, pondered what to do. Initially the board announced the closure of several central and eastside schools, a decision which aroused the anger of people in those sections of town. Early in 1975 the school system established an outline phasing out grade and two junior high schools, busing some of the affected students to other schools, and creating special class or school programs, in large measure to meet federal requirements. No one was happy but no one knew what else to do.

Very early in 1976 the school administration presented an even more comprehensive school closing plan with the eventual elimination of 14 elementary and junior high schools in the Topeka system. Enrollment in 1975-76 stood at 19,500 and officials projected it to be only 15,000 by 1980-81. Thus the school closings could be justified from both an economic view point and one of face saving for local and federal officials. Naturally, the proposed closings disturbed many parents and emphasized that future educational changes in the community would be coming. Some of the changes would be quite painful to all concerned, but, then, a 20th century Topeka board of education faced problems unimaginable to the predecessor of 1867 which settled the educational needs of North Topeka with a $1,350 frame schoolhouse.

J. Butler Chapman in his *History of Kansas and Emigrant's Guide* of 1855 proposed a Manual Labor College for his embryo community

of Whitfield City. He stressed a vocational rather than classical education and declared "neither race or sex will be debarred from its
advantages." Chapman hoped that the nearby Indian nations would
use his institution. Unfortunately the dream of a college never
materialized.

A college was thought to be, in the 1850s, an excellent lure to
migrants heading west—a sign of a town's prosperity, stability, and
permanence. Therefore, in 1857, the territorial legislature incorporated
Buchanan University at Tecumseh. Obviously named for the president, its charter implied that the university would have schools or
departments in law, theology, and medicine as well as a liberal arts
college. Like numerous such schemes, however, nothing came to pass,
no buildings, books, or professors.

The same year the Episcopal church expressed an interest in establishing a girl's seminary in the territory. Tecumseh and Topeka
Episcopalians urged their parish minister, the Rev. Charles M. Callaway, to locate the school in one of those communities. Callaway, from
slave-owning Maryland, weighed the advantages of the two towns—and
their donation pledges—in his mind, and evidently decided in pro-
South Tecumseh's favor.

A report given at the church's August, 1859, convention implied
the land had been secured, a building begun, and three-fourths of the
necessary funds pledged. All would be ready, the paper stated, for a
September, 1860, opening. John Reed, a southern sympathizer, had
given the Episcopalians ten acres south of Tecumseh which townsfolk
called "College Hill." The Rev. Cyrus Rice, who referred to the
seminary as Tecumseh's "biggest enterprise," later remembered that
construction on the school building had gotten up to the first floor
window sills when the church changed the site to Topeka. Hope for
a Tecumseh college revived briefly in 1862 when a legislator proposed
it as an alternative location for the state university but, by then,
Tecumseh had entered its twilight years and the state quickly passed
over it.

By 1860 it had been settled that Topeka would be the home of the
Episcopal seminary. It was a natural choice since it was the county
seat and a possible location for the future state capitol. Too, determined Topekans offered the church a desirable 20 acre tract, later
known as Bethany Square, and 30 town lots. The school's incorporation was the last act of the territorial legislature. The new board
included, among others, Cyrus K. Holliday of Topeka and Rush
Elmore from Tecumseh.

The school opened its doors to 34 students in a wing of the parsonage at Ninth and Topeka in the fall of 1861. As these young girls,

John G. Haskell's 1859 design for the Tecumseh Episcopal Seminary was never constructed. Later the site was changed to Topeka and the school became Bethany College. (Courtesy Episcopal Diocese of Kansas)

Bethany College girls dance in a 1920s May fete. (Courtesy E. V. King)

Wolfe Hall at the College of the Sisters of Bethany was designed by Haskell and built near Ninth and Polk streets in 1871. It was razed in 1959. (Courtesy Episcopal Diocese of Kansas)

mostly from Topeka or Tecumseh, were unprepared for college, the first years of the school's existence were devoted to preparatory work. The Civil War, naturally, interfered with progress and funds from the East and the seminary temporarily closed from March, 1864, to September, 1865. When it reopened, its poverty was evident. "One single piano, which was purchased at a high price for $175," stated the *Commonwealth* in an 1871 history of the school, "represented the music department."

As with similar educational ventures, school promoters tirelessly traveled back East appealing for money. Fortunately, the church possessed a number of wealthy friends in New York and the first bishop of Kansas, the Rt. Rev. Thomas H. Vail, secured $30,000 from John D. Wolfe for a hall on the 20 acre square. Subsequently named for its donor, the enormous H-shaped gothic building contained classrooms, chapel, an art studio, gymnasium, kitchen, room for 50 boarders, and two bathrooms. Such a facility attracted a goodly patronage; Topeka's local aristocracy proudly sent their daughters there, as did the social classes below them.

Following the economic down turn of the early 1870s, the seminary entered its most prosperous decade and a half. In 1870 the charter was changed and the school renamed, this time becoming the College of the Sisters of Bethany, or simply Bethany College. Topeka newspapers extensively reported school work, especially commencement and the public examinations. For a time at least, in the news column the institution overshadowed the other college in town. A number of buildings were added to the college plant. A laundry and stable were built in 1874-75 (the only surviving Bethany building in 1976). Primary school was held in Holmes Hall in 1881. Enrollment strengthened with over 300 students in 1883. For the first time, during the early 1880s, the college operated in the black. Then came disaster.

Bethany College art studio. (Courtesy Episcopal Diocese of Kansas)

The depression which faintly began in 1888-89 and grew in proportion for the next few years crippled Bethany. Over the decades Bishops Thomas, Millspaugh, and Wise tried to liquidate debts while preserving the school's integrity. According to Blanche Mercer Taylor in her history of the Kansas diocese, *Plenteous Harvest,* in 1892 there were 35 students in primary, 84 in preparation, and 38 in collegiate school work for a total of 228. Improvements continued despite economic woes. In 1897 eight women received college diplomas for an education equivalent to that of a modern junior college. In 1907 Bethany opened a Little Girls School for children from ages seven through 12. A girl could enter Bethany for kindergarten either as a boarding or day school pupil and leave with a diploma which admitted her to junior course work at the University of Kansas.

According to a brochure dating from around the turn of the century the annual cost for boarding a girl, including tuition, lights, fuel, "home care," and washing, was $250 to $300. The prices varied according to the rooms.

Regular tuition for a 12-week session, there being three sessions a year, ran $10 to $15 excluding added expenses in music and art. Guitar, zither, banjo and mandolin lessons, for instance, were given at $18.

Bishop Wise optimistically hoped in 1917 that Bethany could become "the Wellesley or the Smith College of the West." Certainly, the school had earned a good reputation, particularly in the music and art departments. Local artist George M. Stone taught drawing and painting there. The bishop presented the idea of making it a full, four year college, possibly by dropping some of the lower grades. An education committee recommended against this proposal and substituted a plan for making Bethany a school of the sixth through 12th grades.

Economic burdens which had built up for a long time forced Bethany's closing after the 1927-28 school year. In its final year there were only three college students and 24 in the high school, the largest department being the kindergarten, the only one which admitted boys. In August, 1928, the *Capital* announced a school would be opened in the fall, not under auspices of the diocese but in the Bethany buildings. It was planned as a coeducational venture from kindergarten to first year high school. As this idea collapsed, Bishop Wise stated for the *Capital,* September 9, 1928, that Bethany would remain closed. However, perhaps in conjunction with the diocese's nursing school at Christ's Hospital, "plans for a larger and more modern school" were considered for the grounds of the hospital.

It was not to be. The Topeka school board took over all but the north-east corner of Bethany Square for its new high school. The college buildings were either removed or torn down although Wolfe Hall served various church functions until it, too, met the wrecking ball in 1959. Like a lesser known Episcopal enterprise in Topeka, the Kansas Theological Seminary,* Bethany College faded from view.

As early as the spring of 1856, so tradition relates, Topeka pioneer John Ritchie dreamed of a college for his newly adopted town. He even selected, in his mind, a site for it on the open prairie about a mile and a half southwest of town. The Congregational church, too, with its strong New England and Kansas ties, desired an educational institution in the West. At a Topeka meeting, April 25, 1857, Congregationalists moved to form a Kansas college and secure its location. Lewis Bodwell later remembered that this action was taken "in a small hired room [by] seven ministers and three laymen, representing eight churches, and a reported constituency of eighty-five members."

Topeka interests, naturally, seized the opportunity, promising the church the 160 acres Ritchie proposed along with a two story stone or brick school structure to be completed by January 1, 1860. Topeka could not fulfill this obligation and in 1859 Lawrence, Burlingame and Wabaunsee all submitted college proposals. The church picked Lawrence calling the new project Monumental College. Monumental it may have been but despite assurances this second scheme also failed and the proposed college site was returned to Topeka in the summer of 1860.

War infringed on the college plans, but its fortunes revived late in 1864. The school was incorporated on February 9, 1865, as Lincoln College. The origin of the title is obvious. Supposedly one of the college trustees, Samuel D. Bowker, spoke to the President about the school and Lincoln nodded his approval.

Initial work was not easy, and though Ritchie obtained the future college site, its distance from town hindered immediate location there. Beginning in the spring of 1865 the school authorities erected a seven-room "preparatory building" on the northeast corner of Tenth and Jackson streets. The *Congregational Record* June, 1865, wrote that this school hall,

fifty-four by thirty-two feet, two stories high, at a cost of $8,000, including site and seats, is now being erected, and according to the stipulations of the contract, to be finished by the first of October next.

*Founded in 1873, the Seminary fulfilled, in the early days at least, the need of the church for new ministers in the West. The school occupied the old Bethany building at Ninth and Topeka. Early students received their non-theological college education at Washburn College, just a couple of blocks away. Reese P. Kendall, ordained in 1876, was the first graduate but enrollment was never large. In 1911 there were 26 men in the seminary. Only five years later the diocese closed it, the Kansas Theological Seminary having "served its purpose and added many a valuable man to the ministry."

It is located on a beautiful spot facing the Capitol grounds, with a view of selling it to the city for a public school edifice, whenever the time shall come to erect the regular college building on the permanent site. Including the preparatory building and the permanent site, the citizens of Topeka will have given the sum of $10,000. . . .

Harvey D. Rice, a prominent Washburn trustee, later reminisced about his role in construction of the building:

I went to work early in the spring of 1865 while United States soldiers were stationed at Topeka, some of whom, from the State of Maine and Massachusetts, I employed to dig trenches for a foundation of the building. The building was to be of stone, with inside work and roof of shingles to be of pine I hauled with my own team the pine lumber from Atchinson [*sic*] and Leavenworth. In the fall the Kansas Pacific railroad was completed to Lawrence and I got the finishing lumber there. I did my hauling with one three yoke ox team and two two-horse teams. . . . The stone for the building were all drawn by my ox team. Native lumber was sawed on the Wakarusa, twelve miles south. With the aid of my two oldest boys and one man in addition to the hauling of material, I raised that year, four thousand bushels of corn. The building was completed on time to the satisfaction of the trustees, to whom it was delivered by me with all bills paid and receipted for.

Trustees originally intended for a November, 1865, opening but postponed it to January 3, 1866. For its enrollment of 22 young men and 16 young ladies, primarily from Topeka and Tecumseh, Lincoln College consisted of a preparatory school subdivided into English and classical departments. The college courses were delayed until the first 38 students had sufficiently prepared themselves for matriculation. For some time to come the preparatory school proved more important than the college. Yet, a circular of 1865 boasted that the collegiate courses would be similar to those "taught in the first colleges of the East, such as Harvard and Yale."

No matter what eastern school Lincoln College patterned its classes after, the curriculum of the late 1860s certainly seemed full. It included 1) Freshman year (in three terms): Greek, Latin, Mathematics, History, and Elocution. 2) Sophomore year: Greek, Latin, Mathematics, and Rhetoric. 3) Junior year: Latin, Greek, any two of French, Italian, German, and Hebrew, Rhetoric, Natural Philosophy, Calculus, and Science (Chemistry, Astronomy, and Botany). 4) Senior year: Rhetoric, Philosophy, Science (Geology), Political economy, Law of Nations, History of Civil Liberty, Old Constitution of the United States, and Theology. However, as Russell K. Hickman states in his history of Lincoln College in the *Kansas Historical Quarterly*, "the listing of so extensive a course of study was almost entirely a theoretical matter, particularly in the year 1866-1867 when only two students were actually enrolled in the collegiate department!"

A writer to the *Kansas State Record*, December 25, 1867, described fully to Topekans the operations of their college. Preparatory classes

From 1865 until 1872 this building on the northeast corner of Tenth and Jackson streets in Topeka was the home of Lincoln College (now Washburn University). When Washburn moved to its present site the building was sold and the building became Jackson grade school. (Courtesy Mrs. Eugene Bowers)

were held in the ground floor audience hall with the library of about 2,000 volumes occupying an upstairs room.

But the bell rings for the opening of the daily session. We enter the audience room, and precisely at nine o'clock the door is closed and fastened. One of the Faculty takes charge of the exercises. First comes the reading by each student of versus from some chapter of the Bible, then a hymn is given out. . . . The *praise* having subsided the *prayer* begins, sometimes brief, sometimes longer . . . and now and then devout, penitential or supplicatory. Devotions ended, recitations commence, and delinquents who have waited in the hall have a chance to come in. We follow the Teacher's class to the south room above. The room is warm and pleasant with its flood of sunshine from without, and the heat from the Stewart stove within.*
. . . This term has been devoted to a drill in the principles of English Grammar. No text book is used, the class study by *topics*; free discussion allowed, the *reasons* of things are sought out. By this drill students are taught independence of thought, which enables them to defend their opinions independently of text books.

A daily program that students probably followed consisted of classes from 9:15 to 12:00 with a 15 minute recess and an afternoon session from 1:30 to 4:00, again with a 15 minute recess. Some pupils, though, occasionally deviated from their schedules during the winter term to attend the legislative sessions. Finally, the college, on paper at least, required its charges "to be in their rooms by ten o'clock P.M., unless permitted to be absent by the Faculty."

Money, of course, worried Lincoln College officials as much as bedtime hours. On February 12 and 13, 1866, the school held a fair which sold tickets and auctioned off various donated items like pictures, books, fancy work, etc. According to the *Congregational Record,*

---

*The stove apparently cost the college $47.50.

March, 1866, "an ordinary broom was bid off at auction for two dollars." The college cleared $600 for furnishing the school. Yet, that was no way to raise huge sums, so early Lincoln—Washburn college presidents frequently went east to raise money from the Congregational strongholds of Massachusetts and Connecticut.

In October, 1868, Prof. Horatio Butterfield persuaded Ichabod Washburn of Worcester, Mass., to give $25,000 as an endowment. Washburn had worked up from apprentice blacksmith to iron wire manufacturer, amassing a fortune in the process. His donation touched Lincoln officials who, knowing there were other institutions named for the late president, renamed the college for its benefactor in May, 1869.

Lincoln college trustees acknowledged the Tenth and Jackson school building to be temporary but at the same time felt Ritchie's 160 acre tract still too far out of town. Several other sites were briefly considered but by 1871 Washburn college settled upon John Ritchie's land, or rather, the northeast corner of it.

The process of moving to the new campus was a slow one. Construction on Main Hall, out on the prairie, began in 1871 but, though it was enclosed late the following year it was not completed until 1874, due to the national economic climate. A plain three story structure with cupola, this general purpose hall stood through one fire

Rice Hall, built in 1872, was Washburn College's first building at the present site. Once partially destroyed by fire it survived only to be demolished by the tornado which struck Topeka in 1966. (Courtesy Kansas State Historical Society)

only to be torn down after the 1966 tornado. Best known as Rice Hall but called Science Hall during the struggling 1870s, it housed male boarders on the top floor and women boarders on the ground floor with classrooms and faculty residents in between.

The late '70s and '80s proved to be an era of considerable growth on campus. Late in the 1870s several frame dormitories were built for both men and women. In the next decade more permanent and impressive structures were added to the scene.

During this same period the college president, Peter MacVicar, frequently took leaves of absence, traveling east to raise money. Usually school patrons, like Miss Mary W. Holbrook of Holbrook, Mass., required a matching sum for their donation. She gave $5,000 provided the school raised a second $5,000 for Holbrook Hall, a girls dormitory (later an administration building and home of various departments). Other school buildings from this period included Boswell Hall (1886), named for its donor Charles W. Boswell, of West Hartford, Conn.; the library and MacVicar Chapel (1889).

School officials for the remainder of the century and afterwards strictly governed activities and student life. They frowned upon the faculty and students playing cards or dancing. According to a college history in the September, 1967, alumni magazine, a student newspaper editor once declared that "a cold and heartless faculty still continue to sit upon us. . . . I believe it is because sated with youthful enjoyments themselves or disappointed, they have grown old and crabbed and take delight in clogging the young blood of the youth around them." Supposedly one rule dictated that young men could escort young ladies from one end of the campus to the dorm—provided they not stop along the way. Since new Boswell library had a circular walk-way surrounding it couples strolled around and around and around the walk before heading home.

Some persons, on the other hand, thought the faculty not strict enough. A Topeka Presbyterian minister, on February 9, 1902, denounced from the pulpit Washburn's teaching Darwinism or the theory of evolution. This he believed wrong for a denominational school, and, according to the following Tuesday's *Capital,* the minister quoted from a Congregational clergyman whose son attended the college. " 'But already the teaching which he is receiving in that school,' " stated the Congregationalist, " 'is weaning him away from the faith of his father, and I fear for what may happen.' "

With the new century came Washburn's greatest expansion. Though still possessing a small enrollment, three important buildings were added in the first decade including the $40,000 Carnegie library.

Dedicated in July, 1905, this was one of the first gifts for a college library made by philanthropist Andrew Carnegie. Besides improving the physical plant, Washburn added a school of law and a school of medicine in 1903. The latter incorporated the old Kansas Medical College (founded in 1890) which in turn, more or less, developed out of the private Topeka physician "colleges" of the early 1870s. The medical college organized in 1889, opened in 1890 with 28 students, and graduated ten doctors of medicine in 1892. Economic problems, however, forced that institution to close in 1913. Many years before the Kansas Medical College, located at 12th and Taylor, had been thrust into Topeka notoriety.

In the second week of December, 1895, a North Topeka resident named Van Sleet suddenly awoke to the premonition that the grave of his recently deceased wife had been robbed. About the same time the Rochester Cemetery sexton noticed a disturbance around Mrs. Van Sleet's grave. He notified the husband and then opened the grave to discover only the woman's clothes. Van Sleet informed the county attorney and police, suspecting that medical students had removed the body for anatomical purposes. The police searched the college dissecting rooms, where, along with several other bodies, they found Mrs. Van Sleet.

Naturally, the story made huge headlines in the morning *Capital,* December 10, 1895. The article disturbed a second North Topekan who had, a couple of weeks before, buried his wife at Rochester Cemetery. Investigating, he, too, found the grave robbed and discovered the body at the medical school. Then a third grave robbery was detected, this time from the Catholic cemetery. These discoveries, one after another, led to an outpouring of anger directed at Topeka physicians and medical students. Rumors of mob violence at the college circulated throughout the day of the 11th and that night Gov. Edmund N. Morrill called out a unit of the national guard from Topeka and another from Lawrence to protect the school. In addition 25 city policemen guarded the place both inside and out. Other than a few demonstrations and a strong denouncement from the Ancient Order of United Workmen nothing apparently happened.

Police soon afterwards arrested the ex-city scavenger as the robber and named three students and the college's dean as receivers of the bodies. Grave robbing, of course, was a particularly important problem during the 19th century, as the need for cadavers grew to advance medical knowledge. One Topeka physician explained to the *Capital* that as students needed the bodies for study, they rarely asked questions of the suppliers. This attitude led Father Henry of Assumption church to demand that the college be closed since "we all know one another [in Topeka] . . . there seldom, if ever is a legitimate subject for a dissecting table." Topeka, he believed, should rely on eastern schools for the city's future doctors. In February, 1897, trial was conducted against one student and the scavenger with both found guilty. Because of its emotional impact, the trial had to be held in Alma, Wabaunsee county. The school was not closed.

More and more, though, people were entering the nation's colleges in the 1900s as more and more of the smaller denominational schools were facing budget problems. But as late as October, 1938, the *Daily Capital* could headline a story "Washburn Finances Best in Years, Cheering Reports are made to Trustees." Two years later, though, Washburn trustees told the city they could not guarantee that the school would open the next fall. As they sank deeper in the red, the board thought about various alternatives—merger, dropping junior and senior years, municipalization or even closure. Only one path was actually satisfactory regardless of the advice in the *Journal*, November 15, 1940, from the superintendent of the Independence (Kans.) Junior College: "I am inclined to think that the University [Lawrence] and the 4-year teacher's college [Emporia] are in a position to take care of the upper years of college quite adequately."

Nevertheless, Washburn chose the rather unusual route of municipalization. Supporters canvassed the city so that at the general election of April, 1941, the issue passed easily, 18,825 to 4,481. Nothing dramatic transpired during the transition except a name change. The new

Washburn College girls sing in Holbrook Hall. (Courtesy Washburn University)

Scrimmage of the Washburn eleven about 1920. (Courtesy Washburn University)

Relaxed Washburn students near Fraternity Row in the 1930s. (Courtesy Cecil Peterson)

institution became known as Washburn Municipal University of Topeka (later "municipal" was dropped).

Disaster struck Washburn at 7:21 P.M., June 8, 1966, as a late spring tornado bore down on the campus. In but a few minutes five major buildings were destroyed eliminating over 120,000 square feet of classroom space. It would be impossible to describe the devastation which struck the school. Once one of the handsomest campuses in Kansas, the tornado denuded it of hundreds of trees with only Carnegie, Benton, Mulvane and Whiting of the older buildings surviving. For several years Washburn made do in part with temporary, portable classrooms until new buildings were finished.

Presently (1976) Washburn consists of a liberal arts college, a graduate school of education, a law school, and a business school. Recognized for quality in a number of departments, the university possesses an exceptionally small library of only 140,000 volumes. While a new library and other needed facilities are in the planning stage, Washburn faces serious financial problems in the 1970s. Area legislators have whispered about possible state takeover, greater state aid, or a broader tax base including all of Shawnee county. Such measures provoked some controversy and what with three major state colleges or universities within 55 miles of Topeka, the Washburn Board of Regents may well be forced into crucial structural changes in the not too distant future.

Washburn and Bethany College's positions in the community in the late 1880s did not deter Topeka Methodists from forming a similar institution. The idea evolved from the city's unprecedented economic growth, when civic leaders seriously believed Topeka would reach a population of 40,000 to 75,000—even 100,000—in the following decade. Organized in 1889, the school was to be built on several hundred acres three miles west of the city, now the site of Mt. Hope cemetery. A church newspaper, *Kansas Church Tidings,* August 28, 1890, supported the plan as Topeka "is the only town in Kansas in which a real University can exist." It added that the city was ideal with so many legal bodies around to benefit from a law school and so many physicians from a medical college.

Not everyone, of course, was pleased with the news. The church conference had not endorsed the project and Baker University officials resisted the idea and a suggestion that their school be moved to the capital. Like Lawrence Congregationalists in the 1850s, regional rivalry often overshadowed spiritual matters.

Had Topeka Methodists contemplated or acted five or seven years before, perhaps the project might have come off. At least there would have been a building. As it developed, the enterprise began in the summer of 1890 just as the cold winds of Topeka's bust were blowing. Only a big hole and some foundation walls were completed west of town when the college stalled. The Topeka *Capital,* July 11, 1890, described the work then in progress. The main hall was to have been approximately 80 by 270 feet long and cost around $150,000. Inside would have been 20 lecture rooms, 20 "professors studies," two "society rooms," and an 800 to 1,000 seat chapel. Surrounding the campus was plotted University Place, "protected from the possibility of having poor or unsightly buildings in their neighborhood by provisions in the Contract made with all purchasers of lots within certain limits."

The reversals of the early '90s doomed the Methodist University, but a small spark was still lit. A supporter of the earlier attempt left money in her will to resurrect the university plan. Topeka Methodists again discussed the idea with some but not enough enthusiasm in February, 1903. They emphasized law, medical, dental, and technical schools, yet nothing was accomplished.

The only important 20th century institution other than the better known "colored institute" was the short lived Topeka Dental College of 1909-1911. It shared facilities and rooms with the Kansas Medical College or Washburn Medical department at 521 Quincy. The first class had only four members, three men and one woman, but the number of students never grew. When it became apparent that the medical college, as constituted, could not survive in Topeka, the dental college transferred its six students to Kansas City's Western Dental College and then folded.

In 1875 the Catholics organized the College of the Sisters of Charity but its history remains obscure. Lutherans announced, through the *Capital,* May 18, 1887, the possibility of a third religious college in town. They were looking for an institution west of the Mississippi, investigating Beloit and Atchison as well as Topeka. The church threw in one hitch: Topekans had to give 40 acres adjacent to the circle railroad and $100,000 for buildings. These things evidently no one provided.

Because of the earlier influx of poorly educated Negroes a special kindergarten for Negroes was begun in the spring of 1895 by Edward Stephaus and Miss Izie Reddick on Washington street. In 1896 it moved to a building on lower Kansas avenue and then in the fall of 1898, purchased its first permanent home "a dilapidated two-story brick and stone building situated on two and one-half lots on Kansas Avenue between Seventeenth and Eighteenth Streets." With growth and public recognition on the part of Topekans over the next five years (not to mention sizeable grants from the state legislature), officials decided to buy a farm of 105 acres one and a half miles east of Topeka in 1903.

On the farm there were erected eight buildings. The largest was the two-story stone Bradford Miller Hall. It contained classrooms, the music department, library, and a spacious auditorium. In addition the campus was composed of two smaller trade buildings, two dormitories, a hospital, gymnasium and a barn. Twice the school changed its name and with each came a raising of its quality. Upon reaching high school level it became Kansas Vocational Institute. In 1951 it became a college and was called the Kansas Technical Institute. It graduated its first college level class in 1954 but closed shortly afterwards as a result of the case of Brown, *et al, vs.* the Board of Education of Topeka. According to its catalogue in 1954 its aim was "to train the whole pupil. While the school is primarily an industrial and normal institute, the spiritual and the moral sides of it receive their full share of attention."

An unidentified Topeka schoolroom, probably in the early 1900s. (Courtesy Kansas State Historical Society)

THE PRINTED WORD; NEWSPAPERS

On June 5, 1855, Topeka tinsmith Joseph C. Miller scribbled in his diary:

A Gentleman by the name of Garvey visited our quiet town to day, he was on a prospective tour and seeking a location for himself and family, where he intends starting a free state paper, which shall be devoted to the interests of the territory and its patrons. Mr. Garvey is quite wealthy, and would no doubt be quite an acquisition to Topeka, as he would be influential enough, to induce people to settle here. . . .

Topekans accepted the stranger quickly, for the next day Miller recorded that the town association voted him lots on Kansas avenue, "quite an eligible situation," where he would immediately have his print shop. A fast and persuasive talker, Edward C. K. Garvey of Milwaukee, Wisc., implied to gullible townsfolk that he had a large steam press coming up the Missouri; therefore Garvey also obtained the promise of a town association-built $400 publishing house, 18 by 24 feet and two stories high. Completed late that summer, the building housed for a time Garvey's family, his print shop, the post office, and a hotel (the Garvey House). The yard around it for a while, according to Giles, was "strewn with furniture, beds, bedding, books, carpets, clothing, medicines, boots and shoes, and numerous other commodities, half hidden by the tall grass, and for weeks and weeks they blackened or bleached, and smoked and steamed, under the alternating influences of dews and showers and burning sun."

One story is that Garvey first stopped at Tecumseh but met a cold reception there and forged on to Topeka where people welcomed him. He printed the first issue of the *Kansas Freeman* on July 4, 1855. Only a handful of the weekly *Freeman* issues survive, up to February, 1856. It was not only the first Shawnee county newspaper but during the Topeka constitutional convention in October and November, 1855, it became, briefly, the first daily in Topeka—the *Daily Kansas Freeman*—with emphasis on convention proceedings and territorial difficulties. Soon afterward Garvey left the newspaper world for other enterprises and built a home, Garvey's Retreat, as a popular gathering place in Tecumseh.

For the next several years the primary Topeka newspaper was John Speer's *Kansas Tribune,* first issued on December 10, 1855. Originally a Lawrence publication, it went through a number of changes before expiring in the late 1860s. For about a week in March, 1856, it was published as a daily and later acquired a new name, the Topeka *Tribune*. Virtually no issues of it or the subsequent *Kansas State Record* exist for the early 1860s, leaving that part of Topeka history somewhat in the dark. Politically, the *Tribune* stood squarely Republican and pro-Negro suffrage but anti-Jim Lane.

Two brothers, Edmund G. and W. W. Ross, published the third city newspaper, the *Kansas State Record,* beginning in 1859. Both eventually sold their interests in the paper, and Edmund became a United States senator. Like the *Tribune,* the *Record* was Republican and later became a daily before being merged into the *Commonwealth* in 1875. J. F. Cummings and Ward Burlingame founded the Topeka *Weekly Leader* in December, 1865, and operated it until 1869. Although it, too, was Republican, the *Leader,* fought the *Record* over party political questions. In 1869, yet another newspaper, the *Kansas Daily Commonwealth,* emerged as the town's premier journal.

Only three other Shawnee county newspapers, two in Tecumseh and one in Auburn, are known to date from the territorial period. J. Butler Chapman of Whitfield City proposed the *Kansas Intelligencer* in 1855, even advertising it in the Topeka press, but no copies are extant; in all likelihood none were ever published. Supposedly an unidentified individual reprinted the Topeka *Record* as the Auburn *Transcript* in late 1859, but the only known and surviving local paper is the *Docket,* founded in June, 1860. Three issues exist, that of November 20, 1860, being the earliest. Editor D. B. Emmert removed the paper in 1861 to Bourbon county where it became the Ft. Scott *Monitor.*

Tecumseh had two newspapers, the Proslave *Note-Book* and the Free-State *Kansas Settler.* The A. T. Andreas *History of Kansas* refers to a third, the *Southerner,* but no record of it exists. Both papers lasted for only a few months, the *Note-Book* in the fall of 1857 and the *Settler* in the winter and spring of 1858. After April 7, 1858, there is no known copy of a Tecumseh paper.

Incomplete as they are, the two provide a significant insight into territorial life with the advertising, market reports and prices, and even a discussion (from eastern sources) of the upcoming marriage of the Princess Royal, Queen Victoria's eldest daughter, to the future German Emperor Frederick William. The *Note-Book's* editor, Samuel G. Reid, held violent southern sympathies; yet, when he quit, the rival Free-State Topeka newspaper, the *Kansas Tribune,* regretted the decision but suggested the founding of a "less radical pro-slavery" publication. However, Thomas Lord's conservative Free-State *Kansas Settler* shared the same fate of disinterest. By 1860 and '61 declining communities like Tecumseh and Auburn could no longer support a newspaper.

In gaining the state capital, Topeka assured herself of attaining an important publishing status if for no other reason than that politics generated headlines. Besides the newspaper printing offices, which themselves did considerable job work, two important 19th century printing firms were the Hall & O'Donald Lithographing Company and George W. Crane & Company. Hall & O'Donald occupied in 1888 the new Thatcher building which Crane and Company later acquired. Though Crane had a large business in blank books, legal blanks, and later office equipment the company was noted for publishing school texts, a line of classic works, and various books like Mary Jackson's 1890 Topeka history, *Pen and Camera Sketches*. Twentieth century economics and transportation improvements, however, would eliminate "home-grown" publishing in favor of the eastern trade.

Samuel S. Prouty established the *Kansas Daily Commonwealth* on May 1, 1869, and it promptly became the most important of young Topeka's journals. An ardently Republican newspaper, the *Commonwealth* was a morning paper publishing a daily edition, except for Monday, and a separate weekly edition. Weeklies of that time often ran as many as 12 pages per issue, but the dailies normally printed only four. Page one was ordinarily divided between local advertising and patent telegraphic news from the east or Europe. On the second page were editorials, mostly on national events, and various long features like reports on other Kansas towns. The editors devoted most of the next page to an advertising spread usually with a fictional or non-fictional series in one column. Finally, the last page contained short local features and ads, sometimes no longer than a sentence. The *Commonwealth* is a chief source of information for Topeka in its second and third decades; it occasionally offered a few engravings illustrating scenes around town.

Nineteenth century newspapermen often descended to the lowest reporting depths, slinging mud every step of the way. But many who contributed this vindictiveness were often highly responsible citizens. All was fair, however, in love, war, and politics and the political statements of the era were very strong.

One Topeka editor, J. Clarke Swayze, stretched the boundaries of good taste as far as he could. Just before the Civil War Swayze moved to Georgia from New York where he published a newspaper. "Pressed" into the Confederate army he later "deserted to the Federals." Following the war he resumed his Georgia newspaper, which the *Commonwealth* later called "a red-hot, peppery, republican sheet." This, along with support for arch Whig Horace Greeley in 1872, caused him some slight difficulty in the South and he left for Kansas, where he founded weekly and daily editions of the Topeka *Blade* in 1873.

Swayze's *Blade* achieved instant notoriety since the editor unswervingly attacked everything and everyone in town except for those persons who agreed with J. Clarke Swayze. Among his first victims was the Rolling Mills, the operation of which he constantly ridiculed. Any situation could be hit with just the right emphasis, a key word or phrase. In 1875 he sarcastically offered the following: "There are thirty-four divorce cases on the District Court Docket for the December term. Who dares to say that Shawnee County ain't progressive?"

He villified anyone he did not like and this especially included competing newspaper editors and local politicians. In doing so Swayze undoubtedly hit upon some truths. Throughout March of 1877 he abused everyone, the anger building to a climax which he never envisioned, much less desired. In mid-month some citizens writing in the *Commonwealth* proposed that Cyrus K. Holliday run again for mayor, enumerating his virtues. On the 14th, under the headline "The Old King Again," Swayze exploded:

> It is the same slobbery sort of stuff which Holliday always succeeds in having said about himself—oldest citizen, property interests, connection with all the public enterprises, etc., etc. If he did ever do anything for Topeka that did not profit himself more than anybody else, the inhabitant don't recollect it. He is one of those grasping men who seem determined that the balance of creation owe them a support. He is of the [F. P.] Baker [of the *Commonwealth*] order; he will enter into schemes to get the money of people which he and Baker think have not sense enough to spend their own money, and if they can get it no other way they concoct lottery schemes and rob the people at large. . . . The day for tricksters and skin-deep men is past for Topeka. Being here first don't constitute a right to rob the people now.*

Baker, of course, received the brunt of Swayze's harrassment as did one John W. "Bubby" Wilson. Early in 1877 the *Commonwealth* lost its status as the official state newspaper, a fact which Swayze gloated over day after day.

---

*Swayze was by no means the first who chipped away at Holliday's pedestal. A writer on behalf of temperance, signed "Faith," discussed the upcoming city elections in the *Leader*, April 1, 1869: "Mr. Holliday, it is well known, is in favor of licensing whiskey shops (and perhaps others still more dishonorable). . . . As Col. Holliday has, by the *Record's* showing, made so many sacrifices in order that the interests of our city would be advanced, is it not unkind and ungenerous for us to *force* this additional personal sacrifice upon him? Has he not done his share? Is it fair that he should build this city, supply it with railroads, and then be compelled to widen our sidewalks, open our gutters, regulate the houses 'with the green blinds,' etc? But before we go further, we ask, is Holliday the only man that has done anything for Topeka? And in doing what he has done, has it been without the surety that it was putting money in his own pockets? He has worked for the up-building of our city, and why should he not when by so doing it would increase the value of real estate, of which he is a large possessor?" As to the references about Baker, Swayze claimed that while the *Commonwealth* editor was in Denison, Texas, 1872-1875, he committed several illegal operations.

Jason Clarke Swayze (1830-1877). (Courtesy Kansas State Historical Society)

The real argument, however, centered upon "Bubby" Wilson. Along with his father V. P. Wilson, a pioneer Kansas editor, Wilson published in the early 1870s the North Topeka *Times*. Selling it in 1876, the junior Wilson dropped out of the business, occasionally working in a fairly low capacity with the *Commonwealth*. The feud with Swayze dated from the *Times* days and the vindictive prose increased throughout March, 1877. On the tenth Wilson and Swayze got into a bloody fight which caused various Kansas newspapers to take up sides, praising one of the participants and damning the other. Excited by the sport, Swayze perhaps went one step too far. After quoting from another Kansas paper about Wilson being a "fancy women's man," the *Blade* editor flatly labled "Bubby" a "gambler and pimp."

On the evening of the 27th Swayze left his office for the post office, returning by way of a rear alley where Wilson came upon him. Anticipating violence Swayze drew a revolver, but Wilson suddenly sprang behind a companion and fired a shot wounding his opponent. Swayze returned the fire but missed and then the two struggled before Wilson fired a third time. By then the *Blade's* editor was dead or dying and the most violent journalistic confrontation in Topeka history was over. Two days later Swayze was buried, his funeral cortege made up of more than 50 carriages, led by the Topeka Cornet Band. Though the accusations were motive enough Wilson was later acquitted

Though Swayze's assassination ended one strident competition, others soon cropped up, but not so vicious or violent. In 1879 two new but very important combatants entered the arena—George W. Reed's *Kansas State Journal* (actually a continuation of the *Blade*) and Joseph K. Hudson's Topeka *Daily Capital*. The evening *Journal* passed through several ownerships, name changes, and political allegiances (in the early 1880s it was Democratic and Greenback) until it went into receivership in 1885. That same year Emporian Frank P. MacLennan purchased the paper publishing it until his death in 1933. Politically independent and frequently outspoken, MacLennan's venture occasionally found itself in legal difficulties. After his death several individuals, including Henry J. Allen of Wichita and the managing editor, Arthur J. Carruth, Jr., controlled the *Journal* as co-owners.

Maj. J. K. Hudson, a Civil War veteran from Ohio and E. E. Ewing printed the first issue of the *Daily Capital* on April 21, 1879. Hudson had prior experience with his home town abolitionist paper, the Salem *Bugle*. The first *Capital* editorial reflected his background: "In the great [presidential] contest of 1880 . . . we believe the duty of every patriot to be to stand by the principles of the Republican party, maintaining the results of the war, the constitutional amendments, and placing all other issues secondary to these." The editors also welcomed the Negro "Exodusters" from the South and embraced prohibition.

Like the *Commonwealth* and the new *State Journal,* Hudson's daily newspaper contained four pages. It originally began as an evening journal, but soon switched to a morning edition in competition with the *Commonwealth.* Page one consisted of the telegraphic news and ads; page two, editorial comment; page three, state news and advertising; and page four, the local events, church services, train schedules, short ads, and personals. The *Journal* more or less resembled it.

On November 1, 1888, Hudson consolidated the old *Commonwealth* into the *Capital* which, with the former's various acquisitions, gave the new paper a heritage dating back to the *State Record* of 1859. Then the walls fell upon Hudson after he had over-extended himself in the previous decade's real estate boom. The *Capital* was sold in 1899 to a syndicate with businessman Frederick O. Popenoe the principal owner. With stock control and Hudson only the editor, Popenoe embarked upon a great "journalistic experiment."

Three years before, the Rev. Charles M. Sheldon of the Central Congregational Church had written a serial which quickly attained tremendous popularity. Entitled *In His Steps,* the book described the consequences befalling a group of people who practiced their lives "as Jesus would." One of their number in the mythical town of

Raymond was Edward Norman, owner-editor of the *Daily News.* Norman eliminated tobacco, alcohol, and patent medicine ads and crime, sporting, theatrical, and other news of a "questionable nature." Revenue and readers, of course, drastically declined, nearly bankrupting the *News* until a millionaire rescued it. This concept of a "Christian" newspaper Popenoe proposed to an astounded *Capital* staff.

Popenoe discussed with Sheldon the possibility of the minister editing the paper for one week according to the principles espoused in *In His Steps.* Naturally surprised, Sheldon nevertheless agreed providing he had complete control. Popenoe set the dates March 13-17, 1900, for the experiment. For this very special event he brought in a publicist who assured that all in the nation, and the world, would become acquainted with Sheldon's "Christian daily."

During the week, the *Capital's* circulation dramatically shot up from around 11,000 to over 360,000, thus attesting to the public's interest if not its approval. Sheldon's strict standards forbade revenue generating stories and ads like the patent medicine notices, a *Capital* staple. He even scrutinized the most innocent things as, for instance, the normal declaration for J. W. Ripley's Topeka Laundry Co. Usually it read "Strictly High Grade Work," but Sheldon changed it to "Claims to do Strictly High Grade Work." As for the quality of his journalism, Frank MacLennan related to the New York *Herald:*

A careful survey of the first page of the *Capital's* first issue under Sheldon shows an entire absence of important news of the day. Not a line about bubonic plague at San Francisco, the dreadful tenement house fire at Newark, N. J., the wounding of eight American soldiers in the Philippines, and the advance of [General] Roberts on the Orange Free State, the death of the Italian boxer Guydo, who died as the result of a blow struck by James Jeffries in a fistic contest. None of those important news items of the day appear, at least, not on the front page. What a chance for Mr. Sheldon to point a moral by exploiting the death of this poor Italian, from a blow . . . on the part of the pugilistic champion.

Two columns on the first page are devoted to the Kansas prohibition law, covered by interviews from prominent people. . . . These views have been published before, and as news are somewhat stale. To all intents and purposes these two columns could have been clipped from a magazine back numbers from '93 and '94.

Sheldon's Christian *Capital* was profitable and for a time Popenoe considered making the experiment permanent. However, enthusiasm and interest would have soon waned eradicating the source of income; it could not have been made up by advertising revenue. As John Ripley in his history of the venture in the spring, 1965, number of the *Kansas Historical Quarterly* stated, Sheldon completely overlooked one very important role. For the Topeka *Capital* "there was no Virginia Page [the heroine of *In His Steps*] waiting in the wings for her cue to step forward with a half-million dollars to save the paper and, in so doing, provide the happy ending typical of Mr. Sheldon's novels." The following year Popenoe lost control of the paper and one year to the day after the first Sheldon issue it was sold to the man with whom the *Capital* has since been identified, Arthur Capper. At the same time Popenoe left for Costa Rica to develop some gold-mining property.

The turn of the century was a crucial time in Topeka's newspaper history. Some matured, some changed directions, and others failed because of the growing influence of the telephone and the coming of the automobile. Many papers possessed only marginal support as they promoted narrow causes, like socialism in the Shawnee County *Socialist* (1913-1914) or prohibition in the *Smashers Mail* (1901).

It would be impossible to list all of Shawnee county's papers or journals. The Kansas State Historical Society in 1916 counted 40 active ones and ten times that number of discontinued papers. Outside of Topeka proper, North Topeka spawned the most important journnals in the county. The weekly North Topeka *Times* was the first in 1871, but the *Mail* founded in 1882 was probably the most influential. Both emphasized local news from surrounding communities, something the south side dailies often ignored. East side Oakland on the other hand, had only three short-lived newspapers, the *Item* and the *News* in the early 1890s and the *Blade*, 1904-1915.

Rossville, Richland, Silver Lake, and Dover all maintained local newspapers at some time. Rossville had the most, with O. L. Sedgwick's *Kansas Valley Times* in 1879 being the oldest, and its descendant, the *Reporter*, surviving until after World War II. The 1916 *History of Kansas Newspapers* inventoried three in Silver Lake, including the *Mirror* of 1911, but only one for Dover, the *Herald* of 1911 to 1913. For several months in 1903 the Carbondale newspaper published the short-lived Richland *Observer* though the earliest journal in town, 1885-1887, was the monthly *Future*. Not really a newspaper, editor C. C. Blake subtitled it "a calculation of the Coming Weather Through Astronomical Mathematics."

Other minor gazettes apparently sprang up from time to time although the 1890s appear to have been the most active years. Some stories in the *Commonwealth* for the 1870s hint at amateur productions in several of the school districts. A well-to-do farmer might own a small printing press and so, with little else to do in his spare time, composed a journal. The Pleasant Hill Lyceum in Soldier township edited *The Echo* while Pauline published the *Leader*. The *Commonwealth*, October 22, 1873, said the latter was "an independent journal, with an extensive circulation, is ably edited by Mr. Shafer. A few select advertisements can be inserted, at 75 cents per quarter section."

Because Topeka was becoming, in a small way at least, a cosmopolitan center in Kansas, several journals concentrated upon the different communities within the city. There were quite a few German, Swedish, and Negro newspapers, with the Germans printing the *Kansas Staats Anzeiger, Neve Pfads in Fernen Westen, Volksblatt,* etc. Swedish publications from Topeka included *Glada Budskapet, Norden* and *Tempel-klockan.* With a sizeable Negro population, Topeka had a half-dozen or more black journals with William Eagleson's *Colored Citizen* and Nick Chiles' *Plaindealer* the most important.

No publishing enterprise in Topeka compared to that begun in the fall of 1893, with $2,500. Arthur Capper obtained work as a printer on the *Capital* on May 16, 1884. Soon he became a reporter with larger goals in mind—namely, the buying and controlling of his own newspaper. His career prospered, and he married well, taking as his wife the only daughter of former governor Samuel J. Crawford. Opportunity knocked in the form of the North Topeka *Mail* which Capper purchased with his own and borrowed money.

Desire did not fade with acquisition of the *Mail*; the new publisher eagerly sought improvements as well as new horizons. Two years later Thomas A. McNeal inquired about a merger of the Capper's *Mail* and his *Kansas Breeze.* Agreed upon, the *Mail and Breeze* became the largest weekly in Kansas, offering local readers fine photographic layouts and substantial county news. It eventually evolved into a strictly rural or farmer's journal after Capper had acquired the *Daily Capital* in March, 1901. Capper, his wife Florence, and three employees purchased the Capital Publishing Company stock for over $50,000.

Capper's empire greatly expanded during the next two decades, emphasizing the rural scene. By 1919 it included, besides the *Capital, Capper's Farmer, Capper's Weekly, Household, Kansas Farmer* (formerly the *Mail and Breeze*), *Missouri Ruralist, Oklahoma Farmer,* and *Nebraska Farm Journal.* In three years he brought in farm papers from Ohio, Michigan, and Pennsylvania. Outside the agricultural world, Capper acquired in 1921 the Kansas City *Kansan,* partly as a challenge to the dominant *Star* and *Times* of the Missouri city.

On July 31, 1941, the *Capital* and *Journal* merged their advertising, circulation, business and mechanical departments into one corporation, the Topeka Newspaper Printing Company. They continued separate editorial and news sections as well as separate identities until 1956 when Stauffer Publications, which by now owned the *Journal*, acquired Capper's Publications. Capper had died in 1951.

The old, familiar columnists which gave a distinctive brand of journalism are gone. Both the *Journal* and the *Capital* had influential

Garnett, Kansas.

AUNT MARY: have not written to the YOUNG FOLKS for a long while. I have been working in the office of the Garnett Journal, for over two months, I like the printer's trade very well I am getting along slowly, I set up a column to-day. We were very busy printing tickets before election, there were a great variety of tickets. Democratic tickets with Greenback men on them, Greenback tickets with Democrats and republicans, and almost every kind you c uld think of. A young man, a printer by trade, told me when I commenced to learn the trade, that it was the poorest trade there was, and that I could not make a living at it. I do not think it can be the poorest trade. Since I have been at this trade I find that a great many printers chew and smoke. and drink. I have been figuring it up, if a man spent ten cents a day for whiskey, that in ten years, without any interest it would amount to $365.00, and for tobacco, if they spent only twenty cents a week, that would amount to $104.00 in ten years, and both together would make $469.00 enough to buy a good second hand press and type. I am now thirteen years old, and I am going to try to put my savings out at interest, in place of spending them for drinks and tobacco, and by the time I am twenty-one do you think I will have enough to buy a good second hand press, or will it turn out as the young man I mentioned said, that printing was the poorest trade in America? Yours Truly,

ARTHUR CAPPER.

Arthur talks in a business-like manner, and Aunt Mary feels quite safe in predicting that printing will not turn out to be the worst trade in America; no trade would in the hands of a boy who makes such sensible calcu'ations and such good resolutions.

political commentators or analyists like A. L. "Dutch" Schultz for the *Journal* who covered primarily state political affairs until retirement in 1962. Even more colorful was Capper Publications' Clifton S. Stratton, whose columns were symbolized by his profile in a Stetson hat. For 30 years, 1926-1956, he served as the *Capital's* Washington correspondent, always within earshot of his boss, Sen. Arthur Capper. A fiercely conservative Republican, Stratton often flailed Franklin Roosevelt's New Deal.

On a less stringent note, every Saturday except two for 38 years until his death on September 29, 1962, Arthur J. Carruth prepared his *Journal* page "Under the Whispering Willow with AJC." Harking back to an older tradition, which has now disappeared altogether, his subtitle supplied its purpose: "Just a Few Shades and Shadows of Anything and Anybody." Mellow and relaxing, appropriate for the week-end, the column related the little events of life in the community and life in general.

People wrote into the "Willow" and in his last column, Carruth explained the origin of the page and the name "Whispering Willow." As a BOC (Bald Old Chief) he objected to a rather trite social column describing mundane civic and charitable club meetings. Termed the " 'Snap Shot' it didn't represent a snap shot view of city brevities. There was nothing in it of an original nature." Thus, he took it upon himself to come up with something better. Planned for a Friday edition, heavy advertising forced it on to the Saturday afternoon paper where it stayed. As to the name, the willow was his father's favorite tree. Carruth related on December 8, 1962:

One day, a good many years ago, . . . [my father] and I were wandering from our car, out southeast of Topeka, not far from Berryton. He had spied a willow in a field. Its branches were waving in the south wind. The grass beneath it seemed cool and inviting. A contented cow munched nearby. We strolled over the field, probably 300 yards from the road, and sat under this willow, my father and I. For an hour or two we idled in its shadows. When we left we understood each other and our philosophies of life better than at any time in our companionship and devoted relationship.

For the woman's view Ada Montgomery, beginning in the *Capital's* woman's department in 1921, presided "Over The Coffee Cup" but probably the best known feature writer is Zula Bennington Greene, "Peggy of the Flint Hills" or elsewhere "Flint Hills Peggy." She began her career in 1928 as a farm wife. She inquired of the Cottonwood Falls *Chase County Leader* publisher, W. C. Austin, if she could write a story about the local fair. He agreed and on October 4, 1928, the paper printed on page two a column entitled "Around the Fair Grounds —by Peggy." The "Peggy" came directly from Austin's imagination, an unwitting but fortunate choice. The paragraphs were simple and homely like the one mentioning "Peter Panish parents, who secretly enjoy the thrill of riding the merry-go-round, though saving their faces by pretending to be bored at having to take the children, who 'just can't be trusted to ride alone.' "

Austin made her feature a regular part of his newspaper, a column called "Flint Hill Fantasies." Within five years 20 to 25 Kansas papers were carrying it and when her husband moved to Topeka in 1933, "Peggy" joined the staff of the *Capital.* Her first assignments concerned the legislature with the feature appropriately labeled "Domesdays." When the legislature adjourned, her regular editorial page column was re-christened "Peggy of the Flint Hills." If Topekans read anything or anybody in the *Capital,* they read "Peggy." Though active in numerous organizations, including local theater, Peggy Greene will always be remembered for her illustrations of such Kansas scenes as a prairie October: "Children's voices will ring clear against the sound of their feet in the new fall of leaves. Leaf smoke will spiral upward in the still air and the nostalgia will be echoed by the cry of wild geese in the night."

Until the mid-20th century Topeka was also the home of a wide variety of journals or periodicals. Far and away the first "magazine" established in the community was the Philomathic Society's *Prairie Star.* Edited by the ladies of that literary group, number one came out on January 24, 1857. All were hand written. It contained the traditional prose and poetry subjects for such a "publication." The next literary publication, entitled *The Kansas Magazine,* was short-lived (1872-1873), but had a tremendous impact since it showed people of the West could offer something substantial to American fiction.

General mass communication like television helped eliminate journals like Capper Publications' *Household* magazine. This monthly publication began in 1902 as *Push* and presented the traditional woman's features of cooking, sewing, gardening, and home decorating. In one of its last issues, November, 1958, the publishers boasted that *Household* was the "Friend of the family in 2,650,000," homes but then it went the way of many other once popular and flourishing magazines.

While some periodicals reflected a fairly narrow constituency some proposed to cover the entire community. A local photography studio published for six issues in late 1946 the *Topeka Magazine* or *TM*. The editors modeled it as a minor-league *Life Magazine* emphasizing photography. It showed numerous scenes and activities about town, the most humorous section being "Pic-Tour of the Nite Clubs"—in dry Kansas. Nevertheless, with its photo essays, cartoons, and ads *TM* revealed something about post-war Topeka, and it did a little soft muckraking on the side by criticising the hypocricy of the liquor laws and pointing out the housing needs of slum districts. In 1974 a second *Topeka* magazine was founded which offered a greater feature variety— cooking hints, garden information, movie reviews, biographical sketches, social calendar, etc. It, too, prints many photographs with a number in color.

Specialist magazines, only a few of which may be mentioned, abounded in the capital city. The state of Kansas, of course, publishes a variety of magazines, two of the better known being the Economic Department's quarterly *Kansas!* and the Historical Society's *Kansas Historical Quarterly*. The different trades, commercial organizations, and professions all have, or have had, journals suited to their needs. These include the Kansas Medical Society's *Journal* (founded 1901), the Kansas Banker's Association *Kansas Banker* (founded 1911), and the Kansas Power and Light Company's house organ *Service Magazine* (founded 1944). Other journals published in Topeka from time to time were the *Legal News* (founded 1897 for court news), the Episcopal church's *Kansas Churchman* (founded 1876), John MacDonald's *Western School Journal* (founded 1885), the monthly *Illustrated Poultry Gazette* (founded in the 1890s, 20 pages, costing 25 cents a year; editor George Gillies claimed it was "the paper that never prints a dull line"), and the international trade journal *Modern Mexico* (founded 1895).

Charles H. Trapp tendered an off-breed but highly personal kind of journalism in the 1920s and 1930s with his paper the *Pink Rag*. Printed on pink newsprint, Trapp, like J. Clark Swayze before him, attacked those people or things which displeased him. J. R. "Doc" Brinkley, the Milford "goat doctor," was his most famous antagonist. Trapp ran one headline during the gubernatorial campaign which stated: "Brinkley Attacks a Woman." Pink, however, was not the only color favored by some journalists with a less than a serious bent; C. B. Arthur in 1915 used yellow for his *Yellow Dog*. Circulated for only two years and "devoted to fun and philosophy," its publisher stated that the "paper is the official organ of the sublime and the ridiculous." A weekly, this humor magazine cost a penny a copy for its four pages. Advertisers apparently did not care too much for it. There were few notices inside, possibly because of Arthur's further explanation of his creation:

And about the name. Why not the Yellow Dog? The thoroughbred bench show animal never has any fun. He is kept on a silk cushion and fed dainty food till he gets indigestion, is never allowed to get his paws wet. When he goes out of the house he is led by a strap down the middle of the sidewalk. The yellow dog steals a bone, gets a swift kick in the slats, and does as he pleases. And to be free to do as you please is worth many a swiftkick.

Column heads of four of Topeka's most popular columnists, always attractions in the "Journal" or "Capital." Last of the old breed of journalists. (Courtesy Kansas State Historical Society)

Irrigation ditches in the San Luis Valley are dry, nearly all of them, but there have been rains, and no rains were ever more welcomed.

River water—the Rio Grande River—is scarce and the "sub," or water level, is dropping all the time. Artesian wells that used to gush high into the air now have to be pumped and some householders can hardly get

Albert T. Reid (1873-1958). (From "The Blue Book of Topeka," 1910)

Merrell Gage working on his statue of Lincoln for the statehouse grounds. (Courtesy Arthur J. Carruth)

THE BEAUX-ARTS; WRITERS AND ARTISTS

The frontier needed settling and settlers needed to cope with inclement weather situations, assert themselves in numerous disagreements with Indians, and negate the low level of education among the majority of eastern, foreign, and black immigrants before any such niceties as writing might be seriously undertaken. Too much time was taken up plowing, sowing, and harvesting, setting up businesses and founding towns to tolerate all the nuances of a growing culture. County residents had to subjugate all adverse human and natural obstructions of their virgin land before turning to literature or art. Fry W. Giles wrote the historical sketch *Thirty Years in Topeka* in 1884, the first respectable piece of writing to be produced in the county but no writers of note appeared in Topeka until around the turn of the century.

At 1534 College Margaret Hill McCarter made her home, reared three children, and turned out 18 books. Mrs. McCarter was the wife of a relatively successful dentist, and she came to Topeka as a high school English teacher in 1888. She made addresses in 22 states and was the first woman to speak before a national political convention (the smoke-filled Harding convention of 1920). She made a memorable statement about the women of her time when she declared that "any woman might write a book in the time wasted in a year or two in useless visiting or lounging around."

Most of Mrs. McCarter's fiction appeared as historical novels. Frankly romantic, their appeal lay in their exciting and suspenseful narratives, colorful descriptions, and adventurous heroes and heroines. Her first novel was *The Price of the Prairies* published in 1910. About her writing she explained:

The money earned by my pen gave my children college educations. When they were babies, while they were children and growing up, I wrote books. I wrote before they were up in the morning. I would get them off to school and then sit down and write. They would come tumbling in from school at noon and clamor to hear what I had written that forenoon, and I would read to them while they ate. I wrote after they were in bed at night. My husband was my best critic. Nearly all of my books are about Kansas, and I have not begun to stir up the wealth of material for books that lies all about us in the state.

The Price of the Prairies poured from presses constantly for the next two decades. Another hometown artist and author, Margaret Whittemore, wrote: "Before she began the book, there had been growing in

Margaret Hill McCarter (1860-1938)
wrote novels around Kansas history.
(Courtesy Kansas State Historical
Society)

the mind of the author a realization of the great price the pioneers had to pay to win the prairie from the Indians. Then a title suggested itself, after which the story took shape rapidly, almost writing itself." The books Mrs. McCarter wrote over the next several years followed a similar historical pattern of a pioneer scene set with rugged characters endowed with matching morals. Her word-pictures of Kansas landscapes and history are enthusiastic and authentic.

A columnist of wide fame was Jay E. House, a native of Illinois who came to Kansas when he was ten years old. He worked on several Kansas newspapers including the Florence *Bulletin,* the Atchison *Champion* and the Erie *Record* before he was hired by the Topeka *Daily Capital* in 1901 to write a column which he called "On Second Thought." No target was too sacred for him and his revelations often caused considerable consternation among public officials. He served as mayor of Topeka two terms (1915-1919) but turned down the chance for a third term when he moved East to write for the Cyrus H. K. Curtis chain. His work appeared regularly in the Philadelphia *Public Ledger,* the New York *Post* and *Saturday Evening Post.* He died suddenly in Topeka in 1936 while he was home on a visit. When he left Kansas in 1919 the Topeka *State Journal* said that even though he was not a native "he speaks the Kansas language, knows the Kansas folk, breathes the Kansas spirit and has the Kansas damficare attitude toward everyone in general."

Another author of the first decades of the 1900s, Nelson Antrim Crawford, published a widely praised but often over-looked novel, *A Man of Learning* in 1928. This book was a succinct satire on midwestern life. Crawford taught journalism at Kansas State College in Manhattan before finally settling down across 17th street from Washburn University. He led a varied editorial and literary career and for over twenty years he edited *Household* magazine for Capper Publications in Topeka. He edited and published *Author and Journalist,* a magazine for writers, and "from the time he began teaching in 1910 until his death in 1963, Crawford wrote poetry, fiction, and non-fiction." It can also be noted that he was an afficiando of cats and often had his home overrun with the creatures.

The most prolific novelist to come from the county was certainly Rex Stout who died late in 1975. He was born December 1, 1886, in Indiana but when he was a small child his parents moved to Wakarusa. Stout received his early education in a rural county school and in 1903 he graduated from Topeka High School as class poet. After that Stout traveled for a while, and sold a few articles. He soon realized that he could turn out a ninety-thousand-word novel "in half the time for twice the money." For the next few years in Paris he wrote serious novels but his real fame began in 1934 when he created the character Nero Wolfe in a detective story entitled *Fer-de-Lance.* A 1973 article in *Publisher's Weekly* described Stout's writing habits:

> Mr. Stout, who proudly claims that he has more books in print (over 50) than any other living writer, lives in a house that straddles the New York-Connecticut state line near Brewster, N.Y. He writes in the afternoons and evenings ("I'm no damn good in the mornings") and always aims to finish a new book within six weeks of starting it.

Shawnee county may lay some claim on the black poet Langston Hughes who spent a part of his childhood in Topeka. He credits the old Topeka Public Library, located on the northeast corner of the statehouse grounds and razed in 1963, as the place where "books began to happen" to him.

Non-fiction writers from Shawnee county did not become prominent until recently, although Dr. Samuel J. Crumbine of the State Board of Health became nationally famous for fighting and controlling diseases such as typhoid and tuberculosis. Crumbine came to Topeka from Dodge City and made a significant contribution to non-fiction with the publication of his autobiography, *Frontier Doctor.* In it he vividly portrays the progress on the Kansas medical frontier. Another nationally-known and respected doctor, Karl Menninger, has dealt with psychiatry in language understood by lay readers in such works as *Love Against Hate* and *Man Against Himself.*

In the realm of historical writing William E. Connelley, who came to Kansas from Kentucky in 1881, produced nine books beginning in 1899. He had been ruined in the banking business and turned to writing histories. In 1914 he became Secretary of the State Historical Society and held that office until his death in 1930. Edgar Langsdorf describes his most noteworthy achievements:

During his years as secretary he continued his research and writing, publishing a five volume *Standard History of Kansas and Kansans* in 1918 and in 1928 a five volume *History of Kansas, State and People,* both "vanity" histories consisting of two volumes of history and three of biographies chiefly of subscribers to the sets.

Nationally-known in the non-fiction field today is John Ripley, editor of and a principal contributor to the Shawnee County Historical Society *Bulletin.* He lived in Potwin during his childhood, and was on the desk of *Business Week* for several years as photo editor. Ripley's main interest is in lantern slides and he has had articles published in several national magazines.

Author and artist Margaret Whittemore was Topeka born and bred. She received her higher education at Washburn College and lived at 1615 College avenue when she did much of her writing and art work. Zoe Myers Siler wrote this description of the artist's work and work shop for the Woman's Kansas Day Club in 1964:

Miss Whittemore outfitted the attic of her home in Topeka as a studio and there she specialized in print making, silk screen prints, lithographs and block prints. She made her drawings in pencil and pen and ink. She had a press in the basement to make imprints on stationery. Christmas cards and any other similar work that presented itself.

The general character of Whittemore's writing took the shape of feature stories and news correspondence. She also did much illustrating for other authors as well as co-authoring several works. But she is probably best known for the sketches incorporated in her three major books, *Sketchbook of Kansas Landmarks, Historic Kansas,* and *One-Way Ticket to Kansas.*

Like Whittemore in the 20th century, early travelers and settlers sketched and painted the great plains. Henry Worrall of Topeka, who began work as an illustrator in the 1860s, was the first artist from Kansas to become nationally recognized. He was known for his contributions to the popular news publications of the day, especially the two foremost magazines, *Harper's Weekly* and *Frank Leslie's Illustrated Newspaper.* Worrall's best drawings have been described as "journalism in print" but he also made use of oils in portraiture and landscapes.

John W. Ripley, Kansas Historian. (Courtesy Kansas State Historical Society)

George M. Stone in his studio. The portrait is that of the Rt. Rev. Elisha Smith Thomas, Second Episcopal Bishop of Kansas, 1889-1895. (From the Topeka "Mail & Breeze," May 22, 1896)

A contemporary of Worrall's, Samuel J. Reader of Indianola, used pigment ground in gum and applied with brush and water to produce some of the best Kansas art about the Civil War. But Reader, who came to Kansas as a territorial pioneer, painted many subjects and drew even more. Most of his work is definitely primitive, but his action scenes of the Battle of the Blue, now held by the Kansas State Historical Society, are the equal of any paintings of battles of the Civil War. One historian has stated that Kansas is in debt to Reader for information on "much of what went on during the territorial period and the Civil War in the West as illustrated only by his unsophisticated art."

The Kansas City *Star* editorialized in 1933: "It is fortunate for Kansas that she had all through the years of her youth a painter who loved her and perhaps idealized her. . . . [George] Stone understood the Kansas of his time." Stone studied in Paris and traveled widely in Europe, but most of his life was spent in Topeka. Here, in company with Albert T. Reid, another celebrated Kansas artist, he opened a school which eventually became Washburn University's art department. A Topeka historian writes:

Stone was the State's foremost portrait painter of governors, judges, businessmen, and their wives. He also earned the title "The Millet of the Prairies," because he represented western farmers in a similar fashion to Millet's French peasants. Stone painted murals, two of which are in the governor's office—*The Pioneers* and *The Spirit of Kansas*.

A student of George Stone as a young girl, Mary Huntoon graduated from Washburn with a degree in art then married a Topeka journalist, Charles B. Hoyt. The Hoyts moved first to New York and then Paris where Miss Huntoon hob-nobbed with the Hemingways and the Steins. She returned to Kansas in the middle of the depression after her husband died. She taught art at Washburn before working as regional director of the Federal Art Project under the New Deal.

A few years ago a nationally prominent psychiatrist said that Mary Huntoon McEntarfer (though married a second time she painted under the family name of Huntoon) "sacrificed a promising art career for art therapy for the mentally ill." After remarrying, she became associated with the Menninger Clinic and became Kansas's first registered art therapist. Dr. Karl Menninger hired her to work at Winter General Hospital previous to its takeover by the Veterans Administration in 1946. Said Menninger: "Mary Huntoon McEntarfer has practised what I've preached for many years. In other words the submission of aggression." Miss Huntoon and her husband moved nine miles north of Topeka to 80 acres of rocky ground after the June, 1966, tornado, and there she lived until her death.

The most controversial piece of painting in Shawnee county was done by a famous artist from neighboring Jefferson county. During the first half of the 20th century John Steuart Curry was a leader of a group of "homespun regionalists" who were most profound after the depression. He was commissioned in 1937 to paint numerous murals in the state capitol. The controversy was based mainly on the amount of artistic freedom to be allowed Curry, but it devolved into ambivalent comments concerning the shade of color of Curry's Hereford bull and the curliness of his pigs' tails. Much of the criticism centered around the artist's depiction of John Brown as an irrational fanatic in a meaningless situation. The climate of opinion, however, rested in the fact that Curry presented the bad side of Kansas history as well as the good. Although the murals were never completely finished nor signed, Curry wrote "I sincerely believe that in these fragments, particular in the panel of John Brown, I have accomplished the greatest painting I have yet done, and they will stand as historic monuments." In an editorial on the death of Curry published August 30, 1946, the Topeka *Daily Capital* expressed its regrets about the murals: "It is too bad the planned series had to be left unfinished and that Curry chose not to sign the panels he did complete. This was his protest against executive council stubborness in denying him the setting he needed. . . ."

Calder M. Picket wrote that "the murals today attract both Kansans and out-of-state visitors, who have heard of the murals and have seen reproductions of the famous painting of John Brown."

Sculpture may be broadly defined as the art of representing observed or imagined objects in solid material and in three dimensions. Robert Merrell Gage, born in Topeka in 1892, is best known for his work in one of the oldest and most widespread of the arts and one of the most difficult, for it requires physical labor, patience and complete control of the materials involved for long periods of time. Gage was educated in Topeka public schools and at Topeka High School. He attended numerous art schools but was most influenced by Gutzon Borglum, famous for his sculpture at Mount Rushmore. After a stay in Paris, he set up his studio in a barn behind his home at 1031 Fillmore street. In 1916-17 he taught at Washburn as instructor of sculpture.

Gage's first public commission is probably his most popular, the seated bronze statue of Lincoln named "the Man of Sorrows." This sculpture was financed by women's clubs, schools, and an appropriation of the Kansas legislature, and is situated near the southeast corner of the statehouse. A short book entitled *Heroic Statues in Bronze of Lincoln,* favorably mentions Gage's work and states: "Agitation was begun early in 1916 and the unveiling took place on Lincoln's birthday, February 12, 1918." This familiar statue seems to have been heavily influenced by a similar Borglum bronze in Newark, N. J., dedicated in 1911. Each has the president seated and each portrays Lincoln as a younger man weighed with worry. Other local pieces done by Gage include the "Pioneer Mother," also on the statehouse grounds, and the "Phil Billard Memorial" in the State Historical Society building. He has also sculpted figures for other state buildings principally in California.

Bradbury Thompson, graphic artist internationally known for his postage stamp, advertisement and book designs, was raised and educated in Topeka. He served as art editor of both the Topeka High *Sunflower* and the Washburn *Kaw* before joining the staff of Capper Publications' art department. For 14 years he was art director of *Mademoiselle* and is the recipient of numerous awards for his outstanding designs. Though he lives in Connecticut, he maintains close ties with Shawnee county and has assisted in the design of several issues of the Shawnee County Historical Society *Bulletin.*

Shawnee county has been well represented in these arts, producing nationally prominent and prolific if not earth-shaking writers and artists. During the 19th century such luxury as expressing these talents was relegated only to the well-to-do who had the spare time to create such work—Kansas pioneers were much too busy carving a homestead out of a wilderness to carve a figure out of stone. However, by the turn of the century art had become a business and the plentiful supply of Shawnee countians making their living by utilizing their talents gives witness to the creativity as well as the practicality of local citizenry.

The Thatcher building, on Eighth between Quincy and Kansas.

The Crawford building, Fifth and Jackson.

Four examples of Topeka's boom of 1888. (From "The Saturday Evening Lance, December 22, 1888, and June 15, 1889)

The Central National Bank building, Seventh and Kansas.

The Knox building, on Sixth between Jackson and Kansas.

RISE OF THE CITY; TOPEKA'S METAMORPHOSIS

Fry Giles in his *Thirty Years in Topeka* wrote:

Most of the settlers [in early 1855] had families at the East whom they were anxious to bring out in the spring, and the all-absorbing question with most of them was, What shall we do for building material? As it became apparent that the sawmill could afford no relief . . . many resorted to the use of rude frames made of hewn poles and weather-boarding rived from oak trees, in Western parlance known as "shakes." In these rude and comfortless shanties many families were under the necessity of living for years, who had been accustomed in their Eastern homes to the highest comforts of civilization.

Some of the more fortunate pioneers built log houses for their comfort but these, too, proved confining. Cyrus Holliday described one to his wife in a letter dated January 7, 1855:

Suffice it to say that today I *am* in the principal house and *hotel* in Topeka. It is 12 x 14 ft.—of logs chincked with turf or sod and roofed with sod. I have known *twenty-four* persons to *sleep* in this house at one time.

I am now writing this sitting on a trunk and writing upon the end board of a wagon which I am holding in my lap. We have no windows. Our door is of 6¼ ct. cotton cloth. Our house is full of boxes, trunks—logs of wood, tools of different trades—men, guns, and the floor is strewn with chips, shavings, stones, earth, coals, ashes and prairie grass—a handful of the latter in one corner together with two buffalo robes and two blankets serves as the bed of a Mr. Giles a fine gentleman from Chicago—and myself Each evening we turn into our humble couch with as much good feeling and peace of mind and conscience, and sleep as soundly and dream as pleasant dreams, as though we were resting our limbs on beds of down in marble halls; and beside our wives as Mr. Giles has just been cruel enough to suggest. We have both agreed to take back that last sentence.

Others, though, were not as fortunate as Holliday and Giles in having a solid roof over their heads. According to the first Topeka history, written in long hand in the 1857 literary paper, *Prairie Star,* by February of 1855 there were only six houses in all of the city: "One log, one board shanty, two a conglomeration of straws, brush, boards and turf, and the remaining two were composed of poles covered with sod." Set perilously close to the river bank, builders strung them out in a row beside the Kansas.

Life on the prairie was difficult. The settler's morning usually beginning with a limited breakfast of bacon scraps and hasty pudding (flour or cornmeal mixed into water or milk). Next he fixed up his premises, washed and mended his clothes, and, perhaps, baked some bread. The rest of the day he spent working his claim or preparing for his vocation. On May 4, 1855, Joseph Miller, in town only a month,

Henry Worrall's drawing of the first Topeka house. The side of beef came from a Tecumseh area farm. (Courtesy Kansas State Historical Society)

wrote in his diary: "Fixed me a sort of bench under a shady tree and manufactured a few articles of tin ware." At night the men* relaxed with a standard dinner of bread, pork, and/or corn meal mush. If two or more ate together, conversation usually turned upon the important topics of the day, politics and the young territory's future. Afterwards the men often sang or engaged in some "other innocent amusements," as Holliday dutifully explained to his wife. Excitement sometimes continued after bedtime, when an occasional wolf poked his head in the door looking for meat.

No known illustrations exist which satisfactorily depict territorial Topeka homelife. Topekans built at random on their lots with great gaps between houses or business buildings. The earliest photos do show isolated structures facing empty, dirt-filled streets. The first permanent stone structure in Topeka was begun by the brothers John and Loring Farnsworth in April, 1855. They broke ground part way up the slope from the Kansas river bottoms, on what is now the west side of the 400 block of Kansas avenue. Stone for the building, which was two stories high and 34 by 44 feet came from a nearby ravine with the lime mortar, according to Loring Farnsworth in 1880, "burnt in a lag heap, down on the Shunganunga." Fairly impressive on the bleak landscape, it served as a home, a printing office, meat shop, grocery and even a liquor store at different times. When the Free-State Topeka legislature met there in 1856, it received the name of Constitution Hall. Long afterwards the state legislature and Topeka school classes met there. People still used it during the 1870s for occasional church festivals or dances but soon afterwards, with a new face, Constitution Hall became lost in a row of younger buildings.

A Congregational minister, passing through town in 1859, described the scene for the *Congregational Record* of October, 1859. He offered

<hr>

*The first woman, whom Giles claimed to be Miss Harriet Hartwell, didn't arrive until January 17, 1855.

an analogy and his opinion about this hamlet on the prairies:

> Topeka shows signs both of vigor and decay. It looks like a tree that had stopped growing and sprouted again. While the sprouts are lively and vigorous, the trunk looks dead and moss-covered. Topeka is evidently growing, and has undoubtedly made sure a successful future. At the same time, it looks like a heap of ruins, from which the city is just emerging and rolling the rubbish off.* If you have ever seen ants at work repairing damages after you have kicked their hill over, you have a pretty just idea of my impression of Topeka in a hasty passage through its main street. It contains a large number of good, substantial buildings, and new ones are going up in all directions. At the same time, buildings and whole blocks of buildings, begun two years ago, and carried to the first or second story, are still "in statu," and likely to be. . . . Thus growth and decay are both going on vigorously side by side. Still the whole impression is that of a live town. The explanation is that they have attempted to push the town beyond the demands of its business, and have been ripped by the hard times; and, at the same time, the *real business* of the place is causing a healthy growth, which promises more than all their spasmodic efforts.

Unlike the first Topeka houses, many of these business buildings huddled along Kansas avenue around Sixth street. Several of the important buildings, like the Ritchie and Gale Blocks, reached up three stories and were built of brick and/or stone from nearby quarries and brickyards. For many years Topeka masons built three walls of a structure of stone but added a brick face to that wall fronting a major thoroughfare.

Early buildings fulfilled a number of functions. The Ritchie Block at Sixth and Kansas may serve as an important example. The *Tribune,* October 3, 1857, reported that its "massive stone columns which support the upper walls . . . are a species of architecture seldom seen in the west." Owned by John Ritchie, Walter Oakley, and L. C. Wilmarth, this three story, 70 by 100 foot business block housed at different times a grocery and queensware (earthen-ware) store, dry goods emporium, bank, business college, and book bindery. In a top floor room the I.O.O.F. met while in the larger auditorium, called Museum or Wilmarth's Hall, various city organizations and clubs held their festivals, dances, and gatherings. Here, in April, 1857, the Philomathic Institute presented the first play in Topeka, "The Drunkard." When fire destroyed the block on November 28, 1869, (the loss estimated at $50,000 to $75,000, with the state of Kansas and Crane's Bindery being the big losers) the disaster awakened Topekans to the need for a fire department.

Hotels also joined the march of business blocks up and down the avenue with the Pioneer House (March, 1855) being the first, though

*From the Topeka *Tribune*, January 15, 1864: "If that pile of rubbish in front of the State House (between Fourth and Fifth and Kansas avenue) was removed it would improve the appearance, and if that pile of stone was removed from the corner this side, several journeys in the mud in the middle of the street, or broken shins produced by climbing over them would be prevented."

it was little more than a temporary shake shelter. Before the end of the decade a number of hotels opened. Enoch Chase, a Topeka founder, erected a three-story hotel on east Sixth which had only ten rooms or so and a kitchen with a dirt floor in the basement. Newspaper publisher Edward C. K. Garvey operated his small hotel on a Fifth and Kansas avenue site. While he was postmaster Garvey kept the postoffice there and managed to have the stage lines stop at his front door. The *Tribune* in February, 1857, advertised that his inn was "conducted on strict temperance principles, 'Touch not taste not the unclean thing is our motto.' " The *State Record*, January 26, 1861, no doubt after a change of hotel management, mentioned that "connected with the House is a bar where the very best and choicest of WINES & LIQUORS, and none others will be kept." A single meal and lodging cost, in 1861, only $1.00 with a month's boarding and meals, $35.00, all to make "it rank as a FIRST CLASS HOTEL."

Walter Oakley chose a Fifth and Kansas site, too, for a hotel later known as the Topeka House. Work commenced in January, 1856, but was not completed until late spring. Its frame ribs consisted of hewn cottonwood timbers since the saw mill was, Giles states, "generally out of order." Following various managerial changes over the years, Hayden D. McMeekin took a lease on the old Topeka House and inventoried the contents. They included eight bedsteads, ten looking glasses, six tables, 44 chairs, 15 stoves, four spittoons, six wash stands, 14 chambers, 26 sheets, 14 comforts, 30 grey blankets, five white blankets, 39 pillows, five cotton mattresses, two spring beds, two feather beds, and other assorted items. A political watering hole until it burned down in 1870, Fry Giles later remembered that "its rooms witnessed many events of interest to Topeka, and some of the most corrupting political influence that Kansas has been cursed with."

War interferred with Kansas' progress. Nevertheless, civic improvement continued though on a greatly reduced scale. The minister who

The Ritchie block on the southeast corner of Sixth and Kansas was the first home of the Kansas state executive offices and state senate. (Courtesy Kansas State Historical Society)

Looking west from the Santa Fe shops over the still rural river bottoms about 1879. (Courtesy Kansas State Historical Society)

viewed Topeka's state of affairs in 1859, returned four years later favorably impressed:

The Main street, along which the business blocks used to be scattered at almost sufficient intervals to have a farming country between, has been "thickening up" till it presents quite a city-like appearance. The recent buildings are of a more cheerful style than the old. That heavy, gloomy, prison-like appearance for which Topeka has been distinguished, is beginning to give way to a lighter and more cheerful aspect. There is really some taste displayed. . . .

For the people who trekked west following the Civil War land agents like Gavitt and Scott extensively advertised city and county property in the local newspapers. In the *Kansas State Record,* November 6, 1867, the following was offered:

Grove Place, situated at the foot of Quincy street, consisting of one and a quarter acres land, a beautiful grove forest shade trees, stone dwelling house 24 x 30, one and a half story high with basement, containing six rooms, pantry, a clothes press, all finished. Good well of water and cistern, frame stable 16 x 24 with hay loft and chicken house. All for $3,000.

Speed of construction was often a hallmark in the late 1860s. It astounded some such as the Topeka paper which reported in February, 1870:

At sunrise yesterday morning the corner at Fifth and Monroe was a vacant lot, not a board or plank being visible about the premises. Tonight at 6 o'clock there had been built on that lot a comfortable four-room dwelling, and a family was in full possession of the premises.

Construction took a down swing in the first half of the 1870s, during the general business slump, but resumed to peak in 1887-88. City expenditures focused upon sidewalk construction and street paving (always a center of attention and controversy) and this intensified throughout the 1880s. The *Weekly Leader* in the summer of 1867 mentioned how the Sage brothers from Dover were laying "hundreds of feet of stone sidewalks, twelve feet wide" on Kansas avenue while

A view from the capitol looking northeast, about 1879. In the center, above the "Commonwealth" office, is the Tefft House hotel, and in the right center the tower of the city building. (Courtesy Kansas State Historical Society)

the *Commonwealth,* in 1871, was still complaining of sink holes in the middle of the street: "If a stage coming to our city and being compelled to pass through that hole [between Crane and Second on Kansas], didn't have *mud*-dled impressions of this city, then we are no judges." Still, these holes did not prevent the almost daily, or so it seemed, horse runaways. "When will people learn to hitch their horses when they go after their beer?" questioned the *Commonwealth,* February 14, 1872.

Topeka's first major area expansion came in April, 1867, with the annexation of Eugene, or North Topeka. This displeased a few, but in a short while more and more North Topekans believed themselves little more than unwanted stepchildren of those on the south side. They saw important business men descend from Union Pacific trains—long the only connection to the East—only to hire cabs to cross over to South Topeka. Independence was not unfeasible, or so North Topekans thought and they elected a prominent banker, Maj. D. M. Adams, to promote the idea of de-annexation in the state legislature. He submitted a bill in January, 1873, but in February the House defeated the measure 44 to 19. With that, the hopes for seccession subsided.

That same month a second siginificant annexation occurred, bringing Crane's east side addition into the city. Dr. Franklin Crane, like many of the other city fathers, pre-empted a farm just outside of the Topeka town-site in the 1850s thus protecting it from injurious outside interests. Ultimately his addition became an industrial center with the King Bridge factory and Santa Fe shops and yards. Soon, prompted by speculation, the city annexed other sub-divisions.

South of the original Topeka plat, John Ritchie obtained property which he fenced and farmed until about 1860. While not one of the city's founders, Ritchie was unquestionably one of its most vigorous and controversial figures. Born in Ohio in 1817 he came to Kansas in March of 1855, and championed the abolitionist cause. He sneaked runaway slaves out of the Topeka area, and on one occasion participated in the terrorist activities at Tecumseh, September, 1855. These Free-State activities led him into serious trouble.

On the eve of statehood political enemies of prominent Free-Staters attempted revenge. On April 20, 1860, Deputy U. S. Marshal Leonard Arms arrived in Topeka to arrest Ritchie at his home. Ritchie immediately turned around and entered his house, picking up a pistol. Once both men were inside, they argued violently with Ritchie protesting that the marshal had no right to arrest him. As Arms demanded that he leave with him, Ritchie fired at the deputy, the ball piercing his neck. Ritchie surrendered himself to Justice of the Peace Joseph C. Miller. Trial was held the following day and because of the tremendous weight of public sympathy he easily got off, the verdict being "that John Ritchie has committed homicide, but one justifiable in the sight of God and man." He continued the advocacy of Negro (and women's) rights until his death on September 1, 1887.

Ritchie subdivided and began selling 75 to 150 foot lots on his farm around the mid-1860s. He even gave land away to those who would improve the property. This the Topeka *Weekly Leader,* January 18, 1866, applauded. "The General calls it the free-soil principle and seems bound to build a city upon his farm, although he does not realize one cent for the land." Despite these superb terms, parts of the area remained deserted. Ritchie did not discriminate against the incoming Negro population, "a circumstance," wrote Giles, "that militated against the sale of lots to white people, and the locality . . . remained comparatively unoccupied from that cause."

In June, 1867, Topeka annexed that area, traditionally called Ritchie's addition, and proceeded with the usual public improvements, streets, sidewalks, schools, police protection, and, of course, taxation. Ritchie subsequently sued, in 1872, claiming his land was outside of Topeka and beyond the pale of the tax collector. He won. Again Topeka annexed it and again lost.

Meantime, several additions grew up beside Ritchie's including the Keith tract and the Western Investment Company's Walnut Grove. In 1885 residents of the three areas decided to incorporate as a third class city called South Topeka. On July 25 voters elected, appropriately enough, John Ritchie as its first mayor.* As the *Capital,* October 9, 1886, explained, South Topeka's boundaries were "very vague in the minds of many." On the north was 12th street, on the west Kansas

---

*J. W. McClure was its second and last mayor.

and Topeka avenues, and on the south and east the Shunganunga. A census of June, 1886, counted 2,193 residents, a large proportion of them Negro.

South Topeka government undoubtedly operated like that of Topeka's. The city officials consisted of a mayor, clerk, treasurer, marshal, road overseer, police judge, assistant marshal, and five councilmen. Both the city ordinances and council minutes survive to indicate that street maintenance and sidewalk building were two of the major headaches of 1880s government. City ordinances were strictly enforced. On July 10, 1886, the council instructed the city attorney to make complaint against and prosecute former mayor John Ritchie for dumping or piling stone on Monroe street and not removing it.

The late 1880s witnessed an unprecedented land boom in Topeka, probably the most significant development and improvement in the city's history. For all practical purposes, the American West had been conquered, now its riches were ready to be exploited. Shawnee countian James L. King got caught up in the exuberance of the day.* In a modest paean titled "A Toast to Topeka," published in Radge's 1887 city directory, King spoke of how Topekans "conspire to beat the brass drum" and "shreik in grand chorus" about their boom. Topeka, he said, "is a collective noun, signifying a boom with wings on it, and a 'get-there' attachment." Topeka, in short, "booms intuitively. Nothing is too good for her."

---

*James L. King (1850-1919) author and journalist wrote *History of Shawnee County* in 1905.

John Ritchie (1817-1887), early Topeka pioneer and developer. (Courtesy Kansas State Historical Society)

The boom's most visible sign was the subdivisions popping up around town in every direction. "Come, gentle reader," wrote King, "let us take a whirl through the suburbs." On his verbal jaunt, King rode through less than two dozen additions, while the *Capital,* in its year's end review, January 1, 1889, counted 69 plats formed in 1888 ranging in size from huge speculation schemes down to tiny farms divided into a block or two. Some of the important additions, those which actually found buyers for lots, still retain their names: Lowman Hill, College Hill, Potwin, Oakland, Quinton Heights and Highland Park. Others passed into relative obscurity, often unsold, like Arlington Heights (south of Sixth street and west of the state hospital) or Gilmore Heights (on Deer creek west of the old Kansas Technical Institute) "where your hair," wrote King, "is brushed by the jagged edges of the clouds."

Street railway expansion coincided with the real estate explosion. Indeed, the two went hand in hand. Either land developers persuaded someone to build or constructed a railway themselves out to their territory. J. K. Hudson did this with his Highland Park farm and East Side Circle Railway. Some railroad magnates purchased property alongside their proposed lines, as did J. B. Bartholomew along the Rapid Transit in Oakland. In many places throughout the city, one can still see where an old rail line once ran, the houses beside it being fractionally older than those built farther away, or roadbeds remain slightly elevated over surrounding lawns.

Potwin or, more correctly, the City of Potwin Place, and College Hill were two of the better known suburbs as well as among the oldest. J. B. Whitaker, county surveyor, laid out and registered the College Hill subdivision on November 5, 1880, for Washburn president Dr. Peter MacVicar. Because the college lay far from the heart of the city, MacVicar hoped his faculty would build homes and board students there. The original College Hill actually occupied but a block or two on College and Boswell streets, directly north of the school, between Elm (later Euclid and finally 17th street) and Walnut (now 15th street). The first houses were built in the early 1880s and a rural school established there as District 22. As its population grew and some of Topeka's leading citizens moved into the district, College Hill came to be bounded on Huntoon, West (Washburn), Washburn (Mac-Vicar), and Euclid streets. Its small commercial center still hugs the intersection of 15th and Lane and was long a town within the city which even included its own movie theatre, the Co-ed.

Potwin Place developer Charles W. Potwin designed his addition to be the residence of the elite. Coming to Topeka in 1869 from Zanesville, Ohio, he purchased 70 acres of land west of town for $14,400, or a little more than $200 an acre. This he farmed, content to wait until the right time to have the land platted. Potwin finally subdivided it in 1882 and gave it the features recognizable today, wide, deep lots with small park-like circles at the street intersections. After planting some 2,000 elms on the spacious lots, originally 122½ feet by 205 feet Potwin again delayed development until the trees matured. He placed properties on the market in the fall of 1885, at prices ranging from $1,250 to $2,000 and then stipulated that the homes cost $2,000 or over.

"Platted in 1882; put on the market in 1885; incorporated in 1888 [June 4th]; a resident city of 600 souls (counting one soul to each person) in 1889, and a thousand dollars in wealth for every man, woman and child within the corporate limits" was the astounding progress of Potwin Place according to the *Capital*, January 1, 1889. The first six houses averaged $5,000 each indicative of the kind of people who chose this bedroom city. No unsightly industrial or commercial establishments blemished its streets. One of the few non-residential structures was the Jane C. Stormont Hospital, built in 1895. A $10,000 brick school house served the district while gas and water mains, telephone lines, and a sewage system were all in or contemplated. A street car line passed along its southern limits so that Potwin had "all of the advantages and none of the disadvantages of a metropolis."*

Not all suburban tracts fared so well as Potwin. Maj. Joseph K. Hudson, founder and editor of the Topeka *Daily Capital*, promoted his farm, Highland Park, in 1887, as choice residential sites conveniently connected to the city by the Highland Park Circle Railway, later the East Side Street Railway. As an added inducement he built five model houses on different sections of the property, each with considerable yard space and eight or more well-sized rooms in two stories. The best six lots sold for $1,000 each while the second choice, again six lots, went for only $600 apiece. Terms were one-fourth down, in cash, and one-quarter payable in each of the next three years at 8% interest.

Hudson's newspaper, naturally enough, publicized the tract during the summer of 1887 detailing its virtues which included plenty of shade trees and an exhilarating view of Topeka's skyline. In the paper's estimation Highland Park would become "a favorite spot for all in search of a quiet, retired home with fine scenery surrounding." Mary E. Jackson concurred in her *Topeka Pen and Camera Sketches*. She described it as "a desirable location for those who wish to be out of

---

*Potwin Place itself expanded in 1890 when the town annexed the Auburndale addition (which had also hoped to be a third class city) and several smaller ones. Both College Hill in 1962 and Potwin in 1968 have been subjects of Shawnee County Historical Society *Bulletins*.

the noise, bustle and smoke of the city." Though she believed "it was selected for residences of a better class," Topeka's old line aristocracy and *nouveau riche* never flocked out there. The bust of 1890-91 swamped Hudson. According to a commentator in the Highland Park *Bulletin* of the Shawnee County Historical Society "as late as 1910 many of the wide streets laid out by him were overgrown with grass they were so little used."*

Later, particularly after World War II, new homes and two major business centers along 29th street (the old shopping center was at 27th and Indiana) made the district a wealthy jewel outside of Topeka's grasp. Unlike some of the other old line subdivisions, Highland Park generally lacked any distinct boundaries and never incorporated. Instead, a Booster Club founded in 1914 acted as an unofficial governing body in conjunction with the Topeka Township Board. Then, in January, 1950, Topeka Mayor Frank J. Warren startled some residents by advocating the annexation of Highland Park. The city tabled the idea for the time being but it was revived and naturally met with the opposition of some Highland Park residents. Nevertheless, the area had been growing at a rate which created water, sewage, fire, and police problems that could only be temporarily alleviated by a local bond issue. On September 5, 1957, Highland Park became the last major parcel of highly developed land brought into the city. The vision, or perhaps the hope, of Hudson had been fulfilled.

Much more exciting and promising and much more of a disaster than J. K. Hudson's dream were the grandiose schemes of the Topeka Land and Development Company, better known as the Boston Syndicate. Beginning in the spring of 1887 a number of Topeka and eastern (primarily Boston) entrepreneurs unobtrusively started buying property west of town. On May 4 the *Capital* announced their intentions:

It is the purpose of the company to make a beautiful summer resort out of Martin's Hill [now Menninger's West Campus]. A grand boulevard will be built out to the hill and around it, where a large hotel, botanical and zoological garden and an observatory station will be established, an artificial lake constructed, and other improvements made which will make it one of the most attractive summer resorts in the west.

It also meant the platting of a considerable amount of ground into lots, construction of an interurban railway, and the formation of a Methodist university.

Such a proposal fired the imaginations of civic leaders who were already busy undertaking new projects. A spokesman for the Boston group maintained "we are not 'boomers'; we invest because we know Topeka is a growing city; it has everything which goes to make up a great business center." For a little over $500,000 the company had

---

Bulletin no. 26 (December, 1956).

purchased approximately 1,500 acres. It intended to lay out two to three million dollars for the Martin Hill scheme and the railway. The *Capital* conservatively speculated that the plan "insures Topeka 45,000 people by July 1,[1887?] and 75,000 by 1890." Promoters even projected a population of 100,000 for the next decade.

The great boom of the '80s was on. The newspapers, particularly the *Capital,* for weeks during the summer of 1887 printed story after story about real estate transactions and the Boston Syndicate. Many of these articles originally came from the eastern press. Topeka's was a "healthy" boom, not merely a cattle, or mining town boom to be immediately followed by a great bust. "Here are no fictitious values," reported the New York *World,* May 13, 1888, "no 'soap bubble' schemes have been concocted to boost up real estate."

In those sunny days of 1888, the boom crested around the first of the year. The *Commonwealth* fervently expressed faith in Topeka, ticking off improvements, one by one:

> The magnificent Rock Island depot, . . . the superb new Throop Hotel, . . . the stately form of Keith's block, which would be considered an ornament to any city in the land, . . . Governor Crawford's office block, . . . Hudson's block, . . . the Central National Bank building. . . .

In that one gilded year alone, four major office buildings were begun or completed which still stand in downtown Topeka. The Thatcher Building, designed by John G. Haskell, had Hall and O'Donald Lithographing Co. as a primary tenant with George W. Crane and Co. occupying it in 1899. Wolf's Jewelry and in 1911-13 the Washburn Law School were important tenants of the Davies Building at 725-727 Kansas avenue, constructed for B. M. Davies. Architect Seymour Davis drew the plans for two structures, the Crawford and the Knox [now the Columbian] Buildings. The former was erected for ex-governor Samuel J. Crawford whose son-in-law, Arthur Capper, published the *Mail and Breeze* there while the latter housed William C. Knox's United States Savings Bank.

Crawford's and Thatcher's buildings cost in the neighborhood of $40,000 while Knox's topped them at $60,000. Local newspapers like the *Kansas Democrat,* June 9, 1888, described the Knox Building at great length. Measuring 50 by 130 feet with a proposed but never built tower reaching up 125 feet, the Sixth street front was faced with Portage red sandstone from Michigan and hauled to Kansas by rail at a cost of $1.25 per cubic foot. Fireproof, the building contained four floors plus basement with the basement and first floor paneled in cherry and the upper floors in hardwoods. The lower floors had eight rooms apiece, the third and fourth ten. Each room had electric light; an elevator ascended to the top. In conclusion, the *Democrat* called

W. C. Knox "one of our youngest but one of our most tireless and energetic young business men."

H. P. Throop, however, well over-spent Knox when he put up his magnificent, $250,000 Throop Hotel at Fourth and Kansas. Architects Hopkins and Holland refitted and rebuilt an earlier hotel in 1887 and 1888 making the four story Throop "the handsomest hotel between the Missouri river and the Pacific slope." Along with the Copeland, it stood as one of the city's most important hostelries. Off the lobby a visitor found the cigar stand, telephone exchange, reading room and post office branch. The floor was tiled, the ceiling frescoed, and, as an 1890 pamphlet declared, "heavy mouldings of natural wood line the sides of the walls." The dining room, the pamphlet continued, seated 125 persons and was "nearly square, of noble proportions, with tiled floor, cherry wood baseboards, and marble slabs running from the base boards to a height of four feet from the floor, giving the room an air of Oriental magnificence." Upstairs the hotel provided a barber shop, banquet room, demonstration rooms, and a second floor parlor for ladies that contained eight pianos. Three elevators—one passenger, one freight, and one laundry—shuttled guests or bags to the 125 rooms. Twenty-five of the best rooms had both bath and water closet. Each floor possessed bathroom facilities. Throop finished each of the guest

The Veale-Thompson block of 1888, on Quincy between Fifth and Sixth. Top view shows construction techniques of the day and the bottom the completed building. (Courtesy Kansas State Historical Society)

The handsome Fifth Avenue hotel, originally called the Morris House, was built in 1869 and 1870 on the southwest corner of Fifth and Quincy. Here January 22, 1872, Topekans entertained the Grand Duke Alexis after his famous American buffalo hunt. (Courtesy Arthur J. Carruth)

rooms in hard wood while "the closet and toilet rooms are laid entirely in marble with finest brass trimmings" which cost $12,000.

The *Commonwealth*, July 20, 1888, summed up the progress and boom:

At least 2,000 residences [have been constructed], . . many of them palatial—all above ordinary. . . . It does seem as if Topeka has made giant strides in the past year. . . . Endowed to a remarkable degree by nature in all the advantages which make greatness possible . . . it is a city whose possibilities are unlimited and whose people are enterprising enough and wealthy enough to work them all out to a glorious realization.

Then the bottom fell out.

Kansas agricultural production suffered a set back after good years when 1886 wheat and corn yields of 14 and 139 million bushels respectively fell to less than ten and 76 million in 1887. This drop led directly to farm failures though a brief reprieve came in 1888. In turn these agricultural failures reduced freight income for railroads like the Santa Fe. Rail lines which had been growing by leaps and bounds with eastern and London capital, found themselves over expanded and debts mounting. Though by 1890 the Santa Fe had achieved its goal of reaching the Pacific Coast, like many another ambitious railroad it went into receivership five years later. As they had once or twice before, some people picked up their scant belongings and silently stole away from Kansas.

As early as April 14, 1888, the Topeka State *Journal* acknowledged that the east had "experienced a slight depression," but Topeka "has through a liberal system of public improvements, given employment to the thousands of workingmen." Yet, just as the farmer was hit with foreclosures, so was the city dweller. Too many lots were laid out and too many deals made without sound financing.

Nothing could stop retrenchment, and the Boston syndicate was only one of the victims. Nearly all of the Topeka Land Company prospects dissipated with the coming of hard times. Its planned lots remained in prairie grass. Other than some landscaping and tree planting on Martin's Hill, only the West Side Circle Railway and a hotel were completed. Unfortunately, the resort idea never materialized and the finished hotel complex on the line did not measure up to the planned $100,000 edifice. Known as the West Side House, exact location unspecified, the *Democrat,* July 28, 1888, reported that it had only two floors, a large veranda on three sides, a waiting room "furnished with rustic seats," a spacious dining room, and an ice cream parlor "which is cool, and overlooks the valley west, which is a pretty sight at sun set." A later newspaperman recalled for the *Capital,* August 24, 1924, that Topekans reveled at the refreshment stand which served "the very best vintage of the hop." The West Side House probably failed before the turn of the century.

The full effects of depression did not really hit Topeka until 1890-91 with the optimists confident until 1891. One barometer, the city's assessed valuation, steadily rose to $10,077,059 in 1890 but slipped slightly the following year and plunged to $9,210,741 in 1892. The population attained a peak of 35,622 in 1889 and dipped to 31,809 the next year. It rose to over 33,000 in 1891 and 1892 only to fall again in 1893, 1894, and in 1895 to 30,151. Several businesses failed

North Kansas avenue in 1888, looking north. Note the Union Pacific depot in center. (Courtesy Kansas State Historical Society)

with George W. Crane's publishing house and William C. Knox's United State Savings Bank going under in 1891.

Outbursts of joy faded into introspection as the *Capital* editorialized on June 8, 1895:

> By the city assessor's report it appears that the population of Topeka has declined slightly in the last year. . . . It is not a great city; but it is great enough for the time. . . We have no millionaires, so wealth has not begun to erect its hurdles in the course of society. We keep pretty well together, like a sensible and intelligent and even tempered democracy should. . . . Ninety per cent of the population are American born and love their state and country. We have over 4,000 colored residents and less than 2 per cent of our total population is illiterate. . . . Taxes are pretty high but they are declining a little every year and where in all the west will you find a more beautiful city, clean, well sewered, almost perfectly paved, tolerably well lighted . . . and embellished with public buildings of which every citizen is proud?
>
> We want more wealth and population and industries as a matter of course, not because they will make this community any happier or more prosperous, but because the struggle to advance is one of the necessary characteristics of a healthy, active human being, and so of a town. But as a sensible people we are moderate in our ambitions. Few of us care to become millionaires—a few hundred thousands invested in first class Kansas farm mortgages, merely to testify our faith in the state would satisfy us. As for brown-stone fronts to our houses we are not vulgarly extravagant in our tastes; pressed brick for the two upper stories and Colorado red sandstone for the lower is good enough for us. . . . The craze for wealth is one of the degenerate signs of the times in big cities. None of it for us.
>
> On the whole, the prospect for these [a few more industries] is fair. The court house and Santa Fe hospital, the wollen mill, two dams and what other little improvements are on will do for this year. Other things can follow. Let us be reasonable and appreciate the blessings we have.

Of all the suburban additions, perhaps none was as important as Oakland, the home of much of Topeka's working and middle classes. The *Daily Herald,* July 29, 1904, commented that unlike some real estate ventures of the '80s "Oakland addition . . . did not go back into farms, nor were the other additions platted in that vicinity vacated when the collapse came." Both J. B. Billard and Freeman Sardou had settled in the area in the 1850s, but it was not until 1887 that J. B. Bartholomew and John Norton bought several neighboring farms. By January 1, 1889, according to the *Capital,* the subdivision's population stood at over 500 with one company having built 211 residences the previous year. The average cost of these initial Oakland homes ran between $1,500 and $5,000.

Mary Jackson outlined some of Oakland's virtues for her *Pen and Camera Sketches:*

> No shanties, and not one poorly-built house has been erected in Oakland. Prosperity seems to reign over the entire place. Temperance flung his banner at the first opening of the [Oakland] Park, and all societies and assemblies are notified . . . not to bring intoxicating liquors into their midst. A large tabernackle

was built in June, 1889, for the Chatauquans, and in frame buildings in north park are the reading rooms of the Chatauquans. During the seasons for out-door entertainments, Oakland Park has been the favorite resort.

The temperance aspect proved crucial since the Oakland *Blade* in 1905 claimed there were 100 joints or dives in Topeka but none in Oakland. It added that "if you want to locate in a town where there are no saloons or joints, come to Oakland; if you must settle where there ARE saloons and joints pass Oakland by and stop off at Topeka, Silver Lake, Willard, Rossville or Leavenworth." Lillian Horton in *Mama Was Pregnant* (1964) aptly summed up this bit of puritanism: "No one ever danced in Oakland. In fact it was almost a sin."

Mrs. Horton remembered the houses being mostly two-story, frame, and "rather naked looking and not more than two or three to a block." Nearly all had gardens with the vacant lots farmed in alfalfa. At the same time, 1904, the *Herald* mentioned that Oakland's business community was "substantial and not of mushroom growth." It embraced four groceries, one drug store "which does not sell whiskey," one general merchandise store, one barber shop, one blacksmith, four physicians, and one important if frequently non-operating woolen mill employing 135 persons. A library, separate school district, and for a time an Oakland High School, as well as Methodist and Presbyterian churches served educational and religious needs.

Oakland incorporated in 1903, holding its first municipal election on February 2, 1904, with F. A. Brigham elected mayor along with five councilmen, a treasurer, clerk, marshal, and street commissioner. Its ordinances were examples of the mundane but necessary legislation of a third class city. Ordinance number five enacted a curfew, for minors under 16, at 9:00 P.M. from March through September and 8:00 P.M. from October through February. It authorized the city marshal "to ring the school bell at the hour of 8:45 o'clock [or 7:45 in the winter] each evening by giving nine [or eight in the winter] successive strokes on the bell . . . as notification to all minors . . . to repair to their home."

Ordinance number eight embodied a number of loosely related provisions. A home owner could not graze livestock, nor could he "allow to be indecently exhibited, any stallion, ass, bull, boor, ram 'with' an animal of the opposite sex." Any Oakland farmer unfortunate enough to be found guilty of breaking this ordinance was fined $25 to $100. The city fined a drunk from three to five dollars for the first offense and up to $50 for subsequent violations. Officials frowned upon spitting on a church carpet or floor and the selling of impure ice. Other ordinances prohibited Sunday sales, football, baseball, and professional entertainments. Still others outlawed gambling and prostitution. Finally, one city law defined cess-pools and privys and specified their construction. They were not to "exceed in depth four (4) feet nor be less than thirty inches in depth." After 20 years of a separate identity, Oakland was merged into Topeka early in 1926.

Until the post World War II era most construction activity concentrated on filling up the gaps in or between older subdivisions. Several individual projects stand out in these years with the mid-1920s being a prolific period. "Topeka this season," reported the *Journal* in March, 1923, "is cramming her guns for the best little building boomlet in fifteen years." Building permits totaled over $4,600,000 or nearly twice the sum of the previous year. Begun or completed in 1923 were the Masonic Temple, Capitol Federal Building, Hotel Kansan, Fidelity State Bank, Mulvane Art Museum and Jayhawk Hotel. Already gracing the growing city skyline were the ten story National Reserve Life Building and the south section of the Santa Fe general offices. The *Capital*, December 30, however, cautioned outsiders from heading to the capital city "in the belief that there is a 'boom on.' " Instead, a number of tradesmen discovered themselves out of work, an ominous foreboding of things to come.

In the early days Topeka's aristocracy often resided east of Kansas avenue. Cyrus K. Holliday, for example, lived in a surprisingly modest home at 300 East Sixth street. Soon, however, the elite preferred an avenue removed from the hustle and bustle of the commercial district so made Harrison, Topeka, and Tyler the streets for their residences. Those disturbed by the crowding in of lesser mortals could pack their belongings and head farther west to more exclusive Potwin Place. By the late 1920s those ready to move again journeyed farther west to Westboro.

Of all of Topeka's suburban tracts, none symbolized wealth or selectivity like Westboro. A quarter section bounded by Gage, Huntoon, Oakley, and 17th streets, prior to 1927 it consisted of farm and dairy land. Local aviators often used the area as an airfield, one early pilot recalling "it was a pretty good strip. . . . About the only obstacle was an occasional cow." Then in 1927 Topeka attorney Tinkam Veale purchased the property from an estate and began development with M. R. Linscott, a former associate of Kansas City's J. C. Nichols Co. Builders chose a myriad of contrasting styles for their homes—English Tudor, Colonial, French Provincial, Italiante, Spanish or an intertwining of different styles for a striking effect. Above all, at the northeast corner, rose a Spanish Colonial tower emphasizing the quality of Westboro and its shopping center—an unmistakable imitation of J. C. Nichols' Country Club Plaza in Kansas City.

Electric and gasoline buses served Topeka when this picture of the 800 block of Kansas avenue was taken in October, 1935. The Mills building, Santa Fe general offices, and the First Baptist spire peak above the avenue store fronts. (Courtesy Kansas State Historical Society)

Business was brisk on the west side of the 700 block of Kansas avenue in October, 1935. The Hotel Jayhawk, Davies building (with Crosby Brothers sign on side), and National Bank of Topeka building are prominent. The depression years were the last time Topeka commercial activity centered upon the "Avenue." (Courtesy Kansas State Historical Society)

A resident who left Topeka in 1925 could have returned a quarter of a century later and still recognize nearly everything in the city. Standing on the corner of 29th and Burlingame road, facing south, he would have gazed upon the same scene of rolling pastures and farm land, broken only here and there by a farm building or two. Immediately in back of him, of course, was the city, a few higher class homes along one side of the Burlingame road and the plush meadows of the Topeka Country Club, the club house itself little more than an over grown farmhouse. West of Gage boulevard would have been found the same thing. North of Highway 24 along Topeka boulevard a few pleasant homes clung along the road but nothing else. The east city boundary still cut at the Sixth and Tenth street intersection with little beyond Golden except some shacks, a trailer park or two, and homes hugging Deer creek and Rice school.

Ten years more, however, and much would have been unrecognizeable to the homecoming visitor. The heart of the city had visibly moved southwest with 29th and Burlingame now a busy residential intersection, not an idylic country crossroad. Stretching well down the road a sea of new housing totally obliterated the area's rural past. The same was fairly true in the other directions of town. New subdivisions popped up everywhere and even climbed the slopes of Burnett's Mound to the displeasure, no doubt, of the Indian Chief's ghost. Only in the east was development retarded, due to the "Eastside's" notorious reputation as the lower class section of town. Growth added greatly to the population of Soldier township and revitalized Tecumseh and Tecumseh township, after a century, into a major community center.

Topeka's core changed markedly during the 1950s and 1960s, particularly around the turn of the decade as higher skyscrapers were constructed. Aristocratic Topeka boulevard was thoroughly destroyed in this period. Wiped away were most traces of its heritage as it was replaced with a motley collection of cheap restaurants, filling stations, parking lots, and in quite a number of circumstances, hideous commercial buildings of jagged architecture.* The state office tower at Tenth and Harrison supplanted a row of mansions of Topeka's elite, the E. H. Crosby home being one of the finest.

Downtown Topeka also radically changed with many established landmarks taken down with new buildings replacing them. Capitol Federal Savings and Loan transferred its headquarters in 1961 from the Sixth and Kansas office, certainly the most important architectural ornament on the avenue. Likewise, the Kansas Power and Light

---

*The Ingleside home, the 1880s experiment in a home for working mothers, was the latest (1975) casualty.

Company moved from the old *Journal* building with its rows of columns to an impressive though otherwise typical 20th century skyscraper. The First National Bank corporation (itself housed in a striking 12 story office built in the 1930s) delayed its final building plans until construction of the Merchants bank commenced. Thus, the largest bank in Topeka could also produce the largest and tallest commercial building in town.

Along with a growing and fairly attractive new skyline—best seen from the Topeka avenue bridge in the north, Interstate Highway 70 from the east, or between 29th and 21st streets on Topeka boulevard from the south—shopkeepers modernized many of their store fronts, Crosby Brothers at 717-23 Kansas being one of the most dramatic alterations

Along with the suburban spread came shopping centers, a phenomenon experienced everywhere in the nation. Before, the different fringes of Topeka such as Oakland, Highland Park and College Hill had their little shopping areas which might include a grocery, drugstore, barber and beauty shop, neighborhood laundry, and one or two other things. However, these establishments catered only to a small region and were little more than a supplement to larger facilities downtown, the places with a greater variety of goods and services.

The first true shopping centers in Topeka were the Westboro Mart and Elmhurst Plaza of the early 1930s. While they, too, catered to a specific area, their developers conceived them as a shopping totality. Here there would be no random building. With the rapid expansion of Topeka to the southwest in the 1950s, the second phase of shopping center construction commenced and soon all four corners of town could claim a neighborhood or regional center. Some, though a unit, followed the older pattern serving a small territory, but the bigger ones—Gage Center, Fairlawn Plaza, Holliday Square, White Lakes, etc.—contained name chain stores, just like downtown, and merchants who could easily compete with their Kansas avenue counterparts in clothing, furniture, and appliances.

Perhaps the largest and most controversial development of the 1960s concerned the vast sea of shanties, low cost housing, second rate businesses, and general slums in the area bounded by Sixth street, Kansas avenue, the river, and the Santa Fe shops. In 1956 Topeka's mayor appointed a committee of five men to serve as an urban renewal commission. For about the next seven years controversy raged over the purpose of urban renewal and its effects upon the people living or working in the district. The NAACP along with some property and business owners loudly objected to the various plans proposed over the years. On the other side of the question stood individuals seeing the redevelopment as a blessing and cure for the deteriorating downtown.

Eventually the residents had to go with most moving to government sponsored low-cost housing in other sections of the city, something which sparked smaller controversies concerning the economic and racial make up of the incoming people. Of course a large percentage of urban renewal's strongest supporters lived in middle or upper class neighborhoods far away from the new low income housing units. By the mid-1960s, with the help of the interstate highway program, most of the land had been cleared and light industries or warehouses, such as Ripley's Cleaners; Duffens Optical; McIntire Brothers mattress factory; H. M. Ives & Sons, printers; and others were established. Like other urban renewal operations of the early 1960s, Topeka's was a simple bulldozing act which stripped away the oldest and perhaps most historic part of the city. No one made a serious attempt to reuse the salvageable structures in the urban renewal area.

The two and a half blocks on the southwest corner of this first urban renewal district was labeled the Townsite Plaza, and this, so planners hoped, would be the landmark of the whole redevelopment scheme. As a part of it, the city was drawn into a questionable arrangement in the construction of an underground parking garage. Beginning in 1963, the urban renewal agency or other interested parties periodically released possible designs for a business and retail center. Frequently anonymous commentators hinted that some entrepreneur was prepared or eager to invest in the Plaza while the local newspapers extolled its proposed wonders—pedestrian ways, malls, and high-rise towers.

After going through several design changes, the *Capital-Journal,* September 26, 1971, announced plans for a portion of the complex. These included an ice-skating rink, twin movie theaters, a central garden court, two or three malls, and 25 shops. Unfortunately, delays and reality set in so that this idea, like others, soon collapsed. Revamped plans eliminated all pretense of architectural unity with nearby structures and any attempt to bring in retail stores. All buildings in the Townsite Plaza are used for business or governmental purposes with the only retail outlet in the area being Montgomery Ward.

One of the goals of urban renewal was the revitalization of downtown Topeka, and in this it has not succeeded. Whether or not it has arrested further decay, there exists little business activity below Sixth street on Kansas avenue (the state government being a major employer in two buildings) or beyond Tenth. More and more stores go empty every year. Downtown Topeka is less important than many shopping complexes, the busiest of which is the stretch between 29th street and 37th street along Topeka boulevard.

As of yet, no significant changes or improvements appear for the heart of the city. One panacea, a downtown civic center, has not elicited much public enthusiasm, the idea having lingered since 1968 with little done beyond talk. "Thus growth and decay are both going on vigorously side by side," commented the visiting Congregational minister a century before in 1859, "if you have ever seen ants at work repairing damages after you have kicked their hill over, you have a pretty just idea of my impression of Topeka."

Kansas avenue's notorious chuckholes as seen by Albert T. Reid. (From the Topeka "Mail and Breeze," August 19, 1905)

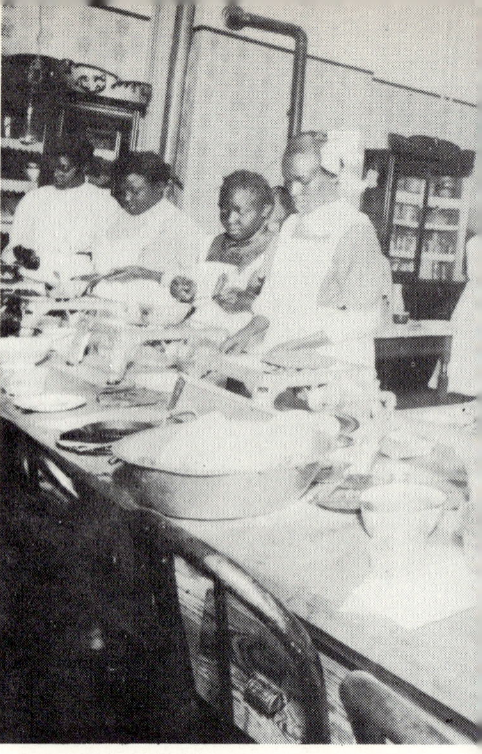

Many Topekans of German origin joined the Turnverein which offered various athletic facilities. (Courtesy Mrs. Fred Gades)

Preparing a meal at the Topeka Provident Association, a charitable society, around the turn of the century. The building was located at Fourth and Jackson streets. (Courtesy ansas State Historical Society)

A Santa Fe section gang with Mexican laborers at Pauline in 1913. (Courtesy Laura Mae Green Bailey)

DIVERGENCE; PEOPLE'S LINEAGES

Germans, Swedes, Negroes, and Mexicans made up the major non-Anglo-Celtic population groups in the 19th and early 20th centuries along with a small but notable early French contingent—the Sardou and Billard families being the most prominent. The Germans, those from the fractured German confederation, had arrived by the 1860s, if not in the 1850s. Both Germans and French Republicans happily celebrated the fall of Paris and Louis Napoleon's Empire in 1870. Swedes came in some strength during the following decade along with the major Negro influx. Santa Fe-employed Mexicans were the last of these, few being in eastern Kansas before World War I.

Nearly all these peoples faced some kind of opposition from the established folk. Even persons from the same background, like Negroes who had settled in the 1860s, feared the poorer late comers who were flooding the community with cheap labor. Topeka newspapers frequently pictured the Swedes as stumbling drunks while the *Commonwealth*, August 1, 1872, noted a particular problem of the city's Negroes:

Several colored people complained to us last evening because they were excluded from an ice cream saloon. They behaved well and had money to pay their way, but they were told that "there was no cream for niggers." Our colored citizens ride in the same 'busses and coaches, with white people, attend the same churches and schools, and it is difficult to understand why they can't eat ice-cream in the same saloon if they conduct themselves properly and pay the bills.

Of course, few whites shared the *Commonwealth's* views and most insulated themselves from the black community except for periods of charity where they could feel socially superior. During the 1920s the Ku Klux Klan paraded on Topeka streets, claiming as many as 5,000 Topeka members in 1923. As late as the 1950s both the Gage Park swimming pool and Lake Shawnee bath houses barred Negroes. Back in 1880, one black individual described a jaunt to the Ritchie's addition south of town and explained the problems of the people. Before a gathering of blacks and whites, one colored man was picking on a banjo, another singing, and a third dancing.

Now I would like to ask our people if they do not think it high time they were dropping all these ignorant practices which are the fruits of slavery, and directing their attention to those things which will reflect credit upon us as a people? It is a fact (and one, indeed, of the greatest wrongs ever done a people) that we are all judged alike. Every man is not taken on merit, as other races, but his color. This being the case it is of the greatest importance that we be careful how we act.

Two significant groups flocked to Kansas in the decades either side of 1880—the German-Russians in 1874 and the southern Negroes, or "Exodusters," in the late 1870s. The Santa Fe and Union Pacific offered for sale a large acreage in central Kansas to the Germans. Many stopped in Topeka with some staying to find employment in the Santa Fe shops. Negroes fled the Jim Crow South to make up, in 1880, according to Fry Giles, approximately 30% of the total population. Both population explosions resulted in considerable difficulties for the settled and immigrant alike, some of them quite humorous like the story from the December 7, 1875, *Blade*:

> People around the old Topeka House where the Mennonites are quartered say that the Russian ladies are not afraid to go out on the sidewalk and wash their legs as far as the knees. A young man who keeps a grocery not far from there, says he watched a manoeuvre of the kind, and continued watching until the lady began to untie some strings about her waist. Then he was afraid to watch any longer.

Exodusters, naturally, had a far rougher time than the Germans or even the "native" Negroes. Most Topekans probably concurred with the Rossville *Kansas Valley Times*, April 23, 1880, "that the Refugees would be much better off back in the south, and that their departure would give general satisfaction." Two weeks later the paper offered a second opinion that the Exodusters were a "lower and more indolent" kind of field hand and "nuisance alike to over-energetic Kansas colored people and whites."

Each group had its own colonies (neighborhoods), churches, clubs, and newspapers. The older, socially superior German population lived on the south side, in the vicinity of the German Catholic (St. Joseph's) church at Third and Van Buren with the Swedes nearby. The Russian born Germans resided in a shack settlement along the Santa Fe tracks in North Topeka, "Little Russia," or just east of the Santa Fe shops in the "Russian shacks." Mexicans later moved into the Russian area beside the shops while Topeka's Negro population spread into pockets all over the city: Redmonsville along the river on the north side, beside the Shunganunga in John Ritchie's South Topeka, and eventually throughout east Topeka. Like the Mexicans, in most if not all cases, Negroes replaced an older, lower class white population which sought a better life on the city's west side.

With the emergence of second and third German and Swedish generations, the old bonds began to dissolve. Nearly all their newspapers and societies were of 19th century origin and few of their separate churches survived beyond the 1920s. The Swedes published at least three Swedish language journals and organized a society called the Norden Benefit Association as early as the mid-1870s. Germans, too, had their distinct newspapers, a German-American bank, and an athletic and social club (with a bar) called the Turnverein. The major newspapers in the 1860s and later frequently commented on German activities, parties, balls, parades, etc.

While the Swedes and Germans quietly assimilated into 20th century Anglo-Celtic society, the Mexicans and Negroes remained outside in semi-isolated communities. Racial differences, of course, created this segregation. It was, and is, more prominent in the city though some rural Shawnee county districts, like Tecumseh, have had sizeable Negro and even tiny Mexican populations.

Samuel Reader, in a letter dated January 19, 1862, wrote to his brother that he had recently been in Topeka where he "saw quite a number of negroes employed by the citizens. They looked intelligent and happy. I believe they have 15 or 20 there but none have come over on this side of the river, yet that is, in this [Soldier] Township." In two decades that condition completely changed.

There existed one prominent Negro district in the city, the King addition to the southwest. Platted in the 1870s, most of the lots, selling for $50 to $100, remained empty. A number of Tennesseeans secured plots in the district bounded by Buchanan, Lincoln, and Lane between 10th and Huntoon; as a result the whites dubbed it Tennesseetown or Little Chattanooga. Fry Giles smugly stated in 1886 that "neatness and good order prevail" in Tennesseetown with "comfortable houses, some of them architectural pretensions." Actually, many of the houses were only "marginal shelters" with the walls bare of paint and plaster. Yet there were exceptions as Tennesseetown matured into an important town within a city.

The boom of 1887-88 passed Tennesseetown by, allowing the quiet residents to pace their own lives in the whirl of a growing Topeka. Such backwaters appeared offensive to some caught in the spirit of expansion. "It is no surprise," wrote one individual to the *Capital,* July 13, 1887, "that capitalists do not wish to invest and build in this place, considering the character of the population." With no street improvements, water mains, or gas lines, the city grew around it. The paper implored "can some way be taken to rid us of this rubbish?"

A special Tennesseetown census taken in 1898 by the Congregational Church furnishes an insight to the community's life just before the turn of the century. It counted 146 families of which over half, 78, owned their homes. Most houses were frame, only seven being brick and three stone. They averaged three and a half rooms though some had as many as eight. A majority of residents kept a small garden (vegetable and/or flower), with a few trees in the yards; some kept horses, cows or pigs.

Many Negroes who migrated to Topeka in 1876 settled in Tennesseetown, named after their native state. This scene was taken on June 20, 1900. (Courtesy Kansas State Historical Society)

This unique census hints at the social conditions—a more thorough survey, in fact, than anything available on Topeka's Europeans. Only 25 families received a pension; in the others one or more family members worked. The women, of course, took in washing or sewing while the men labored at odd jobs or obtained minor positions as day laborers, teamsters, janitors, porters, shoe-shine boys, etc. By this time a few had attained more responsible and visible positions in the city fire or police departments. At or near the top socially and economically stood the local minister. The annual income of the 284 employed workers averaged $399.27 with some incomes as low as $50 and a few earned by ministers and policemen, as high as $1,000.

Out of 585 residents, 167 were slave born, two of them being Sina Wallace, aged 99, and John Williams, aged 61. Sina Wallace typified the impoverished side of Tennesseetown. She, along with four of her 23 children, were entirely dependent on county aid and charity. Her one room house was unpainted, lacked a fence, and had no shrubbery and only "a very few" flowers. Obviously in poor health, she neither owned any books nor subscribed to a city newspaper. Williams, on the other hand, represented the Negro middle class. His yearly earnings totaled approximately $1,200. His five room home was painted and surrounded by a picket fence. The yard contained two shade and

An early black enterprise was the Apex Theater which was located at 122 East Fourth street. These children enjoy ice cream before the movie on June 10, 1933. (Courtesy Paul Boeger)

eight fruit trees with gooseberry bushes and a "good variety of flowers." More significantly, Williams had a piano, a newspaper subscription, and 200 books (the average number of books in Tennesseetown homes was 39—which probably would have compared well with white homes—for a total of 5,306). Son Fred, aged 16, found employment as a stenographer, a good position.

With the passing years and decades of the new century, certain sections in the city became more and more identified as solely Negro. As East Topeka working classes attained social and economic mobility and moved west, Negroes replaced them. At the same time a certain subsection of lower downtown Topeka erected an invisible barrier against whites. Later included in the city's first urban renewal program in the late 1950s it focused upon Fourth and Kansas and then slid north and east into the bottoms as a series of cheap cafes, hotels, and drug stores intermingled with decaying unpainted houses and cottages. A 1934 Negro directory enumerated the efforts of a still quite small business class, here and in other sections of town. It listed six groceries, six barber shops, two beauty parlors, one filling station, two recreation parlors, one coal dealer, one ice company, one theatre (the Apex), two undertakers (Gaines and Bowser), 14 cafes, and five hotels (Dunbar, Overton's, Fourth Ave., Robinson House, and Ransonian). The directory also referred to the black upper classes which were represented by six doctors, six attorneys, and three dentists.

Topeka Klansmen at an undisclosed Ku Klux Klan rally in the 1920s. On occasion the KKK paraded on Topeka streets. (Courtesy Kansas State Historical Society)

Newell home after 1917 Elmont tornado. (Courtesy Kansas State Historical Society)

Eager hands clean up the debris left by the 1903 flood in North Topeka. (Courtesy Kansas State Historical Society)

A Topeka fire engine to the rescue on 500 block of Quincy in 1908. (Courtesy Kansas State Historical Society)

THE TEMPEST; FIRE, FLOOD, AND DISASTER

Fire, flood, wind, and pestilence might be considered Kansas' Four Horsemen of the Apocalypse. Grasshoppers in 1874 were pests for Shawnee county while fires visited Topeka at a very early date. One of the first major blazes broke out in June, 1859, destroying a grain storage barn. Several fires burst forth ten years later with one destroying the *Kansas State Record* office and another the Ritchie block. The latter incident finally provided the impetus to secure a fire engine and some kind of volunteer fire department. In February, 1870, the city obtained a Silby fire engine, two hand cars, 1,500 feet of hose, and the service of 15 volunteers.* Proudly the firemen tested their equipment before interested Topeka spectators, putting out imaginary fires by using water from area cisterns. Then on May 28, 1870, shouts of fire broke the morning air and the first true test for the new department was at hand. The volunteers rushed to the engine's storage barn only a few blocks away from the blaze at the old Topeka House hotel. Unfortunately for the hotel's proprietor, the firemen had stowed the equipment and engine in the omnibus barn—behind the omnibuses and other vehicles!

A sarcastic *Commonwealth* article on the 31st stated that Topeka required a proper carriage (fire) house, and "then they can make it [the engine] effective, instead of being half-an-hour in getting to a fire scarcely a hundred yards" away. Historian George Root noted decades later, "the number of 'superintendents' at the fire considerably exceeded the 'working force.'" The Topeka House, obviously, was a complete loss.

An ever present fear in eastern Kansas revolved around the spring flood, a danger not as frequent but more devastating than fire. "It commenced raining . . . [and] rained all day without a moments cesation," wrote Oregon-bound James Clyman on June 10, 1844, "Knife river [Cross creek] . . . rose 15 feet during the day." Thus grew perhaps the greatest and certainly the most legendary of the Kansas river floods. For several days the rain continued though briefly the sun shone on the 13th. Then "we saw the sun & a general shout was raised through all the camp after 80 hours steady rain we saw the Kanzas river from the Bluffs & it shews 8 or 10 miles wide."

---

*Topeka's second fire chief, George O. Wilmarth, served from 1872 to his death in 1914, a record for such service.

Supposedly the waters stretched as a vast lake from bluff to bluff. Long afterwards early pioneers pointed to rings on some discolored ancient tree trunk where that flood once touched, miles from the Kansas' channel. Other floods struck Shawnee county from time to time, especially on the smaller tributaries. Yet of those subsequent to that great 1844 deluge, the 1903 flood was quite different. Not only was it stronger, but infinitely more people and industries had strung themselves along the river banks.

May of 1903 began quite bright as Topekans planned for President Theodore Roosevelt's imminent visit. It ended with enormous destruction and misery. Heavy rains began in mid-month and then on Memorial Day the Kansas river broke out of its banks quickly spreading throughout the low lying North Topeka residential districts. In a matter of hours water covered North Topeka, the fertile Shawnee county bottoms, and sections of south Topeka and Oakland from five to 25 feet deep. "Secured places became perilous," noted author Margaret Hill McCarter in her account of the flood, *The Overflowing Waters,* "lapping inches of quiet water became swiftest currents on which not a few lives must have ridden to unrecorded deaths; not a few bodies must have floated to unknown burial."

Many stubbornly resisted the tide, choosing to stay in their homes rather than escape either to northern hills or south Topeka. When the danger intensified, these obstinate Topekans scrambled to second floor rooms or attics or to the nearest tree limb. During these first nights citizens safely tucked away on the south side heard frequent bursts of gun fire as the stranded signaled to anyone, anywhere for help.

For some the vigil in the trees proved fatal. Days afterwards Topeka papers printed stories, some undoubtedly false, of witnesses seeing tired, hopeless individuals drop out of branches into the swirling current. At Tecumseh two women were known to have so fallen and drowned; yet, sometimes fairly humorous tales emerged from the otherwise grim scene. Horses and cows climbed voluntarily or were pushed up to second floor sanctuaries. Mrs. McCarter recalled "one waterbound prisoner fed to his cow shut up with him such leaves of trees as he could reach from his window and in turn she furnished all his food." One J. R. Roter of the Lyman district, wrote the *Journal,* spent an evening in a near-by tree. Next morning he waded to the house discovering "his big Newfoundland dog upon his couch, comfortable in a bed of quilts and blankets. The dog was immediately ejected and his place converted to the use of Mr. Roter, who was tired and stiff from his night residence in the tree."

Rescue operations began almost at once as men appropriated boats of all kinds. An approach to the Kansas avenue (Melan) bridge washed out so that a cable had to be strung across the swollen river for use as a guide to the supply boats. One of the heroic spirits in the rescue mission was Santa Fe Chief mechanical engineer Edward Grafstrom. He designed a small powered craft which crossed and re-crossed the river six times saving some 77 lives. On its last voyage, June 2, his launch collided with debris and it capsized. Six passengers reached safety but the swift current pulled Grafstrom under.

Floating debris disrupted many rescue operations and was only one of several problems caused by the flood. Numerous "lakes" formed by the rampaging river up and down the valley were breeding grounds for disease-carrying insects. Dead animals, littering the streets and yards, posed even further problems as a significant source for disease. As soon as it became feasible, health officials built a crematorium for the rotting carcasses.

Human beings accounted for still other difficulties in the restoration of flood-racked areas. Early in the crisis community officials appointed special deputy sheriffs to maintain law and order as well as aid in rescue operations. One newspaper noted that "a lot of unreliable men and boys were sworn in and given badges. They seemed to have the idea that the badges gave them the right to carry firearms and to use them promiscuously." Some of these deputies simply played with their guns discharging them at will; others actually interfered with the salvage work before the badges were recalled.

Outside Topeka the flood waters inundated the other valley towns of Rossville, Silver Lake, and Tecumseh. At least two men from Rossville, living on a river island south of town, drowned, but most if not all Silver Lake people got out in time and the water was never exceptionally high in either place. Newspapers frequently exaggerated stories, partly from poor or incorrect sources of information. Typical was the headline from Valencia which reported, "Farmer Reports That the Town Washed Away." (It very nearly did.) One crucial fact emerged from these various newspaper reports: some of the most

Flood waters of 1951 swirl around Owls baseball park and the Highway 24 cloverleaf. (Courtesy Kansas State Historical Society)

prosperous farms in the county suffered almost total damage. Even landlocked Berryton received a backlash from Lynn creek. Berryton and Monmouth township farmers had sent four wagons of supplies to stricken Topeka. One reporter added upon hearing the news of flood to the south, that perhaps Topekans should now return the favor.

According to James King's Shawnee county history of 1905, over 1,500 residences and 300 public and business buildings of North Topeka were ruined, leaving over $2,200,000 worth of damage. In some places people had to clear from two or three inches to two or three feet of mud, silt, and debris from their ground level floors. Many lost nearly all of their property. Congressman Charles Curtis, for instance, had his library destroyed. At least 24 persons died (14 of them Negroes from the large North Topeka community). The actual number was higher due to uncertain reporting procedures and a large number of unreportable transients. Whole communities like Little Russia were swept away by the tide and their inhabitants had to take refuge in churches, schools, the new city auditorium, or even the mills. "In these places," wrote Mrs. McCarter, "American, Swede, German, Russian and African slept all in one big hall."

Eventually the city recovered, rebuilding homes and restoring farms up and down the valley. Fortunately the Kansas avenue bridge withstood the flood. As protection some dike work was instituted but nothing of a scale to meet total future problems. Overflowing waters returned, with floods in 1908 and 1935 being of some concern. In 1951, however, came the largest (with the possible exception of 1844) and unquestionably the most destructive of all Kansas river floods.

Heavy rains in mid-June created growing apprehension, particularly on the upper reaches of the Kansas and its western and northern tributaries. The rains never let up as the numerous rivers and streams of eastern Kansas overflowed their banks toward the end of the month. Anxiety over the situation eased somewhat the first of the following month but the waters came back with even greater vengeance in mid-month. On June 11 the Topeka *State Journal* announced that taxis, trucks, busses and vehicles of all kinds had began the great and slow exodus out of North Topeka. By the 12th and Friday the 13th the flood waters reached their greatest depth in North Topeka, Oakland, some sections of south Topeka, and all the bottoms with a river crest of over 36 feet, compared to the 1903 flood's 32 feet.

The valley towns were hit far harder in 1951 and most residents had to spend at least some nights in the hills. The Rossville *Reporter*, July 5, 1951, announced that "for the first time in the knowledge of present inhabitants, Main Street south of the U.P. tracks and the highway was covered with water." Cross creek was a serious problem and nearly every basement in town was full. On the eastern end of the county the deluge washed away the Tecumseh Santa Fe depot along with a number of barns, houses, and outbuildings dumping tons of silt across once prosperous farms. Frantically company employees and townspeople worked throughout the day and night of the 13th to save KP&L's Tecumseh power plant by ringing it with a coal dike. Many persons did likewise in shoring up the Topeka water plant and both critical operations were successful.

Fortunately the flood had been expected so that while over 17,000 were homeless in the city, no loss of life was reported. As before, a number of individuals spent one or more nights stranded in upper floor rooms or some tree limb. One major northside institution, the Boys Industrial School, was for a time at least completely isolated from the rest of the world with both electricity and telephones out. The Santa Fe and Rock Island railroads desperately tried to save their river bridges only to lose both (along with the Brickyard and Sardou city bridges). The Santa Fe had four locomotives acting as ballast go into the water along with the span. Hill's packing plant released around 400 of its horses which would otherwise have been trapped at the riverside stockyards. A local saddle club rounded them up but at times they stampeded in downtown Topeka, a rare sight for Kansas avenue where three-quarters of a century before runaway horses were all too common. For a majority of Topekans, on the otherhand, life went on more or less as usual with perhaps only a hint of the situation far away from the dry southside. Like the 1903 flood though only more so, the cleanup was a long and difficult task. Damage figures ran into the millions. Some businesses, like Morrell's, simply quit rather than undertake the expense in restoring operations. For those structures beyond repair or immediate occupancy, the federal government assisted with trailer communities which existed for more than six months. People from all over the country, in a process dating back to 1860 drought relief aided in recovery. Volunteers from Bellevue, Nebr., and Offutt Air Force Base, seeing that the hamlet of Valencia was ignored, promptly formed a brigade of "muckateers" to clean that community.

As a result of the destruction, people of eastern Kansas resumed serious consideration of flood and public works programs more or less forgotten since the early 1930s. Prominent individuals loudly raised their voices in advocating a significantly improved dike program for Topeka along with dam construction up river and on Soldier and

Shunganunga creeks. Naturally, these met with considerable opposition, especially in the fertile Blue river valley. Whether construction will really prevent future flooding is unknown. Some theorize that the Kansas river floods with gigantic proportions approximately every 50 years making the next great flood due around the year 2000. After 20 years' work and over 30 million dollars spent, the Topeka flood control project was completed in 1971.

A clipping from the *Capital*, dated January, 1886, explained in depth the stunning cold of the infamous blizzard of '86. It affected nearly all of Kansas with Topeka temperatures hovering for long periods well below zero. One day the afternoon temperature supposedly never rose above eight degrees below. The newspaper noted how even those who normally would have been most happy at circumstances, the coal dealers, were "not very much pleased; . . . it is almost an impossibility for them to deliver coal." The poor felt the cold the most severely and there was one account of a young man so numbed by it that he fell asleep in his delivery wagon. Fortunately for him the horses complacently strolled back to the market where the proprietor revived him. Street car drivers, however, probably endured the most pain, driving into the wind. One commented to the *Capital* that during a "gale . . . blowing from the north at the rate of about sixty miles an hour":

> My hands are so stiff that I cannot hold the reins; my face is frozen, and I am certain my feet and ears are frosted. I walk most of the time, but it is impossible to keep warm. I started out at 6 o'clock this morning, and I will have to stand it until 10 o'clock to-night.

Periodically, Topeka newspapers reported the extensive damage caused by simple, straight winds or thunderstorms in Topeka and vicinity, usually in the spring. The most frequent victims of such winds were store front plate glass windows, the heavy roof line cornices of 19th century buildings and small, unstable out-buildings. In the country barns were often the greatest casualty though crop damage shared that honor.

One of the most destructive tornadoes in the county struck Menoken and Soldier townships on June 5, 1917. At least three persons in that area were killed and damage to Bishop station (on the Rock Island, south of the river), Welland school house and buildings in Elmont was extensive. Hundreds of workers entered the area cleaning up as best they could, though, explained the *Capital* on June 11, thousands of sightseers followed behind the workers, making reclamation difficult. National guard troops protected property but soon "gave up in despair. . . . It was utterly impossible for them to stop the long line of cars, the drivers of which insisted on driving into the farms to inspect the damage." At times they outnumbered the legitimate workers.

Though numerous legends about Topeka's invulnerability to tornadoes had grown up through the years, those storms did not ignore the town. The first came in the territorial period and knocked some of the stones out of the Congregational Church. Another small tornado danced across the city on April 3, 1897, and caused heavy damage in the southwest and Tennesseetown sections. In the latter, according to the *Capital,* "there was a small-sized panic among the colored people, who ran about crying 'cyclone' at the top of their voices." Outbuildings, shingles and small objects were swept away. One 12-year-old girl was lifted up and carried 50 feet but fortunately was not hurt. No life was lost in the storm.

Such was not the case, however, when the next important tornado passed through the city on the evening of June 8, 1966. Coming off Burnett's mound, which one legend said would protect the city, it headed through the heart of town though it did miss the main downtown business section by a few blocks. The massive storm killed 17 people, injured 500 more and caused untold damage to homes, business buildings, Washburn University and Topeka's beautiful trees. Like a battlefield from World War II the grimmest scenes were found at the college campus, Central Park grade school and the Santa Fe shops east of Branner street. Again the problems of sightseers, looting, and hysteria arose. One fear was that the National Reserve building on the southeast corner of Tenth and Kansas was about to topple. Help from communities over Kansas soon arrived to assist in weatherproofing damaged homes and opening streets to travel. For years afterwards the path of the storm from the southwest to east Topeka and Oakland was clearly marked by the absence of foliage.

Scene of destruction after 1917 tornado which struck Elmont. (Courtesy Kansas State Historical Society)

A binding operation on the Kaw bottoms in eastern Shawnee county about 1910. (Courtesy Mrs. Neta Milliken Wilson)

The Hubert Hall threshing operation in Tecumseh in the early 1900s. (Courtesy Theodore Hall)

TOIL ON THE FARM; COUNTRY LIFE

Health, debt, exhausted soil, free land—all these factors brought early pioneers to Shawnee county which was then part of two billion acres of public domain. Here early settlers found adequate precipitation and proper soil for their agricultural needs. They promptly planted the first year's crop of "sod-corn" to break the surface of the land for future use.

Several federal acts made local land cheap during the territorial and early statehood periods. The Pre-emption act of 1841 gave preferential rights to settlers and squatters. After six months' residence, a settler was allowed to buy as much as 160 acres at $1.25 per acre. The Pre-emption act was not repealed until 1891. In 1847 an act of congress authorized land bounties to veterans of the Mexican War. Subsequent legislation in 1850 and in 1855 permitted the land warrants which were issued to veterans to be assigned to any purchaser. It sold for less than the government's minimum price which was $1.25 per acre. But the most important as well as the most used law was the Homestead Act of 1862 which offered free land to settlers who met certain requirements. These stipulated that the person staking the claim be 21 years old or the head of a household, a citizen or immigrant who had filed a declaration of intent, and did not own as much as 160 acres already. If a pioneer met these requirements and had $10.00 for a filing fee he could homestead up to 160 acres of land, after which he was required to live on the tract, cultivate and improve it for five years before he finally received a deed. The Homestead Act went into effect Jan. 1, 1863, just two years after Kansas became a state. It was amended many times under the prevailing philosophy that public lands should be given to *bona fide* farmers and stockmen whose homesteads would become permanent settlements.

When a new immigrant arrived, he located his claim and marked it by making a foundation of four logs for a cabin and erecting a board with his name on it. He then went to the land office and filed a declaratory statement of intent to homestead or pre-empt the quarter-section. In the Shawnee county region log cabins averaging about ten by twelve feet at the foundation were the most common form of abode.

Even if a new settler had to purchase his land rather than homestead, he could still establish himself easily with minimum expense. An editorial in the March 28, 1879, *Kansas Valley Times* asked "what more independent life can a man of small means ask than a farmer's life in Kansas." The writer then theorized on the approximate cost to settle in the county:

> After thinking the matter over for a long time, we will suppose he takes his $2,000 and comes to Kansas; with that amount of money he can buy 160 acres of land, at say $5 per acre, would be $800. — He then needs a house, but can get along with a smaller one than he had in the east, so he builds an ell of say three rooms for about $200, intending in a year or two to build a front or main house. Having built his house and moved in, he next builds a straw shed, for his two horses and one cow, which is all he needs to start with, and for which he has paid we will say, for the horses, $200; and for the cow $25; wagon $55; harness $30; and plow $25. He now wants a dozen chickens at $1.50, and a pig at $5, and he is well fixed for farming in Kansas. He has expended $1,326.50, besides his labor. He has a balance of nearly $700 to carry him through till he raises a crop. With that 700 he can, if so inclined, build more permanent buildings or invest in young stock or a part of it, and have it returned to him in a short time with a large increase. He has also made a beginning for a farm which will in a few years increase very much in value in case he should want to sell, or a home which will support all and at the same time keep the family together.

Immigrants poured into the county during the first two decades of statehood. The nearness of a ready market in Topeka, as well as the capital, attracted many new settlers who were willing to pay extraordinarily good prices for land in the vicinity. The Topeka *Leader* carried notice of one such purchase in its May 14, 1868, edition. A farmer near the Osage county line was offered "$20 per acre, or $6400.00 for his place. Two years ago he paid just $2 per acre for it. Ten hundred per cent on two years investment is good enough, for the west."

The original log homes on these early homesteads were ones for which the farmers duly gave thanks. It might seem to one looking back that they actually had little for which to give thanks. Most of them lived in hastily constructed, one-room structures with dirt floors and cloth windows and doors. In the severe winter of 1855-56, one pioneer wrote of going to bed as the only escape from freezing, and of awaking the next morning with six inches of snow in his cabin. If the new farmer could endure the hardship of these crude cabins, however, he might prosper enough to build a new house—usually of two-story limestone construction, but if he were particularly successful he might even construct a fine frame farmhouse. Many of these remain in the rural areas of Shawnee county.

The next buildings that would appear in the farmyards were barns. These were often simple log sheds not much different from the houses.

The most important building in any town was the post office. Richland's is shown here shortly after the turn of the century. (Courtesy Mrs. LeRoy Murren)

Richland's main street probably on a Saturday afternoon about 1910. (Courtesy Mrs. LeRoy Murren)

The J. W. Winter store in Dover. (Courtesy Charles Todd)

The variety of barns was tremendous, ranging from mere sheds to stables, hay-barns, and the large structures common today. The latter came in various shapes and styles — round, rectangular, and even octagonal. A pair of the last mentioned still stand, both north of Silver Lake. In 1879, the eastern magazine *Dairy Farming* devoted a chapter to the merits of the "American Octagonal Barn" over the rectangular. Advantages were the economy of material and the open floor, uncluttered by posts, for the free handling and storage of hay. The round-style barn of the Shakers was acclaimed in the 1880s in leading farm journals as sound dairy practice. Cattle could feed head-in on the mooring circle in the center of the barn. Variants on the round barn—hexagonal and octagonal—were built by the more progressive farmers on the Great Plains during the period.

Other out-buildings on the farms were chicken coops, pig sties, ice and spring houses. Foods were kept cool by placing them in a cellar or "cave" usually hollowed from a hillside or dug in the yard. This kept butter, milk, and sometimes cooked food which was saved to serve at the next meal. Some people who had open wells would place butter and milk in a pail lowered into the water by means of a rope. Others had a small shelter or house built near a well. In this structure they had a flat trough. A pipe leading from the pump allowed fresh water to run through the trough at intervals thereby keeping articles which had been placed in the miniature aqueduct cool. In 1926 Mrs. May Moore wrote about the Carter farm near Auburn: "The spring house was built in 1867 with another old neighbor, James Davis, doing the mason work. I can well remember how we used to set our milk there in pans and crocks to cool in the water."

The supply of ice depended on the severity and duration of cold weather the winter before. If ice formed of sufficient thickness on streams, it was cut into blocks and stored in a building erected for that purpose. The blocks were placed on edge and as close together as could be. When a layer was formed saw dust or straw was packed on top of the first and again packed as before. This was continued until the house was full. There was usually enough to supply the community for the next summer as the demand for ice was primarily limited to such occasions as picnics and social gatherings.

In a few years prosperous farms were the rule rather than the exception in much of Shawnee county. An example of this fact is this article from the 1870s concerning the southeastern part of the county:

The farmers, or farm owners of this locality are, first, John Ward, who has the largest, oldest and most fruitful apple orchard in Shawnee county; 360 bearing trees, and shrubbery in abundance. His farm contains 80 acres of very choice land. He will sell for $125 per acre. Ex-mayor McAffee has an extensive plantation,

Separating cream on a Dover area farm about 1946. Soon would come the thankless job of cleaning the separator. (Courtesy Charles Todd)

stock range, etc. here, and one of the largest and most complete barns in the county. Mr. Hartsock, of Topeka, has a $3,000 brick residence, recently completed, on his farm. Dr. Martin, of the city, owns a fortune of land in the form of a well improved farm. Col. Scudder is another extensive farmer, and so is Washburne, and Covell, and A. A. Ward, and Cross, and Tinkam, and others. In this neighborhood also is the extensive and famous nursery, grapery—or vineyard of Messrs. Harvey & Worrall. W. C. Gilpatrick, of revenue notoriety, has a pleasant retreat in this pleasant neighborhood.

Life in the country was often quite rugged, made so by the relative remoteness from Topeka. Horse stealing was one despicable crime often committed in the hinterlands of the county. One deputy sheriff from Auburn who lost a horse trailed the two thieves to Humboldt, caught them and then single-handedly strung them up. More despicable yet was the rape of the daughter of Harrison White south of Topeka in the summer of 1888. A black man ravished Miss White on her father's farm while he worked the fields. The rapist was captured in Wamego, but in the meantime the girl's cousin had shot another black man whom he believed to be the perpetrator of the crime. The black population was indignant and there were fears of mob violence against both the victim's cousin and her father, until the real criminal was returned to Topeka.

Bachelor farming had its drawbacks as Augustus T. Daniels noted in his diaries: "Wonder if I shall ever have a settled opinion on any subject. This doubt, uncertainty, & indecision are the worst results of my Kansas Experience." Later he purchased a farm north of Topeka in Soldier township and supposed that he was doing badly as a farmer. "What a miserable failure I've made of this Kans. biz." and

Charles Todd slops his hogs at his Dover area farm about 1945. (Courtesy Charles Todd)

"O where shall the Exile find a home?" Still later he became quite lonely and morose in his bachelorhood. "O for a letter, a paper or some communication from the outside world."

Usually farm families were large. David Zirkle wrote:

Although we were a large family . . . there were jobs for all. Each boy had a certain job assigned to him, and he knew that particular part of the chores was his responsibility and did not expect anyone else to look after it. Probably the youngest had the task of filling the woodbox with firewood and providing kindling for starting the morning fire. Another looked after filling the stove reservoir and buckets with water that had to be brought from the well. Then there was the table to set. After supper came the job that no one wanted—washing and drying the dishes. This job was usually rotated week to week. The jobs that I have mentioned were for the younger boys. The boys who were old enough to work in the field fed the horses and cattle. My father always fed the hogs.

Garden making was a time of rejoicing for country children, not because they enjoyed the process of preparing the ground and planting the seeds, but because it came at a time of year when the winter was supposed to end. The days were longer, the sun warmed the ground, and children discarded wool socks and the heavy cowhide boots which they had worn for seven or eight months. It was time to go barefoot.

Going to town—meaning Topeka—was a delightful break in the monotony of farming. In the winter the farmer would have everything ready to start by first light. That meant he would have to be up by five o'clock in the morning in order to have the team fed, watered and harnessed in time to leave. When the weather was cold, he would have a stone on the stove where it would get hot. This was placed in the wagon for the traveler to warm his feet. If some of the family were going along they rode in the back of the wagon on straw.

Once at the markets, families traded eggs, butter, and perhaps some cured meat for staples at general stores. They took wheat to the mills in case they needed flour. Sometimes even chickens were taken for trading. Money was tight in these times. Zirkle wrote about his father's financial status: "I never knew of his buying anything, including groceries, which he did not pay for when he got it. Because of thrift and caution he never made much money, but he always had a small surplus of cash on hand; in fact he had some money loaned to neighbors most of the time."

Zirkle also mentioned how many country people obtained important articles without bothering to go to Topeka or one of the rural country stores:

A huckster used to stop at our house. He came on a certain day each week. This one had a light wagon pulled by two horses. He had for sale such things as tin-ware, notions of various kinds, brooms, needles, and pins. One of the items my mother often bought from him was wool yarn used for knitting socks. He was an old Dutchman who spoke with a decided accent. . . . He would take butter, eggs, or chickens in exchange for what he had to sell.

Celebrations were important to country people, simply because they were few and far between. Once in a while a traveling lecturer spoke to local lyceums, but those who enticed one of the learned "professors" into the county outside Topeka were lucky indeed. A topic would be chosen for the Saturday night's discussion and one team argued *pro,* the other *con.* Topics were chosen from major events of the day. One was reported in the *Commonwealth* on December 14, 1871:

Passing the night at Rochester, I accompanied their excellent teacher, Mr. Harvey, to the lyceum, which the enterprising youth of the vicinity have organized. The question, "Resolved, That the newspapers are doing more for the enlightenment of the people of this country than all other literature," was discussed earnestly and

Feeding the chickens on a farm at 29th and Burlingame road about 1912. (Courtesy James D. Wallace)

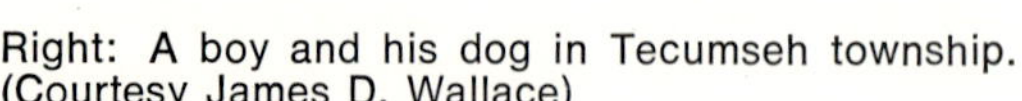

Right: A boy and his dog in Tecumseh township. (Courtesy James D. Wallace)

Center: Sand lot baseball in the country more often meant playing in an unmowed pasture. (Courtesy Roy Gill)

Below, left: Goin' fishin' on Whetstone creek, 1930s. (Courtesy James D. Wallace)

Below, right: Topeka store clerks on a country frolic about 1912. Fay Ritchie is third from left, sister Marian Ritchie far right. (Courtesy James D. Wallace)

intelligently. The local disputants were T. M. James, Dr. Marrow, Owen, Hummer, Hamilton, Cheney and others. Dr. Marrow, in the course of his remarks on the negative of the question, paid as beautiful and eloquent a tribute to the bible as can well be conceived.

The meetings were not always so civilized. A lyceum at Auburn erupted into a regular brawl, although the physical disagreement had nothing to do with the lyceum topic.

Entertainment at home was as inexpensive as possible and limited. It usually involved an activity eventually helpful to the family. For the women sewing and quilting bees were popular if several neighboring ladies could get together. If not, crocheting, knitting, needlepoint, and embroidering were useful and interesting ways of spending an uneventful evening. The men went hunting and fishing. These amusements also provided the family with needed items and welcome supplements to the daily diet. Occasionally the entire family went on an outing for fish. James D. Wallace wrote of such an excursion in his memoirs:

Presumably our family was not talented at fishing, but I do remember one spring Sunday in 1925 when, reacting to one of those strange impulses that we, as a family, so seldom yielded to, the entire family, Dad, Mother, Grandpa, Aunt Mary, Aunt Dicy, we children, including Fay Aleen who was but 2½, and even our hired man, Slim, went fishing in Whetstone [creek]. It was a truly beautiful spring day, as spring days are beautiful occasionally in Kansas, and we spent from right after breakfast until late afternoon at the creek. Our catch was fifty-one, nearly all sun perch, although a few small catfish were caught. The fish ranged from about a half-pound downward to several so small they scarcely made a spot in the skillet, nevertheless we cleaned and fried them all for supper that night. We also cooked a number of crawdads, but everyone agreed that they tasted like a poor quality of rubber. Thus began and ended the Wallace family's greatest fishing excursion, the only one of its kind.

Sunday afternoons and holidays were times for family get-togethers. Sunday often featured a big dinner and conversation until the visitors had to return home and do chores. Holidays offered similar entertainment, and Christmas was an occasion for gift exchanges and church programs.

Most food was home-grown. There were only three staple items that were not raised on the farm and had to be purchased at the store—coffee, salt, and sugar. Coffee was in the bean and until the turn of the century it had to be both roasted and ground at home. Brown sugar was in general use, white sugar was a luxury reserved for company. Meat, often a beef and one or more hogs depending on the size of the family, was butchered on the farm. During the summer months chickens became the principal meat supply. Meat that needed to be kept was either salt-cured or smoked. There was an abundance of home rendered lard which was the only shortening used. Milk and butter were provided by the few dairy cows on each farm.

William Kreipe stirs a boiling caldron of apple butter on his farm near Tecumseh. (Courtesy Mildred Kreipe McAnaw)

Fruit that wasn't eaten fresh was dried. There was no canned fruit for many years as people did not know how to process it in airtight containers. The fruit was peeled, cored, sliced, and placed on canvas or paper in the sun, then turned every day until it was dried completely. Apples could be placed in a shallow hole, covered with straw and about eight inches of earth to keep through the winter. Cider and apple butter were two more ways of preserving apples. Around 1880 preserving fruit and vegetables became simpler through the process of canning. Crocks, jars, and tin cans were used to hold the item being preserved while a lid was placed over the mouth and wax poured over it to make it airtight. Garden produce kept for lengthy periods of time when saved in this manner.

One object seen in the yard of nearly every home in the early history of Shawnee county was an ash hopper. These were often made of boards, about three feet square at the top. The sides were tapered to about six inches at the bottom and rested on a platform of boards. The platform was set on a slant, the back side higher than the front and grooved. The grooves were cut in a fan shape and met at the center at the lower side of the platform. In this hopper were placed wood ashes from the stove. David Zirkle explained the use of his family's hopper:

When soap was needed, the hopper being full of ashes, water was poured in at the top. As it penetrated the ashes and trickled through, the grooves in the platform carried it to a receptacle placed to catch it. This liquid is lye which boiled

At least one of these children en-
joyed their rocking horse near
Wakarusa. (Courtesy Kansas State
Historical Society)

with grease forms a soap, the kind our forebears used for washing clothes, dishes, and for other uses. It was not the kind that makes the housewife's suds as white and soft as a baby's skin.

Farm life was neither all fun nor all work; it was a hard life. Shawnee county was originally populated by farmers and agricultural life was a mainstay of the county years before and after Topeka was a metropolitan area. Today the county is primarily urban but the farms on the outskirts are still representative of the rural heritage of Shawnee county.

Lawn tennis at Camp Tandy near Tecumseh about 1915. (Courtesy E. V. King)

The Palace Clothing Co.
Arthur A. Guettel, Pres.
709~711 Kansas Avenue

Ripley's
A Reliable Firm

LAUNDERERS
CLEANERS
DYERS

"Columbus may have
done a wonderful thing
when he discovered Amer-
ica, but he couldn't have
received a greater kick
out of it than I did, the
day I discovered—

Harry Endlich

"Where You See Tomorrow's Style
Today."

733 Kansas

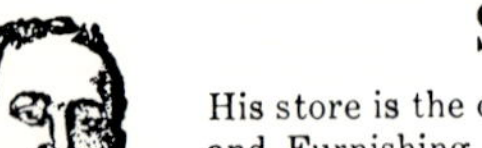

PELLETIER'S

DAVID J. AUGUST

SAYS

His store is the only real Clothing, Shoe
and Furnishing Goods Store in Topeka
AND AUGUST SHOULD KNOW

High Fashions in Misses' and Women's

HAMS
BACON

CONTINUOUS SERVICE
10:30 A.M. to 7:30 P.M.

FROM THE LOWEST RUNG; LIFE IN THE CITY

In 1845 Benjamin Disraeli coined one of the most shattering phrases in the English language: "The Two Nations, The Rich and the Poor." Two nations or two peoples in Britain "who are formed by a different breeding, are fed by a different food, are ordered by different manners, and are not governed by the same laws." As it was with 19th century Britain so it has been (though less drastic and perhaps more complex or subtle) in some areas of 19th and 20th century Kansas. Different people inhabit different spheres in Topeka as they do elsewhere. Charlotte McLellan in her history of the neighborhood declared: "Potwin Place was a paradise for children." However, not all children lived in paradise. To some who lived just over the horizon, even within the shadow of the capitol dome, paradise was only a myth.

The poor barely subsisted and in winter many depended upon charity, either private or organized through the county Poor Commissioner who doled out previously used necessities such as clothes and shoes. In the 19th century most destitute persons were Negroes with only seasonal occupations. The Poor Commissioner reported to the *Commonwealth*, January 3, 1885, that he had supplied 600 colored and 145 white people with $587.10 worth of coal so far that winter. Some well-to-do white families took upon themselves the care of a particular poor family.

Redmonville on the Kaw in North Topeka was one of the worst sights of the 1880s. The *Commonwealth* reporter covered one end of the village to the other for his paper in 1885, conveying the horrors of life there in these words:

In one room of a miserable little shanty, renting for four dollars per month, was found Teenie Hamilton, a widow, whose sole possession consisted of a few dilapidated bed clothes, a little stove, a quart of corn meal, one bucket of coal, and a wen [tumor] on her right shoulder about the size of a man't hat. She had secured some popcorn and was having a royal feast on the full, fluffy grains, and was dividing with a neighbor poorer than she. In the same house was a young man, wife and baby, waiting for something to turn up.

Living in a close, dirty room, not more than 10x12, in which was a bed, stove, tables and chairs, was found a family of six persons, with whom was living a large girl and her ten months old baby, eight people living in this little space, trying to keep warm by an excuse of a fire. The husband is a blacksmith, thrown out of work by the shop closing. This family has suffered for food . . . yet the girl and her child was taken in because no other place was opened to her.

The most appalling exhibition of poverty was found in a little shed-roofed shanty, 12x12. Opening the door upon darkness and coldness, and facing a smell that was stifling, your correspondent went inside. Occupying one corner of the shanty was an old cook stove, in which was feebly burning a match, there stood revealed an old shake down [an improvised bed], which evidently had just been vacated by a woman who might be fifty, and who replied to questions in a dull, apathetic manner, as though neither food or coal, comfort or discomfort were things she cared for.

Conditions at the Shawnee county poor farm, however, seemed a little bit better and quite a bit cleaner than the impoverished areas along the Kaw and Shunganunga. The *Capital* described the facilities in December, 1885, and referred to the recently acquired hospital beds, the good bedding, and the new wash and bath house which the inmates were required to use. Originally built five miles north of Topeka in 1871, the asylum had at that time eight men (five colored, two Germans, and an Irishman) and two women, the latter having "more energy than the men." Though better off than if alone, some lived pitiable lives with no family about or were, as in the case of Julia Haflumboy, a Pottawatomie chief's daughter, destined to "live and die in a poor house." If able the people worked around the 116 acre farm during the summer. At the stroke of 7, 12 and 6 o'clock, a bell summoned them to their meals. They ate at the superintendent's table as much as they needed of light bread, meat, fruit, hominy, rice, beans, and milk.

In the 20th century poverty lingered with fundamental if mundane improvements like sewage lines, water mains, and water closets absent. The Russell Sage Foundation in 1914 made public a survey which showed that approximately 9,000 homes in the city, three-quarters had privys even though many were on or near a sewer line. The east side, with a population of 7,000, was the "largest [area] without sewers in the state of Kansas." There were nearly 5,000 wells in town with quite a few less than ten feet away from the privy. Sixty-four percent of them were considered polluted. Only North Topeka's water was relatively pure and the foundation believed the disease problem potentially serious what with 2,293 horses; 1,392 dogs; 330 cattle; 127 mules; 35 hogs; three goats; and one sheep in the city.

Though some of these lower class residential districts inched their way toward the capitol, a very different breed basked under its copper sheathing. Topeka's upper class grew like that in most western towns, very rapidly without the traditions of a long presence.

Unlike that of the Southeast, Western social position was not based on a long ownership of land. Property, particularly in city lots, was important but only so long as it generated wealth. Another factor

A shanty like that of Teenie Hamilton's.

Slums along the Shunganunga in 1914 showing outside privies, wells, dung heaps, and the creek. (From The Russell Sage Foundation, "Topeka Improvement Survey," 1914)

proved to be the date of one's arrival in town; the earlier, the better. Thus, until his death, Topekans often deferred to Cyrus K. Holliday not only because of his supposed financial position but because few were here any earlier. The same could be said of Fry Giles, John Ritchie, and Franklin Crane.

By the turn of the century, the concept of "first settler" possessed little meaning and so newer individuals were becoming powers in the community. As in other capitals, the professions assumed the leading positions. Law, medicine and journalism were the predominant occupations at that time.

Not all the giants of the city readily showed themselves to the public as did Arthur Capper and Charles Curtis. One of the most important figures, Marcus A. Low, remained fairly anonymous to later generations. Born and raised in Maine he came west and edited a Hamilton, Mo., newspaper. Poor health forced him to travel to California and he later entered into a legal career. As a lawyer he worked for the Rock Island railroad, rising in the firm to general attorney and president of several subsidiaries.

Low maintained a quiet presence in the community despite his importance to the company, and his major public service was as president of the Topeka park board. Yet his influence was important according to the *Journal* when he died in July, 1921. Low carefully "mapped out his battles" on behalf of the railroads with very little fanfare. He rarely attended Republican political functions but he could have had office, even U. S. senator, according to some. Instead, "when the crowds came to town there was always a waiting list in the ante room" of his office in the Rock Island depot. There they sought his advice, his support, or, stated the Kansas City *Times*, "to report what the Kansans called 'the situation.' "*

---

*The *Capital* July 20, 1921, mentioned that "when a man wanted to run for any office from United States senator down to member of the legislature he was always told to go and see 'Hurd, Low and Waggener.' Hurd [of the Santa Fe] and Low looked after the Republican end; Waggener, the Democratic end."

Marcus A. Low (1842-1921), architect of the Rock Island empire through Kansas, and behind-the-scenes political power. (Courtesy Kansas State Historical Society)

From about Third street on the north to Twelfth on the south, the
home of the important lined Topeka boulevard and its environs.
Not every home, however, dazzled since some were for middle-class
folk. Statistics compiled by Preston O. Hale and Arthur Conklin for
the Topeka boulevard *Bulletin* of the Shawnee County Historical
Society (December, 1963) provide an insight to the kind of people
who inhabited the district from the river to Fifteenth street and on
Tyler and Harrison streets, some 45 blocks. The adult population in
1900 was 1,276 with approximately 1,800 children.

Occupations embraced a wide spectrum, reminding one that not
all who lived there possessed large sums of money. Some fields no
longer exist or are unimaginable for that aristocratic boulevard. The
largest number of employees in one category were the downtown
clerks with 110, to be followed by 95 widows. Next came 62 clothiers,
57 domestics ("mostly Swedish girls"), 55 in the printing trade, 49 with
the railroads (this included a number of leading Santa Fe officials
like Edward Wilder, the secretary-treasurer), 38 attorneys, 37 in food
products, 36 in banking, 38 carpenters and painters, 25 educators, 27
students and 22 doctors. Six men acknowledged being laborers, one
was an undertaker, one a pool hall operator and two were cigar makers.
Two were blacksmiths, five were teamsters, nine were coachmen, or
liverymen, and 15 labeled themselves politicians. Among them, also,
lived five artists, 12 clergymen, 13 coach or buggy manufacturers, and
five farmers.

Despite the diversity of exterior trim, houses were either brick or
frame. The interior arrangements usually followed a similar pattern
with a central or side stair hallway, one or possibly two parlors, a
middle sitting room, large dining room, and an equally large kitchen
and pantry in the rear. The downstairs had at least one or two fireplaces in the main rooms and one upstairs, in the main bed chamber
if nowhere else. There were four bedrooms as well as one bath and
water closet on the second floor. If the residents finished the third
floor the large room served as playroom, ballroom or billiard room.
Basements sometimes contained a summer kitchen or servant quarters
(also sometimes on the third floor). In the rear of the property stood,
properly hidden by foliage, the carriage house. Many middle-class
homes had barns but the carriage house was often large and provided
upstairs quarters. The Munn's houseman, William, lived on the
second floor of Dr. L. H. Munn's brick barn at 315 Topeka. There
he acted as butler, gardener, and chauffer who drove Mrs. Munn "in
her smart Victorian buggy."

On opposite page: parlor, exterior, and musicale scene of the S. H. Fairfield residence, 1108 Throop, in the early 1900s. On this page, their cleaning girl. Fairfield was a Wabaunsee county pioneer while daughter Agnes (the woman in the middle of the piano scene) was a Topeka music teacher. (Courtesy Mrs. S. A. Moore)

Different mansions possessed different features like Munn's conservatory and fish pond. Two of Topeka's most spectacular showcases lay off the boulevard, the M. A. Low home at 1271 Fillmore and the Hiram Price Dillon house at Ninth and Harrison. Both incorporated fruit or hardwood paneling, Tiffany windows, imported marble fireplaces, and various art treasures. Low's brick mansion (built in the early 1890s and torn down in 1959) had its own ballroom and private steam heating plant while Dillon's $60,000 to $75,000 house, built in 1910, contained a private elevator. Dillon lavishly decorated his home with Dresden china, French Empire pieces, Ming Dynasty tapestry screens, and an impressive gilt piano. When the contents of the place were sold at auction in 1941, the piano went for $115 and the Ming tapestry screen a mere $16. So ended the testaments of wealth.

Frank G. Ritchie, a laborer in the Santa Fe car shop, never owned a Ming tapestry and probably never saw one. His home on the banks of the Shunganunga in Quinton Heights was fairly typical of working or lower middle-class housing. Located in 1900 on a triangular lot beside the creek, his property included the one story frame home; a

The luxurious dining room of the palatial Hiram Price Dillon home at Ninth and Harrison. (Courtesy Kansas State Historical Society)

small barn; coal and other sheds; a cave on the Shunganunga where the family kept milk, cream, and butter during the summer; a privy and a well. He also owned chickens, a horse and spring wagon, a milk cow, and some pigs usually penned down by the creek, but brought up to the barn when the Shunganunga was on the rise.

Ritchie's family around the turn of the century included five children, all of them living in the five room house. At the front was the parlor and behind it the middle room and then a large kitchen with porches off it. Opening out of the kitchen were two small bedrooms, the bath being the outdoor privy and a portable tub in the kitchen. Their kitchen also had a sink with pitcher pump, some cabinets, a large dining table, and a cook stove. The only other stove in the house was located in the parent's bedroom, or middle room, with the two smaller rooms of the children lacking any kind of heating. The family closed off the parlor when the weather turned cold and they spent all the time either in the kitchen or the middle room. Beneath the house was a dirt floor cellar, accessible only from outside.

Most small houses adhered to that general plan, sometimes using the middle room as a dining room and having the bedrooms upstairs. Few rooms were well decorated. During the 1920s a new architectural style called the airplane bungalow swept the city. Above the kitchen and back porch was a second story. Usually only one room with windows on three, possibly even all four sides, it was used as a sleeping porch in the summer. Come the torrid mid-1930s, this sleeping room became a very valuable asset to a home. After World War II even newer styles, cheese-box cottage, ranch, or split-level, predominated as well as new construction techniques.

Life literally began at home for it was not until well into the 20th century that children, even in upper-class families, were born in local hospitals. Six of the seven Frank Ritchie children saw the light of day in their parents' bedroom; it was so cold at Fay Ritchie's birth in February, 1895, that the parents had to hang quilts across the windows to keep as much of the air out as possible. Along with most fairly large families of the day, the Ritchies had two children die within a matter of months. Infant mortality in 1912, according to the Russell Sage foundation, was only 96 per 1,000 births, not especially high except for the North Topeka and east side districts, but childhood or adult diseases sometimes took a terrible toll. The *Commonwealth,* January 22, 1870, reported the sudden loss of three children of the George Ludington family due to scarlet fever. "It is seldom that three children lie robed in the habiliments of death in the same family the same day," stated the paper. Less than a week later the death of a fourth child occurred.

Accidents, too, played a frightening role for both youngster and adult. For example, in 1869 a four year old girl, "was playing near a cistern and accidentally fell in. Before aid could be summoned she drowned. Four physicians were called, but life was extinct." Runaway horses and fires often killed people. Unquestionably one of the most hazardous jobs in the Topeka of the 1880s and 1890s was the construction of the state capitol, still the tallest structure in the city. Nine men lost their lives during work on it, the most horrible death occuring on July 26, 1890. John Cave, a 24 year old iron worker, fell from the dome to the fourth floor, a distance of 130 feet. The *Capital,* the next day, described the event in gory detail. A wrench slipped and over he tumbled crashing from floor to floor. Where the body finally

The Frank G. Ritchie home in Quinton Heights, 1899. Fay Ritchie is on the right. (Courtesy James D. Wallace)

rested, explained the *Capital,* workmen discovered "his brains had escaped from the skull and fallen through to the basement. . . . His left arm was broken in two places and his right leg was also broken."

The Sage Foundation in discussing Topeka's health conditions in 1912, enumerated the various causes of death for that time comparing the Negro and white communities. The Negro mortality rate generally averaged twice that of the whites in tuberculosis, Bright's disease, organic heart disease, old age, pneumonia, typhoid, homicide, and appendicitis. For the whites major causes included early infancy mortality, accidents, cerebral hemorrhage, circulatory diseases, cancer, diptheria, and diabetes. As for early Topeka, the *State Record* in 1868 printed statistics from the interment book of the Topeka cemetery. It showed 521 burials, 179 under the age of 10 (the highest group, of course) but only one above 90. Causes were known for 289. Of that number consumption (tuberculosis) led with 35. Next came pneumonia, 16; congestive chills, 15; stillborn, 15; killed in battle, 15; typhoid fever, 12; inflamation of bowels, 9; dysentery, 8; whooping cough, 7; congestion of lung, 7; diarrhea, 6; scarlet fever, 5; accident, 5; brain fever, 5; heart disease, 4; and summer complaint, 4. There were other causes, too, like the two suicides and two cases of the croup as well as one each of scalded, hives, and "found hung." Only one person died of old age and one from cancer.

Childhood presented many problems, and many children worked as much as they played. Probably few experienced the party pleasures at the Troutman home in Potwin Place as reported in the *Capital,* August, 1895:

> The young people assembled at seven o'clock [in the evening] and took a ride

A typical working class home in the shop district and hanging out Monday wash, c. 1915. (Courtesy James D. Wallace)

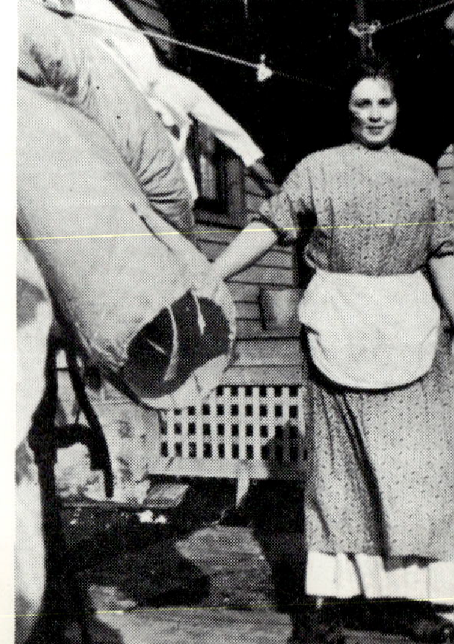

The 1885 census listed 20 Santa Fe employees, laborers, and domestics living at the James D. Wallace boarding house on East First street, next to the A.T.& S.F. shops. (Courtesy James D. Wallace)

of an hour and a half's duration upon their wheels about the city, under the leadership of Mr. Torrence Ewart and Miss Libbie Gregory.* They wore bright colored paper caps and made a gay appearance.

Upon their return the spacious lawn was beautifully illuminated with Chinese lanterns and every convenience provided for an enjoyable evening.

While a lively march was played they marched two by two around the lawn and took their seats in chairs arranged on either side of the broad walk. Refreshments were served and the round of pleasure kept up until ten o'clock.

Fay and Marian Ritchie were not so fortunate in Quinton Heights. They had to perform chores like feeding the chickens, hauling in coal from the shed, cleaning the house, etc. Fay helped her father saw wood. They gathered the logs, placed one on saw horses, and commenced work, Frank Ritchie on one end of the cross-cut saw and his daughter on the other. If Fay did anything wrong, her father shouted, "You're binding, don't do it that way!" Diversions in the home were few, cards and checkers being the most popular. Crokinole, a board game with pockets at the corner on which a variety of different games could be played, afforded children many hours of fun, especially during long winter evenings by the fire. Ultimately, one of the greatest pleasures simply consisted of the family coming together at the stove with the father opening the grate and thrusting a wire basket in the fire to pop popcorn.

The outdoors, of course, offered the most enjoyment. In winter those children residing near the Shunganunga moved on to ice skating or playing shinny on the ice. For shinny, the youngsters simply used discarded cans and battered them from one side to the other, clanging all the way with home made sticks. Late in the afternoon or evening the older ones organized skating parties, building a giant bonfire on the bank to keep warm.

As a different kind of winter pastime, the Ritchie children often intently watched employees of the Baughman ice cream plant hitch up teams of horses which were driven out on the Shunganunga. The

*The bicycle or velocipede had been popular for a generation; "velocipedestrianism" and races proved especially enjoyable though women were barred from an early Topeka velocipede rink.

The Gem grocery at 502-504 West Tenth street. (Courtesy Fritz Leuenberger)

Ice was not always delivered under the most sanitary conditions, but it was welcomed nevertheless, (Courtesy Mrs. Ralph James)

The John Brunt drugstore, 729 Kansas avenue, probably in the 1920s. (Courtesy Roy Gill)

Baughman people sawed off huge chunks of ice and carried it into the plant. There they packed it with sawdust to keep through the summer as storage for ice cream. As a reward or payment for cutting up ice on the Ritchie's side of the creek, the Baughmans sometimes scooped up ice cream in wooden dishes for the children. Baughman's, like Scott Brothers, became a Topeka institution enjoyed by children of all ages. Beginning in 1884, people often traveled out to the fairly inconvenient site for a dish of ice cream after a party or ride—Baughman's was a part of many a Topeka courtship and probably several marriage proposals. Until the 1950s, its horse-drawn ice cream wagons graced Topeka streets, with children flocking to the treats in the wagon itself or just to view the last horse-drawn conveyances in the city.

Summertime granted children the widest assortment of activities and games. The highlight of the year, for many, was the circus. Boys and girls in 1872 had a double thrill. Late in July the New York circus arrived in town only to be followed in mid-August by the "Greatest Show on Earth," P. T. Barnum's "Great Traveling World's Fair." Divided into museum, side show, menagerie, and circus sections, the Barnum circus "presented acres of tents" according to the *Commonwealth* on August 16. As another treat later on in the 19th century several smaller shows wintered in Topeka, including the well known Sells Brothers circus. In April, 1890, the *Capital* featured a small story about a local contractor and a carriage maker who formed the A. K. Fulford & Co's. New London Shows, Aviary, Circus and World's Menagerie—the company planned to use 125 horses, the staple of any circus, and was fixing 27 ornate cages and wagons for the troop, hiring girls for the parade and ring, and sewing band uniforms. "Should the jungles of Wakarusa produce hippopotomi and elephants," reported the paper, Fulford "would much prefer to pay a native Kansan for such specimens than to send to New Orleans, New York or across the water for them."

Sells Brothers, founded in the 1870s but not in Topeka, underwent various changes over the years eventually becoming Sells-Floto circus, one of the largest to survive into the 20th century. Despite an Ohio connection, the Sells circus wintered in Topeka until the early 1900s. Supposedly they housed some of the menagerie in a stone barn on a Quincy street alley between Seventh and Eighth streets. On occasion some of the animals escaped their pens. Once, according to a later newspaper column, a python got loose and cozied up for a nap in a grocery wagon only to frighten the driver the next day. Sometime in 1901, circus officials deliberately allowed an old lion to escape for

Ringling Brothers circus parades Kansas avenue on August 16, 1915. The New England building dominates the skyline. (Courtesy James Simons)

For several years Sells Brothers circus wintered in Topeka. This ad appeared in a local paper in 1883. (Courtesy Kansas State Historical Society)

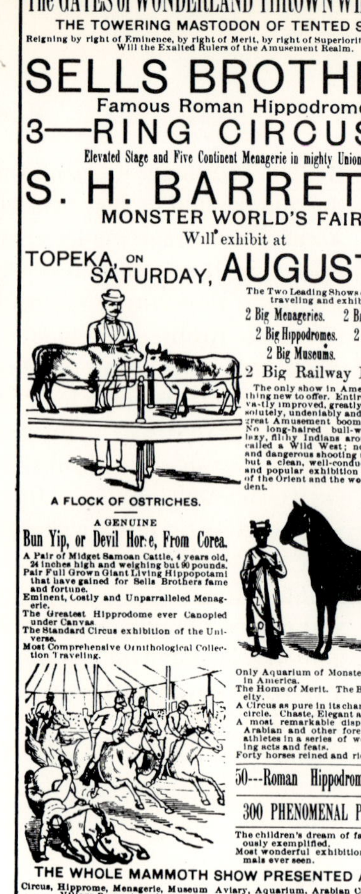

The GATES of WONDERLAND THROWN WIDE APAR[T]

THE TOWERING MASTODON OF TENTED SHOWS.

Reigning by right of Eminence, by right of Merit, by right of Superiority and by Popu[lar] Will the Exalted Rulers of the Amusement Realm.

SELLS BROTHERS

Famous Roman Hippodrome,

3—RING CIRCUS—

Elevated Stage and Five Continent Menagerie in mighty Union with

S. H. BARRETT'S

MONSTER WORLD'S FAIR,

Will exhibit at

TOPEKA, ON SATURDAY, AUGUST 1[?]

The Two Leading Shows of the Nation [now] traveling and exhibiting as one.

2 Big Menageries. 2 Big Elevated Stag[es]
2 Big Hippodromes. 2 Big Circuses.
2 Big Museums. 2 Big Parades.
2 Big Railway Equippag[e]

The only show in America having a[ny]thing new to offer. Entirely reconstruc[ted] va-tly improved, greatly enlarged and [ab]solutely, undeniably and indisputably [the] great Amusement boom of the coun[try] No long-haired bull-whackers chas[ing] lazy, filthy Indians around the ring [and] called a Wild West; no nerve-shock[ing] and dangerous shooting under our canv[as] but a clean, well-conducted, bright, [gay] and popular exhibition of the splend[ors] of the Orient and the wonders of the O[cci]dent.

A FLOCK OF OSTRICHES.

A GENUINE

Bun Yip, or Devil Hor:e, From Corea.

A Pair of Midget Samoan Cattle, 4 years old, 24 inches high and weighing but 90 pounds.
Pair Full Grown Giant Living Hippopotami that have gained for Sells Brothers fame and fortune.
Eminent, Costly and Unparralleled Menagerie.
The Greatest Hipprodome ever Canopied under Canvas.
The Standard Circus exhibition of the Universe.
Most Comprehensive Ornithological Collection Traveling.

Only Aquarium of Monster Marine Mar[vels] in America.
The Home of Merit. The Birthplace of N[ov]elty.
A Circus as pure in its character as the ho[me] circle. Chaste, Elegant and Refined.
A most remarkable display of Japan[ese] Arabian and other foreign acrobats [and] athletes in a series of wonderfully thr[ill]ing acts and feats.
Forty horses reined and ridden by one m[an]

50---Roman Hippodrome Riders.---

300 PHENOMENAL PERFORMERS

The children's dream of fairyland sump[tu]ously exemplified.
Most wonderful exhibition of trained a[ni]mals ever seen.

THE WHOLE MAMMOTH SHOW PRESENTED AT ONCE.

Circus, Hipprome, Menagerie, Museum Aviary, Aquarium, Arabian Caravan, J[apanese] Village Pageants and a world of startling novelties and thrilling featur[es]

—— THE FINEST STREET PARADE EVER GIVEN IN AMER[ICA]

Two Performances daily at 2 and 8 p. m. Doors open one hour [earlier]

Admission to all, only 50 Cents. Children under nir[e]

some publicity. A vigorous young male also broke loose and for a time terrorized the hobo camps along the Shunganunga. William Sells, adopted son of founder Allen Sells, later acquired the show and had the wagons, equipment, costumes, and other paraphenalia manufactured in Topeka. However, early in the new century the Sells-Floto circus became Denver based.

Sports received their fair share of attention in Topeka, too, with buffalo hunting especially popular in the late 1860s and very early 1870s. By 1870 bison were becoming rare on the Kansas High Plains, a testimony to the efficiency of the railroad hunters no doubt. The *Commonwealth,* October 6, 1870, mentioned an excursion to Fort Hays and then on to the Colorado mountains for up to 30 days—the prices for Topeka to Hays $21, and Topeka to Denver $40. "Now ladies and gentlemen," the paper concluded, "gather up your firearms, and go out and kill a buffalo."

Easterners, or even mid-Westerners, often took every detail of the hunt very seriously and dressed up for the occasion. In October of

1872, one hunter enlivened the streets of Topeka with his display. "He carried a double barreled gun," stated the paper, "a powder flask about the size of a canteen, and had on a slouch hat and claw-hammer coat. He drew consolation from a long clay pipe, and glared upon the laughing passersby with wild ferocity." The *Commonwealth* added that it intended to send along a reporter "to see how far they (the excursion party) blow themselves at the first shot." The most regal bison hunter in Topeka history was the Grand Duke Alexis, third surviving son of Czar Alexander II of Russia. After his hunt, the Duke Alexis arrived in Topeka, January 22, 1872, where city and state officials paraded him and other officials, including Gen. Phil Sheridan, through town and honored the party with a state dinner at the Fifth Avenue hotel.

In a few years the buffalo market—along with the numbers of the animals themselves—collapsed. Before that the *Commonwealth* complained, December 20, 1872:

> The market is full of buffalo meat. You can get it in any shape at the restaurants—buffalo cowcumbers; buffalo rampant, with frizzled hair; buffalo sirloin smothered in gopher holes; buffalo giblets garnished with squaw fingers; Cheyenne de Kiowa, garnished with owl sauce and rattlesnake gravy. In fact one may get anything in the shape of 'bufler.' "

Fisticuffs had its share of participants though usually in an unorganized manner. One early match occurred in June, 1873, and the newspaper observed that the prize was to be a North Topeka pony and the "championship of Shawnee county." Fought near the Tefft House, it "attracted quite a crowd of mashers and sports." Another diversion for the spectator was racing and trotting, both of which took place at nearby courses in the 1860s and 1870s. Often they were matches of only two horses and the purse could climb into four figures. The most noted Topeka jockey, who made a large circle through Kansas in the 1870s, was Charles Curtis, the future vice-president of the United States.

Of all sports, baseball was king. "Lawrence has got it, Leavenworth's got it, Topeka's got it, we've *all* got it," announced the *Leader* August 22, 1867. Almost overnight baseball swept across the nation so that in the summer of 1867 Topeka possessed three teams: the Shawnees, the Prairie Club, and the Capitols. The game became a part of the social whirl. When a Topeka club hosted one from Lawrence in 1867, "a number of Topeka ladies honored the game with their presence." In pauses during the match the Topeka Brass Band provided music as they did, along with the string band, when the two teams (Lawrence won) dined together at the Gordon House that evening. "Gayety and good humor prevailed until train time," remarked the *Leader,* August 1.

Old Western League ball park in Highland Park. (Courtesy Roy Gill)

Not everyone, naturally, approved of this new sport. The North Topeka *Times*, April 13, 1871, stated:

> The young men of North Topeka should organize a base ball club. There is nothing that can create nail-less fingers, sprained ankles, and broken noses so numerously nevertheless it is a very fine sport. We notice many athletic young men in this place who, as we have no doubt, would be pleased to lose an eye or have all their teeth knocked down their throats for the fun of the thing, in trying to make home base. . . . South Topeka has a club, therefore, North Topeka should be in the field.

Very soon afterwards groups in the county organized ball clubs. No place was isolated. Tecumseh had her Plowboys and Monmouth township her Modocs. When those two clubs played in July, 1870, Tecumseh slaughtered Monmouth 67 to nine. Such scores were the rule, not the exception though the tally of the Topeka Shawnees against the Lawrence Universitys in September, 1867—96 to 57—was a bit high. Topeka teams usually bested the country talent and during the 1870s sometimes played high-caliber clubs like the St. Louis Brown Stockings. The *Blade*, August 27, 1875, reported that the Topeka Westerns beat the St. Louis club 23 to six only to have the Brown Stockings shut out the Westerns the next day, 27 to nothing.

Universities and colleges also began forming teams with Washburn and K. U. both slugging it out for the first time in 1880. During this decade professionalism dawned and in 1880 Topeka's Westerns joined the Western League, a six club circuit which included Leavenworth, St. Joseph, Lincoln, Denver, and Leadville. Topekans, infused with baseball fever and civic expansion, were determined in 1887 to build the finest ball club in the west. Paying high salaries they hired the best talent for the Golden Giants, or Goldsby's Golden Giants, named for manager W. H. Goldsby. In the club's one year, 1887, the Golden Giants finished as champions with a phenomenal percentage of .775.

Professional baseball had a rough existence in Topeka with no team fielded some years. Around the turn of the century the clubs generally went by the nickname White Sox, though one was called the Cooleycrows, for the two principal owners. In the 1920s a local club became affiliated with the St. Louis Cardinals but a still later team, the Owls, was locally owned. Baseball was revived in 1956 with the Topeka Reds, a Cincinnati farm club but professionalism and the minor league died in 1961. Only in 1906, 1908, 1951, and 1955 did Topeka win the Western Association pennant.

Early professional teams played in a field in Kenwood, near Potwin, at Washburn and Fourth streets. From around 1909 to 1916 Western League teams used a ball park near 15th and Dudley (Hudson), a site conveniently along the Highland Park street car line. A grandstand was built out of lumber from the old city hall in 1939 in North Topeka, now (1976) the site of a shopping center. Those less exalted than the pros and people in the country sometimes commanded a field infrequently mowed with a grandstand consisting of nothing but the earth, a center field sloping drastically toward a brush filled creek, a left field shortened by somebody's barn, and a pitcher's mound lower than home plate. Yet, few minded in the golden age of the game.

Local teams recruited local talent to play arch rivals like Rossville, Valley Falls, Overbrook, Tecumseh, Watson, or Lawrence clubs on summer Sundays, July Fourth, Labor Day, or county fair days. Throughout the 1920s families and friends flocked to the matches, sometimes paying as much as 25 cents to watch. The fees offset expenses and usually provided a little something for the pitcher. Besides the spontaneous teams various local social clubs, such as the American Legion and Kiwanis, sponsored baseball for youngsters or teenagers. An organization for area youth was later formed and named for Ken Berry, former Chicago White Sox outfielder who, along with Cardinal and Montreal pitcher Mike Torrez, are the more prominent native Shawnee county baseball players most recently connected with the major leagues.

Before the widespread use of radio the Topeka "State Journal" annually flashed details of World Series games to those who would gaze at its Eighth and Kansas avenue windows. This crowd gathered in 1928. (Courtesy Kansas State Historical Society)

Softball supposedly originated in Topeka in 1916. A writer recounted the beginnings for the *State Journal,* June 17, 1957. Santa Fe shop employees with nothing to do during lunch breaks needed some kind of recreation. "Springing from some experiments in the Santa Fe upholstering shop," an enterprising individual fabricated a soft ball so that baseball could be played indoors. Whether true or not that is the story.

Not everyone participated in baseball but alternatives existed for those who still wished a colorful avocation. The Topeka *Tribune,* August 23, 1863, announced the formation of one of these alternatives. "We must have a band" it declared and so the Topeka Brass Band came into being. Many people and places immediately followed suit with nearly each town, school district, or social group in the county possessing its own brass.

"One of the pet institutions of Rossville is the cornet band," wrote the *Kansas Valley Times,* November 14, 1879. "It is composed of business men largely, and for a short time in practice, is the best we have ever heard." They and the Silver Lake bandsmen frequently serenaded at weddings or anniversaries and paraded impromptu down their respective main streets. Tecumseh folk also fashioned brass and string bands or "singing" schools in their neighborhoods. According to the *State Record* in November, 1868, Tecumseh's "No. 1 String band" with a scant ten players intended to give concerts in Topeka while the state legislature was in session.

Because everything centered in the capital, there one found the most bands during the 19th century. The German Turners, the Negro community, the political parties, all the fraternal organizations, and the state insane asylum had brass bands even if no one had uniforms and only cornets for instruments. As elsewhere, bandsmen performed at the drop of a hat. In a minor section, the *Commonwealth,* September 9, 1870, noted: "The colored brass band was out on the avenue yesterday afternoon, on top of an omnibus, discoursing some excellent music." So common were these band performances that when no group showed up for a stroll on Topeka streets, newspapers would query "what's the matter?"

Politics spawned a number of bands since they put on rousing displays for campaigns and parades. Marshall's band, Topeka's oldest and most famous, evolved in 1884 from a North Topeka Republican club. John B. Marshall obtained a state charter that year and in six years enlarged it to 50 members who performed popular and classical music. All the members were amateurs but they performed well. In 1889 it participated in President Benjamin Harrison's inauguration

The Democratic Flambeau club. (From Mary Jackson, "Topeka Pen and Camera Sketches," 1890)

Pence's Band, Silver Lake, organized 1894. (From Silver Lake centennial book)

parade. In 1890, Radge's city directory listed nine other bands or orchestras including the Oakland Cornet Band and the Sunflower band for boys. By 1976 Topeka possessed two major civic bands, Marshall's and the Santa Fe band, founded by employees in 1924.

As an adjunct to political bands in the 1880s, hordes of campaign followers carried torches in nighttime parades. A Topeka jailer, John A. McCall, improved upon the grease or oil torch with his flambeau torch, patented in 1879. Both the city Republicans and Democrats adopted the new light source, as did the Lincoln Post of the G.A.R. Thus the torchlight parade heightened every evening of political oratory. Soldier organizations or political clubs of other states frequently invited the Topeka groups to their communities. The local Democrats escorted President Cleveland in Kansas City in 1887 just as the Republicans had done for President Grant seven years before in that city. In 1888 they were at Chicago for Harrison's nomination. For a brief time, Mission township boasted a mounted flambeau club, but with the new campaign tactics of the early 20th century partisan bands and flambeaus disappeared.

Musical lovers in the city founded other bodies, such as choruses, and orchestras to complete the musical spectrum. The Topeka Musical Union organized in the winter of 1869 for "the cultivation and faithful rendering of the better class of musical compositions." Radge's 1876 directory added "that it not only owns a constantly increasing musical library, but a fine piano, furniture, etc., and a nice balance in the treasury for future musical good." Performances were given at private concerts in homes of the local aristocracy or at the Opera House sometimes using pieces written by now obscure Topeka composers.

Even small towns dreamed of full symphony orchestras and Silver Lake tackled the job in 1925. Pitifully small, it consisted of an alto cornet, pianist, three cornets, four violins, and a tenor saxophone. They met every Friday night at the Baptist church for practice and would help at "any social or religious event."

Attempts to organize a permanent orchestra for Topeka in the mid 20th century failed until 1946. That year a young musician, Everett Fetter, joined the music faculty at Washburn. He immediately arranged rehearsals for a possible symphony orchestra and 36 persons showed up. By the time the first concert was given, the Topeka Civic Symphony numbered approximately 60 persons. Like most small city orchestras, Topeka's contains amateurs mixed with professional musicians but none earn a salary for the concert season. The year 1970 was one of its most challenging, culminating with a performance of Beethoven's Ninth Symphony. Fetter retired as conductor six years later.

The Civic Symphony Chorus compliments the Topeka Symphony and they in turn stand in a long tradition of choruses and musical bodies. A *Daily Capital* feature in August, 1890, referred to several of Topeka's better known or active clubs. These included the Schubert club in North Topeka, the German Arion Singing Society and the Ladies Musical Club which met twice a month at member's homes. However, the Modocs towered above them all.

Named after the Modoc Indian tribe this male chorus first performed in Topeka concerts in 1876. They immediately became a hit and Mary Jackson modestly declared that "teachers' associations, conventions and assemblies are always disappointed if they are not favored by its presence" and "they [the Modocs] have assisted in raising more funds for charitable purposes than any other organization in the West." During the 1880s the club identified itself with the G.A.R. They attended national encampments of veterans in Denver, Minneapolis, San Francisco, St. Louis, and Columbus. On August 8, 1890, the Modocs disembarked for the Boston encampment in a special railroad car. "Six pieces of their own special music, composed by members of the club," a "special" piano, and 20 singers went along. In their repertoire for that occasion was the first verse and chorus of "In 1892:"

> We're the boys from Kansas, you bet
> We are a rollicking set,
> We came to the Hub for to sample your grub,
> And swap lies with the jolly old vet
> In eighteen ninety-two
> We hope the boys in blue,
> Will come to our state and we'll treat you first-rate
> For we are loyal through and through.
> Chorus
> We're the Kansas delegation
> We helped to save the nation,
> We joined with the others,
> As comrades and brothers,
> And were the loyal blue.
> The Kansas delegation
> Extends the invitation.
> Now don't think us cheeky,
> But come to Topeka
> In eighteen ninety-two.

While the muse of lyric poetry and music must have been alternately delighted and appalled by music in Topeka, citizens did not ignore the muses of comedy and tragedy. The Kansas *Tribune,* January 23, 1858, briefly noted that a theatrical company had been formed and would perform in a hall in the new Ritchie block. Then on April 2, in the Museum hall of the Ritchie building the Philomathic Institute

The Modoc club preparing for a tour to California, 1886. (Courtesy Kansas State Historical Society)

presented the first play in Topeka, appropriately for a supposedly temperance town, entitled "The Drunkard." A contemporary drama critic in the newspaper praised the theatrical production, "a startling exhibition of the depth and hideousness of human depravity, when ruled by the influence of the intoxicating draught."

Until 1870 most dramatic occasions in the city were amateurish, home-grown affairs of songs and skits. No traveling theater group ventured inland to Topeka and the city for its first decade and a half could not support a resident theatre group or proper theatre facilities. The first important traveling show which visited the city was James A. Lord's Chicago Dramatic Company which arrived in January, 1870.

Lord's dramatic troupe and other similar bodies used, explained James C. Malin in the autumn, 1957, *Kansas Historical Quarterly*, "pairs of first and second leading players of tragedy and comedy." Often they involved husband and wife teams like the Lords who interchanged plays, one night emphasizing comedy and the next tragedy. Each evening they put on several plays, skits, or entertainments. When the Lords returned in December the same year, the *Commonwealth* mentioned two pieces performed, "Ireland as it is" and "Our Gal," claiming that Mrs. Lord "is certainly a lady of rare and versatile talent."

Soon numerous other troupes or individual performers alighted in town offering something different every week if not every night. This rush required a proper theater which Lorenzo Costa built in late 1870. Located at 612-614 Kansas Avenue it opened to the public on January 26, 1871. The *Commonwealth* next day recorded the evening's activities in depth: "Our bright, cosy little Opera House is finished, and the enterprising projector is the toast of our people. Last night . . . one of the most intelligent and brilliant audiences that ever has assembled in our city, lent the encouragement of their presence."

Broken into two sections, the bill of fare for part one included the overture to Boildeau's opera "Caliph of Bagdad," an opening address and the Music Union with a chorus from Rossini's "Moses in Egypt." Part two had the overture of Rossini's "Italians in Algiers," Mendelssohn's "Sky Lark," and concluded with a playlet "abounding in quips and conceits of local humor." Topekans certainly possessed iron wills for all that culture but unfortunately the most fascinating section of the program, "A Scene in the Mayor's Office," did not survive for posterity.

Costa's Opera House booked a variety of entertainment over the years mixing musical programs with lectures. On one night in December, 1872, following piano solos and quartette singing, the entertainment immediately switched to an anthropological lecture:

> Prof. B. F. Mudge was then introduced . . . and proceeded to demonstrate very clearly and logically that at a certain time we were all stones and monuments; he traced the antiquity of man back twelve thousand years beyond nobody and left everybody in doubt as to whether they had ever had an existence or not. The lecture was listened to very attentively throughout.

After pondering the origins of man a certain Prof. Boylse, "closed the entertainment with a humorous local lecture on the dead languages."

Not all Topekans, of course, appreciated erudite exhibitions. "It is a well known fact that a burlesque, untruthful impersonation of low wit of the illiterate darkey that he never possessed, will attract crowds of Topeka denizens," stated the *Commonwealth,* "while a moral, instructive lecture, such as the one last night [about Robert Burns], is but poorly attended, if at all." The great and near great visited Topeka and lectured here, often at the Opera House. Two of the number who came were Horace Greeley and Bret Harte. The newspaper, October 22, 1873, noted "quite a number of the *distingue* of Topeka" called upon Harte at the Fifth Avenue Hotel.

Lester M. Crawford, whom a later writer would declare *"was* the theater in Topeka," purchased the Costa Opera House in 1880 and rechristened it naturally enough, the Crawford Opera House. Within weeks of the transaction fire destroyed the premises, but Crawford rebuilt. Other theaters, too, were erected during the expansive 1880s, most notably the Lukens Opera House in North Topeka and the Topeka or Grand Opera House at 615 Jackson Street.

No other community in Shawnee county boasted of such facilities, but residents outside of Topeka also saw traveling shows, usually in some hall, school house, or church. For instance, the *Commonwealth,* during the winter of 1873, sarcastically noted a second-rate magician performing in Tecumseh. Only 23 persons showed up and the man bypassed Topeka all together. Rossville people, according to the *Kansas Valley Times,* September 5, 1879, had recently heard a live musical program at the Topeka Opera House without leaving their

Looking northwest from the city building to the newly completed Grand Opera House. Just above it are the towers of the English Lutheran church. (Courtesy John W. Ripley)

town. The performance went over the newly mounted telephone wires and over the great distance of 20 miles "the music and singing were heard distinctly."

Formed in October, 1881, a stock company erected Topeka's best known theater, the Grand. It went through a variety of titles but the Grand is the only early theater which survived and is still used as a theater. The structure cost approximately $60,000 and measured 70 by 140 feet with a stage of 60 by 67 feet. Considered by Andreas' *History of Kansas* as "one of the most elegant and commodious temples of amusement to be found in the West," the auditorium was divided into three sections or levels, the *parquette,* dress circle, and family circle, all for a seating capacity of 1,500. With 21 exits, though full to capacity, the place could be emptied "in one minute and a half."

On September 11, 1882, the Topeka House, as it was known, opened to the public. For the occasion the owners engaged the Grand English Opera Company starring Emma Abbot. With a 7:30 curtain, prices ranged from $1.50 for a seat in the *parquette,* to $1.00 for the dress circle, and 50 cents for the gallery. The company originally scheduled Adolph Adam's "brilliant oriental comic opera, 'A King for a Day' " for the opening but an illness forced a substitute with "La Somnarmbula." Also on the bill for that week was "Rigoletto." The *Capital* described the new house in its September 12th issue: "It is indeed a beautiful place, with splendid acoustic properties and affording all required opportunity to see and hear."

Stars of the highest caliber trod the stages at Topeka theaters, particularly Crawford's and the Grand. On October 19, 1888, the *Daily Sunflower* mentioned that Lillie Langtry, the good friend of the Prince of Wales, opened at Crawford's in "As In a Looking Glass" where she "packed the house from pit to dome." The divine Sarah Bernhardt appeared as "Camille" at the old city auditorium on April 7, 1906, a not especially suitable playhouse. Years later the noted *Capital* critic, Jay E. House, remembered how the management "hung up some red cheesecloth curtains to screen the actors not actually on

the stage from public view, and Bernhardt and her support went on. . . .
The red cheesecloth curtains revealed a great deal more than they
concealed. And the spectacle of French gents and ladies en dishabille
was a constantly recurring one to those who did not keep their eyes
on the stage."

The 1912-13 season at the Grand had Maude Adams play Barrie's
"Peter Pan," her most famous role. Jay House on the other hand
cared little for this most famous actress of the day. "The tears are
farcial—the humor is farcial . . . no where does iron or red blood
show," wrote the *Capital's* frequently dissenting social and theatrical
critic on one occasion. John Drew starred in "The Tyranny of Tears"
at the Grand in the 1913-14 season while George Arliss was in "Jacques
Duvall" in 1919. Thus, some of the leading stage figures in America
and Europe appeared in Topeka at one time or another.

Vaudeville also played at the major Topeka theaters, often between
engagements of stock companies. The Novelty, now the Dickinson
theater, was one of the best offering the standard variety of comedy,
singing, dancing, and "novelty" acts. Of course, only the truly top
names appeared at legitimate theaters like the Grand. Certainly one
of the most popular proved to be the Scots comedian, Harry Lauder.
When he played an afternoon and evening performance on March 19,
1918, next day's *Capital* stated "it was undoubtedly the largest audience
gathered in recent years within the portals of the Grand. Every seat
in the house was sold and occupied." The overflow crowd of 200 (the
seating capacity had recently been enlarged) sat in the wings or on
stage just to listen to Lauder's sentimental songs and jokes. Every
year Lauder crossed the United States on his "annual farewell tour"
and the *Capital,* January 16, 1922, again noted how "all local records
for theater attendance are to be broken this afternoon and night at
the Grand Theater with the Topeka appearance of Sir Harry Lauder."

Theatricals faced competition from other quarters, the most notable
being Chautauqua. Beginning in the mid-1870s at Lake Chautauqua
in New York, the assemblies originally proposed to draw church
workers together for lectures and meetings. It soon emerged across
the country as a summer gathering for lectures, entertainment, and
moral uplift. The first Kansas meetings took place at Lawrence's
famous Bismark Grove. Chautauqua came to Topeka in July, 1887,
at Garfield Park. The sessions lasted about a week while numerous
famous personages spoke and the Modocs and Marshall's band entertained the Topeka throngs. By 1910-1920 Topeka had become a
fairly important Chautauqua center but the automobile, movies, and
radio changed the public's tastes.

Statistics for the Chautauqua meeting of June, 1889, were exceptionally impressive. Held at Oakland Grove for the first time, organizers erected a gigantic tabernacle which one newspaper said "looks like an overgrown Hottentot hut." One hundred and 25 feet in diameter and 60 feet high, it supposedly sat 3,000. People from all over the state poured into Topeka where over 200 tents aligned along "avenues" at the park. Even townspeople like the T. B. Sweets spent the week camping out in Oakland. A kitchen contained a brick baking oven capable of turning out pies for a thousand people. Certain days were set aside for special groups, such as Civil War veterans, and the whole show was begun with a lecture on the French Revolution.

The movies, competitor to vaudeville and legitimate theater, entered the picture just prior to the turn of the century. Magic lantern shows had been popular since the 1870s but the first actual moving pictures were presented January 28, 1899, at the Grand theater. According to John W. Ripley an opera company performing "Carmen" stretched a canvas in the back of the stage and flashed scenes of a bull fight upon it. At the end of that year the Corbett-Fitzsimmon fight was shown at Crawford's.

The Oddity, Topeka's first true movie theatre opened around Dec. 1, 1906, and became the first of over 25 such houses in the city. Admission was only five cents for two moving pictures and an illustrated song slide show. An individual could stay as long as he pleased with the performances repeated every half hour. The *State Journal* added that "there will be a complete change of pictures and songs twice a week."

Song slides, combining music played at the theater and color on the screen proved popular at least up until World War I. Theater operators combined them with the motion pictures for an evening's entertainment and also often featured live entertainment on the same bill. By the 1920s, the Grand Theater, Topeka's sole survivor of the major opera houses, had evolved into primarily a movie house. With talking pictures first at the Grand in September, 1927, live entertainment was nearly, but not totally, dead there. At least two or three major stock companies still played in Topeka through the 1920s and on into the '30s, the Norths and the Waddells the best remembered. Because of extensive stays in the city both became identified with Topeka. The *Capital*, November 23, 1926, stated that the Waddell Player's "names are a household word in many Topeka homes." Waddell and other actors in the troupe made their homes here and were "proud to be called 'Topeka's Stock Company,' " concluded the *Capital*, "which title they have justly earned." On September 2, 1939,

Topeka's Waddell Players helped celebrate the opening of the new Union Pacific depot in January, 1927. (Courtesy Kansas State Historical Society)

the Norths gave their last Topeka performance, in a tent in North Topeka with a play aptly called "Home on the Range." Other than amateur civic theater, legitimate theater passed from the Topeka scene.

James D. Wallace, in his reminiscences about life in the 1920s and 1930s, estimated that from 1923 to 1938, or from childhood to marriage, he attended 116 shows at the Grand, 194 at the Jayhawk, 126 at the Orpheum, 31 at the Gem and 28 at the Cozy theaters. Most, though not all, were moving picture shows which for 15 to 40 cents provided a good deal of entertainment. During the heat-struck 1930s movie theaters also provided the first establishments with air conditioning. However, if one wanted to attend a show on Sunday, for a long time he or she had to journey to St. Marys, a community noted for its Catholic institutions.

Motion pictures and the radio, of course, changed the habits of America. During the 1930s motion picture viewing became an important element in courtship with young couples spending much of their time at the movies. Radio, on the other hand, did just the opposite and compelled people to stay at home. In those days broadcasting offered little variety but a wide range of stations, some of them being KOA—Denver; WHB—Kansas City; KFKN—Shennandoah, Iowa; KDKA—Pittsburgh; KNI—Los Angeles; WLS—Chicago; KFKB—Milford, Kansas ("Doc" Brinkley's station); and if the listener were very, very lucky, London, England.

Topeka obtained its first permanent station, WIBW, in 1927. The Capper syndicate received a license for WJAQ in 1922, one of the very earliest, only to lose the station in 1924. Intended for Logansport, Indiana, Capper had WIBW moved to Topeka. The first studio was atop the National Reserve building but in ten years the studios were in Capper's former home on Topeka boulevard. The Jenny

Wren Milling Company of Lawrence received its license for station WREN in April, 1927, with the stipulation that it share air time with WIBW and later the educational stations KFKU, Lawrence, and KSAC, Manhattan. For network reasons it moved to Topeka in 1942, and subsequently the Landon interests gained control. Though a CBS affiliate, WIBW broadcasters long relied on local programming and local talent. Generally it broke down into two broad categories, drama and music, with a strong religious background. The musical end usually revolved about country and western productions with such programs as the "Bar Nothing Ranch," "Dinner Hour Gang" (lunch time performances), "Pleasant Valley Gang," and many others. Music and program director Maudie Butler Carlson, according to Peggy Greene, once had 45 entertainers on the payroll. Blind singer Edmund Denny is one of the last of this breed in 1976.

At the other end of the spectrum, WIBW during the 1930s had its own stock company, the WIBW Players, again made up of local folk. Mrs. Greene recalled their giving as many as four plays a week over the air and shows for the Farm Bureau and Chamber of Commerce. Some works included science fiction stories like "The Soul of the Robot" and Sax Roehmer's "The Day the World Ended."

NBC through its "Blue" and "Red" networks provided Americans with the greatest and best remembered entertainment variety. Topekans tuned into Kansas City's WDAF for Jack Benny's "Jello Program" and the "Chase and Sanborn Hour" on Sunday nights; "Burns and Allen" on Monday; "Fibber McGee and Molly" on Tuesday; Fred Allen's "Town Hall Tonight" and Kay Kayser on Wednesday; the Rudy Vallee and Bing Crosby shows on Thursday; and last but far from least "Amos 'n' Andy," Monday through Friday. CBS had Eddie Cantor but relatively little else so WIBW substituted some of its own programming.

Thus for the "Mercury Theater on the Air" on October 30, 1938, Shawnee county residents listened to the CBS program on KMBC, Kansas City. That night, Halloween Eve, Orson Wells presented H. G. Well's "War of the Worlds." Had people tuned in from the first, they could not have mistaken the show for what it was, a stunning, chilling play. Evidently the hysteria which engulfed other sections of the country did not materialize in Topeka. The *Journal* the next day noted that only a few called the papers and no one called the police about a possible invasion from the planet Mars. Peggy Greene in the *Capital,* November 2, felt "perhaps it was self-control, moral courage, or super-intelligence, but I've an idea that in the back-wash of a hectic political campaign [the Payne Ratner-Walter Huxman gubernatorial contest] a good many Topekans are not just greatly concerned whether the world comes to an end or not."

Television, the latest of the major entertainment forms, came to Topeka in 1953 when WIBW started its TV operations on November 15. The now defunct Dumont network carried its first program at 1:00 P.M., a professional football game between the Cleveland Browns and San Francisco 49ers. Later that day WIBW offered "6-gun Theater" and in the evening the "Jack Benny Program." Capper's already had competition from three major Kansas City stations so WIBW-TV erected its transmitting towers at its studio site on SBA hill west of town, making it the tallest man-made structure in Shawnee county. WIBW's broadcasting monopoly came to an end in late 1967 when KTSB, an NBC affiliate, went on the air.

Sometime in the fall of 1855, according to Giles, several of the women and men in town formed Topeka's first true literary and social organization, the Kansas Philomathic Institute. A paper, the *Prairie Star,* was published, a play was presented in 1858, and culture came to the Plains. The Institute also founded Topeka's first library only to see it destroyed by the Ritchie's block fire in 1869. The *State Record,* December 29, 1860, briefly noted an anniversary program probably given at one of the "halls" in town. It consisted of ten parts commencing with music. Then came an address by the president, an oration, declamation, more music, a poem, the reading of some papers, an essay, still more music, and finally a comedy.

Westerners fully intended to bring Eastern and European culture to the Plains. In spite of the political troubles of the 1850s and attention given to the Civil War they succeeded admirably. Before statehood, men and women were meeting in their homes to discuss literature or scientific matters. Modest, compared to their brethren back East, at no time did their desire for cultural pursuits flicker. Leavenworth and Lawrence led in number and strength of these bodies partly because Topeka did not match the population of those places until the 1880s. Besides the Philomathic in 1860 a Young Men's Lyceum met and the *State Record* noted the formation of a literary body, no doubt short-lived, called the Irving Institute.

Fraternal societies also played an important community role from an early date in Auburn, Tecumseh, and Topeka. A Tecumseh Masonic lodge was founded as early as 1858 but dissolved in 1874 while Topeka's began in 1859. Auburn (1860), Indianola (1862) and Silver Lake (1869 to 1877) also had lodges. The Independent Order of Odd Fellows organized in Tecumseh in 1857 and at Topeka in 1858. The Good Templars, a temperance body, were in the three major towns before statehood.

It would be impossible to delineate the variety and number of all the social or special interest organizations and clubs of Topeka. Their diversity staggers the imagination but unquestionably musical and literary bodies represented a significant number of them. The Avon Club, formed in 1870, was the oldest of the literary bodies and specialized in the study of Shakespeare. Open to men and women, the club met once every two weeks in the winter and held a grand banquet and ball every April 23. During the December, 1870, meeting the society read from *The Merchant of Venice* one night while on the second the program consisted of the reading of an unpublished poem, a discourse on Shakespeare and Milton, the reading of an essay on English character by Emerson, the reading of an essay entitled "Hash," and finally a presentation by J. H. Barrows who "orated for a quarter of an hour on the rights of women."

North Topekans, too, joined in this cultural activity, at least for a short time in the 1870s, with their Pickwick Club. The *Times,* August 31, 1871, commented on its organization and said that they already had "a respectable library open for the use of its members." The group formed committees on drama, music, and literary exercises. "There is musical talent in North Topeka," concluded the *Times,* "and let us develop it. If the ladies do not take an active part we will be compelled to go away from home for musical talent, which would be a just cause of chagrin to all concerned."

Similar 19th century cultural societies included the Topeka Scientific Institute, Nonpariel Club (literary), Our Circle (literary, North Topeka), Atlanteum (history, lierature, and art), the Topeka Society of Natural Sciences, the Chaldean Club (15 women who studied ancient history), and many others. Some were professionally oriented like the Shawnee County Medical Society or ethnic like the Topeka Scottish Society or recreational like the Jackson Street Tennis Club; The Topeka Country Club; Topeka Chess, Checker and Whist Club; Osborn Guards (a Negro military company); and the West Side Gun Club.

"All ladies interested in forming a 'Ladies Library Association' in this city," wrote the *Commonwealth,* November 5, 1870, "are requested to meet at the residence of Mrs. T. L. King . . . to-day at 3 p.m." Thus began one of the more lasting contributions of a Topeka society, the Free Public Library. A week later, on November 12, the ladies formally organized themselves and set about purchasing books for a library to be housed in a store room of Keith & Meyers dry goods emporium. They incorporated in 1872, bringing men into the body, as the Topeka Library Association. For an annual fee of $3.00 ($50.00 life-time) members had the privileges of reading over 250 books (1,766 by 1875). It was opened to the public in 1878. Library premises, like those of many Topeka institutions, floated from one place to another until 1883.

Both the Santa Fe and Union Pacific railroads contributed $25,000 toward construction of a permanent library building. Located oddly, cheaply, but not inappropriately or unattractively, on the northeast corner of the statehouse grounds, the new stone library cost approximately $44,000 and was dedicated on April 20, 1883. Designed by Henry Van Brunt of Kansas City it was described by Mary Jackson in these words:

It is constructed of native limestone, and trimmed with Colorado sandstone and brick, and roofed with red terra cotta tiles. Its dimensions are 116 by 55 feet. The interior of the building is a model of neatness and finished in ash. . . . The lower floor is devoted exclusively to the library and reading rooms, while the upper floor is now used as a hall for private and public entertainments. It is furnished with a concert grand piano, and the walls are hung with engravings. . . . In connection with this hall is a model stage, elegantly furnished, with dressing rooms attached. Two handsome parlors, elegantly furnished, complete the upper floor.

In 1953 the Topeka library moved to new, larger quarters on west 10th street. North Topekans, too, maintained ambitions for a library with their Adams Library Association in 1871. Named for prominent north side citizen Maj. D. M. Adams, members met in Adams' bank building. The North Topeka *Times,* November 2, 1871, explained that a committee would soon canvass the town for books, periodicals, and a bookcase. On occasion, though, the same Adams building was raided for gambling on the premises.

Associated with library and literary groups were the lyceums which primarily served as lecture and debating societies. Every hamlet in the county appears to have had one as did the city. Members or interested persons congregated monthly or weekly to listen to a debate, either on current events or abstract topics. Many printed or wrote in long hand a paper which described the proceedings and essays read before the members. As early as 1860, the *State Record* in discussing the Young Men's Lyceum declared: "It is perhaps the most profitable manner in which the young men of our town could spend their leisure evenings, and should be encouraged."

What with automobiles, the telephone, and radio, the lyceums have long since died out. Indeed of all the 19th century literary bodies one of the few which survived is the Saturday Night Literary Club. Founded February 2, 1883, its program consisted of an essay delivered before the assembly followed by replies or criticism. According to early by-laws, the lectures could last only 45 minutes and the replies ten minutes. Occasionally the critics jumped upon the essayist for bias or poor sources; thus when one member in 1883 concluded his discourse "Scott and Burns" he "then vindicated his own character as well as Burns from the attacks of the president [John MacDonald, a Scotsman]." Today, 1976, the club meets every other week at the Hotel Jayhawk with each member designated as the "gentleman from such and such a state."

Gentlemen's clubs on the order of the renowned London men's clubs existed in Topeka on a minor scale, with the Topeka Club and its palatial quarters at Sixth and Harrison perhaps the most notable. Two local lawyers inspired the idea in 1889 and soon some of the most distinguished leaders of Topeka joined. As a place of relaxation, liquor was merely part of a day's enjoyment there and this fact frequently embroiled the club in law suits or public condemnation as a "bunch of aristocrats and swells." Deaths of prominent leaders forced disbanding in 1921.

Women entered the Topeka Club for periodical ladies' night parties, but they had their own social clubs to look after. In 1897 representatives from several women's bodies organized a federation of clubs, which evolved into The Woman's Club. Social but with a goal of cultural enrichment, the women built an impressive club house in 1924 on Ninth street between Topeka and Harrison. Unlike the edifice belonging to their male counterparts, this building has survived.

Sometime in 1873 at an informal gathering of some of Topeka's elite, one gentleman suddenly jumped up and declared: "We are all such . . . liars that we should form a club." This idea emerged into Topeka's famous or infamous St. Ananias Club, its symbol appropriately being the lyre. Some of Topeka's most famous men belonged to it: Sam Radges, Dr. S. E. Sheldon, Hiram P. Dillon, Judge Samuel Kingman, Daniel Wilder, F. P. Baker, J. G. Waters, Chester Thomas and in all at least 30 members mostly professional men. The by-laws of 1886 indicated a major goal of this social body: "Each member must invent at least one new and wholly original lie at each meeting." Supervising the story telling was not a president but rather the Grand D. L.—Grand Damn Liar.

Their only recreation in the meeting rooms in downtown Topeka was whist, according to the *Capital,* February 16, 1919, "bets they made with the wildest extravagance." Intoxicants were forbidden, a rule which promptly met controversy. One member asked if this included beer and another inquired "if Chapin & Gore's old bourbon had ever been known to intoxicate." According to the *Commonwealth,* August 6, 1886, the Grand D. L. appointed a committee "to investigate, and report results of test experiments." Once an argument broke out with bets supposedly in seven figures about whether or not an electric fan actually could cool a room; the *Capital* failed to record the reaction of the loser. Only one woman was admitted to the club and she was given a masculine *nom de plume*. Honorary memberships were granted to those who told a really big lie. Interest, however, declined with the deaths of the old timers. Upon the demise of Guilford Dudley in the 1920s, it too disbanded.

On May 17, 1855, Topeka settlers celebrated their first social, a picnic on the banks of the Kaw. The day dawned cool as newcomer Joseph Miller described the scene:

In good time the fair sex, of whom there were a good number began to assemble, accompanied by those made of courser material, the table (50 ft. long) was soon spread with rich viands, which creaked & groaned beneath its load of dainty food, there was the mamoth fish, who but the night previous reveled & gamboled in freedom midst the murky waters . . . now stretched at length on a huge platter prepared to grace the festive board. A barbecue & other like substantial food came in for their fare share of attention. A large pyramid cake graced the center of the table surrounded by other minor cakes, from the apex of which as if a natural production a rich profusion of prairie flowers shot forth their smiling petals. . . .

Following the meal came some short speeches, "possessing a good deal of pith" by gentlemen from Topeka and Tecumseh and then "many toasts" which "produced a vast amount of hilarity and meriment." Finally, at dusk they "dispersed each to his own home, well pleased with his day's recreation."

Under the rousing headline "Ho for the Woods!," the *Kansas State Record*, June 9, 1870, noted a Methodist church picnic to be held at Burlingame the next day. With the promise of an exciting excursion over the Santa Fe tracks, the paper warned that "all baskets must be carefully and securely labeled with the owners' names, and delivered to the committee at the baggage car." Round-trip tickets cost participants $1.00 for adults, 50¢ for youth, and 25¢ for children. The *Record*

Outdoor cooking near Tecumseh. (Courtesy E. V. King)

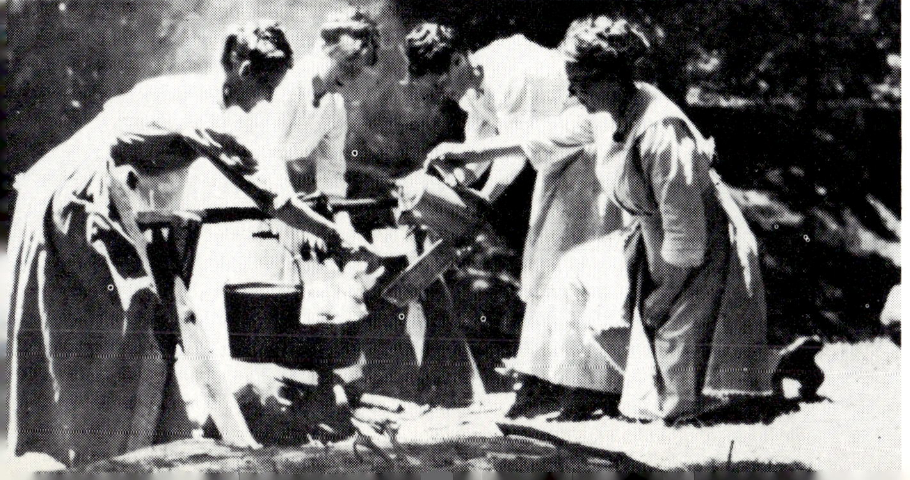

expected a good time for all and further cautioned that "the train will leave the Atchison, Topeka and Santa Fe Depot at 7:45 sharp. Don't be late!"

"Festivals, Oyster suppers, Surprise parties, etc. are in vogue now," declared the North Topeka *Times,* December 14, 1871, with churches especially taking advantage of these socials "to raise the dimes." Nearly every organization at some time or another, formally or spontaneously, had some kind of party or picnic where people could enjoy simple pleasures amidst their work. Picnics were popular, of course, during the summer months with people flocking to any wooded grove near the city. Appropros to this, the *Commonwealth* mentioned one June day, 1873, a new Topeka summer drink called the "Shanghai" which consisted of mixing an egg with a glass of lemonade. When in season, these affairs usually centered around strawberries or peaches.

Obviously, summer activities climaxed on the Fourth of July when everyone, or so it seemed, went somewhere to do something in celebration. Not all Fourths, though, dazzled townsfolk, the one of 1867 being noticeably dull. The *Weekly Leader* reported a picnic dinner at City Park, the scene of so many of these events:

> A dance was got up on the ground and extensively indulged in by our citizens but we are not prepared to say that they enjoyed it. The "Arkansas Traveler" was played very much like a dead march and the dancers waded through the figures with as much animation and showed about as happy faces as if they had been sentenced by a court to be hung, and were marching to the place of execution with no hope of reprieve.

Not everyone was so downcast reported the *Leader,* particularly the black people whose barbecue was on the other side of Kansas avenue from City Park. "Their well known fondness for stump speeches was more than gratified by several colored orators and the irrepressible Col. Ritchie."

In 1873 Topeka appeared gayer to *Commonwealth* reporters who cheerily described the "doin's" all over Shawnee county. Some ventured into the wilds of Big Springs where a tent museum or circus entertained them while others voyaged by way of the Kansas Pacific to Silver Lake, "a Topeka suburb." There, Silver Lake and Topeka men hastily arranged a regatta on the lake for a purse of $50. The boats had been launched and the rowers "stripped to the natural buff" when someone uncovered the fact that one of the racing judges from Topeka was making some unauthorized bets. "Much to the disgust of the Topeka belles and beaux and Silver Lake's lovely mistresses and gallant sons," promoters called the race off. The rowers, on the other hand, saw it a bit differently being glad to get out of the wind blistered water. Afterwards John Martin spoke to the crowd and an original poem and a short address were delivered.

Beating the summer heat at Edgewood park in 1922. (Courtesy Kansas State Historical Society)

Edison electric plant workmen at a watermelon feed in the early 1900s. (Courtesy Kansas State Historical Society)

An outing at Gage Park in early 1900s. (Courtesy Topeka Park Department)

Another group of Topekans assembled at the City Park where "ladies and gents were in their gayest colors, and straw hats and linen goods were all the rage." G. C. Clemens addressed the audience and the paper quoted his concluding paragraph:

When the dark clouds that erstwhiles did wrap the earth as in a funeral pall shall be riven by the light of liberty, and the dying groans of Endymion's lost souls shall pierce the dingy heights of Zenobarba's isle; when the Sclavonic bandies, fresh from the gory fields of Tebulon, shall reach in stern array from Herculaneum's dormant vales to India's hills afar; when the Valscians and their holicausts shall lift up their heads in a last, last gasp; when the triumvirate of Ossian's war chariots shall crush beneath the Roman temple's walls all that is perishable of the bygone age, oh, then shall this fair fabric of freedom's holy shrine go down in all the glory of America's living destiny, until there shall be one universal Fourth of July from the shores of Tartary to where the sun makes his last stand in all his effulgence and beauty!

With autumn "the season for festivals has come round," stated the *Commonwealth* in November of 1870. People resumed attending their local lyceum gatherings and indulged in "the latest novelty," a necktie party, or festival. Comparable to the summer box socials where a master of ceremonies auctioned ladies' picnic baskets to the highest bidder, it bore no relation to a lynching. "Neckties of different patterns," explained the newspaper, "are made by the ladies, sealed up in envelopes, and bought by the gentlemen before unsealing. After one has been sold the buyer hunts up a lady wearing a dress of the same material, and thereafter devotes his attentions to her during the balance of the evening." As an afterthought, the *Commonwealth* added, "we think these festivals would take here in Topeka," and they did.

Regarding early Thanksgiving celebrations, an inquisitive *Capital* editor dispatched a reporter to the most appropriate font for such information, the rooms of the St. Ananias Club. "At this particular spot," the paper stated, November 30, 1899, "one is certain to get reliable information." Several of the very, very old old timers recalled the dinner of 1856. Gathering at the Topeka House, dinner guests ate turkey, bacon, slapjacks, coffee, sugar, and butter—"it would have held up an iron spike, even had it melted." Stated W. L. Gordon: "It was the strongest butter I ever saw." Besides their meal, the group had a bar but no dance because the fiddler who lived six miles south of town could not come up.

Topekans celebrated later Thanksgivings in a variety of ways. In 1869 one group gave a supper and ball, tickets being $5.00 while the Baptists' had a dinner for only $1.00. During the evening, the same Baptists charged only 25¢ for an oyster supper. Two years later the North Topeka *Times* reported things were fairly quiet; the Methodist church conducted services and the post office closed, but the stores remained open all day. About the only major event was a surprise masquerade party at the O. O. Kelsea residence. According to the *Commonwealth* in 1869, "there was more drinking than eating." While "some went to church . . . some went to other places . . ., some ate too much, and some drank too much." Those who "washed down their turkey too freely" paid $3.00 for the privilege to Judge Holmes.

Christmas, of course, was the supreme holiday of the year though little is known of the celebrations in the Topeka of the 1850s. Certainly the first Christmases could hardly have had much in the way of celebration. By the following decade Shawnee countians had achieved enough prosperity to do the season correctly and the stores advertised Christmas items. The *Record* reported in 1868 the festivities at the Grace church with evergreens "procured at considerable expense" from Mill creek. A huge tree filled one end of the sanctuary, "lit up by the hundred tapers" and loaded with presents for children. "The chandeliers and lamps were beautifully festooned, and all with the evergreen, that looks so much more beautiful to Western eyes because it is so rarely that any is seen."

For the 1870 celebration at the Indianola school house, area people had a "plainly decorated" tree according to the *Commonwealth,* but a successful party. Children found plenty of gifts under the tree as the adults were entertained by "some comic dialogues and other performances." Samuel Reader exhibited a magic lantern show "after which old Santa Claus appeared in his usual costume, and distributed the gifts, to the ecstatic delight of all the children present."

Food played an important role in Christmas activity. Jenkin's meat market in 1872 offered turkey, chicken, quail, rabbit, duck, buffalo tongues, mutton, roast beef, and fatted deer. Martha Farnsworth described Christmas with her husband in 1894. Family crowded into her house from all over Kansas, Omaha, and Chicago but after all the cleaning, decorating, and baking "Oh what a jolly happy, Christmas has been this. . . . And this was my dinner. A *14 pound Turkey,* cooked to a turn, *by my own hands,* as *was all my dinner."* She proudly listed the fixings as fried oysters, mashed potatoes, peas, celery, radishes, lettuce, salad dressing, cranberry sauce, apple butter, grape jelly, pumpkin pie, mince pie, layer jell cake, bread, butter, and gravy. "All pronounced my dinner *very good."*

More so than anyone else, Mrs. Farnsworth gave detailed accounts of her holiday affairs. In 1894 she mentioned how on the 20th she and her husband went Christmas shopping for a $275 "plain but pretty" piano and distributed "candy tickets from associated charities" among Topeka's poor. Not all Christmases went smoothly. For example, in 1909 her postman husband "got home from carrying mail at 4 o'clock, after 8 hours, hard work."

Winter snows did not stop people from partying. New Years eve was only one date popular for holding dances or "hops." The Lecompton *Union* in 1857 mentioned a successful New Years ball at Tecumseh while the *Record*, January 6, 1869, featured a story about a Turnverein masquerade on the 31st. People dressed as frontier men, the Ethopian, Hussars, the devil, squaws, Scotch girls, daughter of the regiment, or other figures and the unmasking at midnight "produced considerable amusement, when it was ascertained who personified the different characters."

Snow meant sleighing, a sport which the *Record* in January, 1862, grandiosely noted: "The weather has been cool enough to make buffalo robes comfortable—the snow has been crisp and compact, and the spirits of lads and lassies buoyant, making a combination of circumstances highly auspicious for general enjoyment." Certainly all that sledding implied romantic entanglements. This would have pleased mid-19th century editors who constantly despaired the number of bachelors in town. The frontier required settled families before civilization could take root, and Topekans aimed to recruit as many marriages as possible.

"Come boys, there are plenty of girls in the city who could and would make each one of you a much pleasanter home," wrote the *Commonwealth* in 1871, hoping to spark something. Yet at another time the paper ridiculed those youngsters who were coaxing out a thin mustache. "The young ladies like a manly mustache, and those thin, sickly looking things, with about three hairs on one side of the nose and five on the other are abominable." One Topeka matron July 3, 1870, advised the young folks:

> Give up your cigars and tobacco, and ale and horses, and oysters and ices, as willingly as she will her laces and flowers [and her "lolling on lounges and reading the latest sensations"], and in the struggle of wedded life you will find sure success and happiness.

Courtship took many forms, a buggy ride for Baughman's ice cream, a street car ride from downtown to Oakland, or a simple walk home from church with an evening spent in the parlor. Conrad Swartz explained in his autobiography how he and a friend took their girl friends on an all day excursion around 1900. The four left Topeka on the Kansas City plug (Santa Fe local train) and got off at the Lake View resort in Douglas county. There they "spent the day boating, fishing, had dinner and lounging about the park-like yard and came home on the same train that evening."

Martha Van Orsdol escaped in 1887 to Topeka from a courtship in south central Kansas. Soon, however, she noted in her diary a new beau, a certain mail carrier, "No. 11," who "seems bound to make a *mash* [flirt] on me." The two started going together with long walks from church or conversations in the parlor. Once in a while quarreling broke off the romance, Martha declaring "I *despise* him and told him *never* to come again." Within two weeks, however, they were back together walking home, attending the theater, or, as on July 4, 1888, visiting Garfield Park and a performance of "H.M.S. Pinafore." Then one day after a ride on the East side circle railroad to Cottage Grove and a card game, about midnight, mail carrier No. 11 made her "very happy: the happiest girl that lives. My, dear 'Winnie Boy' *asked me to be his wife.*"

Not all courtships in town ended so joyously. Following a fight between some youths, the Oakland *Blade*, May 11, 1906, acknowledged "that it has been a long standing custom by the young fellows here to allow no one outside of Oakland, especially those from Topeka, Parkdale and North Topeka to wait on any of the young ladies here." Apparently "Oakland boys receive the same treatment when visiting the ladies in those places." If a couple did find some happiness, it left others only jealous. Envy poured forth in a letter dated March, 1870, concerning a newly engaged Bethany student: "So I suppose without a doubt they slept together. I wish you could see them, everyday standing on the porch at noon's recesses, etc. I feel like giving them a pill or physic or some thing of the kind."

In revelry over the exciting occasion of impending matrimony, in 1873 at least, a couple could enjoy dinner at Topeka's "bon ton restaurant" the Avenue Diving Parlors until, however, the proprietors skipped town without paying their debts. But just after the turn of the century young people (and older ones, too) flocked to the community's stellar attraction—Vinewood Park. While different sections of town and county possessed a grove or park well used by the neighborhood residents, Vinewood Park outshone them all as a place for recreation, relaxation, or quiet courtship.

When the expanded park reopened in July, 1903, over 7,000 persons jammed the place causing a mammoth tie-up on the street-railway. Some persons did not get home until after 3:00 o'clock, many after an all night walk from the park. Yet, everything that night proved a success. One concessionaire reported sales of over 40 gallons of ice cream and 100 gallons of lemonade. The *Journal,* on July 27, stated that all the row boats were "busy from morning till night and the remarkable twistings and curves of Deer creek were the cause of an unprecedented destruction of oars."

Highlights at Vinewood included a penny arcade, theater, dance hall, a moving picture theater, carousel, toboggan (roller coaster), and a circle swing. Naturally enough, on opening day several fist fights broke out in the park. All this rushing about caused a tremendous electrical drain. The incandescent lights throughout Vinewood flickered, but as the *Journal* stated, this didn't bother the "innumerable tete-a-tetes" on the park benches. Only the oldsters worried about getting home.

Decades later, long after the Vinewood dance pavilion had rotted away, young couples attended dances at major dance halls like Meadow Acres and the White Lakes Supper Club on south Topeka boulevard. In the "swing" era of the 1940s most of the major big bands in the nation stopped for at least a one night stand. The *Topeka Magazine* in 1946 noted several "night spots" from the well known to smaller road houses such as the Rainbow Club on east Highway 40 or Lake Linge which employed local bands made up of eight to 12 musicians and a female vocalist. According to the *Topeka Magazine,* one of these groups, Del Weidner and his Weidner Wonder Boys, had the motto "Dance with Del . . . the music's swell."

Young women around the turn of the century began thinking more and more seriously of some kind of job to tide them over until marriage. For those of working or middle class backgrounds this became a necessity. There could be no more "lolling on lounges and reading

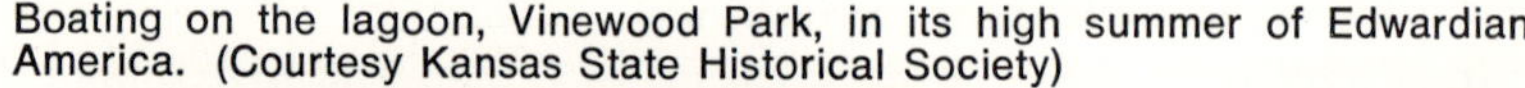

Boating on the lagoon, Vinewood Park, in its high summer of Edwardian America. (Courtesy Kansas State Historical Society)

the latest sensations." Before her sixteenth birthday in 1911, Fay Ritchie started working as a clerk in the Paxton and Paxton dry goods store at Sixth and Quincy. For a job eight to six o'clock, six days a week (to nine o'clock on the 15th of every month, Santa Fe pay day) she earned five dollars a week. Its major compensation was that she met her future husband there. Upon marriage in 1913, like most girls of the day, she quit her job permanently.

Not everyone believed strongly in young female employees. George W. Crane, otherwise quite liberal in employe and race relations, remarked to his board of directors in a letter dater in 1911:

> I advise as an established policy that all new employees of the office be boys instead of girls. With girls there is too much talking, giggling and spooning. Girls as a rule have no object in life but to get married. With boys we have always some coming on to occupy places higher up.*

Freeman Sardou, on the other hand, thought girls the better pickers at his Oakland cherry orchard "because they take more care and pride in their work." "Their fingers are more nimble," he stated to the Oakland *Blade,* June 15, 1906, "and they do not mash and bruise the cherries as much as boys or men. Boys do not care how they do the work so long as they get in ten hours a day."

Before matrimony, Topeka couples undoubtedly did some shopping. If they searched for a ring, Topeka's first jeweler (dating back to 1857), Fred Ortman could supply their need. In the 1880s they would go to E. H. and W. T. Crosby's department store or Auerbach and Guettel's clothing store, the Palace. Once when she went downtown shopping for a new corset and bustle, Martha Van Orsdol accidently ran into her beau and another young man. "It 'plagued me half to death,' " she declared in her diary, "for I was afraid they could tell what I had, but of course 'Boys' don't know that 'girls' wear such things."

Upon marriage, Fay Ritchie and her husband moved in with the family as did many other couples in the 19th and early 20th centuries. Like the so-called family farm, in the city one often found three generations living in the same house, even if the house were small. People made adjustments to the conditions, and grandparents and grandchildren frequently slept together in the same bed.

Marriage for Martha Van Orsdol, however, did not prove a blessing. She sensed things on her wedding day in September, 1889. "He has thought more of how things shall look, at the wedding, than of me." Her expected happiness died a month later at a "Beer Party," a social for drinks and cards, when her husband became

---

*On occasion boys bothered him, too, as in 1910: "I fear we will find it almost a necessity to dispense with Walter __________'s services because of his connection with a lewd woman who annoys us through the telephone."

"*insanely* jealous: he was so nice and kind to me, till the crowd left then he began cursing and abusing me most dreadfully."

"I *always* show the smiling side," she wrote after an arduous year of married life, "however hard it may be to do so." Her husband's temper, verbal abuse, drinking, and illnesses continually wore her down though motherhood in 1892 helped ease some of the burdens. Yet, within months the death of her child added to the troubles. "Oh! God if you would, in mercy," Martha Van Orsdol desperately scribbled in her diary, "take me to my child. I hardly know that I live."

The misery continued into 1894 when, after a prolonged illness, Martha Van Orsdol's husband died, releasing her from a nightmare. She went back to work as nurse in a private home. One of the sons of the household was a bachelor. Like her first husband, Fred Farnsworth was a postman and soon he, too, "made a mash" on her.

Apprehensive, Martha married a second time in May, 1894. On her honeymoon, spent in Kansas City, she picked two four-leaf clovers, "which I take for a 'lucky omen.'" Her extensive and thorough diary, from which these accounts come, takes on a different tone from those during the months of her first marriage. The pages recall days of "dreaming away the hours" or frequent visits in the evening "calling" upon the neighbors—a practice popular in those times but gone by the mid 1900s. When the diary closed for the old year, Martha Van Orsdol Farnsworth quietly added:

1894 has been so happy; one of sweet content because of a husband who is *very* kind; is thoughtful of my comfort and gentle, always; yet the *spectre* of my *wretchedly unhappy* life with another, still haunts me; it *will come up* and make me afraid, that I will awaken to find my present happiness only a dream.

Apparently she—and hopefully many others chronicled in these pages and in this community—never awoke.

Martha Van Orsdol Farnsworth.
(Courtesy Jessie Van Orsdol)

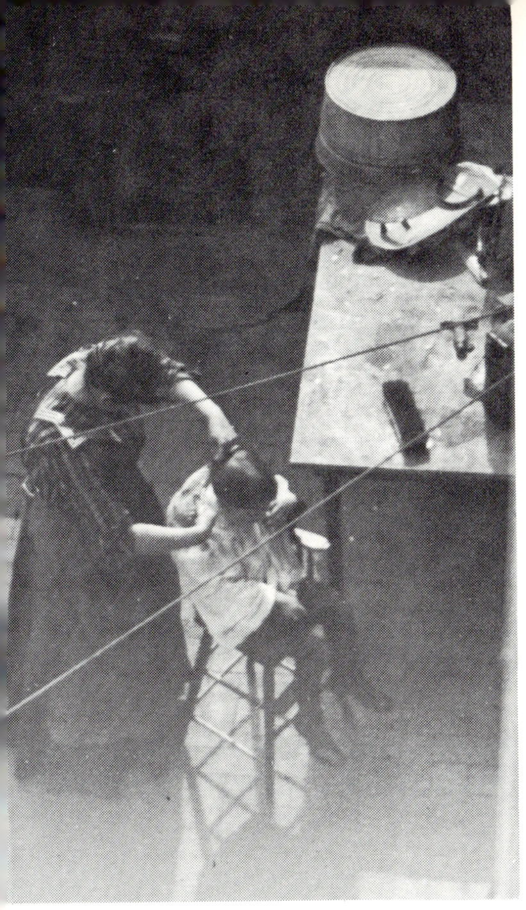

Little boy getting a haircut. (Courtesy Kansas State Historical Society)

Delivering Christmas mail along College avenue. (Courtesy John W. Ripley)

Rossville—1976. (Courtesy Kansas Department of Transportation)

APPENDIX

The following list includes all the known major settlements and proposed towns in Shawnee county along with several but by no means all post office and railroad sub-stations. There may well have been other proposed communities, as well as several duplications, which have not been recorded so that this list cannot be considered definitive.

ARVILLA—East of Burlingame on or near the old Osage county line, projected in 1857. Only a store and two houses were ever erected.

ATCHISON TOWNSHIP—This was one of the three townships formed by the Calhoun county commissioners on October 16, 1855, and named for Atchison, Kansas territory, or Missouri U. S. Senator David Atchison. The northern portion of Soldier township would have been included in this early Calhoun county township.

AUBURN—Next to Topeka and Tecumseh, Auburn has been the most publicized town in the county. Auburn created anxiety among Topekans when it tried to become the county seat. Fry Giles claimed that "repeatedly in subsequent years [Auburn] had measures on foot that, if they had not failed of accomplishment, would have done temporary injury [to Topeka]."

In 1847, white settlers arrived in Shawnee county, the Pottawatomies established a village at the junction of the three streams which form the Wakarusa. A mission run by Father J. B. Hoeken helped the Potawatomies erect a number of cabins on the site, but next year they discovered that they had settled on a Shawnee reserve, so they moved north of the river and Shawnees moved into their cabins. In 1854 three men came to the old mission from Missouri—a Mr. Baker who was a cattleman, a Mr. Cook, and John W. Brown, no relation to the abolitionist. Brown immediately bought a few of the cabins from the Shawnees and 800 acres of land. He, Henry Fox, and two of Topeka's founders, M. C. Dickey and Loring Farnsworth founded a town which they called Brownsville or Brownville since it was located on Brown's land. The new village progressed by leaps and bounds. The first Sunday school in Kansas was established there in 1855 and the first public school in the county was conducted in one of the cabins that same year. The town was located on the California road, "whitened every day by long trains of canvas-covered wagons, laden with freight for the Government, or for Santa Fe traders, the plains resounding with the sharp report of the ox-men's murderous thong, and the carcasses of exhausted animals, like milestones, marking the way," Fry Giles wrote. This travel and the proximity to the Pottawatomie reserve made the expanding hamlet an ideal site for trade. People erected houses, stores, mills, a large hotel, established a paper and there was some talk of building a church. A pair of stage lines connected the town with the East. When Kansas became the 34th state Brownsville, now called Auburn, even vied with Lawrence and Topeka for the state capital.

Auburn had several close calls in its formative years. Once when Jim Lane was scheduled to speak at the Independence Day celebration, Auburnites "borrowed" a cannon from Topeka without telling anyone. The Topeka boys came over and in a brisk fight more than a few eyes were blackened.

In Auburn stands what was once a horse barn which supposedly once saved the town from an Indian attack. One account has it that "as the Indians came over the hill from the north and started down on the town, they saw the barn, long narrow and high with four or five small windows on the north and south. Thinking it to be a fort, the Indians turned and rode away." No one has ever told who these savages might have been or where they might have come from—the Pottawatomies were not hostile and other tribes were near.

When the Auburn citizenry got around to building its first church, the people used brick made in Auburn. While the church was under construction all the men between the ages of 15 and 60 were called into militia service so work was stopped for a time.

Despite apparent prosperity an 1896 Topeka *Mail and Breeze* sketch claimed that the loss of the county seat was the major turning point in Auburn's history.

The growth of Auburn suddenly stopped. Later the location of the Atchison, Topeka and Santa Fe railroad, some seven miles east, still further shut the once thriving little town out from the busy world. The railroad carried the traffic to the west and southwest. With the old established thoroughfare deserted the town fell into a decline, and, today, its population does not exceed 150.

In 1954 the little town had about 115 people plus a bank, two churches, an elementary and a high school, "and a ball field where games are played each weekday night under the lights." By the mid-20th century the bulk of the population were commuters who drove to work in Topeka.

Auburn Township—By the time Kansas was admitted as a state the town of Auburn had passed its zenith in size and industry and had begun its decline. Yet it left its legacy in one of the original townships.

Auburn had a population of 400 and was the only town in Auburn township. A combination saw and grist mill was in operation as were two blacksmith shops, a harness shop, a broom factory, and four brick kilns. There was even a coal mine in operation at one time.

The early settlers of Auburn township were not only industrious but also innovative. For instance, a mile outside of Auburn stood the old "Four Corners House." This was a neat, one-room home made of native lumber and containing two windows on a side and a door in each end. One account in the *Capital* described it this way: "It was built by four young bachelors just over the four corners of their quarter sections, so each young man owned a corner, a window and half a door. And so they filled Uncle Sam's demands for a house on their own farm and had sociability and companionship besides."

Two outstanding contributions to the church life of Kansas and America were made by Auburn township. Edward Gill, for years the Auburn blacksmith, joined the ministry and served the township as a pastor and presiding elder from 1871 to 1905. William Quayle, son of Thomas Quayle, a nephew of the Rev. Mr. Gill, entered Baker University at the age of 14, made a phenomenal rise in the educational and ministerial world and was elected bishop of the Methodist church in 1908. Lewis Dyche was another respected member of the educational community about the same time. The *Capital* said that he "was an Auburn boy and made his first collection of butterflies and insects from the hills and valley he roamed over as a school boy." Dyche was educated in the county and later became a nationally known naturalist and a professor at the University of Kansas.

The most colorful figure to come out of Auburn township must be Frank Stahl who came to Auburn during the territorial days. He served as a lieutenant in the 19th Kansas Volunteer cavalry during the Indian wars. Each June for many years Frank Stahl held a picnic in a grove of trees on his farm. One participant, Elizabeth Virginia Fisher, pictured one of the affairs this way:

Mr. Stahl was very much a temperance man and always had a speaker come for the occasion. The platform was decorated around the top and bottom with bunting which I liked. The seats were big boards held up by some kind of keg. There were no backs, of course. After we had sat still a long time mamma let us children get up and go a ways from that platform to play with the other boys and girls. We enjoyed this very much. After the speaking was over we had dinner and then we were given a dipper of ice-cream on a little wooden dish. We broke off an edge of the dish to eat with.

AVOCA—A bill to incorporate Avoca, introduced in the 1858 territorial legislature, never became a law. Cyrus K. Holliday, John Farnsworth and Milton Dickey of Topeka were "founders." Its location is not known.

BERRYTON—At the age of 88, Berryton ranks as a youngster among county towns. Although located astride the old Sac and Fox Indian trail, the hamlet did not exist until the late nineteenth century. "It got started in 1888, when George W. Berry built a store there," a former resident told a *State Journal* reporter in 1954. "He named it after his father, Wash Berry. The old gentleman came here a long time ago from the South—he was a slave driver there—and lived in a cabin on the Wakarusa."

George Washington Berry—"Wash"—was one of the first settlers in Monmouth township, coming to Kansas soon after it became a territory. Ironically he was related to Abraham Lincoln through Lincoln's mother, Nancy Hanks, and also to Daniel Boone. He was named first sheriff of the county by the 1855 territorial legislature but declined to serve.

In 1886 the Missouri Pacific laid a track through the town site perpendicular to the Indian trail. Wash saw possibilities in the location and with his son, George Webster Berry, built the first store in the area in 1887. George Webster also served as postmaster and agent for the Missouri Pacific. Pauline, Richland, and of course Topeka had been founded long before, but in spite of the competition, Berryton, alternately said to be named for Wash and for his son, soon became a thriving community.

Young Berry made some additions to his store but later sold out. More additions were made under other owners; it burned and was rebuilt. Once the store was operated by a farmer's co-operative, but that phase ended in 1915. The building, now much-changed, remains as the post office.

A second store was established in 1896 by W. F. Havecott. Business was so good the family worked from dawn to dark, rarely having a chance for a quick meal together. Havecott added a lumber yard and operated the post office from his counter. By 1913 children and teen-agers were numerous enough to warrant a high school and when the granger movement swept the midwest a sizeable grange building and fairgrounds were constructed there. Several churches were in close proximity and until the turn of the century Berryton and nearby farmers could even boast a doctor, N. J. Taylor.

In 1928 an article in the *Capital* praised Berryton as the "center of an ideal farming community," a "peaceful village" which kept its citizens. But the paper qualified those statements by noting that "old settlers like Berryton so well they just keep living there, and have (a) fine community of which they are justly proud." The passing of its old citizens and the introduction of the automobile were major contributing factors to the gradual demise of the little village.

The *Capital* article reported 65 people living in Berryton. Subsequent estimates rose to an expansive 83, when the town hit its height. The citizenry began doing their business in the capital so that by 1951 Berryton could no longer support two stores. The Havecott enterprise was sold in that year. A new high school had been built a year previous but is now used as an elementary school since consolidation with Tecumseh to form Shawnee Heights district. The original Berry store closed in the middle 1960s. Presently all that is left is a United Methodist church, the post office, and the school—an example of the agonizingly slow fall of a once prosperous rural community.

BISHOP—Located six miles west of Topeka on the Rock Island, Bishop was a railroad station near the old sugar mill. Like many other such sub-stations for the railroads, this was just a stopping point to pick up produce from local farmers or deliver goods to the neighborhood. Before 1903 it was called Wanamaker. This station was most active in the World War I era. A tornado on June 5, 1917, destroyed the station, then housed in a box car. A possible earlier name for this post-office on Rock Island was Sanford.

BLACKFAU—Incorporated in 1858 by Tecumseh and Shawnee county residents. Its location is unknown but it was either in Douglas or Shawnee counties on the Santa Fe road. It went by several spellings.

BLACKSMITH—A post office from 1871 to 1873 located in Dover township on or near Mission creek; also known in 1871 as Central Grove.

BURLINGAME—In the spring of 1855 this townsite along the Santa Fe trail was platted and called Council City. By September, 1857, it had received its present name and had become a major settlement in southern Shawnee county. According to an 1857 pamphlet, promoters hoped the planned Pacific railroad would pass through there instead of along the Kansas river valley. Townspeople sometimes felt slighted by the Tecumseh or Topeka controlled county board, and Fry Giles believed Burlingame a serious contender in 1858 during the county seat election. Briefly there was a Burlingame township, formed in September, 1857. (Now Osage county.)

CALHOUN—The 1855 territorial legislature incorporated the Calhoun Town Company and created Calhoun county out of the old 12th electoral district. Both were named for John Calhoun, U. S. surveyor general for Kansas and Nebraska. Town founders located it on highlands overlooking the Kansas river, in Kaw half-breed tract no. seven. One commentator, in the Leavenworth *Herald*, June 29, 1855, believed the site had "been selected with more than ordinary care and fore-thought." With coal nearby and an excellent position for a trans-continental railroad, within a year or two the place possessed a general store, blacksmith, shoe shop, saloon, "a first class saw mill," and the James Kuykendall residence.

County officials planned in the fall of 1855 an elaborate 50 by 55 foot courthouse but reduced the size to 25 by 36 feet. For approximately $2,000 the county completed the two-story, half frame, half log structure in 1856. On February 11, 1859, the county's name was changed to Jackson and its offices were transferred to Holton. With that act the community immediately declined and within a few years all traces of it were gone except for the courthouse. The latter survived until the early days of the 20th century, and was used as a farm house. In 1976 only the name remains for a series of bluffs along the Kansas river northeast of Topeka.

Several prominent and interesting figures lived in or near Calhoun during the territorial period. James Kuykendall, one of the three town incorporators, played a significant role in county politics and held a number of offices. Pro-south in feelings, he owned several slaves. For this reason Free-State raiders from Topeka supposedly ransacked his house in 1855 or 1856, searching for a hoard of $12,000 in gold and silver. Forewarned, he had buried it in a stump in the back yard. Kuykendall later bought property in Indianola where he became involved in legal entanglements over ownership of the Clinton hotel.

Infinitely more notorious were the two Edwards brothers who lived in the district between Indianola and Calhoun. They frequently terrorized people and farmers up and down the country-side, always brandishing their guns. Late in March, 1861, Ike Edwards was drinking in a saloon on lower Kansas avenue in Topeka. He followed a Pottawatomie Indian out of the place and with his bowie knife mortally wounded him. Arrogantly, Edwards stayed in the street until a group of citizens were able to get him off to the town's jail. Here, a couple of nights later, three citizens attempted to lynch him. They failed at first but successfully entered the jail the second time. Fry Giles remembered in 1886:

The men returned . . . placed a rope about Edward's neck [apparently the jailer was not interested in his screams], drew him up as high as the low ceiling joists would permit, not quite far enough to relieve his toes from the floor, and left him there.

The expense of burial to the public was slight, and no complaint was made on account of it.

A more famous and valued member of the community was future Union General William Tecumseh Sherman. In the late 1850s, Sherman was involved in a Leavenworth law partnership. In the spring of 1859 he moved to a farm owned by his father-in-law, Thomas Ewing of Ohio, located near the present side of the old county poor farm, half-way between Calhoun and Indianola. Sherman recalled for his *Memoirs*: "I had caused to be erected a small frame house, a barn, and fencing for 100 acres. This helped to pass off time, but afforded little profit." He left that same year, now the most noted resident of Soldier township.

Canema (or Kenamo or Land of Canema)—This paper town was organized by Joseph W. Allen as proprietor in December, 1857. It was located near, if not on, the site of Washington in Tecumseh township.

Carthage—Laid out in northern Monmouth township in 1857, apparently only one house was built there.

Challender's—A Santa Fe railroad station just north of Pauline, discontinued in May, 1871.

Chaumiere—Founded as a Proslave town possibly in Shawnee county in 1857. Thomas Stinson was an incorporator.

Chicago Heights—Early in 1888 H. D. Booge bought land north of Topeka and with associates in Sioux City, New York, and Topeka planned a suburban development. Their surviving plat shows 42 city blocks surrounded by Grant, Sherman, Sheridan, and Garfield boulevards.

The Topeka *State Journal*, September 22, 1916, claimed that Chicago newspapers printed ads from Booge for bids on the construction of several thousand eight room houses on the site opposite ads for Chicago Heights lots. An earlier *Journal* article, May 17, 1888, stated that Booge had already sold 460 lots and was inserting ads in papers in Mexico City, London, Paris, Berlin, and Stockholm. Supposedly, he received letters from the King of Saxony, governors of several Mexican states, and a number of Europeans. However, none of this impressed the locals who knew Chicago Heights to be nothing more than a cow pasture.

Apparently Booge was beginning to feel some pressure to make improvements when he incorporated the Chicago Heights, Potwin Place and South Topeka Electric Motor Railway Company on April 23, 1888. Like the town itself, the inter-urban never materialized and Booge quickly passed out of the picture just at the height of Topeka's boom and just before the sheriff arrived. An old timer interviewed in the *Journal* in 1916 believed Booge profited up to $80,000 before he skipped town to Texas or Mexico. Supposedly Chicago-based unions warned their members "to stay away from the Kansas fake."

Dayton—A territorial settlement, Dayton is shown on several maps as being in northern Monmouth township on a branch of the Oregon road.

Doel—Shown in a 1921 Shawnee county atlas, Doel was a settlement about a quarter mile north of Grove.

Douglas (or Douglass) Township—Named for the sponsor of the Kansas-Nebraska act, U. S. Senator Stephen A. Douglas, Douglas township, Calhoun county, was created on October 16, 1855. Originally it was bounded on the south by the river, the east by the Jefferson county line, on the north by the Fort Leavenworth to Fort Riley military road, and on the west by the Pottawatomie Indian reserve. Atchison township lay north of it.

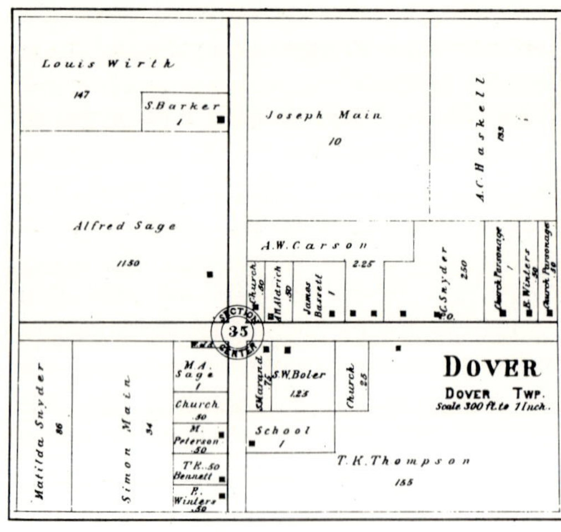

(From "Standard Atlas of Shawnee County," 1898)

Dover—Dover's history began when her premier pioneer, Alfred Sage, built a stone house on the location. Later it became a hostelry for travelers coming through the county.

Dover had several industries in those early days. There was a mill where farmers brought their grain to be ground for family use with the miller withholding a portion of the flour for his pay. There were cheese factories and a blacksmith shop, a bank, a furniture store, a dry goods store, and a weekly newspaper called the Dover *Herald*. Churches came to Dover before there even was a Dover. The Baptists organized in 1868 and built a church in 1869. The Congregationalists and Methodists followed with organizations and buildings. However in the late 1920s the three churches joined hands and built a federated church building where community services were held each Sunday.

From its early days Dover was a country town serving a farming community. In the 20th century it had a telephone office, post office, grocery store, hardware store, a garage, a filling station, a grade and a high school, the church, and a cafe which limited its sales to sodas, ice cream, and candy. There remains a large number of homes owned by families who have retired from farms and commuters who work in Topeka. Dover was once reported to boast a population of nearly 1,000, but this is doubtful. Presently the number hovers around 150. Dover has never been incorporated.

An article from the *Journal* described the business life of Dover:

> Saturday is the only dull day of the week, says one of the merchants. The rest of the time there are lodge meetings, Odd Fellows, Masonic, Eastern Star, Rebekah, or American Legion, baseball games or some social at the church or schools.

The stone house-hotel built by Sage in 1865 still stands today, a reminder of what Dover was at one time. It and one of the old stores in town have been used by those numerous lodge meetings for many years. Dover, though not particularly big, still remains a social center for Dover township.

DOVER TOWNSHIP—In the fall of 1867 Dover township was established on the south side of the Kaw. Uniontown was the first settlement in what was to become Dover township, but it declined and disappeared over a decade before the township was formed. Plowboy came into being shortly thereafter, but the major village in the township wasn't founded until 1870.

The first postmaster was John Sage, appointed in 1863 with permission from local postal authorities. An earlier settler had distributed the mail in the vicinity the previous year. The first township election took place in May, 1868, shortly before Dover was established. The Baptists organized a church in that year and when winter came five persons requested baptism. An article in the Shawnee County Historical Society *Bulletin* described the scene this way:

> Mission Creek was frozen over, so they broke the ice and cleared off a place for baptism. Elder Raymond did the baptizing standing in the ice water through the whole service. After the baptism each person was wrapped in a blanket and helped into a lumber wagon filled with hay, which was provided by Alfred Sage. After the service they all went to Alfred Sage's home which was near by and changed their clothes. Everybody in the community marveled that no one caught cold from this exposure.

The Alfred Sage mentioned in this item was one of the foremost settlers in Dover township. He was born in Somerset, England in 1833 and came to Kansas in 1856. When Dover started in 1870 a store was built and operated by Henry Snyder but was sold the same year to Sage. Another store opened in 1872 which subsequently passed into Sage's and a partner's hands. In 1871, Sage became township postmaster and held the position until 1873.

East of town was a bristling line of bluffs while to the west the Kaw valley, covered with small farms, sloped gently away. Across Mission creek stood the township saw mill which was "buzzing incessantly throughout the day" according to the *Kansas Valley Times*. Dover was named after Dover, New Hampshire, by Jacob Haskell who came to Shawnee county from there. The township is one of the older settled regions in the county. It was originally a portion of Auburn township, from which it was cut off in the fall of 1867. It in turn was carved up to form a part of Mission township in the 1870s.

As one old-timer told a Topeka *State Journal* reporter in 1954: "Dover just grew, but never very much." Like the other rural townships in Shawnee county, Dover reached its high-water mark in the 1870s. Like most others, it was over-shadowed by its metropolitan neighbor. Plowboy, Willard, Valencia, and of course, Dover, appeared, flourished for a while, and then settled down into quiet rural villages with the exception of Plowboy which eventually disappeared entirely.

In 1952 nine school districts in the area combined and a new grade school was built in Dover. By 1954 three buses brought in 90 to 100 students who attended the elementary school and the 60 to 65 in the high school. The 1954 article in the *Journal* pretty well told the story of the township folks: "They like to be easy to get along with, and about the only agitation one of the natives can remember was when they tried to get a cement road to Topeka."

Elmont—The Elmont Town Association, made up of Topeka men, filed for incorporation on October 18, 1886, and platted its Soldier township town in April, 1887. Located to the east of Half Day creek its name apparently refers to elm trees on the side of a hill or mount. This aptly describes the place's geographical position, the community being built on several levels. An 1891 gazetteer reported a population of 16 and listed two carpenters, a station agent, and a general store. The post office functioned from 1887 to 1955, and there was, for a time, an Elmont Telephone Association. The Sinclair Oil Company built a pumping station south of town in 1923.

Disaster has struck Elmont on two occasions: A flood on Half

Day creek in 1902 and a tornado in 1917. The latter practically destroyed the town on June 5 with the Methodist church being completely demolished. A number of individuals were injured. One person later recalled that it, the tornado, "didn't touch any of the women in town, but sure took after the men." Interestingly, records of the area draft board were scattered all over the countryside and two of the draft board members were injured.

Immediately after the 1917 tornado the Methodists rebuilt their church which still (1976) stands. Even before the town was developed religious services were conducted in the district at an 1867 camp meeting on the Half Day school grounds. Only about 30 or so buildings make up the community of Elmont, the church being the most prominent.

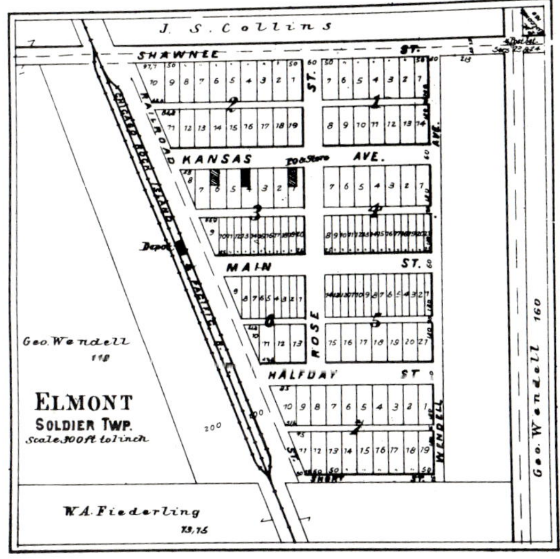

(From "Standard Atlas of Shawnee County," 1898)

Essex—Incorporated in 1858, a town site was never located. Joel Huntoon and Milton Dickey were two of the incorporators.

Esther—A post office from 1891 to 1893 it was located five miles from Richland on the Missouri Pacific, more than likely in Monmouth township.

Eugene (or Eugenia)—"North Topeka [Eugene] only a short time ago," wrote the *Capital*, October 8, 1886, "was looked upon by the

south-siders as a suburb, inhabited by colored people and savages."
For its entire history North Topeka has played a secondary role in
the city's development and was always, or so it seemed, the first scene
of major disasters like the 1903 and 1951 floods. Yet, in many respects
the community was far older than its sister south of the Kaw if one
counts the Papan brothers as early residents. William Curtis and
Louis Laurent laid out the town in 1865, and a post office and boarding
house, for Union Pacific workers, were founded the following year.
On April 9, 1867, a Topeka ordinance annexed Eugene to become the
first such major acquisition and the city's first ward. The first President of the United States to visit Topeka, U. S. Grant, stopped
momentarily at the Kansas Pacific depot in North Topeka on April
25, 1873. According to the next day's *Commonwealth* "the president
came out upon the platform, looked around, shook hands with the
crowd, disbursed a few cigars among the boys, and remarked that
Topeka seemed 'to have considerable bottom.' "

EUREKA—This was a Free-State town laid out on December 9, 1854,
by a party from Pennsylvania and New York. It was located near
Burlingame in Osage county.

EVANS TOWN—Platted in December, 1857, and located in either Williamsport or Monmouth township, Evans Town would have contained
76 blocks with a public square set diagonally in the center of town.
Streets named Shawnee, Martin, Stinson, etc., imply that either Tecumseh residents or pro-southern entrepreneurs promoted it.

EXETER PARK—An 1898 county atlas shows this place in Mission township. Possibly a projected Topeka subdivision, its distance from town
is unusual at such an early date.

FREEMAN'S LAND—A post-Civil War town site, its plat locates Freeman's
Land on Muddy creek and the A. T. & S. F. right of way. This places
it in Soldier township on or near the Jefferson county line.

FREMONT—Established just prior to Topeka's organization in December, 1854, the proposed town was no more than a log cabin, the site
being just east of the present Ward-Meade home.

FREMONT CITY—Mission creek runs through Fremont City's plat
implying a Dover township location. Surveyed by Joel Huntoon in
1857, it might have been placed either in or just outside the Pottawatomie reserve.

GEORGETOWN—A site in present Osage county, it was incorporated in
1858 and abandoned in 1860.

GLASGOW CITY—The Glasgow Town Company was incorporated on February 1, 1858, with a proposed location on the Santa Fe road in southern Shawnee now Osage county.

GLENDALE—Incorporated in 1856, its location is unknown.

GRAND HAVEN—A post office from 1884 to around 1900 Grand Haven was located in the county's southwest corner on the Osage county line. An 1891 gazetteer mentions a post office, blacksmith, and general store, all operated by members of the S. W. or W. K. Sears family.

GROVE—Grove undoubtedly received its name from a nearby grove of trees, a relatively rare sight on the high prairie of northern Shawnee county. Virtually nothing now exists of the town founded in 1905 as a side track on the newly completed Union Pacific branch to Marysville. Activity peaked around 1920 when it possessed a depot, store, grange and township hall, and the Grove State Bank. A Topeka bank formed the latter to serve farmers in this remote section of the county. However, trade never developed and the bank closed after only three years. Apparently one of the cashiers absconded with some funds, and two months after its closure, a burglar blew open the safe to find it empty. The greatest excitement in Grove came in 1946 when five U. S. military prisoners escaped from their train near the depot setting off a two day man hunt. By the 1970s everything was gone except for an elevator and a row of houses which had the prospect of being drowned by the proposed Grove reservoir.

GROVE TOWNSHIP—This is the last township organized in Shawnee county, created out of the northern portion of Silver Lake township on July 15, 1918, the only one formed in the 20th century. Other than Grove hamlet itself, there has´ never been any community of size within the township.

GUMITHORNE—The *Commonwealth*, July 4, 1871, stated a new town would be laid out 12 miles north of Topeka on the proposed Topeka & Lincoln R. R. The Proprietors were to be John Guthrie, Jacob Smith, and Daniel Horne; hence the name Gu/mit/horne.

HALF DAY TOWNSHIP—Formed on October 16, 1855, this Calhoun county township was named for Half Day creek. A portion of Menoken and possibly Silver Lake township occupy the site of Half Day township.

HAVANA—A colony of Germans supposedly laid out this town in 1858 west of Burlingame. Now in Osage county, the site was abandoned sometime in the early 1870s.

HUGHES PARK—Possibly just a subdivision, its plat was filed August 6, 1887, and located about two miles south of Topeka.

INDIANA CITY—Platted in July, 1857, this Osage county site was probably never settled.

INDIANA TOWN—While no specific location was given, its plat map shows the Santa Fe trail going through town, thus making it an Osage county site. The map shows 210 city blocks with public parks, courthouse square, market place, and locations for two depots and four churches Streets were named for presidents, states, and trees.

Sam Reader did this watercolor of Indianola from a sketch he prepared in 1861. The Prusseit house, immediately to the left of the flag pole, was the site of a battle over the local prostitute. (From "Diaries" of Samuel J. Reader)

INDIANOLA—H. D. McMeekin, later a Topeka hotel keeper, and two others bought the Indianola townsite from Louis Vieux, a French-Indian, in 1854. In November of that year they laid out the future town and in 1855 had their town company incorporated. The community did not really begin its developement until 1856 after the government had transferred the post office from nearby Loring in December, 1855. Indianola had one tremendous advantage over its rivals, including Topeka. It straddled the busy Fort Leavenworth-Fort Riley road. Though important for trade and business, Samuel

J. Reader believed the place would never amount to much. In 1862 he complained to his family back East that "instead of laying it out on the prairie the Mo. proprietors laid it out mostly in the timber and bushes." The timber he referred to lay along Soldier creek. Today nothing remains of the town but the name, much of its site being occupied by the Goodyear tire plant.

Indianola, named after Indianola, Texas, had the usual frontier accompaniments: saw mill, blacksmith, two or three stores, a couple of billiard saloons or "whiskey dens," and two hotels, the Milne and Clinton. At the height of its prosperity, lots sold for $250 or $300 with one lot going as high as $500. Reader stated "intemperance is the special vice of this neighborhood" and called Indianola "Whiskey-town." He also associated the town's grog shops with the secessionist movement, all of them being owned by Proslave sympathizers.

Far and away the most prominent feature in town was the Clinton hotel which was built by William Clinton in 1860. Clinton had married an older woman and with her money constructed the 45 by 60 foot building of walnut lumber. A barroom and dining room with the kitchen in an attached room to the main structure were on the ground floor. On the second floor was a large hall stretched across the length of the hotel plus nine small bedrooms. Legend states that in a year or two after he opened the hotel Clinton he robbed the Indianola post office and stole off in the night with the money and a neighbor's wife. Reader wrote in January, 1863, that Clinton's spouse, upon finding her husband missing, "immediately commenced a vigilant search fearing (rightly, perhaps) his affections were being bestowed on some object other than herself." The last great public occasion in the hotel and Indianola, for that matter, occurred in January, 1868, when local Masons gave a ball for townspeople and the state legislators. Long in ruins, the hotel's fractured remains survived until a wind storm blew them down in 1924.

Reader recorded in his surviving diaries and letters numerous local events which give a rich and unparalleled portrait of territorial and early statehood Shawnee county. One day provided him with an unbelievable wealth of material:

On the evening of the 4th of Sept. last [1862] a most terrible battle was fought in Indianola. . . . It appears that a fancy young lady, to use no harsher term, named Jane J— established her headquarters in Billy P[russeit]'s shoemaker shop and . . . she boldly bid definance to all moral restraint and to the respectable ladies of Ind'a in particular. Mrs. B., B., F., O. and T. . . . after holding a council of war determined on a vigorous policy, and forth-with set out for little Billy's house. Billy can hardly be a true German, for he fled at their approach and took refuge in the Clinton house. The attacking force filed through the gate and by a skillful manoeuvre gained possession of the back door without the loss of a man (or woman rather). Having Jane in their power the ladies offered her terms to the effect that she should march out of town with her baggage and equipage, on condition of never returning. A "Big wholesouled Dutchman" named H— endowed with a truly Teutonic courage, now came on the ground, and Jane being thus reinforced refused the terms of capitulation. To fight or to retreat was now the only alternative, and the former was resolved upon. The ladies seized Jane by the dress and in the scuffle she lost nearly all of her clothing, some of them say by her dress catching on the bed post. She fought like a lion and throwing her arms around H—'s neck defended herself mule-fashion with her feet. The battle was raging at its greatest fury when Dr. A— came charging among them, with the greatest gallantry yet shown by any of the combattants. The happy coming of this son of Chivalry turned the tide of battle in Janes favor which was scarcely counter balanced by a reinforcement on the other side. . . . H— put a blanket around Jane and escorted her out of danger to the rear, as she was rather badly "Cut up." The ladies now evacuated the contested field neither defeated nor as victors. It was a drawn fight. The following is a list of the casualties: Killed—Half the men in town morally and politically. Wounded:—Mrs. F. severly in the arm from the blow of a bottle in the hands of Jane J. H—: Several contusions, not dangerous. Missing—Wm P—; during the engagement. The next day all seven of these ladies were arrested by the "harpies of the law," and four of them were fined $1. and costs. . . . I glory in the ladies' spunk—

Originally, Union Pacific officials intended for their track to by-pass both Lawrence and Topeka, on the north side of the river, by one or two miles. This meant, in early 1865, that the railroad would pass near Indianola. Naturally the news pleased residents who eagerly awaited the survey crews and track layers. A story has emerged, per-haps apocryphal, that the ties had already been laid in the Indianola vicinity when the news reached the laborers that the road would go instead, through North Topeka. Senator James Lane and other Law-rence interests, along with three at Topeka, arranged for the change. Over night Indianola's dreams faded as local farmers, supposedly, hauled away the remaining ties of the original route to use them for corncribs. A few people stayed behind but the town quickly disap-peared.

Kilgore—A plat dated June 20, 1889, survives in the Shawnee county register of deeds office but most of the information on it has been torn away. Site owned by S. H. and Georgia C. Kilgore.

Kilmer—Named for C. B. Kilmer who probably laid out the town in the late 1870s or early 1880s. Located on the Santa Fe line to Atchison on the eastern edge of Soldier township, the post office operated from 1886 to 1900. With the possible exception of a store or two, black-smith, etc. the community undoubtedly never amounted to much. In fact, its only claim to fame was Capt. Charles B. Kilmer.

Born in New York, Kilmer went to sea on a whaler for a five year voyage at the age of 16. When he returned Kilmer was a second mate and soon obtained his master's papers. For around 20 years he sailed in whaling operations in the Pacific, stopping in China or the Sandwich Islands. In the early 1860s he wintered in the Hudson Bay area along with Charles Hall, during the latter's expedition searching for the missing Sir John Franklin. Then in 1868 Kilmer moved to Kansas—a dramatic change—to become eventually a land agent for the Santa Fe. Of his home and town, only the house remains, built sometime in the 1870s.

KINGSVILLE (or KINGVILLE)—Located on the Union Pacific between Silver Lake and Rossville, it was founded in the early 1870s and apparently named after Zenas King, who speculated in property in Shawnee county. During the first half of that decade the huge Andrew Wilson ranch made the station an important cattle yard and shipping point. The *Commonwealth*, October 25, 1871, stated that soon 3,000 head of cattle would be shipped from there and buildings and houses would, in the near future, be erected. Eight years later the *Kansas Valley Times* commented that it was "a small place consisting of a store, school house, depot, and stock yards." Population varied over the years from 10 to 20; by 1912 it stood at 15. The government discontinued the post office in 1914, and though the station was still standing in 1925, there had not been an agent for nearly ten years.

KIRO—Possibly named for an early settler, more than likely the Union Pacific chose the name, with creative spelling, after Cairo, Egypt, or Cairo, Illinois. In Menoken township and on the Union Pacific mainline, the Kiro station was built about 1890, burned in 1915, and subsequently rebuilt. Its elevator was erected sometime around 1896 and a general store begun, as a cooperative venture of the Grange and Farmers Union, in 1911. Primarily a shipping point, in 1924 the U. P. loaded at Kiro 318 cars of potatoes, 52 cars of corn, 37 of hay, 17 of wheat, 14 of straw, 9 of hogs, 7 of turnips, 6 of popcorn, 5 of cattle, and one of millet seed. By 1976 all traces of the original station and community were gone, but new housing additions have crept around the site.

Kiro's greatest claim to local fame came in 1933 with the controversy surrounding the proposed Kiro Dam project. In the midst of the depression some officials felt the construction of a dam across the Kaw at Kiro would solve both the unemployment problem and the need for Kaw valley flood control. It would also assure navigation on the Missouri and Mississippi rivers down stream. To be built just west of Kiro, the dam would have stretched from bluff to bluff, a distance of approximately two and one half miles. In turn this would create a lake some 40 miles long, up to St. George, Kans. Costing 45 to 65 million dollars and employing over 17,000 laborers, the lake would also have flooded out the communities of Silver Lake, Rossville, Valencia, Willard, Maple Hill, St. Marys, and Wamego.

Naturally, such a scheme aroused the passions of people located in or just outside the reservoir's path. Initially, Topeka interests and Sen. Arthur Capper were lukewarm or mildly hostile to the dam but they soon became supporters, the lure of $45,000,000 and visions of a grand lake for recreation and industrial development being too much for them. For those upstream in the flood plain, it was an entirely different picture with business and home improvements set aside waiting for the outcome. The Rossville *Reporter,* May 25, 1933, mentioned that at a Wamego public meeting "no levity was indulged" only "grim determination was manifested to fight till Hades freezes over before giving up the fight."

The Kiro dam project waxed and waned during the summer and fall of 1933. The Rossville paper was not especially enthusiastic when it learned the town would be under only 43 feet of water instead of the earlier reported 72 feet. The *Reporter* blamed continuance of the idea on a few "self-appointed great men" of Topeka, and was relieved after the Topeka Junior Chamber of Commerce came out behind the Kiro dam. That was the kiss of death according to the *Reporter* of July 13. It added: "Topeka has nursed at the public teat so long—county, state and federal—it is notorious, and small wonder that the rest of the state loses no opportunity to throw a monkey wrench in their machine at every opportunity." By 1934 the Kiro dam had become history and the "ghost town" went back into obscurity.

LA-VETA—A late settlement of October, 1887, the blocks were a large 680 by 680 feet divided by 20 foot alleys and 80 foot streets. Located just northeast of Auburn in Williamsport township and close to the Santa Fe tracks, the streets had Spanish names.

LEADERVILLE—Apparently a name given to several houses built in the 1880s, located in the vicinity of present day Wanamaker.

LEXINGTON—Founded or platted on April 13, 1857, it was located in Osage county but apparently never existed other than on a map.

MAIRESTOWN (or MAIRESVILLE)—Thomas W. Maires, later a county sheriff, chose a townsite in 1855 or 1857 just east of present day Watson, on the Tecumseh-Monmouth township border. He named it for the family since he and nine other Maires and Edward Hoogland formed a town company. All it could boast in the 1850s, however, was that a Congregational minister preached there.

MASSASOIT—Named for the Indian who aided the Pilgrims, this territorial settlement (and possible post office) was located directly south of Uniontown on Mission creek. Little is known about it.

MENOKEN—This community was one of several strung along the main line of the Kansas (now Union) Pacific which built a side track and depot there in 1876 or 1877. The North Topeka *Times,* January 7, 1877, mentioned that on or near this location was established the town of Farmersville where the "chief occupation thus far is the shipping of corn." Very soon afterwards it probably attained the name Menoken which is derived from an Indian word meaning "fine growth" or "a place for fine growing."

In 1882 a gazetteer alluded to the place's importance as a grain and livestock shipping point and that nearby "wild" or unimproved land sold for $3 to $5 per acre with improved land at $40 to $50. The township erected a hall in 1884 and the Topeka *Mail and Breeze* wrote that the community was well populated by "a thrifty class of intelligent farmers, stock raisers and horticulturists, a number of whom are in good circumstances and a few have model farms and very desirable residences." A store or two operated around the turn of the century, and Menoken obtained telephone service in 1908. The post office founded in 1877 was discontinued in 1910. Its population in 1900 stood at 14 and in 1904, 25. In 1976 the only visible sign of Menoken's existence was a schoolhouse.

MENOKEN TOWNSHIP—One of the last townships formed, it was carved out of Silver Lake township on July 18, 1879. The Kansas Board of Agriculture gave its population in 1885 as 904 of whom 870 were white and 34 colored.

MISSION TOWNSHIP—Until 1871 Mission township was a part of Dover and Topeka townships. In 1870 debate over new townships in the county had flourished. On July 12 a petition signed by Coleman Dudley, Alonson Hurd, John A. White and others asking that a new township be organized was rejected by the county commissioners. Though they failed to give a reason, apparently several of the county commissioners objected to having their own townships divided to form a new one. Mission did not appear on the list of county townships taxed in 1870, but an election return from there did show up. When the returns of the general election were canvassed by the three county commissioners, Commissioner Golden Silvers moved "that the return of election of Mission Precinct be thrown out and not counted. A vote was taken upon the motion with the following result: Golden Silvers, Aye; H. D. Rice and Wm. Wellhouse, No. Motion lost."

The formation of Mission township was ordered on January 7, 1871. The Commissioners Journal recorded the transaction this way:

Ordered by the Board of County Commissioners of Shawnee County Kansas at the regular January term 1871 that a new Township shall and is hereby organized from a portion of Dover and Topeka Townships Shawnee County Kansas bounded and described as follows to wit: Commencing in Section line between Section 34 & 35 at SouthWest corner of Section 35 Town 12 Range 15 thence north to Kansas River thence up the center of the channel of said River to the Section line between Sections 26 & 27 Town 11 Range 14 thence South on the Said Section line to north line of Auburn Tp. thence east to place of beginning. Said Township shall be known and designated as Mission Township Shawnee County Kansas By order of the Board Ja 7, 1871

After the township was formally organized, the first election was held on May 1, 1871. Most of those who had originally petitioned for organization also served as judges and clerks for the election. The first justice of the peace was Frank Crampton, while Coleman Dudley was assessor of the new township. The tax on real and personal property for Mission township was fixed at two mills.

MONIQUE—Incorporated in 1857 in Calhoun county, by a group including Tecumseh's H. J. Strickler. Possibly named for Mrs. Monique LaFromboise, member of a prominent family in the Silver Lake neighborhood.

MONMOUTH TOWNSHIP—Monmouth township in southeast Shawnee county has been settled since 1854, when Charles Matney staked out a claim. There was no town, however, until John Helton platted the site of Richland in 1872. Matney, whose name has alternately been spelled "Matinee" and "Matingly," brought several of his family to Kansas from Virginia, along with a number of friends from Kentucky and Virginia. In the fall of 1857 the first schoolhouse was built on the northeast corner of Matney's property. The same year the first "Sabbath-school," was organized.

Although most of the township was populated by southern people, they were among the first to form a Union "military company" when the Civil War broke out. So many had gone to join volunteer Kansas regiments that by 1864 only older men and young boys responded to the militia call-up. Numerous men were killed and many captured in the attempt to stop Gen. Sterling Price at the Battle of the Big Blue.

After the war the population of Monmouth township increased rapidly. Like David Zirkle's family, most came by railroad. Zirkle wrote about his arrival in *Yesteryears and Yesterdays*:

New as the country was at that time most of the more desirable land which lay in the Wakarusa bottoms was settled, and there were neighbors within not more than half a mile of each other up and down the valley. . . .

Neighbors meant a great deal to each other in those days. They exchanged work, they used each other's tools, they loaned money to each other when one or the other needed it. There never was a note given or interest charged, and it was always repaid promptly.

Zirkle also described the early topography of Monmouth township:

When my folks settled on the Wakarusa, a large part of the country lying away from the streams on higher ground was still prairie with no fences. Anyone was at liberty to use it for grazing which all of the settlers did. Roads did not follow section or quarter lines over this prairie. In going from one place to Topeka as they did frequently, the distance to be traveled was not as far as it is now because they angled across the prairie part way.

Each corner of the county had areas where major celebrations took place. For example, in Monmouth township on Independence Day, 1880, this notice appeared:

At Linn Creek

A celebration will occur at Clark's grove, on Linn Creek, at which Capt. J. H. Moss will orate. The programme will be similar to the usual custom.

One of the notable landmarks in Monmouth township was a stone bridge built in 1878. Margaret Whittemore wrote of it: "Pioneer stonemasons of Kansas built with their own hands many rock bridges with graceful curves. Such a one was the triple-arched span near Berryton, part of which fell into the water in the spring of 1952, after serving for seventy-four years as a scenic crossing."

The best known person to come from the township was Georgia Neese Clark Gray. King's *History of Shawnee County* says her father, Albert Neese, was a life-long resident of Richland. His father, David, came to Kansas from Ohio with his parents at age 12. The original homestead still exists. David, Albert, and Georgia were all of Democratic persuasion, and Georgia was appointed United States Treasurer by President Harry Truman. David ran the store in Richland and Georgia helped until it closed. She presently (1976) is vice-chairman of the board of the Capital City State Bank.

MUDDY CREEK—A Santa Fe station in Soldier township, no doubt on Muddy creek, in the 1870s.

NARROWS—Possibly a wagon camp site on the Oregon trail, now in Osage county.

NEW LEXINGTON—No location given but probably a site now in Osage county. A surviving plat shows two public parks in town squares.

OAKLAND—A separate third class city from 1903 to 1926, the original Topeka-Oakland boundary was Sardou street. Now everything north

of Seward and east of the Santa Fe shops is considered to be Oakland.
After failing twice, annexation passed in Oakland in October, 1925,
by a vote of 505 to 206. Many residents feared annexation would
deprive them of their school system and high school, which it did.
The latter was housed in a fine building with an enrollment in 1922
of 165 students in grades nine through 12. Some Topeka city commissioners feared it, too, would eventually cost over a million dollars
to bring sewers, water, and fire protection to Oakland.

One Hundred and Ten—The creek crossing the Santa Fe trail on this
site was called 110 creek because it was 110 miles from Westport
Landing in Missouri, a starting point for the road. A small settlement
was established here by that name and the place receives mentions in
many accounts of early territorial life. It also went by the name of
McGee's, after the founder Frye P. McGee. People noted it as a proslavery community. Site is now in Osage county.

Paris—Supposedly an 1856 town in Shawnee county, no location is
given.

Pauline—Another town which sprouted from the seed of a railroad
stop was Pauline. The little hamlet was named after one of its first
residents, W. D. Paul. Now little more than a suburb of Topeka,
Pauline was once the thriving center of Williamsport township and
a rival for local business with Berryton, several miles east.

The railroad stop which began as a water and coaling location
became a station in the 1870s. Paul donated a part of his property to
establish the Union Congregational Church, probably in 1894. Pauline
supported several country stores and a post office. An elevator was
constructed and local farmers shipped their produce to Topeka. When
the Farmers' Union movement spread through the state a co-op came
into being which still services the surrounding agricultural community.

Even though numerous ornate homes were erected in the late 19th
century and even though all indications were that Pauline would continue to be prosperous, its close proximity to Topeka and the arrival
of the automobile caused a decline in Pauline fortunes similar to those
suffered by other villages in the southeastern portion of Shawnee
county. In 1942, however, the town was re-vitalized when Topeka
Army Air Field, later Forbes Air Force Base was established on the
east edge of Pauline.

The air base expanded Pauline greatly in the next three decades.
Nearby schools consolidated to form the Washburn Rural High School
district. Cullen Village, housing for air force personnel, cropped up to

fill schools and help support the small businesses along U. S. Highway 75. But even Forbes could not prevent the slow deterioration of the town. The population increased, but so had mobility; most folks in Pauline went to Topeka to do their business and go to church.

In 1970 the Topeka *State Journal* told the story of the Union Congregational Church: "The church was used by the congregation until . . . Clyde Smalley, owner of the building, let the school district remodel the building into a two room school and use it for free." The school board bought the building in 1932 from Mrs. Fred Hill, Smalley's daughter.

Today the church is a craft and curio shop. The post office is still operational, as is the Co-op elevator, and there remain a few small shops along the highway. By 1976 Topeka had stretched itself down the highway to touch the outskirts of Pauline.

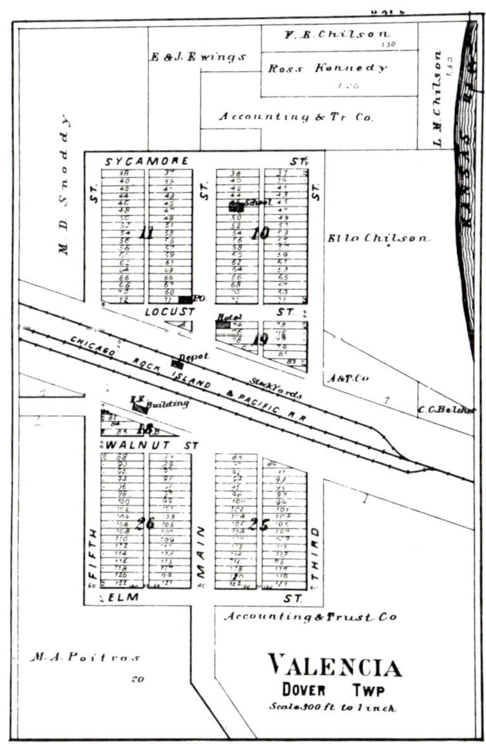

(From "Standard Atlas of Shawnee County," 1898)

PLOWBOY AND VALENCIA—In 1925, Blaine Crow wrote in *A Community Survey of Silver Lake Rural High School District* that the earliest settlement and post office in the district was Plowboy. Apparently both town and post office were little more than a private home.

About 1880 a store was built and Frank Fievy, a Silver Lake school teacher but a Plowboy resident, rechristened the post office and store Valencia. That name had been applied before. As early as 1872 the *Kansas Daily Commonwealth* carried an article concerning a lyceum at Pleasant Grove and the article was signed "Valencia."

The Rock Island graded its roadway past Valencia in 1882-1883, but did not build the line or a depot until 1887. The old Valencia store was transferred to the present Valencia site about the same time. A frame school was built there in 1894. Unlike most small towns in Shawnee county, Valencia reached its pinnacle in the 1920s. In 1925 it contained two general stores, a depot, and a telephone office. From then on it declined as did other rural villages. One by one the businesses closed up, leaving for posterity only the cluster of homes which is presently Valencia.

POTWIN—A third class city from 1888 to 1899, the town once included the Auburndale subdivision to the west but now the district is considered to be Greenwood and Woodlawn streets and one or two blocks to the east.

PRAIRIE CITY—Platted in 1856 in what is now Osage City, its Broadway street is listed as the Santa Fe road. Of its 128 blocks, four public squares were set aside for the courthouse, a college, Fort Riley railroad depot, and the Independence railroad depot.

REDMONDVILLE—This was the Negro settlement of North Topeka in the 1880s. While it can never be considered a separate town, the North Topeka *Times,* January 10, 1879, noted that a distillery was being erected on the site with the houses of Redmondville the workers' homes.

RICHLAND—The most populous and prosperous community in Monmouth township was Richland which was in the extreme southeast corner of the county. Richland has been described as "just an ordinary country town," an accurate description. The little town was the social and to some extent the business center of the rural Monmouth township population. It was also the first town settled in the township.

There was no settlement in the vicinity until John Helton platted Richland in 1872, after the Lawrence, Leavenworth, and Emporia Railroad established a depot on Camp creek less than half a mile from where it empties into the Wakarusa. The local post office had been set up in a pioneer's cabin in the fall of 1856, one mile north of the future town site. After Helton laid out the town, the office was moved into the village. At one time Richland boasted a pair of neat little churches, Methodist and United Brethren, the former built in 1883 and the latter in 1890. The second structure erected in town housed both a home and a grocery store and later a small hotel for the railroad.

Richland was the center of a rich agricultural region and did a large amount of business for a place of its size. Both Camp creek and the Wakarusa were skirted with heavy timber, and a lumber trade among local farmers flourished. In 1896 the Topeka *Mail and Breeze* reported that "a creamery was started about eighteen months ago with a capital stock of $7,500, $5,000 of which has been paid up. It is now making cheese and in the summer will use the milk from fully 200 cows."

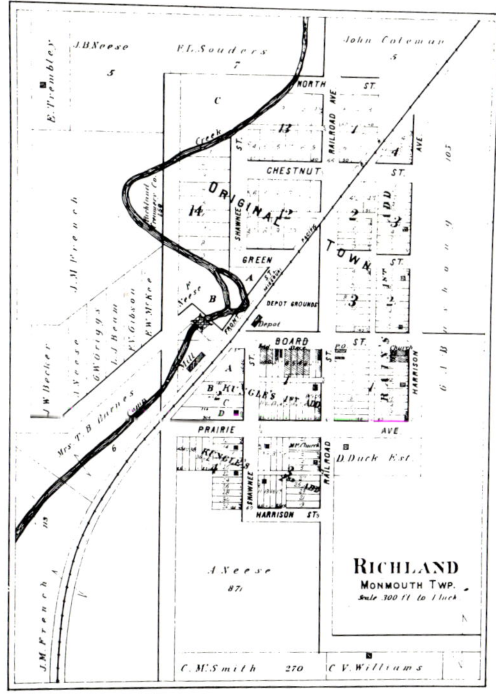

(From "Standard Atlas of Shawnee County," 1898)

The year before this report the Lawrence, Leavenworth, and Emporia folded and the tracks were torn up in 1899. One old-time resident commented on the decline of the railroad through Richland:

I heard the fellows about that time say there was a disagreement between two politicians—one at Lawrence and one at Emporia. The railroad was going to go to Texas, but the fellow at Emporia said the other one had double crossed him and wouldn't let it go there.

At the site where the town once stood, only an empty diagonal street running through the center of the one-time downtown area and some pilings from an old trestle are all that remain of the road. The Missouri Pacific line came to Richland later but all hope of being a major stopping-point had died.

In the meantime the community had grown to be a thriving town. The main township post office was in the village, and David Neese had built a store there. For the most part Richland remained an "ordinary country town" until recently. Time and progress finally overcame the rural community. On August 17, 1967, a final sale of most everything in the grocery store owned by Mrs. Georga Neese Gray marked the end of Richland and the beginning of a reservoir on the Wakarusa. Richland's population had dwindled to less than 100 and the remaining families moved as quickly as their accounts were settled. The post office closed. The elevator owned by Georgia's husband, Andrew Gray, closed at the same time. Today Richland is only a small grocery and a gas station about a mile and one-half north of the former town site.

RIDGEWAY—An 1858 settlement, or post office, the site is now located in Osage county.

ROSSVILLE—Though one of the last major towns founded in Shawnee county, since the 1850s there had been Pottawatomie settlements on or near this Cross creek site. The United States established a post office there in 1862, inside the Indian reserve, and named it Rossville after Agent W. W. Ross (brother of Edmund G. Ross and a Topeka newspaper editor). Rossville also went by the name of Cross Creek well into the 1870s.

Topekan George W. Veale and three other men purchased one hundred acres on the east bank of Cross creek from Anthony Navarre and his Indian wife in 1870. They platted a village, calling it Edna, which the *Commonwealth,* mentioned on May 19, 1870:

> A generous policy has been adopted by the proprietors towards settlers. To those who will erect substantial buildings and engage in any legitimate business, lots will be given them sufficient to place their buildings: but lots will neither be given nor sold to those contemplating a traffic in whisky.

Confusion, however, soon developed over the two names Edna and Rossville, so within a year or two the founders reverted to the older name.

Rossville possessed several natural advantages which eventually made it second in size to Topeka. First, it was safely well away from the capital, not to be over-shadowed like miniscule Tecumseh, but with a strong rail connection to the metropolis of Shawnee county. Secondly, the community was centered, in 1871, in the newly opened Pottawatomie lands. Among its assets were its inhabitants whom the

North Topeka *Times,* September 14, 1871, complimented: "The citizens of Rossville and vicinity, though not entirely virtuous and industrious, are to a great extent religious, educated and practical business men and farmers." Eight years later a Rossville newspaper, the *Kansas Valley Times,* February 7, 1879, reported on the town's rapid growth by enumerating its business enterprises:

Railroad depot, stock yards, express office, telegraph office, money order post-office, railroad water tank and wind mill, lumber yard, steam flouring mill, livery stable, painter, tailor, shoemaker, real estate office, newspaper, tinware, milliner, four general stores, two blacksmiths, three carpenters, barber shop, stone mason, two doctors, two drug stores, three grain dealers, two stock dealers, two hotels, one plasterer, justice of the peace, two notary publics—no lawyers, no saloons—none are required.

The restriction against saloons was important because, unlike its neighbor, Silver Lake, Rossville was a temperance town. During the fall of 1880 townspeople debated among themselves the pros and cons of incorporation. Fearing the "liquor interests" would gain control of a future town council, the *Kansas Valley Times* felt "if that element were to prevail, we had better remain as we are." Nevertheless, Rossville incorporated and its inhabitants elected their first mayor in June, 1881. The reform or temperance spirit continued when they voted, in 1889, their first and only all-women town council and mayor. A month after their election, the women passed an ordinance outlawing gambling saloons and devices in town. Purity, however, did not win out, and on August 11, 1904, the Topeka *Herald* announced how two local men had been "running an open joint in Rossville for two years."

ROSSVILLE TOWNSHIP—Rossville township was carved out of the western part of Silver Lake township on January 16, 1871. Like Silver Lake township, this area was long settled by Pottawatomies and those whites working for them or for the government as traders or agricultural experts. White settlement began, for all practical purposes, in 1847 but inclusion in the Pottawatomie reserve delayed significant development until after the Civil War. The 1885 census, excluding the town of Rossville, was 1,032 with 570 males and 813 whites and 219 colored (undoubtedly both Indian and Negro).

SAQUA (or SAWQUA or OSAWAQUE)—These various spelling combinations may all refer to the same 1870s post office in northern Shawnee county, possibly on Indian creek.

SHAWNEE COUNTY—On August 30, 1855, the territorial legislature created the first counties in Kansas, two of them being Shawnee and Calhoun. Named for the Shawnee Indians, the boundary stretched from the Kansas river south to a line just below present day Burlingame. On February 23, 1860, the legislature changed these boundaries granting some nine miles on the south to Osage county and shifting the northern limit approximately four miles north of the river. This made the new county seat of Topeka more centrally located. In February, 1868, the present northern line was established.

In 1976 Shawnee county consists of 12 townships: Rossville, Grove, Silver Lake, Menoken, and Soldier north of the Kansas and Dover, Auburn, Mission, Topeka, Williamsport, Monmouth, and Tecumseh south of the river. There are five incorporated towns: Rossville, Silver Lake, Willard, Auburn, and Topeka.

SEABROOK—A post office established southwest of Topeka in 1887 in Mission township. An 1891 gazetteer lists a grocer, a nursery, and a neighborhood population of 25. This later became a nucleus of Topeka's growth to the southwest in the 1950s with a shopping center at 21st and Gage boulevard.

SHOREY—Located about a mile north of Topeka, Shorey lay alongside the Chicago, Rock Island, and Pacific railroad tracks. Its post office was established February 18, 1889, but discontinued in 1908. An 1891 gazetteer gave the population as 400 and listed a number of businesses including a confectioner, restaurant, and bankers (Smith and Norton). Other than the Rock Island, the only industry of note in the 19th century appears to have been the Shorey Wind Mill and Pump Company. A price list from 1889 indicates that the mills cost $50.00 for a 10-foot, one horse power model and $75.00 for a 12-foot, two horse power mill. The towers ranged in size from 30 feet to 50, the cost being 75 cents per foot. Long a modest suburb the name since nearly forgotten, the only major structure in the district is the old Seaman Rural High School, built in the 1920s.

SILVER LAKE—Some forgotten Kansas river flood created a new channel leaving behind a crescent-shaped lake. Perhaps because of its shimmering properties, people began calling it Silver Lake. Nevertheless, the area surrounding it had long been inhabited with stores established beside the lake during the 1850s to serve Indians and Oregon-bound immigrants. By March, 1866, the Union Pacific, Eastern Division, had reached the settlement and two years later the village of Silver Lake was platted.

One of its two promoters, Medore (or Madore) B. Beaubien, had arrived in Kansas as early as 1847, acting as interpreter and trader to the Pottawatomies. He had been in the fur trade and was one of the first residents of the future Chicago, Ill. Until his death in 1889, he was the first citizen of Silver Lake. He also served as the town's first mayor in 1871, and built the community's finest residence at a cost of $6,000.

While in its youth, Silver Lake earned a less than gracious reputation. In the 1870s there was at least one, possibly three, saloons going "full blast." In reviewing the town's history, the *Mail and Breeze,* May 22, 1896, possibly exaggerated, yet, the saloons supposedly served "the vilest rot-gut that ever irrigated the throat of an old toper." Whiskey "flowed like water at nearly all hours of the day and night. Disgraceful street brawls, accompanied by the most blasphemous oaths were a common occurrence." One citizen claimed "he once witnessed four drunken street fights inside of five minutes." In its first city election, the *Kansas State Record,* April 4, 1871, stated there were two opposing political camps, the "whisky ring" and a temperance group.

If whiskey vending upset Silver Lake's neighbors then the small-pox frightened them even more. Periodically, epidemics broke out in nearly every community during the 19th century. They were a common if disturbing feature of western life. Topeka's *Commonwealth* on December 19, 1872, published several different versions of how that dreaded disease came to plague the small town of Silver Lake. Evidently an employee of cattle magnate Andrew Wilson was identified with the smallpox late in October or early November. Supposedly, the town's doctor, who also owned a store, nursed the ranch worker in his upstairs room. Without notifying the townspeople, the doctor and clerk continued with business as usual until the truth about the sick man's condition could no longer be hidden. Another individual contracted the disease and the problem came out in the open.

When the Topeka newspaper printed the story the Silver Lake doctor immediately fired back a reply absolving himself of any responsibility. He sought help from Wilson, but finding none, kept the small-pox victim in a small frame house near town. "There has been no case or symptom of smallpox in or about Ward's store," Dr. C. D. Ward claimed, "yet some men have threatened him and his place of business in case he did not immediately close up, to the extent he has decided to do so."

Whatever the truth, at least two or three persons died in Silver Lake and countless individuals were ill during this epidemic. It spread to other towns such as St. Marys and caused worry in Rossville and Topeka. Rossville citizens met in the schoolhouse on December 12 and passed a resolution requesting "that the citizens of those places now infected with the smallpox, keep entirely from us, and that we do not wish any communication with them" until the plague was entirely gone. For several weeks before Christmas the *Commonwealth* noted that rumors of smallpox were circulating in the city, particularly North Topeka. Several Topeka physicians attended the sick at Silver Lake and as a precaution, the newspaper pleaded with them to stay there for a time: "There may be no risk to us . . . but we know the people would feel better contented with their remaining at Silver Lake while their services are required there."

By Christmas the disease had subsided but some people were still apprehensive. Topeka doctors reported these conditions in Silver Lake just before Christmas: three adults were confined in one poorly ventilated room less than ten feet square while another man lay seriously ill in an unfinished house about ten by 12 feet. There his family "consisting of six had to sleep in the same room." News about smallpox excited everyone.

The Topeka *Mail and Breeze,* May 22, 1896, reported that "everything is now quiet. . . . There are not over half the number of places of business there was there fifteen years ago. A great many of the buildings are deserted, their former owners or occupants having moved to Topeka, and other points, while a large number have died." Into the 20th century businesses were limited though the town did possess a bank. Always, however, it stood in the shadow of its larger neighbors, Rossville and Topeka. Real growth in the area did not occur until the late 1960s as more and more families moved there for the small town environment.

SILVER LAKE TOWNSHIP—Now the smallest township in Shawnee county, Silver Lake has been reduced over the years through the creation of surrounding townships. Immediately after the board of county commissioners extended the northern county boundary in 1868, a petition was "signed by more than fifty citizens and by more than a majority of the legal voters thereof." Thus on March 16, 1868, Silver Lake township was formed out of the western portion of Soldier township.

SOLDIER TOWNSHIP—Evidently from February 23, 1860, when the county boundaries were shifted north across the river, or from the township re-organization of March 17 to April 2 Topeka township included that area which became Soldier township. Then on April 2, 1860, Soldier township was organized. Until March 16, 1868, when Silver Lake township was formed, everything on the north side of the river belonged to Soldier township. Its 1885 population of 2,827 made it the largest township in the county outside Topeka township. Its Negro population was also the largest outside of Topeka township with 918.

South Tecumseh—Tecumseh promoters organized a South Tecumseh town association to develop this suburb in 1858; a community which probably never materialized.

South Topeka—A third class city in the 1880s, just south of the then city limits of Topeka.

Spencer (or Spencerville)—A stop on the Santa Fe east of Tecumseh.

Sumner City—This was a proposed all Negro city of the mid-1890s, between Topeka and Tecumseh near the river. Some preliminary land negotiations took place but no activity followed.

Superior—Apparently a territorial paper town in present Osage county, three of the four public squares were named after the Great Lakes—Ontario, Huron, and Erie.

Swinburn—A 1900 gazetteer describes this Grove township post office as having three livestock breeders, a livery, blacksmith, and grocer.

Switzer—A small community with no location or date specified but probably an Osage county site on Switzer creek.

Tecumseh—Thomas Stinson settled in the Tecumseh neighborhood in the spring of 1854 though he evidently had been farming some in the area since the previous year. By September 1, 1854, he had a townsite platted and named for chief Tecumseh, the great leader of the Shawnee nation. As a Proslave town and county seat, Tecumseh enjoyed a brief prosperity, but upon the ascendancy of Topeka the community rapidly declined. It received only one vote for state capital in 1861.

Soldiers passing through to or from Fort Riley during the Civil War frequently commented on its deserted appearance. "The old Brick Courthouse," wrote one man in 1862, "is now going fast to ruin. Its windows above and below are badly broken both glass and sash—so likewise is the brick church which was formerly occupied by the Southern Methodist church." Fry Giles stated in 1886 that the courthouse was sold for $500 and "its dissevered parts were carried away, to reappear in modest farm cottages, and now—where scenes of commerce and social gaiety filled the day—there wave rich fields of ripening grain, that reconvert the abandoned town to its primitive picturesqueness."

An 1891 gazetteer, however, referred to some business activity in the place with a grocer and confectioner, a blacksmith, sand and coal operation, two physicians, a carpenter, and a music dealer. A renaissance of sorts occurred in 1924 and 1925 with the construction there of the Kansas Power & Light Co. power plant and in 1957 with the establishment of the Du Pont cellophane plant east of town. A dramatic population rise in both town and township occurred in the 1960s as people escaped city living for the comforts and security of country life.

Tecumseh Township—The oldest township in Shawnee county, it was organized on September 17, 1855, to encompass all the country from the Kansas to the Wakarusa rivers with Yocum township south of the Wakarusa. Eventually, Topeka (1857) and Monmouth (1860) townships were carved out of it. Like the other townships in the county, the governing township board consists of a clerk, treasurer, and trustee. Though the least powerful political unit, the board oversees road, cemetery, and park maintenance along with fire protection in the joint Topeka [township] Tecumseh Fire District with the fire station at 29th and California. In 1969 the township built a special maintenance shop on Ward road. The only smaller governmental units are the several separate rural water districts in the county.

Tevis—A Missouri Pacific station named after the Tevis family. At one time the Tevis name was particularly numerous in the middle of Monmouth township and is well-remembered in the Berryton community. The station was never much more than a simple depot along the tracks.

Looking north on Kansas avenue from Seventh, March 20, 1935, during a dust storm. In the height of dust bowl Kansas, 1936, Topeka experienced a record 59 days on which temperatures rose above 100°. (Courtesy Kansas State Historical Society)

Topeka—Established in 1854, the town founders considered such names as Webster, Mid-Continent, or Papan's Ferry before selecting this anglicized Indian word. Naturalist Thomas Say in 1819-1820 recorded an Otoe word for the river of the Kansa: to-pe-o-ka, which meant good potatoe river. Supposedly this word also stood for and was used for the Smoky Hill river to the west. Thus, it was in common usage before 1854 when Cyrus K. Holliday first used it in a letter dated December 17, 1854, to describe the new settlement he had just helped to found. A similar word or words exist in various other languages. For example "top" and "eka" in Lettish (the language of Latvia) literally would mean "to become a building."

Topeka Township—Formed on February 23, 1857, by carving out the western portion of Tecumseh township, the electorate voted at the Garvey House hotel in Topeka. Over the years the township boundaries have been radically reduced due to the creation of newer townships and the encroaching city of Topeka. By the 1970s very little of the township remains.

Trenton—Incorporated in 1858, location unknown.

Uniontown—Settlement for Indian traders in 1848, the site was still mentioned as late as the 1860s. First white town in Shawnee county. It was located in the NE¼ of Sec. 23, T. 11 S., R. 13 E., near the western boundary of the county.

Urbana—This was an end of track town on the A. T. & S. F. in 1869. On the Wakarusa, it must have been side by side with Wakarusa. A writer to the *Commonwealth,* June 18, 1869, mentioned it as being a beautiful place for picnics and that "improvements are in progress there."

Valley Town—A town company was formed, supposedly by Proslave individuals, to obtain land away from Free-State Topeka.

Versailles—Platted April 13, 1857, it was a town of 48 rectangular blocks. In Osage county and never actually settled, it was on the same site as Lexington.

Vidette—A post office established in 1887 in Mission township. An 1891 gazetteer reported a population of 46 for the area along with the only industry, the Vidette Sorghum and Corn Mills.

Wagner (or Wagener)—A post office in northern Shawnee county, it was established in 1880 and discontinued two years later. Apparently it was located in Silver Lake township though it was also listed in Jackson county in the 1880s. There was a grocery store there.

Wakarusa, Kingston and Williamsport—The name Wakarusa, though spelled Warrunza, was first mentioned by Dr. Edwin James in an account of the Stephen H. Long exploration expedition of 1819-1820. A railroad survey map of 1850 spelled it Wahkarussi. The name has been translated as meaning "the river of big weeds," and, more frequently, "hip deep." The tale behind the latter is a romantic tale involving the inevitable Indian chief or beautiful maiden who tried to ride his or her pony across the stream in high water and on reaching its deepest point exclaimed "Wakarusa!" George Root wrote in a 1937 *Kansas Historical Quarterly* that a literal translation of the word cannot be printed without giving offense, although in the Indian tongue there was no vulgarity and the definition was a perfectly proper one."

Despite all this, the town of Wakarusa came into being when two Topekans platted a townsite in 1868. Like many other successful speculators the founders had learned the Santa Fe would be coming that way. These men, named Mills and Smith, were soon joined by G. T. Lockard, J. P. Ennis, and Zenas King from Topeka. The town was first named Kingston.

Another town, Williamsport, had previously been founded near Kingston, but that town's company was composed entirely of citizens of Williamsport, Pa., and of the 25 members of that company only three, T. U. Thompson, Dr. A. J. Huntoon, and Joel Huntoon, ever came to Kansas. Joel Huntoon built a house on the site in 1857. Williamsport was never much and all that remains in 1976 are a few gravestones on a farm.

After the Santa Fe built its line through town in 1869 and established it as a major watering stop, a county post office moved from along the banks of the Wakarusa into town and it soon became known as Wakarusa.

By 1871 Mills built a hotel and a store at the station. A church was constructed by Presbyterians, and another by Methodists. Andreas' *History of Kansas* noted: "Wakarusa village claims to have the finest district schoolhouse in the county, if not in the State. It contains over a hundred inhabitants, and has the usual number of village industries, besides the business of crushing stone for railroad ballast. The Sherman Stone Crushing Company have located one of their machines at the village, and employ from fifty to one hundred men."

An article in the January 18, 1872, *Commonwealth* had this to say about the four-year-old settlement:

This city is small, but mighty wicked. Hence, the farmers residing contiguous have re-christened it "Sodom." It certainly is not a model town, if reports are to be credited, but a sort of modern Sodom sure enough, containing many lots but "nary" lot. Yet the writer claims that this place will soon become a thrifty and business town. Located on the line of one of the most important railways of the

West, and in the midst of a rich agricultural and growing community, its course soon, is bound, in the nature of things, to be upward.

To most of its 1976 residents Wakarusa is a small, peaceful town. It still carries on its business much the same as it did when it was known as Kingston.

WANAMAKER—In 1891 it was a post office and grocery store, never an actual settlement.

WASHINGTON—Capt. Eli Allen, W. Y. Roberts and three other men organized this town on the hills immediately west of Big Springs in the spring of 1855. Straddling the Oregon road it boasted a hotel but competition from Big Springs proved too great. A tourist through there in 1859 stated that Washington contained only two log houses. Incidentally, for sometime in the 1850s, Big Springs was thought to be in Shawnee county.

WASHINGTON—Now an Osage county site and another speculative venture which immediately failed.

WATSON—A postoffice, named after and operated by G. H. Watson, was established in 1883 but discontinued in 1899. An 1891 gazetteer listed a grocer (Watson), two carpenters, and a physician (J. Z. Hils). The Watson Mutual Telephone Co., of 1914 served Tecumseh, Berryton, Richland, Big Springs, Stull, and even Lecompton customers. Located on the Tecumseh-Monmouth township line, it revived in the 1960s as a Topeka suburb, with the new Shawnee Heights school on the north side of the border and the old Watson grange hall on the south.

WAVELAND—"This thriving community," wrote a reporter for the *Kansas Daily Commonwealth* on January 18, 1872, "is located on the Wakarusa about thirteen miles southwest of Topeka, and lies partly in Osage county." It had been settled early in county history and at one time the county line divided it. The settlement prospered for a while, as most little settlements did, so long as there was a rural population to support it. By the time of the *Commonwealth* article, Waveland was the home of "J. G. Clarke & Co.'s famous Waveland Nursery, the oldest and most complete in the state. They have in the nursery, aside from thousands of plants, shrubs, trees, etc., of every variety, some 50,000 large fruit trees—apple and peach, which must be sold the present season, being too large to keep over...."

For a time Waveland was the only settlement between Pauline and Burlingame. As such it had aspirations of being the trade center for southern Shawnee county. On February 27, 1873, the *Commonwealth* reported the need for a store and a blacksmith shop in the settlement and "substantial inducements (were) offered." There was a local lyceum, a farmer's club which met on Saturday nights and Milt Walt-mire conducted a singing school in the 1870s.

When the Atchison, Topeka, and Santa Fe was built south to Burlingame it went through Wakarusa rather than Waveland. A railroad was essential to a 19th century village, and the lack of one marked the end of Waveland's aspirations.

WHITEFIELD (or WHITFIELD)—Post office and grocery store 14 miles southwest of Topeka in Dover township in the 1890s.

WHITFIELD CITY (or DELAWARE CITY, KANSAPOLIS or ROCHESTER)—Between Calhoun and Indianola, on the Fort Leavenworth-Fort Riley military road, lay the much named town of Whitfield City. One John Butler Chapman from Indiana founded the community in August, 1854, and promptly wrote a book, *History of Kansas and Emigrant's Guide* to promote the place. Unquestionably, Chapman was one of the most colorful and fascinating figures in early Shawnee county and Kansas history. A lawyer and "persistent meddler" in Democratic politics, Chapman traveled extensively in California and the Pacific northwest before coming to Kansas. Attempts to win a territorial political office failed as did an embarrassing May-December romance (he was already married) in which the bride-to-be "diddled . . . the scamp" out of $9,000. He left Kansas sometime in 1859 with the ghost of his settlement behind him.

Chapman originally named the town Delaware City but as there already existed a post office called Delaware he changed it to Whitfield City. This second choice honored 18th century Methodist leader George Whitefield.* By 1856 he had given up on that title and people were calling it Kansapolis, or Kansaspolis or Kansasapolis. In two or three years it had attained its last name, Rochester, probably after Rochester, N. Y. "Death soon followed—of too much name," wrote Fry W. Giles 30 years later.

J. Butler Chapman's *History of Kansas* amounted to little as a history. He devoted three of his 19 chapters to Whitfield City, extolling the surroundings and natural resources of the town on the banks of the Conda river (Soldier creek):

Whitfield City is laid out with a view of encouraging scientific, literary and religious institutions; liberal donations are made for school houses and churches, and the fine springs ensure comfort and convenience. The central position to any part of the territory will render Whitfield a convenient location for men of business. The Kansas river, navigable only a small portion of the year, is near enough for

---

*"Whitfield City, a name of ancient remembrance among all Christian denominations," wrote Chapman. However, the spelling error of Whitefield led some individuals to believe the name comes from Gen. John W. Whitfield, the Kansas congressional representative. Chapman was Free-State and Whitfield Proslave; still, politics and town promotion made strange bedfellows.

all commercial purposes. The road leading to the river is a beautiful dry sandy ground, without any obstruction from mud and ravine, or other matter. . . . No country in the world contains a richer soil than in the vicinity of this town. . . . A railroad up the Kansas river will soon supercede every other thoroughfare.

A later historian remarked that "his intentions seem sincere" though "only his enthusiasm for it is too unbounded." That enthusiasm, however, lured a number of people to an unhappy prospect. One man who trekked to Kansas recalled for the *Commonwealth*:

It happened to be the very nucleus of literary, scientific and religious progress which drew me . . . to Kansas in the summer of 1855. Instead of entering another St. Louis, we found a rather pretty hillock, with numerous stakes driven about it, plainly indicating that this was the metropolis, Whitfield.

At this time there was not a single building in the place. The first public improvement, we believe, consisted in the erection, by J. Butler C., of a stately edifice, five logs high, which was shortly followed by two or three others of similar dimensions.

At least Chapman and the disappointed settler agreed upon one item, Whitfield had a pretty setting.

Chapman promised other material advantages for the embryo town, including a newspaper entitled the *Kansas Intelligencer*. He may have published, sometime in late 1855 or early 1856, one or two issues of the paper but none have survived. Chapman also envisioned churches, hotels, stores, etc. but other than a few houses and a saw mill, they never materialized. People who did settle down in Whitfield or Kansapolis or Rochester formed a town association with president, secretary, and treasurer, which donated 50 lots for a rail line. Unfortunately, it was all for naught since people soon drifted away; Chapman himself sold out and moved in 1857. When the town association levied a tax for bridge building, only five members paid, the rest were delinquent. By 1860, except for a schoolhouse built the year before, and few farms, Whitfield City went back to being a "pretty hillock."

For perhaps a decade one could speak of a Rochester community; afterwards the name came to signify only the school and the cemetery. In June, 1860, the Congregational church organized in the schoolhouse with Peter MacVicar as its first minister, but the *Congregational Record* in January, 1866, called it "one of our feeblest churches." After World War II and especially beginning in the 1960s, Rochester's fortunes revived with more and more Topekans moving into the district from the city.

WILLARD—When the westernmost bridge across the Kaw in Shawnee county was built south of Rossville, the little hamlet of Willard was on the south end. Willard never grew much even with this beneficial structure.

Less than a mile southeast of Willard lies the old Uniontown cemetery, filled with the first white settlers of Shawnee county. Across the gravel road rests the empty field where Uniontown once stood.

There was a school located in Willard from its earliest habitation. The last one, built in the 1920s, was a two-room frame structure which still (in 1976) stands, empty, on the south side of Willard. The stone school on West Union road was called, appropriately, West Union school and in 1976 was a residence southeast of Willard. Aside from the schools, Willard was only a collection of houses inhabited by Topeka commuters.

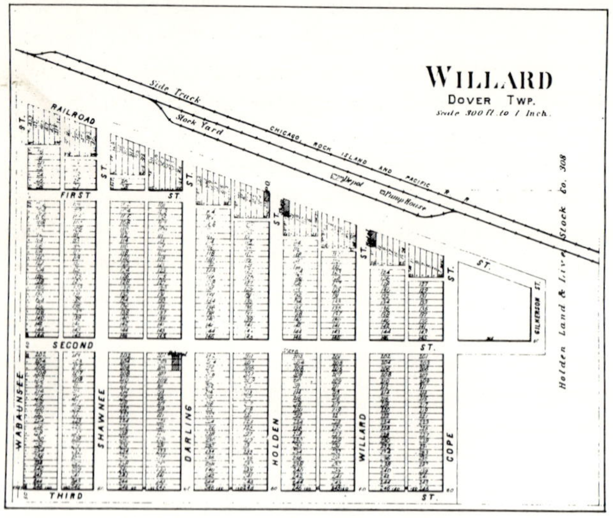

(From "Standard Atlas of Shawnee County," 1898)

WILLIAMSPORT TOWNSHIP—Williamsport township in southern Shawnee county was established in 1860. Robert Simerwell, who helped establish the Baptist Indian mission near Topeka, was the first known settler. He arrived in 1854 and opened a blacksmith shop. William Matney of Virginia and William Cokes from Missouri located in the township in August and September respectively. The new township grew considerably during territorial days.

Williamsport was named for Williamsport, Pa., the home of the first town company to locate in the township. The company was organized in Lycoming county, Pa., in 1857 with 25 members, but only three ever came to settle.

On December 16, 1854, in the cabin of the Rev. Mr. Simerwell, the first Baptist sermon was preached in the township by the Rev. Mr. James Gilpatrick. Early the next year the first birth was recorded, the child of Mr. and Mrs. Darius W. Herald. Mrs. Herald's death, which came only a month later, was also a first in Williamsport.

As with most frontier communities in Kansas territory Williamsport township measured its progress in homes, schools, and churches. The Porter school, later Pleasant Valley District No. 4, was organized July 25, 1859, with Elizabeth Simerwell as the first teacher. The district functioned until April, 1955. The limestone one-room school, built in 1871, was the oldest schoolhouse in use in the county in that year. In 1857 a school was built at Shawnee Center, west of Wakarusa, by subscription. It was so named because in those days it was within a quarter-mile of the geographic center of old Shawnee county. "The building served the community as a place for public meetings, school, church, lectures, theatricals, and various political and social parties," wrote Bessie Moore, granddaughter of Robert Simerwell, in an issue of the Shawnee County Historical Society *Bulletin*. She continued: "It was a recruiting station for a company of militia men who served under Captain Perry Tice, who led a company of state militia into Missouri during the Price raid at Lexington." Shawnee Center was disbanded as a school in the 1940s but served for over twenty years afterwards as a community building.

A Congregational church was established at Wakarusa about May, 1860. Another Congregational church was organized in 1880 but was disbanded when the church building was partly destroyed. The remains of the structure were used in the construction of Seaman Congregational Church in Shorey. Lois Johnson Cone wrote for the *Bulletin* that "a place of worship is always one of the first concerns in a community. On November 20, 1939 over 200 people met at Wakarusa to celebrate the founding of their church April 17, 1869." She wrote:

> It was continued as a union church until 1876 when a vote was taken to disband it and issue letters for the members to other churches. This, however, was not a happy solution to their problems and they met again at the home of William S. Hibbard to organize the Society of the Wakarusa Presbyterian Church. The deacons were Hibbard, William McCoy, T. B. Gamble and George D. Neill.

Williamsport township was interested in local education as a letter to the *Commonwealth* on January 14, 1873, stated that there had for some time been talk about a township library. Topeka was too far away. The writer said those who preferred good literature to "the trashy periodicals of the day should form an association without delay." Apparently, however, the people in Williamsport could never agree on the project, the writer implied.

Jessie D. Wood was an old fashioned family doctor and was probably the best-known man in the township. He made his first professional call on the night of December 22, 1854, when he rode bareback over an unmarked prairie road to deliver Mollie Cook, who may have been the first white female born in Shawnee county. (Others have also made that claim.) Another noted citizen of the township was Thomas Reynolds, a farmer, glass-blower and forty-niner. He settled in Kansas in 1854 and joined Captain Tice's company to help repel Price's rebels in 1864. Mrs. Cone wrote that Reynolds "loved nature and he spent a great deal of time in the woods. He was called the "Poet of Wakarusa! although he was more nature lover than poet." Nevertheless he contributed numerous articles to the *Commonwealth* and thus recorded much valuable information about the township in its formative years.

Williamsport township contained three towns of note: Waveland, Williamsport, and Wakarusa, but only Wakarusa remains today. Briefly, in 1857, Wakarusa township preceded it.

WILLMINGTON—The plat for this town was filed at Tecumseh on September 1, 1857. Located in Osage county, the town was located at the junction of the Westport and Leavenworth branches of the Santa Fe road.

WYOMING—Probably named for Wyoming Valley, Pa. The Leavenworth *Herald,* April 26, 1856, briefly mentioned the proposed town which was to be located on the Fort Leavenworth-Fort Riley military road. It was in extreme northeastern Shawnee county (or then, Calhoun county) and sometimes reported to be in Jefferson county. Some early maps show it, but the town never amounted to much and probably ceased to exist before 1861.

YOCUM TOWNSHIP—Named after early county commissioner William Yocum, this township was formed September 17, 1855, and located south of the Wakarusa river.

YOUNG AMERICA—A projected town of 1857 in what is now Osage county.

BIBLIOGRAPHICAL NOTE

A comprehensive bibliography of Shawnee county source materials would amount to a full chapter. This note can serve only as a general display of the more important works consulted. Many, if not most, of the quotes and newspaper sources are documented in the text. Articles in the *Kansas Historical Collections* and *Kansas Historical Quarterly* have been immensely valuable as have those in the *Bulletins* of the Shawnee County Historical Society, especially those edited by John W. Ripley.

Nearly all the primary sources used are in the library and archives of the Kansas State Historical Society. These include the incomparable diaries of Samuel J. Reader for the 1850s and '60s along with his "Autobiography" written in the 1890s (both illustrated with his water-colors). The multi-volumed diaries of Martha Van Orsdol Farnsworth offer an unparalleled view of Topeka life from the 1880s to the 1920s. The diaries of Joseph C. Miller (1855) and Charles Thresher (from Monmouth township) and the letters of Cyrus K. Holliday and Bethany College student Ovella Dunn (1870) were also helpful. A unique collection contains the various scribbles of George Root, also in the Historical Society's manuscript division.

General Shawnee county histories include William Cone's *Historical Sketch of Shawnee County* (1877), a section in the A. T. Andreas *History of Kansas* (1883), and James L. King's *History of Shawnee County* (1905). The most comprehensive Topeka history remains Fry W. Giles' *Thirty Years in Topeka* (1886, reprinted in 1960). For a sometimes eccentric Topeka history, see Mary E. Jackson's entertaining *Topeka Pen and Camera Sketches* (1890). A number of the country communities have produced local histories, two of them being Blaine Crow, *A Community Survey of the Silver Lake . . . District* (1925) and Douglass W. Wallace, *Things Ended and Things Begun, A History of Tecumseh* (1975). Kansas histories consulted were William Zornow's *Kansas, A History of the Jayhawk State* (1961) and Robert W. Richmond's *Kansas, A Land of Contrasts* (1974).

Louise Barry's *The Beginning of the West* (1972) serves as a guide and bibliography to the pre-territorial period. Worthy industrial histories include Edward G. Nelson, *KPL in Kansas* (1964) and the Russell Sage Foundation's unusual social document, *The Topeka*

Improvement Survey (1914). Interestingly, the Santa Fe railroad in Topeka has not been thoroughly covered; the only satisfactory discussion of the general offices and shops is Tom MacRae, "The Santa Fe in Topeka," *Santa Fe Employee's Magazine* (May, July, 1911).

Topeka and Shawnee county's social history has been featured in numerous works, far too many for all to be mentioned here. Important, however, are Lillian Horton, *Mama Was Pregnant* (1964) which tells about Topeka and Oakland in the early decades of the 20th century; and David Zirkle, *Yesteryears and Yesterdays* (1956) which does much the same thing for Richland and Monmouth township. *Sixty-Two Years of History in the Topeka High School* (1932) is the only significant publication dealing with all aspects of high school life. Margaret Whittemore's *Historic Kansas* (1958) besides discussing local artists offers her own sketches of the state as a complement.

INDEX

(Italicized page numbers indicate photos)

**Kansas Avenue,
North from Sixth Street,
East Side of Avenue.**

First National Bank.	534
(later, 732 Kansas)	
American District Telegraph.	
Hugo Felitz, Tents &	526
Awnings.	
Burkhardt & Oswald,	518
Harness & Saddlery.	
Reed & Son, Furniture &	510
Carpets.	
George M. Hammel,	508
Merchant Tailor.	
Hardt & McMillan,	506
Gents Furnishings.	
Durein & Kreipe,	502
Grocery & Bakery.	
Frank Durein,	500
Real Estate & Loans.	

★ ★ ★

Postoffice. 430 – 434

**Kansas Avenue,
South from Sixth Street,
West Side of Avenue.**

W. A. Stout, Cigars & Tobacco.	601
T. J. Kellam, Stationery & Books.	603
Merchants National Bank.	605
Barnes & Sim, Druggists.	607
Bartholomew & Co., Real Estate.	609
O. A. Peck & Co., Groceries.	611
Baker & Wardin,	613
Watchmakers & Jewelry.	
Hay, Wiggin & Co., Dry Goods.	615
S. Barnum, Clothier.	617 – 619
Geo. Downing, Photographer.	
Western Union;	621
Kansas Electric Co.	
Topeka Rapid Transit Co.	623
Scott Smith, Barber Shop & Baths.	625
Stevenson & Peckham,	627 – 629
Dry Goods.	
Bernheim & Levi,	631
Ladies' Furnishings.	
Windsor Hotel.	633 – 635
(later, National Hotel)	

★ ★ ★

City Hall. 701 – 703